COVENANT

WHAT THE
BIBLE SAYS
ABOUT

COVENANT

By

Mont W. Smith

College Press Publishing Company, Joplin, Missouri

Table of Contents

Table of Contents

Introduction

WHAT THE BIBLE SAYS ABOUT COVENANT

I can not recall when I first became conscious of covenant. I had read several debates by Alexander Campbell, and discovered later he used covenant as hermeneutic in an essential way. Two professors in undergraduate school, when I recalled it, made frequent references to the covenants. My graduate school professors were, for the most part, fine Christian existentialists. They were preoccupied with modern theology, and that did not include covenants. They were interested in Christian unity, and systematic theologies were a source of difficulty to their interests.

After being out of the United States for six years for service in Ethiopia, I returned and eventually took a doctorate at Fuller Seminary in Pasadena. There a search was done that would lay a sound theological basis for church growth. It seemed to me incredible that God's stated purpose should be the reestablishment of fellowship with man and it not be taken seriously by the church. What was wrong? Christians I had known were, by and large, good people; they prayed, gave, sought the guidance of the Lord, went to church, and loved their neighbor, but the church did not seem to grow. They gave some, but relatively scant, attention to missions.

After I had become a professor of missions and church growth, I was further shaken by the stout resistance I received from some students while laying a Biblical and theological foundation for mission and church growth. The same resistance came from some in the Bible department itself!

Then it jelled for me. I saw that Paul interchanged covenant with the word service! That meant the terms of pardon were not the terms of a covenant. Entry into covenant was not execution of the terms of a covenant. That was the beginning of the rethinking on covenant. The thing Christians swear to do because they are in the covenant is execute the covenant. Execute is ministry—the same word Paul used in II Corinthians 3:6ff. Failure to be an active part of the ministry of reconciliation was breach of covenant. Beginning there, the concept was totally redeveloped with all the tools at my disposal. Fortunately for me, the President of the college was an excellent theologian. And he was a man deeply influenced by and dedicated to covenant. He had been years ahead of me in his own thinking on the matter. When I began to advance both mission and church growth in a covenant context he encouraged me during transitional times. I am most grateful to Dr. Medford Jones for that.

At this writing I am chairman of the Bible Faculty. We are trying to ground all students in the Biblical doctrine of covenant for no other purpose than to create a ministry for obedience to God's great command: Make disciples. We have in mind to place in every kind of church, regardless of denomination and theological orientation, men and women competent to lead churches to disciple the nations. For that same reason I am writing this book.

In a more personal vein, I believe had it not been for the very concept of covenant I would not have been able to have remained a worker in the church and perhaps not a believer. In the objective assurance I had from the long history of God's being faithful to His own covenanted commitments, a confidence in God more deep and secure grew in my soul. I have found God good at His word. We swore to serve Christ well. I want to be good at my word too. Since the study of covenant has helped me so much, I wanted to share that joy with you.

Mont W. Smith
February 1981

Chapter One

COVENANT AS TREATY

The Bible's Covenant Story

The story of Biblical faith is the story of a relationship. The basis of that relationship was an agreement called covenant. Biblical history is the record of how that relationship fared. Covenanted relationship represents a certain approach to life and is therefore properly called a philosophy. History reflects a philosophy—the historian must choose out of thousands of happenings those which have unusual significance. Thus Hebrew-Christian philosophy is expressed in their books of history. Their histories were a record of how the covenant worked out—of the heroes, those who kept the covenant, and the villains, those who worked against or who broke the covenant. The divisions within the Hebrew community have always been related to contrary views of covenant. Theological divisions within the larger Christian movement relate in significant ways to how each sect understood covenant, and especially how each related the Old Covenant to the New.

Testament and Covenant

When one says testament it is usually understood to mean the documents of the covenant, the Books of the Bible. These are known as the Old Testament, from Genesis to Malachi, and the New Testament, from Matthew to Revelation. The word covenant is usually used, at least in our own times, to mean the specific agreement, treaty or promises made. This distinction is not completely satisfactory, however, as the terms testament and covenant are proper translations

1

of the same Hebrew word. In Biblical vocabulary, the agreement was called the covenant and the documents that carried it and explained it were called the scriptures. Even in the scriptures themselves the distinction is often blurred, but it is essential to keep the distinction in mind as it will have significant ramifications later in the study.

An Overview of Covenant-History

The real story of covenant began with God choosing "a wandering Aramean" called Abraham to be God's agent to initiate a reconciliation with mankind. The events prior to Abraham tell how the alienation between God and mankind came about. One can read about that in the first eleven chapters of Genesis. God made an agreement with Abraham. It was an uncomplicated covenant. Abraham was to make God his own God and to walk in trust of Him. God agreed to care for the descendants of Abraham through whom He intended to bless all mankind.

The descendants of Abraham went into the Egyptian captivity according to agreement. God rescued Israel from Egypt, an event that was forever stamped upon the consciousness of the Hebrew. Shortly after the rescue God added to the original covenant a great many additional requirements, regulations and promises. This covenant became, in effect, the constitution of the future Hebrew nation. It was called the Torah, or the Law of God, and it was duly ratified by God and the people in a meaningful oath-swearing ceremony. The nation bound itself and its children to be the people of God and to live according to the agreement.

For the next ten or fifteen centuries, the Biblical record traces the progress of the people of the covenant as they attempted to administrate the Law of Moses. They had their ups and downs, their heroes and failures. And at last they had David.

With David and his son, Solomon, the Hebrews entered into what they came to regard as their golden age. The people were unified under a devout king. They passed from a shepherding society to a more urban military theocracy. They entered into the political arena of the near east and became a buffer state between Egypt on the south and Assyria-Persia to the north and east. Their remaining history was connected closely with the fortunes of those two neighbors. The moral destiny of Israel as God's chosen people did not keep pace with her political advance, however. Tension between God and His kingdom of Israel grew. The united monarchy of David split into the northern region called thereafter Israel. The southern part took the name Judah. Each then had a king and a separate history. Both states were alternately faithful and faithless to the covenant they continued to support, at least in pretense. In vain the prophets urged each nation to a change of heart with vivid recounting of the curses contained in the very text of the covenant.

Finally, after centuries of appeal and minor punishments for breech of agreement and periods of prosperity for faithfulness, it was obvious the covenant was not going to work. God announced a coming captivity in Babylon as punishment for covenant breaking. That event was traumatic for Israel, so much so it was identified in metaphor as the death of God's people. At the same time as the announced captivity God also announced a return to Canaan and the initiation of a "new" covenant. The prophet called the captivity and return the death and resurrection of Israel.

The New Covenant was not what was expected at all! The Son of God Himself entered the plane of human history. He was to be the very model of the new covenant. His life the new Law, his death the ultimate sacrifice for sin. His resurrection was the summation of God's hope for Israel and all mankind. He commanded the new covenant be proclaimed to all nations. The Hebrews were split in their opinion of the new order. Some moved at once to the side of Christ. Others could not believe the radical character of the new covenant presented by Jesus. They rejected it, had the Messiah killed and, in spite of the resurrection and the fact that the first members of the church, the new covenanters, were themselves Hebrews, they actively worked against the fledgling group.

The New Testament scriptures tell the story of the beginnings of what came to be known as Christianity. The last book of the New Testament foresees grave difficulties facing God's new people, as terrifying as dragons, strange beasts, wicked cities, and as dangerous to men of faith as a cultured, beautiful and available woman. In spite of all such difficulties, the Messiah is shown to win in the end, bring history to a halt, judge all men and give to each his due, reunite heaven with earth and restore men to fellowship with God. Such is the Biblical story. It is the story of a magnificent God and His God-creature, man, their difficulties and their reconciliation. It is the story of a relationship and of the agreement that made the relationship possible. It is the story of covenant.

The Hebrew Root of Covenant

(The following section contains some technical information about Hebrew words which may be beyond the needs

4

of the average reader. The material is provided in some detail to stress the importance of the concept of covenant in ancient times, and to illustrate exactly what a covenant included. The important points are reviewed in the questions at the end of this chapter.)

The Hebrew word for covenant was *berith*, or the more ancient form *b'rth*. Its etymology allows some breadth of view. It may have come from the basic form *b-r-h*, to dine and also to select. More likely, however is the root *b-r-t*, to bind together. That root developed into the term treaty, pact, or alliance. For instance, the Amorite terms for "make a covenant" is literally, "to kill a young donkey" referring to the form of ancient oath taking. The Hebrew for "enter a treaty" is actually "to cut a covenant." We may be fairly certain, therefore, that the stem *b-r-t* (*berith*) meant "to bind together in an alliance." The best translation is undoubtedly the English word "treaty." The manner of taking ancient oaths, reflected in scripture will be discussed at length in a later section.

It will be necessary to study briefly several other words that are closely related to *berith*. When they were spoken, the context of *berith* was present. *'Alah* is the Hebrew word for oath of covenant. Its own stem is *'hl*, which, traced out, moved from *ahdat* to *adot* to *edot* and finally became *edut*, a word translated covenant, as W. F. Albright has shown.[1] The root meant to bind together, a confederation, covenant or agreement, and corresponds to the Akkadian *a'alu/e'elu* meaning to bind together and also to the Arabic *'ahd* meaning covenant. The later Aramaic was *adayya* and was

---

1. W. F. Albright, "The Hebrew Expression for 'Making a Covenant,'" *Bulletin of the American Schools of Oriental Research*, 121:21f., 1951.

rendered covenant.[2] *Alah,* then was the act of entering a covenant, a ceremony, pledge or oath. Because the form of the oath involved a self-curse, the same word has the negative meaning of curse, and is so rendered in several Old Testament passages. Nonetheless, *alah,* oath, meant the taking of an oath to perform a covenant, and can come to mean what *berith* itself meant. To perform one's oath was to perform one's covenant. To break a covenant was to break one's oath as well.

The word *yada* in Hebrew was also a covenant term. The most frequently used word to translate it was "know." *Yada* meant having a covenanted relationship with, or behaving in a way consistent with being a covenanted partner. In the Amarna Tablets, "know" was rendered, "May the king, my lord, take care of me," but the more accurate rendering, as Huffman demonstrated, would have been, "May the king, my lord, recognize me as a legitimate vassal (and therefore provide proper support)."[3] To know someone was to have a formal relationship to him. Thus "Adam knew Eve and she conceived and bore Cain" (Gen. 4:1). YHWH said, "You Israel alone have I known of all nations on earth (Amos 3:2)." A parallelism is used by Jeremiah which constitutes a definition of *yada.* "I had known you" was used in parallel with "I had set you apart as holy" (Jer. 1:5). To "know" was to "be in a covenanted relationship with." In Near Eastern international treaties, *yada* was used as a technical term for "be in a covenant." The same use was employed by Moses and other Hebrew writers.

---

2. Frank M. Cross, *Canaanite Myth and Hebrew Epic,* Harvard University Press, 1973, p. 265f.

3. Herbert B. Huffman, "The Treaty Background of Hebrew YADA," *Bulletin of the American School of Oriental Research,* 181:31, 1966.

One other word deserves attention here although it is so significant as to warrant a rather complete examination later in the study. It was the term *hesed* in Hebrew. The *H* sound is gutteral or harsh, as with certain Germanic pronunciations. Nelson Glueck, the Jewish archeologist and scholar, has done the new definitive study of *hesed*. He demonstrated its meaning to be covenant keeping, or acting in a proper supportive way to a partner in covenant. He concluded that one not in a covenant could not show *hesed*. *Hesed*, he said, was the very essence of a covenant, the doing of what was pledged. In that sense it is parallel to faithfulness, being true to, or keeping faith with. It is most frequently used in parallelism with "covenant keeping," and therefore is another word for keeping agreements made to support the covenant partner. It is a moral term. The morality expressed is doing what one committed himself to when he entered a covenant. Thus when *hesed* is used, it implies that a covenant exists between the parties, whether the pact is formal or natural.

A Survey of the Uses of B'rth

Covenants were entered into by God and Noah's group. God obligated Noah and his family to eight matters, and then pledged that He would never again destroy the earth by flood (Gen. 9:1-17). Abraham and Abimelech entered into a covenant (Gen. 21:27). A marriage was considered a kind of covenant (Mal. 2:14), as covenant-related terms such as *yada'* and *hesed* are frequently employed in discussions of marriages. Marriage and "entered a covenant with" are used in parallelism in Ezekiel 16:8. Jeremiah, Hosea and other prophets frequently used the marriage metaphor when discussing the covenant Israel had with YHWH.

7

A treaty was suggested between tribes such as the Ammonites and the men of Jabesh Gilead (I Sam. 11:1). The Law of Moses forbad the making of covenants with the pagan tribes inhabiting Canaan (Exod. 23:32). But when the people of Gibeon tricked Joshua into making a covenant with them, so sacred was the covenant oath, especially when made in the name of YHWH, Joshua felt obligated to keep it (Josh. 9:3ff.). There is an example of two kings making a covenant (I Kgs. 20:34). There is an example of a covenant between a king and his subjects (II Chron. 23:16). In another case, a military commander, as part of a group who remained loyal to the royal family after a coup, enlisted other commanders and the palace guard to rally to the support of the child Prince Joash who was secreted with a nurse in the temple.

> He made a covenant with them and put them under oath at the temple of the Lord. Then he showed them the king's son. He commanded them saying, "This is what you are to do . . ." (II Kgs. 11:1ff.).

The three most important covenants in the Old Testament were made between God and first Abraham (Gen. 12:1-3 and then the people of Israel (Exod. 24:1-7) and finally with David (I Chron. 28:7 and II Chron. 7:17). It is interesting that the record of God's *b'rth* with David and his royal household found in the Book of Kings, and in the early chapters of Chronicles, did not use the word covenant. All the elements of a typical covenant were there: the parties having been specified, the stipulations or obligations listed, and the promises or rewards then stated. But the word covenant itself was not used. Was it then a true covenant? The word *hesed* (covenant keeping) was used in regard to God's

8

faithfulness to his promise to David, which implied a covenant, but the word covenant was absent. However, when the entire affair was recounted in II Chronicles, this statement appears.

> As for you, if you walk before me as your father did, and do all I command, and observe my decrees and laws, I will establish your royal throne, as I covenanted with David your father when I said, "You shall never fail to have a man rule over Israel" (II Chron. 7:18).

In the same way we may imply a covenant between God and Adam, although the term covenant does not appear in the Genesis account. Adam had limitations and God had made promises, conditioned upon Adam's *hesed*. When Adam broke the terms, God invoked the promise, "In the day that thou sinnest, thou shalt surely die" (Gen. 3:3). It was not until Hosea's time the actual word covenant was applied to that situation. Hosea wrote, "Like Adam they have broken the covenant" (Hos. 6:7).

The importance of any doctrine or idea is not the frequency of appearance of the term itself, it is the relationship the term, or rather, the idea expressed in the term, has to the central thrust of the Bible. The idea of covenant is inseparably connected to every major idea in the Bible.

There is one other matter before we leave the word study on covenant. The problem is conditionality. Did covenant include the idea of "conditions"? Granted that covenant has the idea of commitment or promise in it; does it also have the idea of reciprocal commitment or conditional promise? Theologians range in their opinion from covenant meaning only one-sided promise to rather legalistic conditionality. A quotation from Canon Wilson, the Hebrew-Chaldee authority, will show the correct ancient understanding.

Berith was used . . . of any covenant of God with man, or of man with man; and also of any promise or stipulation; as also of any fixed arrangement (Jer. 33:20) or precept to be observed (Jer. 34:15). It is also put for the conditions of a covenant, as the Decalogue (Deut. 4:13; 9:9; Is. 28:18), and for the sign of the covenant (Gen. 17:13).[4]

I think it is safe to say one could bind himself to do something apart from any concession by the other, and call it covenant. But it is also apparent the normal use of covenant required mutual promise or mutual commitment. It may be well to list at this point some verbs associated with *b'rth*. They show its context. Such verbs are: *bara'*, "enter into"; *'amad*, "to be in"; *'avar*, "transgress"; *parar*, "break." The following verbs are used when observance of covenant is discussed: *'asah* "institute"; *nathan*, "make or do"; *hagag*, "keep" and/or "establish"; *shamar*, "maintain or continue." It seems to me the assumption of mutual commitment must be made when *b'rth* is used and exceptions, if claimed, must be supported with evidence from context. It will not do to support a meaning, in the absence of other evidence, by a prior theological assumption.

Hittite Treaty Discoveries

Modern Biblical scholarship, particularly among Old Testament authorities, received a considerable benefit when the Hittite language code was broken as widely reported by Ceram.[5] The translation of the Hittite texts revealed many similarities between their normal treaties of alliance and the

---

4. William Wilson, *Old Testament Word Studies*, Grand Rapids: Kregel Publications, 1978, p. 99.

5. C. Ceram, *The Secret of the Hittites*, Tr. by R. Wilson, AA Knopf, 1956.

the covenants of the Old Testament. The impact of the treaty text discovery has caused a revolution in Biblical theology, providing additional support for the date and authenticity of Old Tesatament documents. (See sources listed below.)

V. Korosec thoroughly examined the texts and reported on them as early as 1931.[6] He remains the almost uncontradicted authority in that field. The first scholar to bring the treaty texts to wide public view was D. A. Wiseman, who read a paper on the parallels between the Hittite and Hebrew treaty forms before the Society of Old Testament Studies in January of 1948.[7] In 1954 the most influential of the early leaders, George E. Mendenhall, published in the Biblical Archeologist an article, "Covenant Forms in Israelite Traditions." It was reprinted as a fine monograph in 1955 and was widely circulated.[8] Other writers began to produce a variety of books and articles on the topic. The brilliant Jesuit Old Testament authority, D. J. McCarthy, published at Rome in 1963 *Treaty and Covenant.*[9] D. R. Hillars, writing for the Johns Hopkins Series, published in 1969, *Covenant: The History of a Biblical Idea.*[10] Meredeth Kline produced *three fine books on aspects of the topic, in 1963 The Treaty of the Great King, in 1968 By Oath Consigned,* and in 1972 *The Structure of Biblical Authority.*[11]

---

6. V. Korosec, *Hethitische Staatsvertrage Ein Beitrag zu ihrer juristischen Wertung,* Rectswissenschaftliche, Studen 60, Leipzig, 1931.

7. D. J. Wiseman, *The Vassal-Treaties of Esarhadden,* London, 1978, p. 60.

8. George E. Mendenhall, *Law and Covenant in the Ancient Near East,* Monograph, Pittsburg, 1955.

_____ "Covenant Forms," in *The Biblical Archeologist,* #15, 1954: 50-76.

9. D. J. McCarthy, *Treaty and Covenant,* Rome, 1963.

10. D. R. Hillars, *Covenant: The History of a Biblical Idea,* Johns Hopkins, Baltimore, 1969.

11. Meredeth G. Kline, *The Treaty of the Great King,* Grand Rapids: Eerdmans, 1963.

_____ *By Oath Consigned,* Grand Rapids: Eerdmans, 1968.

_____ *The Structure of Biblical Authority,* same, 1972.

The Suzerainty-Vassal Treaty

The ancient Hittite and Neo-Assyrian type of Alliance Treaty had seven distinct features. Many scholars have found these same features in the Israelite covenants.

1. *The Preamble* The parties to the pact were here identified clearly, by name and sometimes by position or status.

2. *Historical Prologue* The previous status or history of the two parties was discussed here. How they came to know the other or how the stronger party had been helpful to the weaker, or a list of previous relationships or obligations was presented. This form of covenant was deeply moral. The parties were entering a personal as well as a legal relationship. Their honor, and in many cases, their very lives were at stake in fulfillment of the treaty terms. Thus, both the sovereign and the vassal needed full moral and spiritual commitment by the other. Each intended to give heart, soul, and life to the success of the relationship. Mendenhall summarized it well. "The covenant form is still thought of as a personal relationship, rather than an objective statement of law."[12]

3. *Stipulations* These refer to the obligations of the weaker party, or the party of the second part, if equals. These were often stated in detail, with frequent use of moral terms, such as "to love" and "to walk before with the whole heart." Total loyalty was demanded. Usually the vassal was forbidden to make alliances with anyone else. He was

---

12. George E. Mendenhall, *Law and Covenant in the Ancient Near East*, Monograph, Pittsburg, 1955.

———— "Covenant Forms," in *The Biblical Archeologist*, #15, 1954: 50-76.

obligated to come to the aid of the king upon call. He was to be supportive not only in policy, but in attitude, in heart, and in personal concern as well. Gifts, tribute, service to the lord and master were spelled out. No hint of disloyalty, of disinterest, or emotional detachment was permitted on the part of the vassal.

The king or superior party was also obligated to "love" the vassal. He was to provide support, direction, aid in military matters if someone should attack the vassal, etc. Such aid was absolute and the vassal was sometimes spoken of as the "son" or "child" of the king.

4. *Depository* The text of the treaty was most sacred. The oath of the covenant was sworn before the many gods. To breach the pact was an offense to the gods. Accordingly, the actual treaty text was kept in a temple—in the presence of the gods. There was a provision for the public reading, often once a year, before the people in a public place. This was to insure all of the continued good will of each party. It was to remind all of the specific stipulations of the pact. For a vassal, it served his purposes both to reaffirm to the crown his loyalty and to remind ambitious nobles of his own personal, warm and continued relationship to the king.

5. *Witnesses* A list of witnesses, often a long list of respected gods of both parties, was inscribed as part of the treaty. In the early treaties, the vassal's gods were listed in full, but this practice gave way in later centuries. Honored men, rivers, holy mountains, the sky or other objects of nature were also called upon to be witnesses.

6. *Curses and Blessings* Both parties, the witnesses, and the entire population were made aware of the results of both treason and loyalty. The vassal agreed to receive as just punishment the curses that were listed. The sovereign was

declared just if he inflicted upon the vassal the punishments listed if the vassal proved to be faithless and immoral in regard to covenant. The punishments were specified.

The blessings of covenanted love and political support were also detailed. In a sense these were the obligation of the party of the first part, or the sovereign. They were not spoken of as obligation, however. They were blessings, or kindnesses the master would show to his servant. The master did, however, agree to love and regard as his own family the vassal and his heirs.

7. *The Covenant Oath* This was the actual pledge made by the vassal to the lord. It involved the killing of an animal or animals and each party touching blood. This affirmed the idea they were one blood and had a shared life. It also indicated the type of punishment fitting for one who broke his oath and betrayed his covenant lord.

Treaty Forms Compared

Neo-Assyrian	Israelite
1. *Preamble*	
"Thus saith NN . . . the valiant, the great king, song of NN, king of Hattiland. . . ."	"I am the Lord your God, . . . the God of your fathers . . . Jehovah" (Exod. 20).
2. *Historical Prologue*	
"I sought after you . . . sick and ailing, . . . but I put you in the place of your father (as King) and took your brothers and sisters and . . . Amurruland in oath for you."	"You have seen what I did to the Egyptians . . . brought you out of the land of Egypt, out of the house of bondage . . ." (Exod. 19, 20).
3. *The Stipulations Upon Vassal*	
a) No vassal shall make a treaty with a foreign power.	"Thou shalt have no other Gods before Me" (Deut. 5:7).

b) No vassal is to war against another vassal.

". . . make no covenants with them . . ." (Deut. 7:2).

c) Must answer the King's call to arms.

". . . the Lord your God shall deliver them before you, and you shall utterly destroy them" (Deut. 7:2).

d) Unlimited trust, love, and no "murmuring" against the King, no "rumors" . . . etc.

"You shall not put the Lord your God to the test, as you tested Him at Massah" (Deut. 6:16; Exod. 17:7).

e) No vassal may give refuge to anyone fleeing the King's wrath.

"You shall consume all the peoples whom the Lord your God shall deliver to you; your eye shall not pity them . . . " (Deut. 7:16).

f) Must appear before the king once a year.

"Every year" (Deut. 15:20; Lev. 16:34).

g) The King was the final judicial authority.

"As the Lord may appoint" (Deut. 17:9-17, etc.).

4. Provision for the deposit of the treaty text and public review of the treaty text.

"The book of the covenant was put in the Ark of the Covenant . . ." (Exod. 25:16).

5. Lists of witnesses to the Treaty. These were the chief gods of the area.

"I call upon heaven and earth to witness . . ." (Deut. 4:26).

6. A Blessing and Curses section.

"A curse if you kept not all the words . . ." (Deut. 27:26).

7. The Formal Oath-Taking.

"All that is written in the book we shall do. And Moses took the blood and threw it upon the people . . ." (Exod. 24:8).

It is easy to see why great interest was generated when the treaties were translated. Interpretation of the data has been varied, but it is now a matter of almost universal consensus among Old Testament scholars that the Old Testament Covenant is related in some way to the Hittite International Treaty form. Scholars have usually fallen into groups of shared opinions when a matter of uncertainty about the Old Testament has arisen. There are schools of thought about most subjects in the Bible.

Liberal scholars who were influenced by the presuppositions of what is called "form criticism" tended to take a view that was evolutionary. They believed the Hebrew writers borrowed Near Eastern *forms* and gave them their own meanings and projected this understanding back onto the characters in the earlier myths and legends. The Hebrew ideas about religion, they say, grew at about the same time and with the same ideas as their pagan neighbors. Julius Wellhausen represented well the rather "low view" of scripture. Those interested in understanding more of it can read either his own works translated[13] or can read a history of Old Testament interpretation such as Martin Noth's *A History of Pentateuchal Traditions.*[14] Those who may wish to read about the same material from a covenant point of view, supporting, in the main, the text as traditionally understood, and accepting it at face value, may read Walter Eichrodt's *Theology of the Old Testament.*[15]

We may say with some certainty, when all the dust of academic debate has settled, the prophets of the Old Testament, and Moses in particular, followed by his friend Joshua, understood they had a treaty with YHWH, the Creator of the universe. They understood that His covenant was a serious matter. A relationship to God was as important as

---

13. Julius Wellhausen, *Die Composition des Hexateuchs,* Jahrbucher duer Deutch Theologie 21 1876:392-450.

14. Martin Noth, *A History of Pentateuchal Traditions,* Englewood Cliffs, N.J.: Prentice Hall, 1972.

15. Walter Eichrodt, *Theology of the Old Testament,* Vol. 1, Philadelphia: Westminster Press, 1961.

any with kings and pharaohs. The fidelity given to God was no less important than that given to the lords of this earth.

"Religious Language" is Treaty Language

One is also impressed with the kind of language found in the ancient treaty formulas. It was what we would associate with religious vocabulary. For instance, in the Annals of Ashurbanipal this statement occurs, "The people of Arabia asked one another saying: 'Why has such an evil befallen Arabia?' and they answered, 'Because they did not observe the valid covenant sworn to the God of Ashur'" (Rassam Cylinder 9:68-72). At the end of chapter twenty-nine of Deuteronomy the same kind of question is asked: "And the generations to come, . . . and the foreigners . . . will ask 'Why did the Lord do thus to the land?' . . . and they will be told, 'Because they forsook the covenant of the Lord'" (Deut. 29:21-24).

In the giving of grants to a loyal vassal, much of the same kind of language as is used in scripture can be found. A grant to an Assyrian servant read: "Balta, whose heart is whole to his master, stood before me with truthfulness, and walked in perfection in my palace . . . and kept the charge of my kingship . . . I considered his good relations to me and established therefore this gift." Identical formulas were found in connection with the covenants given to both David and Abraham. To Isaac, God said, "I will multiply your descendants . . . and will give to your descendants all these lands . . . because Abraham obeyed my voice and kept my charge, and my commandments, statutes, and laws." (Gen. 26:4, 5). Of David, Solomon said: "Thou hast shown great and steadfast love to thy servant David, my father, because he walked before thee in faithfulness, righteousness of heart, and uprightness, and Thou hast kept for him this great and steadfast love . . ." (I Kgs. 3:6).

In W. L. Moran's splendid work, it was shown that the concept of the "love of God" actually expressed loyalty.[16]

It was in this sense we find the same word used in almost all extant documents. It was a political expression. Deuteronomy abounds in expressions originating in the diplomatic language of the Ancient Near East. "To follow with the whole heart," "to cleave with the whole soul and strength," "to harken to the voice of," "to be perfect with," "to go after," "to serve with a perfect heart," "to fear or revere," "to put these words in your heart," "to turn neither to the left nor to the right,"—all were expressions common in diplomatic language 2,000 years before Christ.

Land was distributed to vassals by the great kings and warlords of the ancient world. Such phrases abound as: "Behold I have given you the Seha-river-land . . . but unto Mashuiluwas I have given the land Mira." In another Hittite treaty, a vassal was rewarded as follows: "See, I gave you the Sippasla Mountain land. Occupy it." God said to Joshua: "See, I have given you Jericho . . . you shall . . ." (Josh. 6:2). God said to Abraham: "Look . . . for all the land that you see I shall give to you . . ." (Gen. 13:14).

The blessing and curses sections of the Hittite treaties are of special interest. They were remarkably similar to those of the Law of Moses. The blessings of being a faithful vassal were described in detail in the treaties. The evils that were sworn to befall the unfaithful vassal were stipulated in detail. McCarthy has translated this treaty curse from an ancient text:

---

16. W. L. Moran, "Love of God," *Catholic Biblical Quarterly*, 25:77-87, 1963.

This head is not the head of a ram, it is the head of the Matiilu, and the head of his sons, his nobles, and his people. If those sin against this treaty, as the head of this ram is cut off, and his leg put in his mouth, so may the head of those named be cut off. This shoulder is not the shoulder of a ram. It is the shoulder of the one named, and of his sons, nobles, and the people of his land. If Matiilu sins against this treaty, as the shoulder of this ram is torn out, so may be the shoulder of the one named, his sons, nobles, and the people of his land be torn out.

A reading of the blessings and curses of Deuteronomy leaves one feeling much the same way. Death and sorrow were to follow all who broke the covenant sworn to Jehovah. Making a covenant with Jehovah and sealing it with a solemn oath was no less binding or dangerous than making a treaty with a powerful king. Jehovah intended to be the Great King of His people. He expected His people to give the same kind of service and "treaty love" to Him as they would to any earthly king or governor. Malachi made that matter clear:

And if I am master, where is my fear, says the Lord of hosts to you priests, you who despise my name. You say, "How have we despised thy name?" By offering polluted food upon my altar. And you say, "How have we polluted it?" When you offer blind animals in sacrifice, is that no evil thing? And when you offer those that are lame and sick, is that no evil? Present that to your governor; will he be pleased with you or do you favors? says the Lord of hosts (Mal. 1:6ff.).

Treaties in Perpetuity

In normal international affairs, as well as contracts between cities, tribes, and individuals, the length of time a treaty is to be in force is important. There are two types of duration treaties. The pact may run for a stated number of years, in which case the duration is part of the treaty itself. It may or may not be renewed after it has expired. On the other hand a treaty may be open-ended or, as diplomatic language has it, "in perpetuity." How long is that? When such a statement as "in perpetuity" occurs in the body of the treaty it means the treaty is to stand until mutually agreed, or until circumstances force a change as mutually agreed, or until one party breaks it so seriously as to make it null and void. In pacts between nations, "in perpetuity," is intended to bind not only the present administration but succeeding ones as well. The son of the king with whom a treaty is made is expected to continue any treaty made "in perpetuity."

The Hebrew words *ad olam*, meaning "for ever" mean "in perpetuity" when in the context of treaty. That is to say, in the Bible, a promise is associated with a covenant and lasts as long as the treaty lasts. Few promises of the Old Testament, made in connection with a specific treaty, are regarded as in force in the New Testament. Thus Canaan was to be a promised land *ad olam* (Gen. 17:8), David's throne (II Sam. 7:13), circumcision (Gen. 17:13), the Sabbath day (Exod. 31:16), the Passover (Exod. 12:14), the House of Eli as priesthood (I Sam. 2:30ff.), the vestments of Aaron (Exod. 28:43), and the scapegoat ceremony (Lev. 16:29) are all spoken of as "forever." Yet all these passed away if the Apostles of Christ are to be believed. The Hebrew *ad olam*, when used in connection with covenanted matters, means, "as long as the covenant lasts." When the Old Covenant was discontinued, as the Apostles understood, all promises made under it also ended.

20

Covenant Formulary

Covenant "formulary" refers to the parts of a covenant. Ashley Johnson, who had written in the late nineteen hundreds a splendid series of lectures on the two covenants, used the three category system of analysis. I think it is the same system used by the Apostles. The typical covenant form has *Parties*, *Stipulations*, and *Promises*. Almost every passage of scripture is a discussion of some aspect of these three parts. If one were not a party to a particular covenant, he need not worry about keeping the stipulations and he need not expect any blessing for keeping them or any curse for their violation. Covenants were a complete package. There is a popular church song that goes something like this:

> Every promise in the Book is mine,
> Every chapter, every verse, every line,
> All the blessings of His love Divine,
> Every promise in the Book is mine.

While that is good rhyming, it is not good theology. Unless one were, for instance, a blood descendant of Abraham, he had no part in the promised inheritance of Canaan as his homeland. He was not obligated to circumcise his sons, and neither should he expect, as a Bible believer, to be part of a great nation. Those stipulations and promises were part of a covenant which was not a universal kind. It was a particular covenant made with a particular man and his blood descendants. One must be very careful to read the Bible as he would a treaty document, not as a tool for divination, or as a document that carries some magical power to reveal privately some message from God. It is a treaty paper and is straightforward in language and means

21

what it says in the very words of the text. It means to communicate the same idea to every reader. That is why treaties
were written and commanded to be read to the common
man each year. The common man understands such language. The normal rules of grammar prevail, and when
the text is put in context, the original and true meaning
emerges.

Hesed

In the Hebrew word *hesed* there is a marvelous idea.
Before defining it, I want to establish its very high place in
Biblical thinking. It was a covenant-related term of greatest
importance. Nelson Glueck has done the definitive study of
the term. It was published in English in 1975.[17] An American
student of Hebrew at Yale University wrote his dissertation
on the same word. In 1935, Bowen defined *hesed* as

A beneficient expression of a relationship growing out of
some tie or bond, such as a family, or bond, or covenant,
or guest-host pattern.[18]

Although the term was used to describe human qualities,
in Deuteronomy it was used exclusively to describe YHWH.
It was always used in association with the word *berith*,
"covenant." It was a moral term but used in covenant context. A later writer, Aubrey Johnson in his book, *Hesed and
Hasid*, defined *hesed* always in relation to covenanted
stipulations or "loyalty to covenantal terms."[19] One could

---

17. Nelson Glueck, *Hesed*, Hebrew Union College Press, Also KVAL,
New York City, 1927 and 1975.

18. Boone A. Bowen, *A Study of Hesed*, unpublished doctoral dissertation,
Yale Univeristy School, 1935.

19. Aubrey Johnson, *Hesed and Hasid*, Oslo: Fabritus and Sonner, 1955,
p. 100-112.

expect *hesed* from Jehovah simply because He was as good as His word. One owed *hesed* to Jehovah if he had accepted a covenanted relationship. Johnson differed slightly from Glueck in that, for Johnson, *hesed* had an element of affection in it, and could not be translated simply "loyalty." In covenant, whether that of host and guest, or of ruler and vassal, the partner had an element of trust and love or concern for the other. The core meaning, accepted by both Johnson and Glueck, was "faithfulness to commitments and to legitimate expectations."

Jehovah as Covenant-Keeper God

Glueck came to the conclusion, from a rather radical form-critical position, that the word *hesed* when applied to YHWH meant "covenant keeping."

> In everyday life, *hesed* was the reciprocal conduct expected in the relationship between master and servant. Similarly, *hesed* characterizes the reciprocal relationship between Yahweh and his servants. Yahweh keeps his promise and thus shows *hesed* to those who walk before him . . . The covenant concluded between Yahweh and the patriarchs, established through an oath, had *hesed* as a consequence. *Hesed* was the content of every *b'rth* as well as every covenantal relationship.

> Thus *hesed* can be translated as "loyalty" and "love" so as to emphasize that it is Yahweh's *hesed*. However, one must remain aware that a very particular kind of love is meant, conforming to loyalty and obligation and thereby fulfilling the conditions of the covenant.

Several passages of scripture where parallelism is used will help demonstrate how scholars come to define Hebrew words the way they do.

23

Your God is God, a faithful God who keeps covenant and *hesed* with those who . . . (Deut. 7:9).

We see that *faithful* means *covenant keeping* and that means having *hesed* too. Much the same is seen below.

"I will maintain my *hesed* to him forever, and my covenant with him shall never fail" (Ps. 89:28)

We see that *forever* is used in parallel with *never fail* and *hesed* is parallel with *covenant*. To continue the same passage will reveal several parallelisms.

> "If his sons forsake my law
> and do not follow my statutes,
> if they violate my decrees,
> and fail to keep my commands,
> I will punish their sins with a rod
> and their iniquity with flogging.
> But I will not take my *hesed* from him,
> nor will I betray my faithfulness.
> I will not violate my covenant.

It is apparent that *forsake* means what *do not follow* meant. We see that *law, statutes, decrees,* and *commands* all mean the same thing in Hebrew. It is also clear that *sins* and *iniquity* both mean exactly the same thing. And we see again that *hesed* means *faithfulness* and also *not violate covenant*. In the two passages below the same ideas are expressed.

"For thy *hesed* is before my eyes, and I walk in *faithfulness* to Thee" (Ps. 26:3).

"Let Thy *steadfast love* (*hesed*) and Thy *faithfulness* preserve me" (Ps. 40:11).

In the great prayers addressed to God by Solomon, Daniel and Nehemiah, the same pattern of address was used. Several hundred years separated these prayers, yet they have essentially the same theme: God's valid behavior according to His covenanted promises.

Solomon addressed God, "God . . . you who keep your covenant and *hesed*" (I Kgs. 8:23).

Daniel addressed God, "Oh, God . . . who keeps His covenant and *hesed*" (Dan. 9:4).

Nehemiah the same, "God . . . keeping covenant and *hesed* to all . . ." (Neh. 1:5).

The use of parallelism has fallen into bad times recently, to the loss of sound Biblical thinking. If Bible students began to recognize parallels when they see them, and understand their original use by the writers of the Bible texts, they would begin to think as the writers did and to adopt the same category system. Parallelism was used by recent scholars to aid in understanding ancient Hebrew.

By this method we find that *hesed* has two aspects. They are related, and the one implies the other, yet there are two elements joined. No Greek word could carry BOTH elements. Neither could Latin nor English. Therefore we have difficulty correctly carrying the true meaning of *hesed* out of the Hebrew into other languages unless a good deal of explanation is used.

Hebrew hesed

Follow-thru on obligation is the root idea. And "follow-thru" must be some BEHAVIOR. It is not an emotion that leads to action. It is the action itself. Since "obligation" is part of the definition, there must have been some kind of commitment previously made or implied. For this reason, Nelson Glueck, the leading authority on *hesed* (having done exhaustive study of that one word for his doctoral dissertation) says that *hesed* is the "essence of a covenant." That means the doing of a covenant is the *hesed* of it. If a commitment was made and not done, there was a lack of *hesed*.

Greek eleos

The Greek-speaking Jews used the word *eleos* to translate *hesed*. In the English *eleos* became *mercy*. *Mercy, steadfast love,* and *lovingkindness* are the chief ways *hesed-eleos* has been translated. Why did the Greeks use *eleos*? We are not sure. One thing is sure, however. *Eleos* must mean exactly what *hesed* meant, for translators are not to re-define the content of a word, but only "translate" it. But why "mercy" for "faithfulness"? Well, when one makes an agreement, it is usually to his own advantage. He is to be benefited by the performance of the other partner to the agreement. If my partner fails to follow through I am damaged. It is to my benefit that he follow through on his commitments. Thus the follow-through is translated by some beneficial term: love, mercy, steadfast love, or loving-kindness. We must remember, however, that our word *mercy* is being slightly redefined. (We do not redefine the original—*hesed*.) When one hears "mercy" being read in scripture, it must be understood to mean: "follow-through on commitments so the other partner may not suffer because of my unfaithfulness."

Types of Obligations

There were in Hebrew, as with any culture, two or more kinds of obligations. Some were formal. In Hebrew these were called "*covenant.*" Some were informal: returning good to one who had done good to us.

Formal Obligations Formal obligations were such as arise when one enters a league or confederation. There is usually a written, or at least, a well understood covenant or treaty in such cases. Contracts, marriages, and treaties all are formal type agreements and from them arises obligation. *Hesed* was the word for keeping those obligations. Words that mean "follow-through" on obligation are always found in abundance wherever covenant type words are found. It is sufficient here to say because the two phrases, "Who keeps covenant" and "*hesed*" are used together, some kind of obligation meeting must be understood when translating *hesed* as *eleos.* It is unfortunate for Bible understanding that the English language has no word that includes meeting obligation, married, as it were, to being bound to help the covenanted partner.

Informal obligations arise when we are 1) *Parents* who have an unstated but moral obligation to care for the children. Such care for the *best interest of* includes instruction, discipline, degrees of freedom and such, as well as mere physical care. 2) *Host* has the obligation to make the guest feel at ease, be safe, and have such needs cared for as good order might require. The guest has an obligation to the host. He may not be demanding, rude, or return evil to one "with whom he has dipped the bread." 3) A *king* has moral obligations that transcend any statement of law. He is *responsible* for the basic welfare of the people. He is to be an example to the entire land: "Like King, like subject." The *citizen* is to honor and support the king—not in evil, but to his *best interest.* Tribal elders, (and later all leaders) were to act in the best intersts of the people. The people were to care for the needs and best interests of the leaders. 4) *Friends* who had aided me were to find the same kind of treatment from me. This is expected in every culture. The Hebrews also called that kind of *good will hesed.*

Since help given in return for help received is the essence of *hesed,* and since help is needed most when we can not perform by ourselves, we see why *mercy,* or *lovingkindness,* or *steadfast love* is used to translate *hesed.*

Moral Obligations

Because Abraham was going into a dangerous land, where men were regularly killed for their attractive wives, Abraham asked Sarah to show him the *hesed* to be passed off as his sister if that should be necessary to save his life (Gen. 20:13).

When Joseph correctly interpreted the dream for the baker who was thereby restored to favor, Joseph reminded him to remember his *hesed* to Joseph when he came into favor (Gen. 40:14).

The people of Israel were criticized for not having cared for the family of the great Gideon who had so aided them all in their own quest for freedom. The scripture says they "forgot God" and in parallelism, they "did not show *hesed* to the family of Gideon *in return for all the good he had done to Israel"* (Judg. 8:35).

Rahab asked the spies to swear an oath (formal covenant) that they would honor their promises in exchange for her own help, and that honoring of commitment was called *hesed* (Josh. 2:12-14).

Abner was angry with the son of Saul who accused him of an error in respect, at which Abner affirmed that he had shown great *hesed* to "the house of Saul, your father." He was loyal to Saul as his obligation. He was paying it (II Sam. 3:8).

David asked Solomon to remember his obligation to return kindness to the house of Barzillai, who had so aided David after his early defeat by Absalom. The obligation Solomon was to remember was called his *hesed* to Barzillai" (I Kgs. 2:7).

Friends showed *hesed* to friends. Hushai was asked by Absalom whether he had shown *hesed* to David, his friend (II Sam. 16:17). David repaid the *hesed* shown to him by Nahash by coming to the aid of the sons of Nahash (II Sam. 10:2).

It was regarded as a grave error and breach of *hesed* for Joash to have slain, however unwittingly, the son of his friend, Jehoida (II Chron. 24:22).

Ruth was complimented by Boaz for having been faithful to her mother-in-law, Naomi, in caring for her. Such "mercy" was called *hesed* in the text (Ruth 3:10).

Naomi blessed Boaz for having been faithful to the law of succession in Israel in taking Ruth as wife. That was *hesed* on the part of Boaz (Ruth 2:20).

We may say that *hesed* arose from relationships that exist, whether by birth, marriage, or any other by common social assent. The obligation was tantamount to moral compulsion. To call one "friend," "family," "wife," "lord," "partner," "servant," or "guest" placed upon the individual an obligation to act in the other's best interest: to show *hesed*.

Covenant as Theological Core

A Hebrew dictionary of theological terms or a dictionary of religion could be created by using covenant as core. Every major philosophic and theological idea in the Bible is related in some way to covenant. It is a rare religious idea in the Bible that is not tied in some way to an aspect of a covenant. Consider the following:

GOD liked to be known as a covenant-making and covenant-keeping Creator. The most frequently used word to describe YHWH or, to put it another way, the most frequently used word used to modify the term God in the Old Testament was "covenant keeper" (Deut. 7:7-9).

MAN was made in God's image and differed from animals in that he could make moral choices. A dog has some ability to choose. He will choose a piece of meat over a dry stick every time! But man can make a moral commitment and choose ways to keep it or break it. In this way he differs from all creatures. Micah asked what God required of man. He answered, "To act justly, to love mercy, and to walk humbly with God" (Mic. 6:8). Each of those words is a treaty related word! Each has no real substance except as part of a previously made commitment.

RIGHTEOUSNESS was keeping covenant. So with Adam. So in the law of Moses (Deut. 6:25). So in the New Testament (I John 3:7). "He that does what is right is righteous." What is "right" is always stipulated in a covenant.

JUSTICE, the word mishpath in Hebrew, meant "making judgments or decisions that are in harmony with the covenant." Another way of saying it is "deciding rightly" (Deut. 33:21).

HEARING the Lord was doing what He had said to do (Deut. 28:2, 13, 15). What He had said to do was in the treaty.

SIN was breach of the covenant, or disobedience (Deut. 28:58-61). John said that sin was disobedience. Offerings

30

for sins were for breach of the Law of God whether one realized he was doing it or not (Lev. 4:2, 13, 22, 27).

SACRIFICES were for sins committed. The entire sacrificial system was one which provided for "atonement" for sins committed. The system was a vital part of the Old Covenant, and when the Old Covenant was done away, the entire sacrificial system was done away with it (Heb. 10:1-10).

THE LAW was the statement of stipulations for Israel. It was a word having a broader and milder connotation than European or American concepts of law. Law was a tool to help maintain good relationships. It helped one covenant partner know what the other could not abide. It allowed great areas of freedom. That which was not forbidden was presumed to be permitted. The Law in Israel later came to mean the covenant itself, and later yet the entire body of scripture of the Old Testament.

THE PEOPLE OF GOD, a very significant idea in both Testaments, came into being by having a convenanted relationship with God. God chose Abraham and Israel as his own special people and made a covenant with them. The status was a result of their relationship to God, identified and defined by the covenant (Deut. 26:16-19).

BLESSINGS from God were convenanted. Some common blessings were given to all descendants of Adam, but others were special and limited to the people of the covenant. They were extensive, specific, and related to each individual covenant (Deut. 28:1-14).

CURSES from God were almost always related to covenant. There is a long list in the Old Testament in various places, all part of the Old Covenant (Deut. 28:15ff.). When neighboring tribes about Israel were cursed by God it was to

31

insure the survival of Israel as a covenant people and to make good the promises made to their fathers (Deut. 9:1-6).

PROPHETS were not ecstatic visionaries, but sober lawyers of the covenant, pressing YHWH's lawsuit against a sinful and covenant-breaking nation. They were to aid Israel in keeping their relationship with YHWH sound and secure. All the thunderings about sin by the prophets were related to the Law of Moses. This fact was confessed by them (Dan. 9:7-19).

THE LORD'S SUPPER was a covenant renewal ceremony, as was one aspect of the old sacrifices.

LOVING THE LORD was used in parallel with keeping His statutes, walking in His ways and cleaving to Him. All these phrases were diplomatic terms for keeping a treaty.

In the word studies below, I have taken several words from the Theological Dictionary edited by Alan Richardson, Canon of Durham. Note the wide references to covenant in representative words, contributed by several different authorities.[20]

CALLED, ELECT, ELECTED, CHOSEN are all words used frequently in the scripture and "all trace back to the covenant with Abraham" (p. 43).

DETERMINATE, PREDETERMINED, PREDESTINATED all trace back to the determination of God to bless all mankind in Christ who was the seed of woman and of Abraham. This determination began with "the choice of Abraham" (p. 64).

GRACE "The grace of God in the Old Testament is closely connected with the idea of covenant." It represented the forbearance with which God dealt with man and His offer

---

20. Alan Canon Richardson, *A Theological Dictionary of the Bible,* New York: Macmillan Company, 1953.

of a way out. "Paul's approach (to grace) was through the idea of covenant-love, *hesed*, which has broken down all barriers" (p. 100).

INHERITANCE is a concept of receiving the blessings from God as within His family and "traces back to God's promise to Abraham in Gen. 12:7" (p. 112).

KINDNESS "is used once in the sense of a good deed (II Sam. 2:6) and elsewhere (36 times) for the Hebrew *hesed*, the covenant-word which Cloverdale translated by 'loving-kindness'" (p. 119).

LOVING-KINDNESS "Sir Adam Smith suggested the rendering of 'leal-love.' The merit of this translation is that it combines both the two ideas of love and loyalty, both of which are essential. The theological importance of the word *hesed* is that it stands more than any other word for the attitude that both parties to a covenant ought to maintain toward each other" (p. 136).

MERCY "thus signifies that continued forbearance of God by which he 'keepeth covenant' with Israel even when Israel is slow to keep His commandments to a degree" (p. 143).

OBEY is from the Hebrew *shema* meaning to hear and "to conform in humility to that which God prescribes by way of claim or of promise." It is directly opposite of the conduct of "revolt and rebellion of those who broke the Old Covenant" (p. 160).

PEACE was a very complex concept that involved a covenanted peace with God. "Peace is a normal and proper condition of men in relationship with one another in family first and extended to others by a covenant which determines relationships and is also a 'covenant of peace'" (p. 165).

PROMISE is most frequently related to a covenanted agreement, "i.e., strangers to the covenants of promise" (p. 172).

It is not necessary to carry the concept further, at least in this same procedure. Before this discussion of covenant as "theological core" is terminated, however, it is well to examine an example of a respected theologian who has undertaken to place all Old Testament matters within a covenant perspective. W. Eichrodt was asked to contribute the first two volumes to the very impressive and well received Westminster Series on the Old Testament. Volume one reviews the religion of Israel in the following outlined form. This is the Table of Contents.

   I. Old Testament Theology: Problem and Method

  II. The Covenant Relationship
    1. The Meaning of the Covenant Concept
    2. The History of the Covenant Concept

 III. The Covenant Statutes
    A. The Secular Law

 IV. The Covenant Statutes (continued)
    B. The CULTUS
      Sacred rites
      Sacred objects
      Sacred seasons
      Sacred actions
      Synthesis

  V. The Name of the Covenant God

 VI. The Nature of the Covenant God: Being

VII. The Nature of the Covenant God: Activity

VIII. The Instruments of the Covenant
    A. The Charismatic Leaders
      Moses   Nabism
      Seers   Classical prophecy
      Nazarites

It is obvious to any casual reader of the Old Testament that the documents of scripture are not laid out in as neat a fashion as Eichrodt's. The documents grew up around the covenant over a long period of time. The books of the Old Covenant are certainly not written in legal style. Most of the Torah itself, the five books of Moses, are understandings of history, covenant, exhortation, records of failure, and success all mixed together. Nonetheless the presumption of Eichrodt is sound. There is a core to the Old Testament, and the New Testament writers called the entire package of documents the Old Testament (II Cor. 3:14). Gerhart Hasel has denied that the idea of covenant can give structural unity to the Old Testament. He further denied that covenant stood as the foremost idea from which all others are explained.[21] I think the fact that the documents were identified as Covenant Documents puts the presumption in favor of a covenant orientation as core. If covenant is not the foremost

---

21. Gerhart Hasel, *Old Testament Theology: Basic Issues in the Current Debate*, Grand Rapids: Eerdmans, 1972, p. 79.

idea of the Old Testament, by which all other ideas become related, what is? History is a careful selection of data in support of a principle, thus salvation-history itself cannot be the subject of its own observation or report. In selecting New Testament (covenant) as the name for the books of the Apostles, the ancient church also signaled their understanding of covenant as the prime philosophic concept of the documents.

Conclusion

In this first chapter we have attempted to define the key words in the study: covenant and covenant keeping. These were carried in the Hebrew as *b'rth* and *hesed,* respectively. Two methods were used in defining them. First, the word as used in the Testament, as understood by its context, and as used by the authors was reviewed. Second, the method was to examine parallels of the same word, whether in its original Hebraic form or a translation of it. By this study it was learned that *b'rth* was a diplomatic term meaning covenant. That meaning fit most uses of the word in the Old Testament, especially the Sinai Covenant. We understood that covenants had three elements: Parties, Terms, and Promises. A key idea was mutual commitment or mutual promise. Another concept was conditionality. Promises were conditioned upon the faithfulness of the other party. This was modified slightly by the concept of *hesed.*

A comparison of the ancient Near Eastern Treaty forms also supported the idea of Israel's Treaty with God. No effort was made to elaborate on the implications of the similarity other than the necessary implication that a relationship with God was structured to an extent, and that the fact of covenant was taken very seriously by the Hebrews. Care for that relationship was to be as serious as the care given to any lord. The basis of a relationship with God was to receive the same legal and moral attention any pact between men or nations was to receive.

The third major concept treated in this first chapter was covenant as core of Biblical theology or Hebrew philosophy. All major ideas and elements of religion were part of a covenant. The nation itself was the "people of the covenant." The priesthood, sacrifices, worship and administration were all used to promote and protect the covenant and the keeping of the covenant.

The last idea presented in the chapter was a study of the word *hesed*. It was the chief Hebrew word for covenant keeping. It was used in parallelism with words which meant both keeping covenant or faithfulness and also in situations where support of the other was needed or given. *Hesed* has the twin ideas of faithfulness both to the terms of the treaty and the individual with whom one was encovenanted.

Questions on Chapter One

1. The frame of reference of Biblical theology was provided by
   a) Hebrews   b) Romans   c) Greeks   d) English
2. The Hebrew word for covenant was
   a) *Hesed*   b) *b'rth*   c) *shalom*   d) *messiah*
3. T F The usual meaning of covenant was "promise."
4. T F "Treaty" is a good way to understand *b'rth*.

5. Treaties bound when
   a) Both agreed on the terms
   b) Both understood it
   c) One said, "Agreed."
   d) Oath was sworn
6. Name the three elements all covenants had.

   _____

   _____

   _____

7. T F "Mutual commitment" is a good way to understand covenant.
8. T F "Grace" meant something apart from and unconnected with covenants.
9. T F Covenants are conditional promises.
10. T F Keeping covenant was the root meaning of "righteousness."
11. T F Hebrew covenant-keeping had in it the element of affection.
12. The main word for keeping-covenant-with-affection for the other was
    a) *b'rth*   b) *ahab*   c) *hesed*   d) *yada*
13. *Hesed* was composed of two ideas. Describe each.
    A._____
    B._____
14. What concept other than "treaty" could be used to harmonize Biblical revelation? Discuss it.
15. Explain why the documents of the Bible, composed of history, law, poetry and prophetic sermons were all called the Old Testament.

38

1. a) Hebrew frame of reference is the Biblical category system.
1. b) *B'rth* was the word translated into "covenant."
3. F The meaning of b'rth was *conditional promise,* not mere unilateral promise.
4. T The New International Version translated *b'rth* as treaty.
5. d) Oath bound both parties. Until oath was sworn, either party could negotiate, urge additions to the text, or back out.
6. *Parties, Stipulations,* and *Promises.*
   >Terms
   >Conditions
   >"Laws"
7. T Covenant meant that two parties each made commitments to the other.
8. F Grace was often used for keeping covenant and for supporting the other party even when he was slack or was neglecting his duty.
9. T The first party is technically freed from obligation if the second utterly abandons his part.
10. T Both Deuteronomy and John so state.
11. T Part of Hebrew covenant was the element of *hesed.*
12. *Hesed* is used in parallel with covenant keeping very frequently.
13. A) Keeping my part of the bargain faithfully.
    B) Helping my partner to keep his part, coming to his aid, etc.
14.
15. Because all these are related to and held together by the Covenant.

TURN THE BOOK OVER FOR ANSWERS.

COVENANT AS TREATY

Chapter Two

PLATO OR MOSES?

Who shall guide us in our attempt to understand God and His covenants—Plato or Moses? Who shall tell us the meaning of life and the nature of mankind—Plato or Moses? Who shall teach us reality, choice, and destiny—Plato or Moses? It may surprise you as you read this chapter to discover how much of the Christian world has chosen . . . Plato!

It is my own opinion that Moses was far ahead of Plato in matters of philosophy that really count. Moses had moved from the category system preoccupied with the *nature* of things to an examination of the *ethic* or the *purpose* of things. When we approach God and His message, we will do well to turn from Plato and the Greeks, and listen to Moses.

In this chapter the presuppositions of covenant religion will be examined. These presuppositions will be compared and contrasted with those of the Hellenistic world. A great deal of wrong thinking in theology has occurred because of the practice of accepting the presuppositions of the Greeks and recasting the Biblical concepts into that mold. Many problems arise in reading the Bible if one believes the assumptions of the Greeks and then tries to make sense of the Bible. The Bible carries its own category system. It places its related elements into its own frame of reference. It has, in a word, its own philosophy. All its philosophy is harmonized with the notion of covenant.

Reality

Plato does not represent all possible Greek philosophies, but because his writings have survived and have been widely discussed, his name has been used almost as a synonym for Greek philosophy. I am using it in that same way, although aware of the limitations of the practice.

The Greeks held two different views of ultimate reality. One was represented by Plato who rejected the "analogy of the gods" explanation of reality and sought it in nature itself. He studied the laws of nature and of human behavior and concluded that true reality was composed of the appearances that made up individual facts and the laws of nature that allowed, directed, or produced the facts. The enduring reality was the laws of being. This was "spirit" for Plato. Spiritual was the word or concept for the unseen reality that underlies all nature. Matter, for Plato, was a transitory sub-reality. It was real, to be sure, but not eternal, because all manifestations of the law of reproduction, for instance, passed away while the law itself remained. For Plato, the nearest thing to a god was the overall orderliness he found in nature. Plato was a pantheist of sorts. There was for Plato no separate deity apart from the very nature of matter and its "forms" or ideas that organized it. The student of Plato who took this view further was Aristotle. Plato and Aristotle's scientific approach to reality has been almost universally accepted as true by non-Christian western philosophers and by the overwhelming majority of teachers of science. It is the presupposition of materialism: nature is all there is to reality.

Other ancient Greeks held the "analogy of the gods" philosophy. What happened on earth was not caused by laws of nature, but was a reflection of the activity of the gods. The rain god did his job. The sun god his. The goddess of love hers. When a god was angry or tired things went bad in nature. When there was confusion or warfare between the gods, that situation was reflected in similar dislocations on earth. Ancient Baalism operated on the same basic presupposition, as did the religions of Egypt, and for that

41

matter, the rest of the world at that time. Man, then, was captive to either nature or the gods.

The Hebrews were not interested in the philosophy of nature. Nor did they believe in the "analogy of the gods." For them reality consisted of both the supernatural and the natural. We must turn to Moses for his statement of philosophy. It is found in the early chapters of Genesis. Reality is composed, according to Moses, of both matter and Spirit, both nature and the world of God. Moses was neither a materialist nor a pantheist. God created nature out of nothing. He simply willed it into existence. He said, "Let there be light. And there was light!" In the same way God made the rest of the universe. He established the order of things: the orbits, the reproductive styles, the basic orderliness found in nature. Man did not look to nature for any real knowledge about God! Nature was not God. Paul, a Mosaic type philosopher, stated that one could know only two things about God from looking at nature: the fact that God exists and that He is all powerful (Rom. 1:20). Implications flowed from that admission, which Paul pursued, but he rested his case there. We see at once that the very fact God offered to Abraham a covenant implied that God existed and was not a part of nature itself, that He was conversant, intelligent, compassionate, able to speak man's language, made plans, so limited His own power as to approach man and not "blow him away," and had some plans.

Plato was preoccupied with the problem of HOW god could relate to nature. Moses was content to take the common sense approach and ask WHAT God wanted in nature and in man. Covenant took the emphasis away from other topics, and put it on God's interests in history and His interest in man's part in it. When God made a covenant with Abraham, He established the AGENDA of philosophy and history. It was perhaps interesting to discover how nature worked, but that was not as important as having a right relationship with the ultimate Reality.

The Eden Episode

Moses elaborated upon the implications of covenant in the Eden account. Many factors were worked together to give an entire picture. That was a typical Hebrew way of doing things: wholly. Let us see how nature worked. It was from God. It was not God Himself. How God, as spirit, could connect with nature was not a matter of interest. God established an order, "Let each bear fruit after its own kind." Man was to subdue the world and "dress it." He was, in a word, to learn to live with nature, and not to be dominated by nature. He was in nature and also above it. This is exactly the opposite view taken by the Baalites and Plato. For them, man was to submit to nature, "do what came naturally," harmonize with the cycles of nature and thus find peace and security. That is also the philosophy of materialism. If nature is all there is to reality, then to follow the dictates of nature is the best way to survival and a happy adjustment. This view is reflected in such statements as, "He is more the product of evil, than evil himself. For he is the result of his gene patterning and of his social status. He did what he had to do under the circumstances." Moses would view that philosophy with alarm. Nature was not as inflexible for the Hebrew as for the Aristotelian Greek. For Aristotle nature was a *machana*, or spelled differently, a "machine." This brittle and mechanistic view of nature has been accepted by most of the scientific world. The Bible has an alternative view. Nature was composed of regularity and interruptibility.

43

To be sure, nature had regularity. If that were not so, one could not bake bread! Things have to be regular enough to enable man to learn the pattern and use it well. Interruptibility was also a part of nature. Breeds of cattle are interruptions of otherwise random breeding patterns. The sowing of wheat in a field is the planned interruption of otherwise random spreading of seeds. Medicine and first-aid are the timely interposition of forces that serve to avert or delay the otherwise normal course of decay or continued ill.

Just as God can interrupt nature in an act of revelation, such as an appearance to Abraham, so man can interrupt nature by placing a hand in the water and see the water flow in a disrupted pattern. As soon as the disruption is removed, the normal pattern continues. Laws of nature, in other words, are not properly stated without an assumed priviso. For instance, the law as stated here is not correct.

"Objects in motion tend to stay in motion and objects at rest tend to stay at rest."

It must be understood as having a hidden proviso to be completely true. With the assumed proviso openly stated it would read something as this:

"Objects in motion tend to stay in motion unless other forces intervene, and

Objects at rest tend to stay at rest unless other forces intervene."

Similarly, this maxim is at fault:

"Falling objects accelerate at the rate of 32 feet per second per second."

The truth is this:

"Falling objects accelerate at the rate of 32 feet per second per second unless other forces intervene."

The "other forces" may be wind and such, or may be a hand that reaches out stopping the falling object in midflight. All living beings have some ability as an "other force." According to Moses, man had almost God-like potential. He could think and plan ahead. He could greatly modify otherwise random processes and thus "subdue the earth."

Massive interventions in nature must be explained by forces sufficient to have caused the disruption. Many disruptions in nature, once thought to have been caused by the gods or even the true God, have been explained by other forces in nature, by psychology, or as having been the work of a human. Yet, there certainly were, and perhaps are those interruptions that can be only attributed to God. Alleged "revelations" of God, classified here as interruptions, ought to be carefully supported by evidence, but we ought not doubt our senses when they testify to an interruption any more than when they tell us of regularity. All such claims are subject, of course, to sound testimony and common sense. To conclude, the Hebrew had a more reasonable and less mechanistic view of nature than we inherited from the Greeks.

Choice and Consequence

Adam had a great deal of freedom. He was allowed to do whatever he liked except that he was forbidden to eat of a certain tree. Man was free to choose what he wanted, but he was not free to determine the consequences! God, nature, or later, society, helped determine the consequence. This was true in all things. It was true in nature. Pain was present in the garden if man had a body as men have now. Pain in the foot is less a problem than infection in the foot. If a tree in the garden had tannic acid in its bark, Adam would have gotten sick if he brewed a tea from that! He could put his hand forth to either fire or water. He got what he chose, but he did not determine the consequences. God did that.

In the arena of morals the same was true. God told man what he may and may not do—as a matter of morals. He ought not eat of one tree. The concept of "ought" is a moral idea. The Bible teaches that man was morally capable and morally responsible from the very beginning and that morality is from God and not merely a reflection of social values or the way societies maintain good order. Man was free; he *ought not* eat of the tree, but he *could* eat if he so chose. Morality had to do with choices, and no morality arose where there was no freedom of choice. As with nature, the consequences of choice were out of man's hands.

The Hebrews understood that all men were morally responsible, for all were descended from Adam and bore the stamp of his image. So all men were held to be in sin and error when they acted against the "right," whether the right was declared by God, or the Law of Moses, or by one's own conscience (Rom. 2:12-16). Furthermore, all men who do wrong will suffer the consequences, whether by nature, "who bear in their bodies the marks of their shame" (Rom. 1:27), by society, "for there is no authority except what God has established" (Rom. 13:1), or in the last judgment "when God will judge men's secrets through Jesus Christ, according to my gospel" (Rom. 2:16). In speaking as he did, Paul expressed the ancient Mosaic concept of universal human moral responsibility.

The responsibility of mankind extended to at least three arenas. First, man was responsible to God. That is expressed in the command about the fruit itself. Second, man was responsible for his world at large. That is carried in the command to dress and keep the garden. Third, mankind was responsible for the other parts of mankind. That is carried by Adam having got into difficulty through Eve, for which she was given special consequences. It was also expressed through God's reaction to the serpent who, because he lied about God and led someone else to believe it to their doom, was made the lowest of the low in God's sight, and also in man's sight. The serpent was to creep low, live low to the ground, and "eat dust." Anyone who led astray another was morally responsible for that act, according to the philosophy of Moses.

The Greeks had little concept of responsibility on such a grand scale. Their behaviors were philosophically DETER-MINED. They did what nature, and for Plato, the best in nature, caused them to do. Or man did what the gods had determined to be one's course, one's fate. On the practical level, the Greeks had slaves, practiced homosexuality, exposed infants to death (and attempted to blame their dying on the gods) and practiced what animals do: the survival of US survivors! In a mechanistic and deterministic universe, there is little need to discuss morality. One wills as he is made to will.

Ideas About God

Greek and Hebrew ideas about God were very different. Such Greeks as were religious had many gods. The Hebrews had one. The Greeks had a grand system of inferior and superior gods. They had their myths explaining the seasons. The Hebrew had none. The gods of the Greeks were much like the Greeks. They had virtues and vices; they won and they lost conflicts; they were a mixture of good and evil. The Greeks attributed "causes" to the gods. One caused springtime, another happiness. There was a god of wine. Idols, pictoral representations of these mythical gods, were accorded an honored place in the family. For the more philosophic Greek, the idol was not a god and did not represent a god at all. It represented an idea such as love or hope, or personal honor, or enduring friendship, and the like. The Hebrew was to have no image of God. Man and mankind alone was in the image of God.

The Greeks and Hebrews also differed in a more fundamental way. It had to do with power and its use. While many potential contrasts between Greek and Hebrew thinking are possible, none are more important than the one related to power.

For the Greeks power was the greatest divine attribute. Greeks loved and longed for power. They idealized this longing in their gods. Power became a more important attribute than morality. You see, if a god were to submit to some moral code, he would be inferior to that code. He would be inferior to the author or enforcer of the code. Thus a Greek god, to be god at all, must practice *both* good and evil. That will show him to be the greatest power in the universe. It was in this vein that the serpent suggested to Eve that being like God was "knowing both good and evil." "Knowing" for the Hebrew meant active and intimate participation in!

In the very act of approaching Abraham with a covenant, God was offering to seriously *limit* His power. For when one makes a promise, he has eliminated a great many possible future actions. He must do that one act. God was commited to a whole series of actions as a result of the covenant with Abraham. His ethic forced Him to do what He had promised. God's option to bless the world or not bless the world in Abraham's seed was gone. His only option now was to bless the world. That was a limitation.

When one thinks about it, God made a habit of limiting His power. It may be that God wanted to convey the notion that "restraint of power" is a greater attribute of character than power!

God's Restraint of Power

God gave up some power when He made the universe. At least he was restricted from interference and still have nature proceed on its normal course. It was a voluntary restraint certainly, but creation itself constituted a limitation on God's future potential actions. As long as He permitted nature to exist God had to make room for it.

God gave up considerable power when he made man with a spiritual nature: thinking, feeling and willing. He risked becoming the laughing stock of heaven in giving man free will. Allowing man to sin and to choose contrary to God's own stated will placed upon God a limitation. As long as man existed God had some accommodations to make. God did not get His own way about the fruit His man ate. To not get one's own way is a limitation certainly. The reader ought not be offended by talk like this—unless he also believes, as did the Greeks, that power is God's greatest attribute!

God limited His power when He communicated with man in language. He and Adam talked in words. If Adam was as human then as he is now, the conversation had to be out loud! They talked together. God taught Adam language. At least they named the animals. They created vocabulary.

49

Note that language is a type of covenant. We each agree that a given word means the same thing. Two can not have conversation unless the pattern of sounds is meant to convey what both agree. If one party to a conversation were to exercise some power and redefine all the words, and then forget the original, the two could no longer talk! God's Spirit communicated through words. This is the root source of the Hebrew high theology of "word of God." What God speaks is what God's Spirit is saying. God must also confine His revelation to human syntax. He must use verbs correctly. He must submit to the rules of grammar. Is that a weakness as the Greeks would believe? Or is it God's true glory and honor? Is the limiting of one's power a type of Godliness?

The greatest way God had limited His power was in covenant. He made commitments for a very long period of time. His *hesed* limited Him to fulfilling these. He could do nothing else, for as Paul said, "He cannot deny Himself" (II Tim. 2:13).

Sin, Righteousness, and Restraint of Power

Adam was limited in the garden. As long as he was content to live with that limitation he was godly—Godlike. When he exercised his power to chose either good or evil, he lost his godliness. Thus sin became, for the Hebrew, some aspect of unrestrained exercise of power. For instance, saying anything—the truth or lies, is free exercise of power. Limiting one's speech to the truth is restraint of the power of speech. Unrestricted and free use of sex was sin. Limiting sex to marriage was righteousness. Possessing things by any means, whether manufacture, borrowing, or stealing is an example

50

of free and unrestrained use of ability. Limiting the gaining of possessions to "lawful gain" is righteousness. It is difficult to think of any sin listed in either the Old or the New Testaments that does not involve the excessive use of power or ability. It is also difficult to find a matter regarded as righteous that does not require some sort of restraint of one's full powers.

Moses challenged the basic assumptions of the Greeks, through their forebears, when he produced Genesis for all to read. He challenged what was thought about God's relationship to nature, how nature itself worked, and what God's true power and glory were.

Persuasion and Programming

God set about repairing the ruptured relationship caused by the deliberate rejection of God's word and therefore rejection of His very nature. Adam had but one flaw. It was his lot to have been created. He did not choose his relationship to God. He was born to it, as it were. He had never chosen fellowship with God. And when he sinned, he chose not to remain in fellowship with God. From then until now, God determined that none should have His fellowship except those who sought it. Renewed fellowship would be with only such as wanted it. God was generous to man. If man did not want fellowship with God he was not forced into it. He could suffer, as Paul later put it, "Eternal separation from the presence of the Lord, and from the majesty of His power" (II Th. 1:9), but if he disliked God's company he wasn't forced into it.

The offer of a covenant to Abraham was consistent with God's nature and the situation. God, in grace and compassion, offered to mankind, through Abraham, an opportunity for reconciliation. But man must agree. That problem was solved in the idea of covenant. God had a part and man had a part. This set the style of relationship from then until now. In every dealing with God, man has a responsible part and God has a part. To be sure, God's part is by far the greater and full of good will, but man must join the hand of God and exercise his mind, and use his will, and move his body and enter the covenant. God will not program man to say, "I love you." He is willing to persuade man with mercies. He is willing to warn man with prediction and demonstration, but He will not destroy His handiwork by programming man to think, feel or will anything. He will use the medium of history, objective revelation, and words to reach man. God uses mediation. A covenant stands between God and man and joins together all who accept its terms and it separates all who refuse.

When viewed in that light, it takes more power to persuade than to program a reconciliation with free human beings. It took much more risk on God's part to make man with free will than with a spiritual reflex system. God risked something when He populated the earth with potential enemies. It would have been no risk to have programmed man to obedience. It was a superior God who revealed Himself to Moses. Lacking God's revelation, the Greeks did the best they could. They made their gods in their own image.

Man

For the Hebrew it was not possible to discuss God apart from man. The Hebrews experienced God in a relationship, not as a philosophic postulate. As a consequence, we have discussed man to a degree in the section about God. The Greeks and the Hebrews had such radically opposing views of man it seems advisable to devote more time to it here. The Greeks had a very low view of man. He came from evil, and as long as he was in a body he was bound to be evil to an extent. This view was expressed in their mythology. In the Delphi myth of the creation of man, the Hellenes had Zeus at war with Titan. Titan was cast to earth and burned with lightning. Out of the ashes of Titan, the evil one, man came. Man was therefore something evil—for the Greek. Plato typified man by his body. The head was called *nous*, the upper torso the *thumos*, and the lower torso *epithumia*. The head was "mind," the chest "spirit" or "courage," and the lower body "appetite" or "lust." For Plato as for most of the Greek writers who have claimed to follow him, *nous* was the word used for God. Plato's *nous* was the eternal "life-force." The implication was clear. Man's mind was like God and his body was like Titan. This was the philosophic root of the pagan dualism that characterized Greek thinking. For the Greeks,

> Man'd duty is to free himself from the chains of the body in which the soul lies fast bound like a prisoner in his cell.[1]

Plutarch in *Consolations to a Wife,* described the dual nature of man in terms of a bird held in a cage. The soul was imprisoned in the body as a bird in a cage. The duty of the soul, like the bird, was to escape. The soul often became so weak and lifeless that it actually returned to the cage as might a poor, captive bird, without spirit or zest for life.[2]

---

1. Phaedrus 250C, Phaedo 66B, Republic 517B, Cratylus 400C, Gorgias 493a.
2. Plutarch, *Consolations* 611E.

That kind of dualism was to cause the ancient church much concern. The Gnostics had the same philosophic presuppositions: the body was evil and the soul was good. It is not entirely fair to identify Plato with the Gnostics, especially understanding that Plato made a major philosophic shift in his later writings.[3] The popular understanding of Plato, however, leaves most authorities agreeing with Ladd: Platonic dualism is roughly similar to Gnostic dualism.[4] Man was like a charioteer driving two different horses across the heavens.

One was straining to fly downward into limitation, captivity, and loss. The other wanted to fly upward. For Plato, upward was ultimately "formless, colorless, intangible, truly existing essence (*ousia ontōs ousa*) with which all knowledge is concerned."[5] The downward pull, toward earth— evil in itself, assured man a status where "the utmost toil and struggle awaits the soul."[6] Plato's low view of man can be seen from four statements made about man: 1) The body is an enemy of the soul and is a "mass of evil."[7] 2) The body of man is the prisonhouse of the soul.[8] 3) The body hinders the soul in the acquisition of "knowledge" or philosophic understanding based upon science, the life of contemplation and abstraction.[9] 4) The mind ought to have as little as possible to do with the body.[10]

---

3. Leonard J. Eslick, *op. cit.*, 191.
4. George Eldon Ladd, *The Pattern of New Testament Truth*, Grand Rapids: Eerdmans, 1968, pp. 13, 14.
5. Phaedrus 247C.
6. Phaedrus 247B.
7. Phaedo 66B.
8. Phaedo 82E.
9. Phaedo 66.
10. Phaedo 65B.

For the Gnostics, who pressed pagan dualism to its logical conclusion, matter was evil. Flesh itself was evil. Gnostics, when attempting to harmonize Hebraic-Christian views with their own, saw Christ as a "redeemer." The Gnostic "redeemer" was one who came from God as a shaft of light and showed man the way to heaven. Salvation was escape from the body into oneness with the "divine mind." Salvation was extinction of personality.

The ethics of the Gnostics took two radically different forms. First, some claimed that the Christian faith freed them from the body "by faith." The body was "dead" with Christ. Therefore, if one's thinking was right and he had the will to do right, but his body sinned, it was of no real consequence. It was merely one's wretched body doing what bodies do. Paul and John both combatted that false conclusion (I John 1:8-10). Second, some held that since the body was evil, it ought to be "put to death." These deprived the body when it asked for food or shelter. They did whatever the body did not like. The body was abused as an evil. Paul argued against that view in Colossians 2:16-23.

Hebrew View of Man

Man was created in God's image for fellowship with God. Man was God's own reflection, the last and the best of all creation.

> And God made man from the dust of the earth and blew into his nostrils the breath of life, and man became a living soul (Gen. 2:7; cf. Isa. 42:5).

Man did not "have" a soul but rather WAS a soul. Breath or spirit was life, animation, power to make a difference on earth. Man was an integrated whole, for the Hebrew. The mind and the body were so bound up together that it was not possible to distinguish them, except to measure strength. *Nepes* or *nepesh* was soul. The same word was translated as "throat" (Ps. 69:1), "breath" (Gen. 35:18), and "life" (Gen. 9:4, Lev. 17:11). *Nepes* meant "me" as a living individual being. Another word the Hebrews used for man was *N'sama* or "breath." When man's breath went away, he died (Ps. 104:29ff.). In Job, it was the "breath" that made a man "understand" (Job 32:8). Breath meant life-force or an evidence of life. *Basar* was Hebrew for body. There was no thought that the body was evil; however, the body was weak. The "arm of flesh shall fail." Man's life "in the flesh" was contrasted with God's eternal type life (Gen. 6:4). There was no dualism as with the Greeks, however. Man's flesh and man's spirit acted together. The spirit could fail and the flesh suffer (Isa. 19:3). The flesh may fail, and the spirit suffer, "and when he drank, his spirit returned and he revived" (I Kings 17:22).

Ru'ah was the word in Hebrew for "spirit." It was a synonym for "soul" and for "breath." It is nonetheless the most frequently found word for describing man's moral nature. The word "heart," in Hebrew *leb* was used in many parallelisms with "spirit." A Hebrew could be "vexed in spirit" and "be of broken spirit" and be of "broken heart" and have a "faithful spirit" or a "spirit of whoredom," and also have "a haughty spirit." An individual may be a soul with "thy spirit against God." One could have a "spirit of sorrow," or have a "wounded spirit." In all events, the basic mindset of the Hebrew was that man was an integrated whole. He was somehow deficient when not "all together."

Sheol, for instance, was the separation of man from his life, or spirit. His soul perished. To the Hebrew, death or

56

"perish" was not extinction. It was a bad thing. It was a "meaningless, dreary existence, cut off from the living and from the presence of Jehovah."[11] In contrast with the Greek, the Hebrew believed that "life" was a basic and Godlike quality. Both his spirit and his body, and consequently his soul could be either good or bad. Nothing was evil in itself, except separation from Jehovah. The Hebrew had the only view of man that is consistent with a concept of covenant.

Free Will and Depravity

When men assumed the absolute sovereignty of God, without the quality of restraint of power for fellowship, then God became the very "cause" of everything. The Greeks had the philosophical problem of evil in man. If God were all powerful, and there was evil in man, then God must be the author of evil. The "fall of Adam" has afforded some the opportunity to substitute the Greek low view of man for Hebraic high view. After Adam fell, they allege, mankind became what the Greeks had always believed him to be: no good. The resulting idea is called "total depravity." Here is a statement by Martin Luther in his early days.

> Since the nature of man is corrupted through and through by original sin and is damned within and without, in body and soul, and flees from God when it really feels its sin, what becomes of free will and human powers? . . . Spiritual powers are not only corrupted, but even totally destroyed in both men and devils, and that nothing remains but a corrupted intellect and a will which is hostile and opposed to God at every point, which thinks and desires nothing but that alone which is contrary and opposed to God.[12]

11. Alan R. Richardson, *A Theological Wordbook of the Bible*, New York: Macmillan Co., 1953.
12. Martin Luther, *The Bondage of the Will*, n.d., Westwood, N.J.: Revel

Such a view reflects not the Hebrew philosophy of man, but that of the pagan Greek. Adam may or may not have had all his intellectual powers and the power of will destroyed. The text does not state it explicitly. The text does say that man felt ashamed, that he hid, that he suffered the loss of Eden, that he must work by the sweat of his brow, that Eve would have pain in childbirth, that woman was to serve man. Nothing was said as to general depravity in the text. Some examples may be given showing God assumed that man, both before and after the sin in the Garden, had full mental, emotional, and volitional powers, as well as continued moral responsibility.

1) God said to Cain:

Why are you angry? . . . If you do well, is it not accepted? And if you do not do well, sin is lurking at your door; its desire is for you, but you must master it (Gen. 4:7).

2) Moses assumed that the children of Israel had both the mental ability and the freedom of will to accept or reject the covenant.

The Lord will prosper you if you obey the voice of your God so as to keep His commandments . . . The word is very near you; it is in your mouth and in your heart, so that you can do it . . . I have set before you life and death, blessing and curses; therefore choose life that you and your descendants may live, loving the Lord and obeying His voice (Deut. 30:20).

3) Joshua called upon the people to make the choice that would lead to life and security in the promised land. He said, "Choose ye this day whom ye shall serve, whether it be the gods . . . left across the river . . . but as for me and my house, we shall serve the Lord" (Josh. 24:15).

4) Isaiah also assumed that man could be reasoned with, "Come saith the Lord, let us reason together . . . why will ye perish?" (Isa. 1:18). The Hebrew had also an age of accountability, ". . . For before the child knows to refuse the evil and choose the good . . ." (Isa. 7:14-16).

5) Elijah called upon the people to choose YHWH and not Baal:

How long go ye limping between the two sides? If Baal be God, serve him; but if YHWH be God, then serve Him (I Kings 18:21).

6) It may be well to cite an extra-canonical text in support of Hebrew-type thinking. This comes from Ecclesiasticus 15:14-18:

God made man from the beginning and left him in the hands of his own counsel. He added his commands and precepts. If thou wilt keep the commandments, and perform acceptable fidelity forever, they will preserve thee. He hath set water and fire before thee; stretch forth thy hand to which thou wilt. Before man is life and death, good and evil, that which he shall choose shall be given him.

7) Jesus also indicated the basic Hebrew mind-set when He lamented over Jerusalem, ". . . How often I would have gathered you under my wing as a hen gathers her chicks and you would not" (Matt. 23:37ff.). In another case, Jesus indicated the basic reason why men refused to believe his message. "How can you believe, when you seek the honor that comes from man and do not seek the honor that comes from the only God?" (John 5:44). This reflects the statement of Jeremiah:

Return every one of you from his evil ways and mend your ways and your doings. But they say, "That is in vain, we will follow our own plans, and will everyone act according to the stubbornness of his own evil heart" (18:11).

Common sense was reflected in all these statements. The Hebrew was a common sense philosopher. Covenant presupposed both the power of God and the free will in man.

Hebrew Words for Free Will

There were five major words used by the Hebrews to indicate the making of choices. These same words were also applied to God's ability to make decisions according to goals, pressures or preferences.

1. *'avah*   This meant "willing inclination" according to the Hebrew Lexicons. It was rendered *boulomai* and *thelo* in the Greek translations. Following are examples of its usage in the Old Testament.

Exod. 10:27   "He would not let them go" ("was not inclined to")

Deut. 1:26   "He would not go up as commanded."

Deut. 10:10   "The Lord was unwilling to destroy you."

Isa. 1:19   "If you are willing to"

2. *Hafes*   This word was rendered "to delight in," "to prefer," "to choose" or "will" or "to be willing to" in various places. It can be used in its negative form.

Ruth 3:13   "If he will not do. . . ."

Prov. 21:1   "He turns it where ever he wills"

Prov. 31:13   "and works with willing hands"

Isa. 42:21   "The Lord was pleased to magnify His Law."

II Sam. 20:11 "whoever favors David and Joab, let him. . . ."
I Sam. 15:22 "Has the Lord as great a deight in. . . ."

3. *Ratson*

Neh. 9:24 ". . . they would do with them *as they pleased.*
Ps. 40:8 "I *delight to* do your will O Lord."
Dan. 8:4 "He did *as he pleased.*"
Ps. 143:10 "teach me thy *will.* . . ."

4. *Nadav*

Ps. 54:6 "I will freely sacrifice"
Ps. 110:3 "My people will be willing in that day. . . ."
II Cor. 8:11ff. "If there be a willingness to . . ."

5. *Ya'al*

Hos. 5:11 "He willingly walked before me"
Gen. 18:11 "I have 'taken upon myself' to speak to the Lord"
Judg. 17:11 "and the Levite *was content to* dwell with. . . ."
I Sam. 17:39 "and he *tried to* go but could not"

The conclusion must surely be since man is held responsible, he must possess sufficient ability to choose the right and reject the evil. His captivity, if any, would have to be that he is in the clutches of an evil generation and a society dominated by evil men who teach us to love what is wrong and to choose against our best interests. That is certainly a kind of depravity, although it is not genetic depravity.

The doctrine of total depravity is an unnecessary and artificial means of defending God's honor. There is certainly a depravity of relationship when man, as with Adam, leaves fellowship for power and his Godlikeness for uncontrolled self-expression. Godlike abilities wrongly used begin depravity. The habitual misuse will harden man's will to evil and he will use mind to justify wrong rather than judge it wrong. When evil is compounded by habit and reinforced by society which teaches us to love evil and to call evil good, and reward sin with advancement and pleasures, man is all but trapped and utterly lost. Only divine intervention could have saved him. Genetic depravity was not emphasized in either the Old Testament or the New. The words "total depravity" are absent from scripture. One might assume the concept those terms bear is also absent. The low philosophy of man came from Athens, not Jerusalem!

The doctrine of depravity is solidly entrenched in certain strains of evangelical theology. B. B. Warfield has declared the doctrine of depravity to be the main truth advanced by the Reformation:

> The issue of total depravity is the root doctrine of the Reformation. It is the source of Reformed theology. . . .
>
> It is . . . in a true sense the manifesto of the Reformation.[13]

H. J. Iwald added, ". . . Evangelical theology stands or falls with the doctrine of the bondage of the will."[14]

Pressing a stated premise to its logical conclusion was a typical Greek way of approaching truth. The Hebrew saw things in a target sort of way. The core or center was vital. As a matter was less related to the core, its importance diminished. Sin as "missing the mark," reflected that imagery. The Hebrew thought pictorially. The Greek thought analytically. Jesus taught in the Hebrew model: parables and illustrations. For a Hebrew, the further removed from fellowship with God one was, the more "depraved" he became. For Greek type theologians, using the two-category system of thought, the spirit was always good, but depravity was genetic and transmitted in the body. Hebrew philosophy was rather matter of fact and rooted in common sense, and they gave no attention to such philosophic interests.

---

13. J. I Packer and O. R. Johnson, in *The Bondage of the Will*, by Luther, n.d., Westwood, N.J.: Revel, p. 41.

14. J. I. Packer. *Op. cit.*, p. 58.

Common sense forces us all to admit that we have the ability to choose between varieties of perceived good and evil. That we must respond to stimuli is not questioned. We may choose which stimuli have our better attention. How we respond to stimuli will depend not only upon our social "programming" but upon our own goals. The emotional impact of stimuli can be mitigated or enhanced, depending upon what we want. What we want is not always what our society has taught us to want. If we have had unfortunate experiences, common sense says to repeat such is foolish. As a person changes his mind, he changes his goals and the ways he reacts to stimuli.

At any rate God held man accountable for responding to reasonable evidence. The fact that he offered man a treaty is surely evidence that He regarded man as sufficiently competent to respond satisfactorily. In a sense, whether man is depraved is irrelevant. "Abraham believed God and it was credited to him as righteousness" (Gen. 15:6). If God is prepared to count an honest response to his word as satisfactory righteousness, then depravity is, whether true or false, not relevant.

A summary of the contrasts between typical Greek and Mosaic views on several subjects is shown below:

Greek Emphasis	Hebrew Emphasis
1. God is pure idea. Power is the best and greatest expression of God.	1. God is spirit who thinks, feels and wills. His glory is in His restraint of power.
2. Man came from the ashes of the evil Titan. Man is prone to evil. He is of "matter" and matter is somehow wrong.	2. Man was made in the image of God. He can do both good and evil. He can think, feel and will.
3. Matter is in the wrong. It is solid whereas spirit is idea or	3. Matter was made by God as part of a system that was said

light. The more density, the more error.

4. Nature is like a machine. All parts interconnect. All things in nature are "determined" by things in nature. Man is trapped and wills as he is made to will.

5. Sin is failure to seek the "wisdom" or the idea or laws governing nature and men, failure to find or act according to such natural law.

6. Salvation is the loss of the body and living in an idea-only kind of formless, colorless, non-material, "no-substance" extinction.

7. Religion is determining who controls what, and then practicing divination to find out things in advance.

to have been "good." Matter can be used for good or evil.

4. Nature has regularity and interruptability. Man is not to be slave of but the master of nature. Man must respond to stimuli, but can control and redirect his response.

5. Sin is breach of fellowship or breach of God's word or doing anything to aid such lawlessness.

6. Salvation is reconciliation to God, living in the world for ever, having sins forgiven.

7. Religion is living a life in harmony with the laws or will of God, and responding in every situation as God would also have responded.

Moses' Philosophy of Society

Moses continued his story of mankind's journey from God into the real world, the world as we know it today. Mankind, after leaving the garden spread throughout the world. Cain killed Abel, his brother. It might have come as a real shock to discover that beatings can bring not only pain but also death. In accordance with God's concept of moral responsibility, Cain was held accountable for the death of his brother. "Am I my brother's keeper?" he asked God. The answer was, of course, "Yes."

64

The story continued. Man became more and more wicked. He formalized wickedness and error in society. There had been a few unusually good men in the previous history. Enoch "walked with God and was not, for God took him" (Gen. 5:24). We are not told what a "walking with God" meant in those days, but he satisfied God and did not die.

In the main, however, mankind became increasingly wicked. At last God had enough. He was utterly disgusted. And He was sorry he had made man at all. He was emotional. He was heartsick. It looked as if He might lose the great experiment. One translation said, "God repented that he had made man." Another said, "I am grieved that I have made them." He intended to destroy all living things, animals, birds and "creatures that move along the ground." As we know from the account, He eventually saved Noah and his family and enough animals to begin again.

What is important to philosophy is that Moses is saying society is not a law unto itself. Society may not set its own course apart from its God-given mandate and not be accountable. That was a radical view of society in an age when the state and the gods were one! His view rested upon the principle that man after the garden was as responsible to God as he was when in the garden. All mankind was equally responsible.

A second element in the philosophic statement being made here is that God can, does, and will get utterly "fed up" with man. He is not all grace and kindness. He is what He is: a moral God who expected those made in His image to amount to something more than being mere animals. He had the emotional capability to wipe it all out. He had the courage to start all over again.

65

The Covenants with Noah

There were two covenants involved with Noah. One had reference to Noah and his own immediate family. The other had reference to his family as it represented the future generations of mankind. The formulary for the earlier covenant was this.

Parties: Noah with the other seven people and God.
Terms: Build an ark of specified size and in a prescribed way.
           Collect representative animals to enter the ark.
           When the time comes, get in and keep others out.
Promises: Survive the flood and escape the death-judgment of God.

The formulary for the later post-flood covenant was this.

Parties: Noah and his family and "all generations to come," and God.
Terms: "Be fruitful and increase in number."
           "Fill the earth."
           Take possession of all animals, birds, and fish and use for food.
           Use all plant life for your benefit.
           Do not eat blood.
           Do not kill a fellow man.
Promises: Everything that lives and moves shall be food for you.
           An accounting for any animal or man that slays a human.
           Never again to destroy the world in a flood.
           The giving of the rainbow as sign of the covenant.

Note that all mankind, just as in the case with Adam, is RESPONSIBLE to God for care of three areas of life: 1. Covenanted relationships to God. 2. Care and use of the earth.

66

3. Care for one's fellow man. This is an obligation upon every soul. All men will give account to God. This covenant was, in fact, a renewal of the Adamic mandate. If there is any one idea Moses intended to get across it was that man is a morally responsible being. He is not an animal, but is in the image of God, and an attack on man is an attack on God! Whoever assaults a fellow man will answer to God, be he man or beast!

The book of Genesis is a book of beginning from the Covenant point of view. The beginning of nature, of man and woman, of language and fellowship, of doubt and temptation, of sin and shame, of alienation and expulsion, of the growth of society and compounded sinfulness, and then the beginning of worldwide judgment in the flood. Finally there is the beginning of covenant with the call of Abram, the beginning of real history in covenant fulfillment in the Exodus.

Genesis is a great book of philosophy and history. It leaves us wondering about a lot of things. It raises questions that it does not answer. Its real agenda is not familiar to all. What it does give is enough to get a frame of reference for what was yet to come. It shows us the basic assumptions the Bible authors accepted as true and to which they harmonized their thinking. It helps us see how it all started. We shall now proceed to how the great experiment fared.

The last thing to be said here is a reminder to keep all things in perspective. God made man for fellowship. Man alienated himself in an insane grasp for power. God is now beginning His program of reconciliation with the call of Abraham.

Conclusion

The philosophic statement made by Moses—and we who are Christian believe he received it in revelation from God as the scripture says (Heb. 1:1)—was in the form of story. A true story to be sure, but an unusual method for a philosopher. How Moses presented his philosophy was well suited to his purpose. He was harmonizing the major ideas of philosophy with the concept of covenant. Covenant presupposed several things. In the offer of a covenant to Abraham, for instance, one knew at once God was a personality with certain personality traits. He was not impersonal POWER. This was in sharp contrast to the pagan Greeks. They concluded that raw power was what God must be.

If two philosophers were to take as their presuppositions the contrasting ideas of "Power is God's greatest attribute" and "Restraint of power is God's greatest attribute," and each followed those assumptions down their respective paths, those two thinkers would never meet again. One assumption leads to determinism. The other leads to covenant.

Man was viewed in different ways by the two philosophies. For the Greeks man was, at least while in the body, almost wholly evil. For the Hebrew man was in God's own image. He had the ability to do good or evil. He was not predetermined to either. Free will must be true if accountability is to be part of a philosophy. Accountability had a very heavy part in the philosophy of Moses.

Man had a God-given destiny; he could cooperate and be benefitted or rebel and suffer the consequences. Nature was to be man's servant. Man was not to consider himself a child of nature or be captive to its seasons, forms, or patterns. Societies of man did not change that truth. Men could not join together and annul the stated will of God. Society was also accountable.

Man did, however, exercise his ability and chose to tear up the good relationship he had with God. God did not leave him in utter hopelessness, for He planned to intervene in history and make every effort to restore the ruptured relationship before man became utterly and completely alienated. God began His organized plan of reconciliation with Abraham.

Questions for Chapter Two

1. The Hebrew regarded _____ of power as superior to power.
2. Name three ways God limited Himself for fellowship with man.

_____

_____

_____

3. Emphasizing God's POWER and nothing else leads to philosophic
   a) honor
   b) praise of God's glory
   c) determinism
   d) apriori
4. T F Adam had the power of choice.
5. T F Cain had the power of choice.
6. T F Moses believed that man was utterly depraved in body and soul.
7. T F The Law of Moses expected men to choose the right and live.
8. T F The Greeks believed that man was basically evil.
9. T F For the Greeks, matter tended to be evil and spirit good.
10. T F "Spirit" for the Hebrews could think, feel, and choose.

11. T F Soul or spirit for the Greeks was a living being.
12. T F For the Hebrew, "spirit," "soul," and "heart" meant one whole person.
13. T F Total depravity was a Hebrew idea.
14. Explain how the concept of "total depravity" entered Christian thought.
15. The philosophic problem of God's power and man's freedom were harmonized in the Hebrew idea of

_____.

16. Jesus said the reason man did not believe was
   a) they were depraved
   b) they did not understand
   c) they did not want to
   d) they preferred man's praise
17. Name two ways man can escape being controlled by every stimulus.

_____

_____

18. The realm of nature as a machine was whose idea?

_____

19. T F Accountability assumed both free will and some kind of law.
20. To be accountable for one's own acts, one must be

_____.

TURN THE BOOK OVER FOR ANSWERS.

1. Restraint
2. A) In making nature and man
   B) In giving man free will
   C) In speaking language
   D) In making covenant

3. c) determinism. If God is all powerful then nothing then happens that He did not cause to happen. But for Hebrews, God had several kinds of will: intended will, natural will, permissive will, covenanted will, and ultimate will.

4. T
5. T
6. F
7. T
8. T
9. T
10. T
11. F Soul was the idea that lay behind the seen object. It was the spiritualized or idealized true essence of a category. It was the perfect pattern that all produced objects shared in flawed ways. It was not personality as with the Hebrews.
12. T
13. F They never used the word.
14. When pagan Greeks were converted to Judaism and later to Christianity, they carried with them their basic low view of man. In the sin of Adam they found a way to justify their low view.
15. Covenant
16. d)
17. He can choose among many stimuli which he will give most attention.
   He can lower or raise his response according to his purposes.
   He can respond in unexpected new ways to old stimuli.
18. Aristotle, who was Plato's student.
19. T
20. Free to act in harmony with or against some precept.

Chapter Three

MAJOR COVENANTS OF THE OLD TESTAMENT

There were two covenants in the Old Testament that received treatment in the New Testament. There were constant references to them by Christ, the Apostles, especially Paul, and the other writers. One other suzerainty-vassal type treaty having minor attention in the New Testament, and in respect of which the term covenant was not used, was the covenant with David. Its importance was major, but overt references to it were few. These three covenants form the theological base of the entire New Covenant theology. Alexander Campbell accurately wrote a century ago.

All the leading terms and phrases of the New Testament are to be understood and explained by the history of the Jewish nation and God's government of them.[1]

Each of these Old Testament covenants was associated with one man. The covenants had to do with Abraham, Moses and David. These men rose as mountain peaks in the history of God's will. They stand out from all others despite the fact they were less moral, less impressive politically, and less known in the larger ancient world than many.

The Abrahamic Covenant

As far as the Israelites were concerned their history began with Abraham (formerly called Abram). When an Israelite brought an offering to God he was required to say the "shema of Abraham." It was a kind of early creed. It was a confession of faith.

---

1. Alexander Campbell, ed. *The Christian System*, Nashville, 1835, Reprinted, Cincinnati: Standard Publishing.

My father was a wandering Aramean, and he went down into Egypt with a few people and lived there and became a great nation, powerful and numerous. But the Egyptians mistreated us and made us suffer, putting us to hard labor. But the Lord brought us out of Egypt with a mighty hand . . . and gave us this land (Deut. 26:5).

When an explanation was given of such events as the exodus from Egypt, or the displacement of the Canaanite peoples, or the distribution of land to Israelites, or the blessings of homeland and peace, writers called attention to Abraham. They did not go back into history any further. They did not refer to Adam or Noah or Enoch. They did not recount the flood. For the Hebrew, real history began with Abraham. This was true of all the ancient documents.

See, I have given you this land. Go in and take possession of the land that the Lord swore He would give to our fathers, to Abraham, Isaac and Jacob and to their descendants after them (Deut. 1:8).

In the prayer of intercession Moses pleaded with God to forgive the wayward refugees in the wilderness.

O Lord, why should your anger burn against your people . . .? Turn your fierce anger, relent and do not bring disaster on your people. Remember your servants Abraham, Isaac and Israel to whom you swore by your own self, "I will make your descendants as numerous as the stars in the sky, and I will give your descendants all this land . . ." (Exod. 32:11ff.).

God promised to forgive the nation if they would repent and keep the covenant. He promised forgiveness because of His previous commitment to Abraham.

But if they will confess their sins . . . then I will remember my covenant with Jacob and my covenant with Isaac, and my

73

covenant with Abraham and I will remember the land (Lev. 26:42).

As the Israelites were preparing to leave Sinai, after Aaron's sin, these words were spoken by YHWH to Moses.

> Leave this place, you and the people you brought out of Egypt, and go to the land I promised on oath to Abraham, Isaac, and Jacob (Exod. 33:1).

The most explicit statement of God's motivation in saving Israel and giving them the land of Canaan is to be found in Deuteronomy.

> After the Lord has driven them out before you, do not say to yourself, "The Lord has brought me here to take possession of this land because of my righteousness." . . . . . The Lord will drive them out before you to accomplish what he swore to your fathers, to Abraham, Isaac and Jacob. Understand then it is not because of your righteousness that the Lord your God is giving you this good land to possess, for you are a stiff-necked people (Deut. 9:4ff.).

In the New Testament the same understanding was expressed by early preachers. Stephen began his recounting of events with the call of Abraham. The exodus was explained, as Moses did, with reference to covenanted promises.

> When the time drew near for God to fulfill his promise to Abraham, the number of our people greatly increased (Acts 7:17).

It was for the above reasons I have regarded redemption history as having begun in earnest with the Abrahamic covenant. Prior events had little interest and no recounting in later Old Testament passages. The call of Abraham and the covenant with him was of supreme importance in Biblical theology and history.

Briefly summarized, God called Abraham, for reasons He did not disclose and after testing his obedience, cut a covenant with him.

> Go from your country and your kindred and your father's house to a land I will show you. And I will make you a great nation. And I will bless you and make your name great, so that you will be a blessing. I will bless those that bless you and him who curses you, I will curse. And by you all the families of the earth shall be blessed (Gen. 12:1-3).

The exact details of the relationship and of the covenant were disclosed as events progressed. God tested Abraham's faithfulness several times. He was satisfied sufficiently to modify and expand the covenant and to make it the basis of future events. A composite summary of the covenant can be made.

Parties: God and Abraham, his posterity through Isaac, and all slaves who were affixed to that family (Gen. 17:1ff.).

Terms: Dwell in Canaan (12:4)
Continue to trust God and Him only (14:22 and 15:4-7).
Circumcise all males (17:9)
Establish Isaac as covenant heir (17:19)
"Know for certain that your descendants will be strangers in a country not their own and they will be enslaved and mistreated four hundred years" (15:13).

Promises: Canaan was to belong to the heirs of Abraham (15:18ff.).
They were to become a great nation (15:4).

75

> God was to rescue them from the Egyptian cap-
> tivity (17:16).
> Sarah was to have a "son of promise" (17:15).
> Isaac was to become the father of twelve nations
> (17:20).
> The covenant with Abraham was to be renewed
> with Isaac (17:21).
> "And in thy seed shall all nations of the earth be
> blessed" (12:3).

Abraham was certainly human. He had only a very few visits with God and so can be excused for his need for reassurance. He asked God how he could be sure God would keep all the promises He had been making to him. God then, in an unusual gesture of good will, swore formally to the covenant.

He asked Abraham to prepare the oath-swearing animals. Abraham killed several and cut them completely apart from head to tail. He then laid the carcasses "side to side." That procedure allowed the two contracting parties to "pass between the halves." In so doing, each was swearing to become one body with the other. It also illustrated the punishment due one who broke faith. He ought to die. So God swore the covenant oath.

> As the sun was setting Abram fell into deep sleep and a
> thick and dreadful darkness came over him. The Lord said
> to him, "Know for certain that your descendants . . ." and
> when the sun had set and darkness had fallen, a smoking
> fire pot with a blazing torch appeared and passed between
> the pieces. On that day the Lord made a covenant with
> Abram (Gen. 15:8).

Some of the conditions and promises were restated variously in the text. There were some parallelisms not

76

listed in both forms. So, the promises given to Abraham are usually grouped into three main ones: possessing Canaan, becoming a great nation, and blessing all the earth. I shall use this shorter form when speaking of the promises in the future.

God tested Abraham several times. His responses to God were used by New Testament writers as evidence of what God really wanted in man. For instance, God had said to Abraham his posterity would number as the sands of the sea. He said once to Abraham, "Look up and count the stars in the heavens, Abraham." Abraham looked up. "Count them for me," said God. "No one can count the stars of the heavens, Lord, they are far too many." God answered, "So shall your offspring be!" And Abraham believed God and it was regarded by God as his righteousness (15:4). The one supreme characteristic of people who satisfy God is they believe what he says. For the Hebrew belief was the same as "hearing." Hearing meant both the getting of information, understanding it, and acting upon it. The older English versions have translated the Hebrew shema as "harken to" and the later versions correctly rendered it "obey."

In another and related instance, God commanded Abraham to sacrifice his son of promise, Isaac. Abraham set out to obey. He took Isaac and some wood and proceeded to the mountain for the offering—of his own son. The place where it was to have been done is almost universally thought to be Jerusalem and the very spot where the temple was later built or the spot where Jesus was later crucified. At any rate, Abraham took the one through whom God had covenanted to bless the world as well as fill it with his children, and in obedience to God, intended to kill him. He believed God's promises were so sure he expected God to raise Isaac from the dead (Heb. 11:16). And, in a sense, he did receive him back from the dead. Both Paul and James later used the events here as proper understandings of faith. Paul emphasized the inner confidence in God. James called attention to Abraham's *actions* in confidence of God.

> Was not our ancestor Abraham considered righteous by what he did when he offered his son Isaac on the altar? You see that his faith and his actions were working together. . . . You see a person is justified by what he does and not by faith alone (Jam. 2:21ff.).

Sons of the Covenant

One had a special status when in a covenanted relationship to God. The sons of Abraham, with a few exceptions, were not necessarily the best of men. Isaac was a moral man, as was Joseph, his grandson. The rest of the family were for several generations none too pretty. The covenant passed to Isaac as God had said.

> . . . I will give all these lands and will confirm the oath I swore to your father Abraham . . . because Abraham obeyed me and kept my requirements, my commandments, my decrees and my laws (Gen. 26:1-5).

Jacob was a rascal. He tricked his father who was blind. He had trouble with his brother. He had difficulty with Laban, his father-in-law. He cheated him (Gen. 30:31ff.). He was regarded as a great man, however, because of his attitude toward the covenant. He took it seriously.

When Esau and Jacob had their now famous exchange about the "birthright," something profound was being discussed. Here is a summary of what was happening. Esau was always going away hunting for game and women. He neglected the people of the covenant and their welfare. He was a rather free spirit. But he was not always successful at hunting and came in one time and asked to be fed by Jacob. Put in current vernacular the conversation might have been as follows:

"I am almost dead of hunger, Jacob. Can you have something fixed for me?"

"Esau, why don't you stay home and take care of yourself and the family's business? You leave for days at a time and come home smelling like a goat."

"I like wild meat. I do not like sheep. And I certainly don't like sitting day after day watching sheep and goats," replied Esau.

"What about the family? What about the land? What about the promise?"

"Ah, the land. Have you seen a sunset from the far west, Jacob? Have you ever tracked a deer in the early morning? Have you ever been really free? That is life, Jacob. To travel and be free."

"What about the family and the covenant? What about Abraham's oath?"

Esau might have replied, "Not that again. Do you still believe that? How many years has it been? Do we own any land? Are your flocks spread as far as Damascus? Leave it, Jacob, and bring me something to eat before I die in your tent."

"This land is to be ours. All of it. And you don't seem to care. You chase deer and who-knows-what-else across it. We own this land, Esau, and you don't seem to care."

"Yeh, tell that to the elders of Beersheva. Go to the next valley and say to all of them there, 'You men get off our land.' See what it gets you. Or better yet go to Jerusalem. Pound on the gates. Tell the guards you own the place.

Tell the king to give you a thousand gold coins rent. And see how far you can run with a spear in your backside."

"If it doesn't mean anything to you, then give it to me," said Jacob.

"Take it."

"I'm serious. If you do not want the birthright. Give it to me. Officially. With witness. I'll pay you something for it. I want it. It would break Isaac's heart to have the birthright pass to someone who didn't take it seriously. Sell it to me."

"All right. I'll sell it to you. With witness. I'll sell you the promises of the covenant. Poor old Isaac. Poor dear father Isaac. He still believes that stuff about Canaan and great nation, and stars and sand. Yes, I will sell you Jerusalem and Beersheva, and Ashdod, and all the valleys and the vineyards of Samaria, and all those lovely ladies therein. How much can you pay?"

"What do you ask?"

"I tell you what, dear brother Jacob. I will sell you it all for exactly what it is worth. I will sell it to you, the whole mess, rights, lands, the stars in the heavens—all the covenant—for just what those promises are worth. One good bowl of Jabobite stew! What do you say?"

"Are you serious?"

"I am."

"I'll get the witnesses," replied Jacob.

One can read the rest in the account of Moses. The covenant passed in a rough and tumble way down through the years. Those who thought it important came down in history as heroes, be they moral men or bad. Those who regarded the promises of the covenant to be empty dreams were to disappear. If they were remembered, it was as evil men, regardless of their specific morals. This is not to say God ignored morals. It is to say that at this stage of the program, it was more important for the covenant to survive than for isolated morals to be perfectly in place.

Believing in, supporting and enhancing the success of the covenant was morality then. It has ever been so, from then until now.

Jacob had an encounter with God. His name was changed to Israel. He had twelve sons. Those twelve boys later became great tribes. The morals of the sons, at least the older ten, were none too good. All the family eventually went into Egypt as honored guests. They stayed there for the agreed time. Their status changed while there. It was carried in the record by these simple words, "Then a new king, who did not know Joseph, came into power" (Exod. 1:8).

As God had said to Abraham, the people were mistreated there. They became slaves. As slaves they degenerated into a beastly kind of humanity. A few held to the old ideas and kept the name of God and the covenant dreams alive. The majority degenerated. Survival had higher priority than quality of life for the slaves. When they finally came out of Egypt, most were rebellious, unstable, preoccupied with things bad for them, without faith, morals, or education. They were an ignorant, disorganized, flighty, rag-tag lot. But they were the people of the covenant. It was through them God intended to bless all mankind. At that time, things did not appear too hopeful.

Moses

Moses was the greatest of all the ancient fathers. He was, in turn, a slave, a child marked for death, a fugitive from the law (in a basket floating in the reeds), a son of the princess, an educated and wealthy member of the royal family, a murderer, outcast, shepherd, husband and father. Then he was called by God to continue the history-of-salvation. God

81

appeared to him. It had been five hundred years since it all began, but God sounded as if it were yesterday. From a bush on fire but not burning, God said to Moses,

I am the God of your father, the God of Abraham, the God of Isaac, and the God of Jacob. . . . I have indeed seen the misery of MY PEOPLE in Egypt. I have heard them crying . . . (Exod. 3:7).

The great lawgiver confronted the power of the gods and the royal house of Egypt. God chose him to set His people free.

The Passover

The rescue from Egypt was for the Hebrews the greatest event in history since the covenant with Abraham. It represented, more than anything else, God's *hesed*. He had promised Abraham specifically He would bring Israel out of captivity. He did so in a remarkable way. They remembered it down through the years. The Feast of the Passover commemorated it. The Atonement pictured it. They sang of it. When their faith was weak they recalled it. When they had reason to doubt the validity of their covenant and their faith and their separateness, they looked to the Passover event for reassurance.

You can read for yourselves God's challenge of the power of the gods of Egypt and the power of Pharaoh's state in the ten plagues (Exod. 7-12). In the tenth plague all the firstborn of the land were to die. Israel was God's "firstborn." He was not to die, however. On that dread night, an angel of death was to pass through Egypt. God commanded the Israelites through Moses to prepare for the awaited exodus by gathering up their possessions, eating well, if in haste, and doing something strange with the blood of the lamb eaten that night.

> Take some of the blood and put it on the sides and tops of the doorframes of the houses where they eat the lambs. . . . This is how you are to eat it: with your cloak tucked into your belt, your sandals on your feet and your staff in your hand. Eat it in haste; it is the Lord's Passover (Exod. 12:1ff.).

Wailing was heard from one end of the Nile to the other. Every firstborn was dying. No one of Israel died. The death angel passed over Israel. Every one who was inside a house marked with blood was passed over by death. In the house of God's people that night there was no death. Later, when the exiles were safely in Canaan, had their own land and king, and had become a great nation as God had promised, fathers were to tell their sons the story.

> In the future when your son asks you, "What is the meaning of the stipulations, decrees and laws the Lord our God has commanded you?" tell him, "We were slaves of Pharaoh's in Egypt, but the Lord brought us out of Egypt with a mighty hand. Before our eyes the Lord sent miraculous signs and wonders—great and terrible—upon Egypt and Pharaoh and his whole household. But He brought us out from there to bring us in and give us the land that he had promised on oath to our forefathers" (Deut. 7:20ff.).

He led the people out into the wilderness. They were a great company. It must have been a confused yet wonderful sight. They went into the wilderness, a far worse place than Egypt had been. But, God had said He was taking them into that promised land flowing with milk and honey. They arrived, but not all the original ones who exited Egypt. God was angry with most of them. Those who had not trusted Him to bring them safely through left their bones in the desert (Heb. 3:7ff.).

An observation and a conclusion ought to be stated here. The covenant promises were to a group. God's covenant was with a group of people related by blood to Abraham. An individual could lose his part in the promises by unbelief or disobedience (for the Hebrew it was the same thing). God's promises were for the category, the group. No individual could claim God was dishonoring His promise if he individually, for whatever reason, did not see the fulfillment of the promise. We are faced with a category system unfamiliar to the western philosophic world: the promise to a group could be virtually unconditional with God. That is, He would do what He had promised—with the group. An individual's right to the promise was very conditional. He had to keep the covenant. He might fall outside the blessings himself because of unbelief, but the group that was faithful could indeed inherit the benefit of the covenanted promise. This principle, if understood, will make Biblical theology considerably easier to grasp.

The group arrived at Mount Sinai in Arabia. There the covenant called the Old Covenant was given. It was added to the Abrahamic covenant, Paul said (Gal. 3:19). The two became one. They merged. Except for the promise to bless all nations in the seed of Abraham—as yet an unfilled promise—Christ and the Apostles regarded the covenants in the Old Testament to be one covenant and it was called *The Old Covenant.*

The covenant at Sinai has been described in four of the five books of the Pentateuch. Some summary will be necessary. This very brief analysis is helpful because it is essentially accurate and easily remembered. We shall analyze the covenant by the usual formulary.

Parties: God and the Children of Israel (Lev. 26:46).
Terms: Keep the 613 Laws of Moses (Lev. 26:14).
Promises: All physical, national, earthly (Lev. 26:1-13).

The Oath Swearing of the Old Covenant

All major Treaties were sworn with an *alah*, an oath of covenant. As with Abraham's covenant, so with this pact, the people signed the treaty with an act which would be forever etched upon their minds. They assembled. If usual custom was followed they came tribe by tribe and clan by clan. Clans were subdivided into "houses" or extended-family groups. At last came isolated individuals of small nuclear family groups. Moses had already prepared the site. The clans were gathered and all was ready.

Moses killed the animals. The blood was drawn off into basins. The carcasses were laid back to back with enough space between them to allow the clans to pass. They numbered some 600,000 in all. They were to pass, clan by clan, through the pieces as God had at Abraham's ceremony.

The Book of the Covenant was read. All the people responded with loud voice:

We will do everything the Lord has said. We will obey . . . (Exod. 24:7).

The blood was separated into two lots. One half of it was poured upon the altar. God was signing the Treaty! The other half was mixed with water—to extend it hundreds of times. Moses had cut a stout stick of wood and had securely fastened a bundle of wool to it. This he dipped into the tubs of bloody water. He shouted the formal words of covenant oath:

This is the blood of the covenant (Exod. 24:8).

85

The people passed in order and were sprinkled with bloody water as Moses threw it at them. When blood touched them, they had formally signed the pact. They had chosen to be sons of God and members of his kingdom! No covenant of status was ratified without a kind of blood ceremony. The details of each oath taking may have been slightly adjusted to the situation, but all Hebrews understood that without blood a covenant was not ratified (Heb. 9:18ff.).

The Old Covenant: Parties

One had to be of the blood of Abraham to be in this covenant. It was possible for slaves to enter, but they became part of the covenant because they became part of the family of Abraham. Although intermarriage with non-Israelites was forbidden in the law (Deut. 7:3) we find David's grandmother to have been a Moabitess (Ruth 1:4). The children of mixed marriages could become Israelite after the tenth generation. This was for children of "forbidden marriages" or illegitimate children. If such a child came from an Edomite or Egyptian illicit relationship or marriage with an Israelite he could become a member, (literally "enter the assembly") in the third generation (Deut. 23:1-8). Aside from these passages, there seems to be no way according to the Law itself any ethnic could be part of Israel.

The covenant was with the flesh and blood of Abraham. Being in the covenant was not a matter of choice. It was based upon flesh and blood, the flesh and blood of Abraham.

There are many passages indicating the understanding of the Hebrews themselves about the extent of the parties to this treaty.

These are the words Moses spoke to all Israel in the desert east of the Jordan (Deut. 1:1).

86

The Hittites, Girgashites, Amorites, Canaanites, Perizzites Hivites, and Jebusites, seven nations stronger and larger than you, and when the Lord your God has delivered them over to you and you have defeated them, then you must destroy them totally. Make no treaty with them and show them no mercy (Deut. 7:1, 2).

The Lord has chosen you out of all peoples on the face of the earth to be his people, his treasured possession. The Lord did not set his affection on you because you were more numerous than other peoples, . . . but it was because the Lord loved you and kept the oath he swore to your forefathers (Deut. 7:6-8).

O Lord God, did you not drive out the inhabitants of this land before your people Israel and give it forever to the descendants of Abraham your friend? (II Chron. 20:7).

The time is coming when I will make a new covenant with the house of Israel and the house of Judah. It will not be like the covenant I made with their forefathers when I took them by the hand to lead them out of Egypt (Jer. 31:32).

In the New Testament Paul was quite emphatic about the limitation of the Old Covenant. He wrote the following passages.

Indeed, when Gentiles, who do not have the Law (Rom. 2:14).

What advantage is there in being a Jew? Much in every way. First of all they have been entrusted with the very words of God (Rom. 2:1).

What if God did this to make the riches of His glory known to the objects of His mercy, even us, whom he also called, not only from the Jews, but also from the Gentiles. As He says in Hosea: "I will call them, MY PEOPLE, who are not my people" (Rom. 9:23f.).

The word "gentile" is a translation of the Hebrew *goi* and of the Greek, *ethne*, from which our word ethnic also comes. It meant any distinct people, usually, though not always, applied to non-Israelites. With Paul the terms Greek and ethnic are used interchangeably and referred to any one not a blood descendant of Abraham. He understood the Law, his way of saying the Old Treaty, separated the Jew and the gentile. In Christ, the Law, i.e., the Old Treaty, was taken away and thus the two kinds of peoples on earth could come together. In other words, no ethnic had part in the Law. It was the Law that made him an ethnic!

> For He himself is our peace, who has made the two one and has destroyed the barrier, . . . by abolishing the Law with its commandments and regulations. His purpose was to create one new man out of the two (Eph. 2:14f.).

> Remember that formerly you who are Gentiles by birth, and called "uncircumcision" by those that call themselves "the circumcision" . . . remember that at that time you were separate from Christ, excluded from citizenship in Israel and foreigners to the covenants of promise (Eph. 2:11).

God never intended all nations on earth to keep the Law of Moses. No place can be found in the Treaty where Israel was to teach or impose the law upon other nations. They were not commanded to be "evangelistic" about their religion, as far as non-Israelites were concerned. We can summarize by stating again, the Sinai Treaty was made with the flesh and blood descendants of Abraham and none other. No one and no nation could simply opt into membership. One had to be born into the Old Covenant.

That fact accounts for the confusion of Nicodemus when he was in conversation with Jesus. Christ would have said, "One can no longer be considered a member of God's Israel (Kingdom) simply by being born of Abraham."

"But," Nicodemus replied, "I am already born and in His kingdom."

Jesus said, "No, one must be born a second time to enter God's kingdom."

"How can I enter again my mother's womb and be born?"

"You must be born of water and the Spirit," Jesus answered. When Jesus said water and spirit, he meant by choice and personal allegiance giving.

"The flesh of Abraham gains a man nothing," Jesus continued, "every man must now choose to be a child of God. You can't be born into it (John 3:1ff.)."

The Old Covenant: Terms

The terms of the Mosaic covenant numbered 613 according to Jewish count. There were several parallel names for the entire set. By the use of parallel words for the terms of the treaty, God meant to urge that all be kept. Below is a sample of ways of saying the obligations of the Treaty.

Moses wrote down everything the Lord had said . . . then he took the Book of the Covenant and read it to all the people. They responded, "We will do everything the Lord has commanded. We will obey" (Exod. 24:4ff.).

This is the Law Moses set before the Israelites. These are the stipulations, decrees, and laws Moses gave them when they came out of Egypt (Num. 4:44).

But if you will not listen to me and carry out all these commands, and if you reject my decrees, and abhor my laws, and fail to carry out all my commands and so violate my covenant, then I will do this to you (Lev. 27:14).

Be careful that you do not forget the Lord your God failing to observe His commands, His laws and His decrees that I am giving you this day (Deut. 8:11).

The Lord will establish you as His holy people as He promised you on oath, if you keep the commandments of the Lord your God, and walk in His ways (Deut. 28:9).

Perhaps the greatest and most comprehensive passage in the Old Testament regarding "walking with God" is found at the end of the Pentateuch. It is an excellent statement of the essential philosophy of religion of the Hebrews. A short summary will first be given, followed by a longer one. Here is the short form.

The Lord will again delight in you and make you prosperous, just as he delighted in your fathers, if you obey the Lord your God, and keep his commands and decrees that are written in the Book of the Law, and turn to the Lord your God with all your heart and with all your soul (Deut. 30:9-10).

The longer form has almost all the elements necessary to build a balanced idea of what made Israel what she was. Parts of this passage have been quoted in the New Testament.

Now what I am commanding you today is not too difficult for you or beyond your reach. It is not up in heaven so that you may ask, "Who will ascend into heaven and get it, and proclaim it so that we may obey it?" Nor is it beyond the sea so that you have to ask, "Who will cross the sea and get it and proclaim it to us so that we may obey it?" No, the word is very near you; it is in your mouth and in your heart so you may obey it.

See, I set before you this day life and prosperity, death and destruction. For I command you today to love the Lord your God, to walk in his ways, and to keep his commands, decrees, and laws; that you will live and increase, and the Lord your God will bless you in the land you are entering to possess.

But if your heart turns away and you are not obedient, and if you are drawn away to bow down to other gods and worship them, I declare to you this day that you will certainly be destroyed. You will not live long in the land you are crossing the Jordan to enter and possess.

This day I call heaven and earth as witnesses against you that I have set before you life and death, blessings and curses, Now choose life, so that you and your children may live and that you may love the Lord your God, listen to his voice and hold fast to Him. For the Lord is your life, and he will give you many years in the land he swore to give to your fathers, Abraham, Isaac, and Jacob (Deut. 30:11-20).

We see that obeying the covenant was identical with loving the Lord, and walking in His ways, listening to his voice, and clinging to Him. They are parallels. The Law was declared to have been able to be clearly understood. It was not too difficult for them. On the basis of keeping the covenant they were assured of God's aid in prosperity and long life in their new land. The foregoing clause was understood to be a formal statement of covenant, as it called upon witnesses to verify its formality and acceptance.

The Unity of the Law

The law was a single whole. It was meant by the Israelite authors of the Bible to be administered as a whole. To be sure, it was given in the scriptural texts in a very disjointed fashion. Certain groups in the nation may have been more preoccupied with some parts of it than others.

They almost certainly memorized only the parts that affected them most directly. The priesthood, for instance, may have had copies of relevant sections for instruction of new candidates, or sent to regional centers for study. The Levites, who acted as local judges, might have copies of the subsections governing matters over which they had jurisdiction. But all sections of the nation, in both Judah and Israel, before and after the great reform, from king to prophet all agreed: the Law was one whole law and was to be taken seriously by all.

As far as we know, they did not break the law into European type subdivisions. There was no "moral law" as against the "ceremonial law," as opposed to the "judicial law," as apart from the "national laws," or "laws of family" apart from the "laws of a community." There were individual laws addressing such, but it would be unfair to them and unwise for our own understanding to divide them in a manner differing from their own.

One thing the Law of Moses (another way of saying the Law of God) did was create a theocracy. It was a nation where God was the King. Religion and culture were one. Faith in God and governmental administration were linked in the covenant. There was no freedom of religion in such a state. Everything was religion. There was no difference between the sacred and the secular. The laws of the land were the laws of God. The Law, God's Torah, involved every aspect of life, from duties of king (Deut. 17:14ff.), to public health (Lev. 13-14), to marriage and divorce (Deut. 22:13ff.), to public holidays (Lev. 23:1ff.), to types of sacrifices (Lev. 1-7), to approved and forbidden relationships (Lev. 18-19), foods (Lev. 11:1ff.), sexual practices (Lev. 12 and 18), inheritance (Num. 36), public worship (Deut. 12 & 13), administration of justice (Deut. 19:15ff.), conscription for war (Deut. 20ff.) camp sanitation (Deut. 23:12ff.), slavery (Deut. 15:12) public finance (Deut. 14:22), care of the poor (Deut. 24:19), and many others.

Some of the laws seem to us to be "primitive." Some seem almost superstitious, "Do not wear clothes of linen and wool woven together (Deut. 22:11), and "Do not boil a kid in its own mother's milk" (Deut. 14:21). We must not be too hasty to judge the Torah. It may well be the command was to wipe out superstitions, replacing them with trust in God and the law. For instance, a pagan divination-rite may have been popular which said, "If you want a man-child, boil a kid in its own mother's milk." An effort to destroy the practices of magic may have been the root of some laws. Maybe a superstition said, "If you want protection from demons, wear an inner cloth woven of one-half wool and one-half linen." Some who read the various laws regarding the purification of women have been offended by the implication that normal functions of womanhood were regarded as needing purification. The laws about such things may have been designed to protect her. At least after her purification she was completely free of any taint. If men in that age believed, falsely of course, that menstrual flow was a curse of God and a sign of woman's sub-human status with God and hence man, the purification would take care of that. It might also set at ease her own mind about the matter.

The law that says, "An eye for an eye and a tooth for a tooth (Exod. 21:22ff.) has caused many to feel the law of Moses was brutal and allowed vengeance taking to thrive. Far from it. The command was given to limit, not expand damages. For instance we can find passages that allude to compounding of retribution.

Cain may be avenged seven times, but Lamech seventy-seven (Gen. 4:24).

The law limited damages to retribution in kind, and ought to be read "Only an eye for an eye and only a tooth for a tooth."

The Law of Moses was full of remarkably humane regulations.

Do not take advantage of a hired man who is poor and needy, whether he is an Israelite or an alien living in one of your towns (Deut. 24:14).

Do not deprive the alien and the fatherless of justice or take the cloak of a widow as a pledge. Remember you were slaves in Egypt and God redeemed you from there (Deut. 24:17).

When you beat the olives from your trees, do not go over the branches a second time. Leave it for the alien, the fatherless and the widow (Deut. 24:20).

Do not have two different weights in your bag, one light and one heavy. . . . For the Lord detests anyone who does these things, anyone who deals dishonestly (Deut. 24:13).

Whatever your lips utter you must be sure to do, because you have made your vow freely to the Lord with your own mouth (Deut. 23:23).

Do not take a pair of millstones, not even the upper one, for security for a debt, for that would be taking a man's livelihood for security (Deut. 24:6).

If a slave has taken refuge with you, do not hand him over to his master. Let him live among you wherever he likes and in whatever town he chooses. Do not oppress him (Deut. 23:15ff.).

If there is a poor man living among your brothers . . . do not be hard hearted or tightfisted toward your poor brother. Be open handed and lend him whatever he needs (Deut. 16:7ff.).

Do not seek revenge or bear a grudge against one of your people, but love your neighbor as yourself. I am the Lord (Lev. 19:18).

94

Do not pervert justice; do not show partiality to the poor or favoritism to the great, but judge your neighbor fairly (Lev. 19:15).

The Sacrificial System

There was another wonderful part of the Old Covenant: the sacrificial system. In it, and in the variety of sacrifices it provided, there was opportunity for both the individual and community to come before God. In connection with the sacrifices the Hebrew came the closest to God. The high priest took the blood of the sacrifice into the Most Holy Place, the inner part of the tabernacle, into the very presence of God. During the sacrifice itself, confession was made to God. Man reaffirmed his commitment to the Torah. Sins had atonement: covering the wrong and securing the sinner from punishment.[2] In a meaningful ceremony one goat was sacrificed and another was sent far away—as far away as Israel had wished their sins removed.

He is to lay both hands on the head of the live goat and confess over it all the wickedness and rebellion of the Israelites —all their sins—and put them on the goat's head. He shall send the goat away into the desert in the care of a man appointed for the task. The goat will carry on itself all their sins to a solitary place (Lev. 16:20ff.).

The High Priest carried the blood of atonement into the presence of God. He sprinkled it seven times on the mercy-seat of the Ark of the Covenant. No one was allowed to be in the Tabernacle during that time except the High Priest. It was a lonely, awesome responsibility. When he had finished

---

2. William Wilson, *Old Testament Word Studies*, Grand Rapids: Kregel, 1978.

inside, he came out and announced that atonement was done according to the Torah, and that the sins of the people were gone, at least for another year (Heb. 9:21ff.).

There were a lot of sacrifices and offerings. A sacrifice was also an offering to God. It was giving to God one's life, and by substitution, one's life blood. Grain kept men alive. There was a grain offering. Wine was the sign of the good life. There was a wine offering, a fermented drink offering. The firstborn son of a family was offered to God, not as a body to be killed, as in the former pagan days, but to live for God. There were five major offerings, each having both similarities and differences. They were the Burnt Offering, the Grain Offering, the Fellowship or Peace Offering, the Sin Offering and the Guilt Offering (Lev. 1-7).

At the sacrifice, the common Hebrew was doing several things. He was "coming before the Lord." He was participating in the community of faith. He was thanking God for blessings received. He was cleansing his conscience. He was receiving mercy from God.

There was no magic in Hebrew sacrifice. It was convenanted and straight forward. God had agreed when sacrifice was offered He would respond in heaven, as it were. An animal, the Hebrew understood, could stand in his place and receive the punishment man deserved only if God agreed to it. As God had so covenanted, He accepted the death of the animal as the "death" of the man. It cleaned the slate—for a year. It postponed the punishment man had agreed was just. It postponed it for a year. The sacrifices were annual. So the sins and guilt of a man were rolled ahead, as it were, year after year, growing higher and higher. As long as the Hebrew sacrificed, he had God's assurance that his status with God was secure. He must

96

sacrifice with a good and repentant heart. He must be quite sincere. The sacrifices had to be done in faith (Heb. 11:28). The sacrifice cleansed the conscience. If a man believed God was good at his word, and understood God as agreeing to allow the blood of the innocent and perfect lamb to be the blood of the sinner, and that blood was shed, then man was freed from guilt, and had a clean slate before God. His conscience was made clean—if he really believed God was honest.

Greek and Hebrew Sacrifice Contrasted

There was a real difference between the sacrificial practices of the Greeks and that of the Hebrews. The Hebrew word for sacrifice would be translated into the Greek word in the Septuagint (Greek) Version of the Old Testament. One would make a fatal mistake to go to Plato's dictionary for the true meaning, however. The meaning of the Greek word in the Old Testament had the Hebrew meaning. If this were not so, the translators were redefining sacrifice and not merely translating. To put it another way, when a Greek heard the word sacrifice in the context of Hebrew or later Christian discussions, he must not picture in his mind what they did in Athens, but what was done in Jerusalem. What was done in either place looked similar from afar. But the meaning of each part of the sacrifices was vastly different in Athens and Jerusalem.

A Greek sacrifice looked something as this. There was an altar. On it an animal was placed. There was a priest with a knife in his hand. Beside him was a "prophet" with a book in his hand. It was the cult's Oracle. It may have been a book of Zodiac type meanings. "Signs" obtained from the sacrifice itself were found in the book and their meanings announced to the public. There was a prayer. It went something as this:

O ye gods that dwell on Olympus and elsewhere, We have come to obtain wisdom from you. Tell us what your determination of our future has been. In this sacrifice tell us your will and give us your wisdom. We believe in your Book of Signs and we will act upon your answers.

The priest would then cut open the animal from throat to pelvis. The blood would flow. The flow would be "read," the sign told to the prophet who would consult his book and announce the meaning, "Rapid blood flowing to the left means do not sign contracts with anyone for three weeks." Or some such thing. They looked at the heart, the liver and the intestines for signs. One could characterize their entire system as divination.

The Hebrew sacrifice was vastly different. It was a covenant renewal ceremony. As with the other, there was a priest with a knife, and a prophet, as it were, with a book. In this case the "book" was the Book of the Torah.

There would be a prayer. It would have been something as this:

O Lord God, God of our father Abraham, we have come before you to confess our sins. We have sinned against you in this and this and this way. We are truly sorry. We know that we ought to die here today. For you had said and we had agreed, "The soul that sinneth, it shall die." Not only have we ourselves sinned, but all our family, the whole nation. Forgive us and them, Lord. We thank you that it is this guiltless and perfect lamb that is to die here. We know it ought to have been us. When its own blood is shed and it dies, we know it ought to have been us. We thank you for your grace and covenant-keeping. We pledge a better year before your face. We will do better.

The priest would then cut the throat of the animal and as the blood flowed and its life ebbed away, the Hebrew, if he had confidence in God's promises, would feel a wave of relief. He was cleansed. He could start over for another year. The contrasts between the two can be seen clearly:

Greek Sacrifice		*Hebrew Sacrifice*	
Objects:	Altar, animal, priest, prophet, Book of Oracles	Objects:	Altar, animal, priest, prophet, Book of Covenant
Prayer:	For information "Tell us" "Inform us" "Show us."	Prayer:	Confession Thanksgiving Intercession Covenant renewal pledge Praise of God's *hesed*
Purpose:	Outwit the fates by obtaining information gained privately	Purpose:	Renew the Covenant Cover the sins Cleanse the conscience
Basis:	A clever invention by man to help him control factors beyond him	Basis:	A matter of Treaty with God whereby man can remain in fellowship with God and each other.
Philosophic Assumption:	A deterministic, programed world view. An effort to see events in advance and gain for selves. A contradiction between above.	Philosophic Assumption:	Being in and remaining in a covenanted relationship with God is life and security. The Covenant was all the real information man needed.

The Old Covenant: Promises

The promises written as part of the covenant are easily cataloged. They were all physical, national, and immediate. They were classified by the Hebrews themselves as the positive promises, called blessings, and the negative ones called curses.

They were physical blessings. A partial list from Deuteronomy is shown here.

All these blessings will come upon you and accompany you if you obey the Lord your God. You will be blessed in the city and blessed in the country,

.... in the fruit of your womb,

.... and the crops of your land,

.... and the young of your livestock,

.... your basket and your kneeding trough,

.... your enemies defeated before you,

.... abundant prosperity,

.... you will lend, not borrow,

.... you will be the head and not the tail (Deut. 28:1ff.).

From Leviticus comes this partial list. It is but another way of saying what was said in Deuteronomy.

I will send you rain in its season, and the ground will yield its crops, and the trees their fruit. Your threshing will continue till grape harvest and the grape harvest will continue until planting, and you will eat all the food you want and you will live in safety in the land. I will grant peace in the land, and you will lie down and no one will make you afraid (Lev. 26:4ff.).

The promises were all national. That is, they related to the entire nation and not simply to an individual. An individual might be very faithful amid a wicked generation and

100

suffer defeat and imprisonment along with the rest. The promises related to Canaan, the land of promise. It was never promised to those who were outside the land. It was Canaan where the promises of covenant were to take place. The promises were immediate in the sense of life now here on earth. There is no mention of eternal life in the entire covenant. It simply was not a part of the Treaty of Moses. There may have been a concept of life after death. Some or all may have expected it. Many may have assumed it was to be true if they kept the covenant as individuals. It was simply not mentioned in the covenant text. That is perhaps why when Jesus came and preached eternal life as a promise of the new era, people flocked to him. The Sadducees rejected any hope of life after death. Josephus said, "They take away the belief of the immortal duration of the soul and the punishments and rewards in hades."[3] The Sadducees would not likely have denied an explicit doctrine of the Torah. They were, to quote Patten, "actually conservative in regard to the Law."[4] They rejected any doctrine that could not be justified by the Torah.[5] Jesus sided on the same question with the Pharisees, who did believe in resurrection. They both did it on grounds other than the Treaty Text, however. The Sadducees were correct; the Torah was silent on the matter. Jesus did side with the Sadducees in one aspect of the issue. He declared the Old Covenant could not impart eternal life (John 5:39-40).

The blood of Christ, the last sacrifice under the Law, imparted life to all who had lived in good faith under the former system (Heb. 9:15).

---

3. Flavius Josephus, *Wars*, ii, 8, 14.
4. Prescilla Patten and Rebecca Patten, *Before the Times*, San Francisco: Strawberry Hill Press, 1980, p. 86.
5. David S. Russell, *The Jews from Alexander to Herod*, London: Oxford University Press, 1967, p. 159.

Torah

The word Law or Torah meant something less threatening than some have assumed. It meant instruction from God, whether as statute itself or explanation of context by God (history). The Torah was not meant to put the nation under such a strain it was bound to fail. True and enduring relationships are based upon mutual understanding. The people had to know, explicitly, what God could and could not abide. No relationship will last if one party is chafing. By disclosing to Israel not only His essential requirement, but also matters to be carefully avoided, God showed true *hesed*. He was aiding the partner in the covenant to do what was in the Lord's best interest.

When dealing in formal and important matters, long human experience has shown man to be weak at his best. It is almost axiomatic if one wants to lose a friend or the good will of a close relative, he will enter a deal with him with nothing in writing! A good many friends have been lost that way. The Law was not ideal, far from it, but it was satisfactory enough to get the nation started and held on a steady course. In spite of all the failures in it, it did accomplish God's purpose for it.

The Growth of the Torah

The word Law grew in meaning throughout the history of Israel. Since it was used by the Apostles of Christ so frequently, and has been the source of many theological disputes, and the cause of some division in the churches, Bible students ought to have a clear idea of how the word was used in scripture. By limiting their own use of it to correspond to that usage in scripture, much confusion can be avoided.

102

It had in scripture four applications. It grew from the narrow meaning it had in the beginning to the largest meaning, assigned by the Apostles.

The original meaning of Torah was "terms of the covenant." It referred to that part of the covenant obligating man. It was a short form of commandment. When used in the singular and without a prefix, it meant any law or a law. When the words "the law" were used it referred to the stipulations of the Mosaic Treaty. It was often found in parallel with other words commonly understood to mean the requirements of the Code of Moses.

> When you have crossed the Jordan, into the land the Lord your God is giving you, set up some large stones and coat them with plaster. Write on them all the words of this law (Deut. 27:3). . . . You shall write very clearly all the words of this law on the stones you have set up (v. 8).
>
> On the same day Moses commanded the people: (v. 11).

What follows in the passage is a list of commands of the Treaty in oath-curse form. The people hear as each is read aloud to them. After each command, the people were to shout, "Amen." In this instance, the term Law referred specifically to the commandments of the Covenant.

Paul used the term in the same way. In Romans Seven there is a discussion of the "law." The "law," Paul affirmed, was dead and gone. A Christian was dead to the law. He used the words "released from the law." Continuing the discussion he said.

> What shall we say then? Is the law sin? By no means. Indeed I would not have known what sin was except through the law. For I would not have known what it was to covet if the law had not said, "Do not covet." But sin, seizing the opportunity afforded by the commandment, produced in me every kind of covetous desire (Rom. 7:7ff.).

In selecting one of the ten commandments and identifying it as an example of the "law," he was using the word in its narrow meaning. In the same way, the word commandments can be understood as "the law."

James also used the word in the narrow sense when he spoke of the "perfect law of liberty" (James 1:25). Later he wrote this:

> For whoever keeps the whole law, but stumbles at just one point is guilty of breaking all of it. For He who said, "Do not commit adultery," also said, "Do not murder" (James 2:10).

James did not limit the meaning of "the law" to the Ten Commandments only, for he said:

> But if you show favoritism you are convicted by the law as lawbreakers (2:9).

The law regarding judging without regard to whether one was high born or low, rich or poor, alien or native is found in several places in the code (Lev. 19:15). The narrow meaning of Law is stipulation of a covenant.

The second expanded meaning of the word Law was covenant itself. It was used at times to refer to the entire Mosaic Treaty. John summed it all up and used the term law in a broad sense.

> The law was given through Moses; grace and truth came through Jesus Christ (John 1:17).

He was using the word to include all that Moses said, and was referring not only to the stipulations, but to the entire treaty, parties and promises as well as terms. He had just said, "Yet to all who received him, to those who believe in his name, he gave the right to become children of God— children born not of natural descent . . . but of God (John

1:12)." That had reference to parties. The Law, as used in II Chron. 35:12, had reference to the sacrificial system and specifically to material found in Lev. 3:3. The source of the information was called "The book of the Law of Moses," meaning the entire Old System. In John 7:19-23 Jesus distinguished between what came from Moses and what came from the "Patriarchs." Paul used the term "the Law" when he asked, "Is the Law therefore opposed to the promises of God?" He meant here to include the entire package, inasmuch as he mentioned "promises." He had asked earlier, "Did God give you His spirit and work miracles among you because you observe the Law?" (Gal. 3:5ff.). In a later passage in Galatians, he used the word "covenant" where he had previously used the word Law.

> These things may be taken figuratively, for the women represent two covenants, One covenant is from Mt. Sinai and bears children who are to be slaves: this is Hagar. Now Hagar stands for Mt. Sinai in Arabia. . . . But the Jerusalem that is above is free and she is our mother (Gal. 4:24).

The concept developed further to a third meaning. It came to refer to the Pentateuch, the five books of Moses. It was in this sense Jesus frequently used the words.

> This is what I told you while I was still with you. Everything must be fulfilled that is written about me in the Law of Moses, the prophets and the Psalms (Luke 24:44).

The practice of including all five of the early books of the Old Testament scriptures as the Law of Moses was common long before the time of Christ. The chart below will list passages refering to something in one of the books of the Pentateuch. How the author identified the source will give their understanding of the Pentateuch as the Law.

Source	Identification	Book Cited
II Kings 14:6	"the book of the Law of Moses"	Deut. 24:16
II Chr. 25:12	"the book of the Law of Moses"	Lev. 3:3
Ezra 6:8	"the book of Moses"	Num. 3:6
Joshua 8:31	"the book of the Law"	Exod. 20:25
Neh. 8:1	"the book of the Law of Moses"	The exact passage was not identified.
Neh. 8:8	"the book of the Law of God"	
Neh. 8:9	"the words of the Law"	
Neh. 8:14	"the Law which the Lord had commanded through Moses"	
Neh. 8:18	"the book of the Law of God"	
Gal. 4:21, 22	"the Law"	Gen. 21:1ff.
Luke 2:22	"Law of Moses"	Exod. 13:2
Luke 2:24	"Law of the Lord"	Lev. 12:8
II Cor. 3:14	"Old Covenant"	Exod. 34:33

Several conclusions can be drawn. The Episode of giving the Ten Commandments was called the "Old Covenant." The Law of Moses and the Law of God referred to the same documents. In the Old Testament era before the coming of John, the Law was a term used to denote the Pentateuch. You will note in the study above all five books of the Pentateuch find representation in "the law."

Finally, "the Law" came to mean the entire old covenant system. It was used this way over 150 times. When Paul or Jesus used the words, they usually meant all scripture before the time of Christ.

The Law and the prophets were proclaimed before John, since that time the good news of the kingdom has been preached (Luke 16:16).

106

The former regulation is set aside because it was weak and useless (for the Law made nothing perfect) and a better hope is introduced by which we draw near to God (Heb. 7:18).

But the ministry Jesus has received is as superior to theirs as the covenant of which he is mediator is superior to the old one, and is founded on better promises (Heb. 8:6).

If perfection could have been attained through the Levitical Priesthood, for on the basis of it the Law was given to the people, why was there need for another priest to come? . . . For when there is a change in the priesthood there must also be a change of the Law (Heb. 7:12).

The classic passage indicating the kind of thinking by the Apostles is Paul's declaration that all the ministry or administration of the things related to Moses, including the Ten Commandments, were done away as surely as the radiation from the face of Moses faded away. As Moses had a veil over his face, so the entire old covenant is veiled in meaning. It cannot be fully understood, said Paul, except through understanding Christ's meaning for it all.

But their minds were made dull, for to this day the same veil remains when the Old Testament is read. It has not been removed, because only in Christ is it removed. Even to this day when Moses is read a veil covers their hearts (II Cor. 3:14ff.).

Jesus quoted from the Psalms (82:6) identifying it as "the Law."

Jesus answered them, "Is it not written in your law, 'I have said you are gods?' If he called them gods—to whom the word of God came, and the scripture cannot be broken, what about . . ." (John 10:34).

107

Here is a fine example of the early church's habit of calling all the documents of the Old Testament the Scripture. Anything found in the Canon of the Old Testament could be referred to as the Law, since it had all passed away.

The reader can picture a funnel and understand the words "the Law" as sometimes used to represent the wide opening, the entire Old Testament. It was also used to denote the neck of the funnel, a subsection of the Old Testament scriptures known as the Pentateuch. The meaning was further narrowed to mean the Treaty of Moses as opposed to the previous history and covenants and subsequent developments. The spout of the funnel, the narrowest use of the Law, referred to the stipulations of the Treaty of Moses. That was a subsection of the Treaty itself. In Paul's mind and in the mind of Christ, I think, the words "the Law" meant everything about the old covenant as it rooted in the stipulations of the Treaty at Sinai. There was no scripture in the Old Testament that could escape the modification in meaning brought by its relationship to the Mosaic Treaty.

The Administration of Death

Paul called the Old Covenant the administration of death. He had good reason. Chiefly because the law of the land was also the law of religion, the administrators of the covenant were also required to act on behalf of civil administration and execute judgment upon breakers of the Law. There is no way around the problem. In a theocracy, there is no room for religious failure without it also being civil rebellion.

For instance, for each of the Ten Commandments there was an attendant command to kill the offender. This was true of all but the last: covetousness. That fault was too subjective to be established by witnesses. For the rest there was punishment, swift and fatal. Below is a list of the commandments and the passages where offenders were commanded to be put to death.

1. "No other gods" . . . . "Shall be utterly destroyed" (Exod. 22:20) "But you shall kill him" (Deut. 13:6-10)
2. "No graven images" . . . . . "Shall be put to death" (Deut. 17:6)
3. "Not take . . . name in vain" "Shall be put to death" (Lev. 24:16)
4. "Remember the Sabbath" . "Stoned to death" (Num. 15:36)
5. "Honor father and mother" "Shall be put to death" (Exod. 21:17)
6. "Do not kill" . . . . "Shall be put to death" (Exod. 21:12-14)
7. "Do not commit adultery" "Both . . . put to death" (Lev. 20:10)
8. "Do not steal" . . . . "He dies" (Exod. 22:2) "the kidnapper must die" (Deut. 24:7)
9. "False witness" . . . . "Purge the evil" (Deut. 19:19)
10. "Covetousness is idolatry" "Idolators . . . put to death" Paul (Col. 3:5) (Deut. 17:6)

"Whoever strikes a man so that he dies shall be put to death" (Exod. 21:12). "If a man owns an ox known to gore, and it gore a man, and the man die, the ox shall be stoned and the owner put to death" (Exod. 21:28). "You shall put to death any sorceress" (Exod. 22:18). "Anyone who has sexual relations with an animal shall be put to death" (Exod. 22:19). "If a prophet presumes to speak a word in my name that I have not commanded him to speak . . . he shall die"

(Deut. 18:20). "When the judge . . . a Levite . . . gives a verdict, any man, who by not obeying the priest or the judge . . . that man shall die" (Deut. 17:8-12). "If two men are fighting and the wife of one of them comes to rescue one of them from his assailant, and she reaches out and seizes him by his private parts, you shall cut off her hand. Show her no pity" (Deut. 25:11).

Little wonder Paul called it the administration of death! To be true to the Law one was required to administrate death to friend and neighbor. To be free from the law was to be free from death. It was in that perspective Paul called the Treaty of Moses "the law of sin and death (Rom. 8:3)." He wrote in another letter the Law was "against us" (Col. 2:14). Christ came, he said, "to redeem them that were under the Law" (Gal. 4:5). Paul was astounded that any should want to return to "those weak and beggarly elements" (Gal. 4:9). He had concluded none could keep the Law, whether an individual or a nation. No one could be justified by the Law as long as this one curse remained in force. Every Israelite had agreed to it. Paul reminded all.

> All those who rely on the works of the law are under a curse; for it is written, "Cursed be everyone who does not abide in all that is written in the Book of the Law" (Gal. 3:10).

The Tent and the Ark

There were two objects that were called for in the Law. About these the entire religion grew. They became the most sacred things in Israel. One was the tent of meeting or the Tabernacle. Its specifications were explicitly delivered to Moses. The furnishings were carefully described. The service within the Tabernacle was detailed. How to approach it and who may approach it were clearly stated. The tribes camped about it when at rest. It traveled with tribes, moving with

110

protective care, in the center of procession when they migrated. God had promised to be with them when they traveled. He had led them with a pillar of smoke by day and a flaming pillar by night. Now he was at home "in their midst." The light of His glory shown through the walls of the tent for all to see. It glowed at night. God was in the center of Israel and that meant all was well. Later the tent became the Temple at Jerusalem.

The Ark was a wooden box, elaborately carved and over-laid with beaten gold. On the Ark was a "mercy seat." On it the priest poured the blood of the high sacrifices. In the Ark were several objects. All had important meaning in the history of Israel. The Tables of Stone were placed inside (Exod. 25:16) and Aaron's rod that budded (Heb. 9:4). The Book of the Covenant was placed on the outside for easy access.

> After Moses had finished writing in the book the words of this law, from beginning to end, he gave this command to the Levites who carried the Ark of the Covenant of the Lord: "Take this Book of the Law and place it beside the Ark of the Covenant of your Lord God" (Deut. 31:24ff.).

You will recall the ancient treaties required the Text of the Treaty to be held in a most sacred place and be read to all the people each year. Since no one was allowed to open the Ark, and since the reason for the safekeeping of the Text was its availability, it was placed outside the Ark, but within the Most Holy Place of the Tabernacle. One implication of its location was all members of the nation were responsible to both know and keep the covenant. It was the presence of the Covenant that made the Ark and the Tabernacle holy and sacred. God was party to the covenant.

111

The covenant was in His immediate presence, as it were, so all might be assured of its success. The covenant, of course, brought the Ark into existence. It was father of both the Ark and the Tabernacle.

Later in history we shall find Paul speaking of the church as the Temple or Tabernacle of God, and that God's Spirit dwells in it. The old tabernacle was a kind of foreshadowing of later things. It was a glorious thing to see in those days, and it is a glorious thing to see in ours.

The Conquest and the Judges

United by a common treaty with the God of all nature, that band of unskilled, poorly clad, and almost weaponless wanderers crossed the river and entered Canaan. They fully expected to conquer it! Their leader was by that time Joshua. Moses had died. The magnificent old lawgiver had passed away. We shall see him once more, but that is getting ahead of the story.

Joshua was himself an old man by then. He had been one of the original band to exit Egypt. He had been one of the spies who brought back the report terrifying the people (Deut. 1:22ff.). He and Caleb had brought a minority report, however. The other ten reported the land flowed with milk and honey and brought back produce to prove it. But they were astounded at the population, the strength of the cities and the size of the inhabitants. "We look like grasshoppers next to them," they said. The people rebelled and God reacted by killing the ten spies on the spot and forcing the rest of the band of adult age to perish over a forty-year span in the desert country. Joshua had seen the manna and the quail which fed the people. He saw the brass serpent standing on the hill and how all who simply saw it were healed of the terrible snake bites. He was in several battles and tasted victory. He survived several attempted coups. He was a good and loyal man. Now he was the commander-in-chief of this very dubious army! As a skinny old man with sagging armor he challenged a stranger wandering too close to camp.

"Are you friend or foe?" he shouted, drawing his sword.

"I am the commander of the armies of heaven," replied the Stranger. Joshua, knees a bit stiff with age, and leaning on his sword point, first knelt and then fully prostrated himself before the Being. Grand old man. Beautiful, toothless old warrior. With men like him God had set out to conquer the whole world!

Under his leadership the land of promise was taken. Little by little, each province was entered, fierce battles waged, with good men and bad dying. Walled cities were taken. For the most part the original inhabitants were put to death: men, women, children, and in some cases, livestock and pets. The land was given to each tribe as their turn came. The wives and children, older men and youths were left to begin their new life. The others went on with the army to regions yet to be conquered. It was bloody and it was brutal. It was what life had become on earth after the Garden. And God was in the very middle of it. He commanded it. Let there be no mistake about the character of God. He is just what He is. He thinks, feels, and works out plans, just as we all do. He had plans. He was not going to force anyone back into a relationship with Him. He would convince men and angels of the validity of His nature. He could be gentle and understanding. But when He had plans, He went about them as men go about plans at times. He could get angry. He is not all sweetness and soft words. It is not right to think the God of the Old Testament was a vengeful tribal Deity and the Jesus of the New Testament a kind fatherly type. They were one and the same person, according to Jesus (John 14:6-9). When God elected to work out His plans on the plain of history, He understood it would come to this. Make no mistakes about God. He has the emotional strength to carry out His plans.

He said He would give the land of Canaan to Abraham's descendants, and He was doing it. We ought to note that, consistent with the basic philosophy expressed in the philosophy section of Genesis, God used man to work out His plans. God gave Canaan to them, but they had to also take it! That was covenant at work: God had a part and man had a part. But man could not have done it without God. He had the greater and essential part.

Rahab and Jericho

In the list of all-time greats of God's salvation-history (Heb. 11:1ff.) there appears an unlikely name: Rahab. She was a harlot. She "operated a house," as they said in the old west. Her name appeared because of a very slim but significant connection to the covenant. Her story is worth considering. It is almost the story of mankind.

Spies had been sent by Joshua into the region west of Jericho. That city was in a prosperous valley, had natural springs, as it has today, and was well populated. It was walled. The spies came into the city. Word got out they were there. They were in frightful danger and they went to the madam of the house and asked for aid. They were able to persuade her they were in the special care of the God who had brought them into this land. They explained

114

to her the fact the city was to fall. Of that she may be assured they would have said. Their God had confounded Egypt and the six kings and had declared on a blood oath he would give all this land to them.

She agreed to help them in exchange for their own care of her and her family when the city fell. They struck a bargain. They made a covenant. Parties: The spies and Rahab. Terms: Hide the spies and let them down the outside wall. Then hang a long, clearly visible scarlet cord from her window. Promises: She, her family, and "all who belonged to her" were to be spared when the city fell. See how a covenant worked. Note the terminology.

"Swear to me by the Lord," she said.

"Our lives for your lives," the men assured her.

"This oath we swear will not be binding on us unless . . . cord."

"But if you tell what we are doing we will be released from the oath."

"Agreed," she replied, "let it be as you say."

> Joshua said to the two men who had spied out the land, "Go into the prostitute's house and bring her out and all who belong to her in accordance to your oath to her" . . . They brought out her entire family and put them in a safe place outside the camp of Israel. . . . Then they burned the city. . . . But Joshua spared Rahab the prostitute, . . . and she lives among the Israelites to this day (Josh. 6:22f.).

Several principles can be gained from this episode. Aiding the people of the covenant is aiding Jehovah. The people of God and the covenant of God are almost inseparable. One, the covenant, made them a nation; the other, the people keep, promote and protect the covenant. Another principle is the fact that covenant keeping is really what makes any society function. Each must be able to depend on the other. Morality, the keeping of covenant, is empty unless there is a specific commitment made and received. Religion, therefore, must not be only subjective. That allows one to write both sides of the agreement and keep only what he wrote for himself. Morality requires a stated standard to which all parties have agreed. A third principle is that the specific ethic one has at the time of covenanted contact with God or the people of God is less important than the trust given to the God of the covenant or the covenant or the people of the covenant. Rahab was saved because she came into contact with God's plans and she supported them. In God's salvation-history, those who support His plans come down in history as heroes, regardless of their morals.

The same thing was true of Samson. He was a great judge (Judg. 15:20). He had a problem with women (Judg. 20:1). He died in captivity, blinded, and far from friends and homeland. He was, nonetheless, a hero to the Hebrews. Why? He was for the Law and the people of Israel, and against the enemies of God's people, and that fact overshadowed all his human failings. He was a "judge" in Israel. He rendered verdicts in justice and according to Torah.

In the case of the sons of Eli, an old and famous priest, the point is again illustrated. The sons were rascals. They served at the altar. They were to have a share of what was being sacrificed. Contrary to the Torah, they took by intimidation (I Sam. 2:12ff.) choice parts already dedicated as sacrificial meat. That meat the Lord's. It was a dangerous business. They also took advantage of women who came to sacrifice or work about the Tabernacle. Eli knew about it and he talked to the sons. "If man sins against another man, judges may mediate for him, but if a man sins against the Lord who will intercede for him?" God at last had enough. He recalled the fact He had promised the ancestors of the clan of Eli they would be priests, "forever." Then He said these words:

> I promised that your house and your father's house would minister before me forever. But now the Lord declares, far be it from me! Those who honor me, I will honor, but those who despise me will be disdained. The time is coming when I will cut short . . . your house. I will raise up for Myself a faithful priest (I Sam. 2:30ff.).

Why, we might ask, were the sons of Eli so offensive to God, and Samson, sharing as he did the same weaknesses, regarded so highly? The answer is that Samson's error was a sin, to be sure, and forbidden by Torah. But it did not represent a rebellion against God and was not an attack on any of the people of God. It did not represent abandonment of covenant, only breach of it. To be in the very presence of God and flagrantly violate a matter so closely related to direct honor, as was a sacrifice, was deeply offensive to God.

And so the history of the people of the covenant went. It had its ups and its downs. The people were unskilled at farming, and so it seemed at times, almost anything else. They were forbidden by Greek-Philistine law from smelting iron or even being blacksmiths (I Sam. 13:19). Saul became a king. He did a great deal of good for the land. He and Samuel had difficulty. Saul was moody and unstable. He did work for the best interests of Israel. But the higher in rank one goes the more responsibility he carries. That is simply the way it is with God. Jesus said, "To whom much is given, much will be required" (Luke 12:48). God holds people responsible. At last Saul became increasing incorrigible. He disobeyed a direct order from God (I Sam. 15:3), he consulted witches, (I Sam. 28:8) but worst of all, he raised his hand against the king God had appointed. That young man's name was David.

The Davidic Covenant

David became the most famous king in Hebrew history. His story, at least the major highlights, is too familiar to repeat. He was from a simple farming community at Lehem's Place: Bethlehem. He became famous for the killing of the giant. He married the king's daughter. His best friend was the son of the king. He lived, after his falling out with Saul, and his anointing as king, as the leader of what we would now call a guerrilla band. For a time he commanded a unit in a Philistine army (I Sam. 27:1ff.). He became King of the two hill tribes after the death of Saul and his dear friend, Jonathan.

David attempted to be conciliatory toward the northern tribes. Their new king, a son of Saul, ruled in Israel to the north. The land of Banjamin lay between Judah and the other tribes. Most of the Benjamites came over to David. When Abner, the commander of the army of the North, was falsely accused by the King Ish-Bosheth of breach of faith, Abner went over to David's side, bringing many Benjaminites with him. He had also spoken to many Israelite tribal leaders urging them to unite with David as God's own king.

Abner was murdered by David's cousin and commander-in-chief, Joab, as he was returning to Israel to call a conference of national reconciliation. David was deeply embarrassed and mourned publicly. The tribes of the North were convinced David was not involved in the murder and began to speak of unity. At that time Ish-Bosheth was murdered and the Senate of the Northern region ratified David as their king. He had ruled in the south for about seven years and now ruled the united kingdom.

His rule was successful. The kingdom extended to embrace all the lands promised to Abraham. David established justice and held the Torah in greatest honor. He had the support of all factions in the land: the priests with their power bloc; the army, commanded by old comrades in arms; the tribal elders who needed peace and a time of rebuilding; the common people who lived without fear of raiding Philistines. He collected documents. He had captured the great Jebusite fortress city in Judah and made it the capital of the united kingdom. To it, Jerusalem, he returned the Ark, dancing in the street before it, to the hill of Zion. He began plans to build the temple. He instituted the Torah as the law of the land with central enforcement. The promises made to Abraham had all come to pass, except one. They were a great nation. Isaac had his twelve "peoples"; they were indeed dwelling in the land flowing with milk and honey. Their King was an experienced warrior, a very sensitive musician, a good administrator, and best of all, he was loyal to YHWH and loved the Torah. One last promise given to Abraham remained. That one—the one for which all others existed—was not fulfilled. That would take another nine hundred years to even begin.

God's Suzerainty Grant to David

In spite of the fact that David had a shameful episode with Bathsheba he is well remembered as a great king. He learned in that unfortunate series of sins he was not above the Torah. The king and the common man were equal before

119

the Lord, and before the Law. David's sin was more serious only because it was true in that day more than now, probably, the people tended to imitate closely the king. He was their life and the life of the entire land. Like king, like people was true, as history tended to show.

God initiated the grant to David. Through Nathan the prophet God spoke to David. In abbreviated form the essentials can be seen.

> I took you from the pasture and from following the flock to be the ruler over my people Israel.

> The Lord declares to you that the Lord himself will establish a house for you. When your days are over and you rest with your fathers, I will raise up your offspring to succeed you. . . .

> He is the one who will build a house for my name, and I will establish the throne of his kingdom for ever. I will be his father and he will be my son.

> When he does wrong I will punish him . . . but my love will never be taken from him. . . .

> Your throne will be established forever (II Sam. 7:8ff.).

This case is an example of the old treaty-grants. It differed in significant ways from national treaties, but followed the suzerainty treaty formulary. In the grant of Ashurbanipol to his servant Balta this language occurred.

> Balta . . . whose heart is whole to his master, stood before me in truthfulness, walked in perfection in my palace . . . and kept the charge of my kingship. I considered his good relations with me, and established therefore this gift.[6]

The references to "he will be my son" were also familiar phases in other ancient suzerainty grants. The vassal was a

---

6. Moshe Weinfeld, "Covenant," *Encyclopaedica Judaica*, V, Jerusalem: Keter Publishing House, 1971, p. 1018.

sort of adopted son. His station would pass on to the vassal's heir upon his death.

David called Solomon to give him one last charge before he died. David understood the ancient treaties. No son of a vassal could expect to stand in the place of his father before the suzerain unless he also keep the same fidelity that brought the grant to the father.

I am about to go the way of all the earth. Be strong, show yourself a man, and observe what the Lord God requires: walk in His ways, and keep his decrees and commands, his laws and requirements, as written in the Law of Moses . . . so the Lord may keep his promise to me,

"If your descendants watch how they live, and if they walk faithfully before me with all their heart and soul, you will never fail to have a man on the throne of Israel"

Now you yourself know . . .   (I Kgs. 2:2ff.).

This is another example of the "group" promise and the "individual in the group" separation. David understood well the grant was conditional. Solomon must stand in the responsibility place of David as well as in the privileged places. This was made clear when Solomon himself began to drift away from God. He lost for the House of David the northern states.

Solomon did not keep the Lord's command. So the Lord said to Solomon, "Since this is your attitude and you have not kept my covenant and my decrees which I commanded you, I will most certainly tear the kingdom away from you and give it to one of your subordinates. I will tear it out of the hand of your son. Yet I will not tear the whole kingdom from him, but I will give him one tribe for the sake of David my servant and for the sake of Jerusalem, which I have chosen" (I Kgs. 11:9ff.).

121

God chose an energetic young steward of the administration of Solomon and gave to him the same kind of suzerainty grant he had given to David, with the exception of the Tribe of Judah. Solomon tried to kill him, but he escaped to Egypt and lived with Solomon's enemy until Solomon died. Then he ascended to the throne of the northern tribes.

A brief summary of the Davidic covenant is shown here.

Parties: God and David (II Sam. 7:12-17).

Terms: Keep the Law of Moses satisfactorily (I Kgs. 2:2).
Stay away from idols (I Kgs. 11:9).
Protect and promote the Covenant (I Kgs. 11:33).

Promises: "A descendant of David to be king" (II Sam. 7:13).
To punish but not forsake the royal house (II Sam. 7:15).
Be ruler over one state only (I Kgs. 11:36).
"and of his kingdom there shall be no end" (I Kgs. 11:39; Luke 1:33).

Covenants and "Sign of a Covenant"

Beginning with God's covenant with Noah, the idea of covenant sign was introduced. A "sign" was not the same as an "oath." A sign may have been a pile of rocks, or a stone placed upright, or anything agreeable to both parties or imposed upon the other by the stronger party.

The sign of the covenant with Noah was a rainbow. "This is the sign of the covenant I am making between me and you," God declared (Gen. 9:12).

The sign of the Abrahamic covenant was circumcision. "You are to undergo circumcision and it will be the sign of the covenant between me and you" (Gen. 17:11).

The sign of the Mosaic covenant was keeping the Sabbath. "It will be a sign between me and the Israelites for ever" (Exod. 31:13). The next verses end the giving of the tablets of stone, so we conclude the Sabbath was the sign for the entire old treaty.

There was no sign mentioned in connection with the Davidic covenant.

The keeping of signs was directly related to the covenant of which one was a part. Since the Mosaic covenant was added to the Abrahamic, the blood descendants of Abraham kept both.

When one had a relationship with God, be it formal or prophetic (that is, God appearing to him from time to time), he simply had to understand how God thought. God treated people as if they were made in His image: as responsible people. As Adam had to learn to live with nature in the garden of Eden, so humanity had to learn to live with God. One cannot say, considering the long history of patient forbearance of God with Israel all the years, that God is overdemanding or quick to punish. How long did the sons of Eli insult Him at the very gates of the Tabernacle before God acted? But God is serious with mankind. They must behave as responsible divine-like beings. For such they are; "In our image." God's patience was great with Solomon, for, reminded of His *hesed* to David, He left Solomon on the throne until he died a natural death! (I Kgs. 3:6-14). It is true, "God is slow to anger" (Ps. 103:8), but He will only take so much.

David had many descendants who were qualified by blood to sit on his throne. Many did. Not all were satisfactory to God. Those who were in gross violation God removed. For some He simply allowed their own foolishness and error to overtake and destroy them. But until the great exile several hundreds of years later, God kept a son of David on the throne. An individual may have been put off, but a different son of David was used to replace him. In short, being in an heir-group never excused the individual from faithfulness. God kept faith with that family patiently for decade after decade until the entire nation was taken out of the land into captivity and there was no more kingdom.

What is significant for later history is the final enthronement of Jesus, blood descendant of David, over God's new Israel. The Lord was faithful to David and his household. A son of David now sits on the throne of his father and also at the right hand of God (Luke 1:32).

Conditionality

Covenants were instruments of conditionality. They were mutual commitments. The very word "if" implied it. Clear statements of scripture reinforce the idea. Israel's happy life and her very status with God were conditional.

> If you fully obey the Lord your God and carefully follow all his commands I give you this day, the Lord your God will set you high above all the nations on earth (Deut. 28:1).

The formulary of covenant had conditionality built into it. One aspect of the form of covenant was the fact it had terms.

> These are the terms of the covenant the Lord commanded Moses to make with the Israelites in Moab in addition to the Covenant He had made with them at Horeb (Deut. 29:1).

> Carefully follow the terms of this covenant so that you may prosper in everything you do (29:9).

124

When such a person hears the words of this oath and . . . thinks, "I will be safe even if I persist in going my own way," this will bring disaster . . . (Deut. 29:19).

All the nations will ask, "Why has the Lord done this to this land? Why this fierce burning anger?" The answer will be, "It is because the people abandoned the covenant of the Lord" (Deut. 29:24, 25).

Even the promise given to Abraham, now fully executed in all matters regarding Israel's becoming a great nation, was conditioned upon Abraham's heirs having the same faith as Abraham's.

In furious anger and in great wrath the Lord uprooted them from their land and thrust them into another land as it is now (Deut. 29:28).

A return to the land was also promised upon full repentance.

And when you and your children return to the Lord, your God, and obey him with all your heart and all your soul as I have commanded you today, then the Lord your God will restore your fortunes and have compassion on you, and gather you again from all the nations where he scattered you (Deut. 30:2).

It was in full confidence in God's integrity the prophets later quoted these very passages in reminding Israel of the conditionality of the covenant with God. Abraham was faithful and so by His own oath, God was obligated to rescue the posterity from the Egyptian captivity. He did so and was thereby faithful to the Abrahamic covenant. But now, God added to that covenant other stipulations for the descendants of Abraham. Their land and status would be forfeited upon gross disobedience. This made the continuation of being

125

a great nation and possessing the land conditional. From that time forward, God was free from the charge he had broken faith with Abraham if Israel suffered loss.

The same was true for the sons of David. They also were required to remain faithful. God was free to modify the covenant upon gross violation. We saw that He did so in regard to the ten tribes being given to Jeroboam and his posterity. This dynasty in turn lost it. The conclusion must be that covenants are conditional. All God's promises are related to a specific covenant. Thus all God's promises are conditional. We will find this true in both the Old and the New Testaments.

Conclusion

The first eleven chapters of Genesis were history. Since history is philosophy, they were also philosophy. Israel regarded her own history to have begun with the call and election of Abraham. Whom God calls, He elects. He made a covenant with Abraham, the promises of which essentially combined to three. God was to give his posterity Canaan. They were to become a great nation. They were to be the agency through whom God intended to bless all mankind. Abraham was faithful. God was faithful. Joshua reminded all, "Every promise has been fulfilled, not one has failed" (Josh. 23:14). As regarded Israel as a nation all promises were kept. One was yet to be kept: blessing all nations by Abraham's seed.

Then the great Old Covenant, the Mosaic Covenant, was written and formally accepted. By it God made specific promises—all related to the good life in Canaan. The people promised to make continued peace with God conditioned

126

upon their own faithfulness. That covenant created a Theocracy. That fact, necessary as it was at the time, eventually became the greatest problem for people under the Old Covenant.

The third covenant examined was the grant to David and his family. It provided for a dynastic succession to Israel's throne. The pact was hardly instituted before it was broken and therefore modified. Upon faithful keeping of the Law, a descendant was always to sit on the throne of David.

In the early history of Israel a man or woman was accorded a respectable place in the record based upon their belief in and support of God and the covenant. While God was certainly interested in ethics, His immediate concern, at that time, was the success of the people of the covenant, their entering, possessing, and living in Canaan as He had promised.

Covenants imply several things. They imply God is a person. He is Spirit to be sure (John 4:24) but He can think, and He made plans, modified procedures as necessary to complete those plans, and felt joy, frustration, satisfaction and anger throughout it all. Covenant presupposed free moral agency in man. He was accountable. Covenant became the objective standard by which man became morally responsible. Thus far in Biblical history any relationship to God was first and foremost a covenanted relationship.

MAJOR OLD TESTAMENT COVENANTS

	Parties	Terms	Promises
Abrahamic:	God, Abraham, Isaac, posterity and slaves	Trust God, obey, circumcise, live in Canaan, die in faith. Circumcise as "sign."	1. Canaan 2. Great Nation 3. ta ethne blessed
Mosaic:	God and the tribes of Israel	Keep the 613 Laws of Moses. Be a theocracy. Keep Sabbath as "sign."	Prosperity, physical needs, national in character, related to Canaan
Davidic:	David and his sons	Keep the Law of Moses faithfully.	A son of David to always be king of Israel, at least one tribe.

127

Questions on Chapter Three

1. Where did the Biblical writers usually begin salvation-history?
2. Why did God choose Abraham and not someone else?
3. What was Abraham's (Abram) first test of belief?
   a) Was asked to go to Canaan and live.
   b) Was told to marry Sarah.
   c) Was to sacrifice Isaac.
   d) Was to prepare a sacrifice.
4. T F   Abraham had several wives and several children.
5. T F   Ishmael was to be the one through whom the covenant passed.
6. T F   The lineage of Abraham was a morally upstanding one.
7. T F   God set the captives free because they were so faithful.
8. T F   God got angry a lot in the Old Testament.
9. T F   God's promises are unconditional.
10. T F   The Law of Moses and the law of God are two different laws.
11. Define "parallelism" _____
    _____ .

12. A man could become a Jew by accepting circumcision. Discuss.
13. Summarize the Gentile's standing and responsibility to keep the Torah.
14. Law was translated a) *shema*   c) *hesed*
                         b) *b'rth*   d) *torah*
15. Explain how God can promise to bring Israel into Canaan and yet leave almost all of them dead in the wilderness.

16. What one thing can God not abide in His followers?
17. Why did Paul call the Old Covenant the Administration of Death?
18. Men whose morals were not always perfect were counted as heroes. Why?

PLEASE TURN THE BOOK OVER FOR ANSWERS.

1. With the call of Abraham

2. The text does not say:
God chooses many things without reference to any known matters. He simply works out His plans, with-in covenanted limitations, if any, as He sees fit.

3. a) He was asked to go to Canaan. He did so and got the covenant promised. We do not know exactly what God would have done if he had refused. Presumably He would have offered it to another (Rom. 11:48).

4. T
5. F
6. F
7. F
8. F
9. F
10. F

11. It is a literary form wherein a second word or phrase is repeating and defining the meaning of the first. No new idea is meant to be represented in the second word or line.

12. No one could simply join Israel. One had to be born a Jew. Some did become Jews by slavery, illegal marriage, and by grace of God and Joshua, but those cases

were exceptions. The Old Testament was built upon the flesh and blood of Abraham.

13. They had no standing and hence no responsibility whatever.

14. d) Torah

15. The promise was to the group and any individual must remain faithful to the covenant and God to gain for himself a place in the promise.

16. Failure to treat God as the one true God.

17. It required the servants of the covenant to kill offenders.

18. Because there are two kinds of sin. One is massive: being out of fellowship with God or insulting or ignoring Him. The other kind of sin is sin just the same but represents human weakness and can be corrected with faith. The other lacks faith, the basis of correction.

Chapter Four

PROPHET AND COVENANT

The people of God were created by the covenant. Without that, they had no identity. John Bright, one of America's finest scholars understood the uniqueness of Israel.

Israel seems in fact to have to have entered history as a covenant society. From some two hundred years after her first appearance in Palestine, she had no statehood, no organized government, no administrative machinery, and above all, she had no king. She was a sacred league of tribes united in covenant with Jehovah. The focal point of the league was the shrine that housed its most sacred object, the Ark of the Covenant, the portable throne of the invisible Deity, which at least by the end of the earliest period was located at Shiloh.[1]

We saw in the last chapter the development from that league of isolated tribes into a very great nation. David had unified them into a strong Middle-Eastern kingdom. They changed rapidly under the administration of Solomon and his son, Rehoboam. A reflection of that shift in culture and society can be seen by a passage of scripture. "But Rehoboam rejected the advice the elders gave him and consulted the young men who had grown up with him" (I Kgs. 12:8). They passed rapidly from an agricultural and herding society located in thousands of small villages to an urban society with its contracts, specializations, and bureaucracy. They became a small but powerful military kingdom. Yet they were the people of God and the children of the covenant. That was their root, their moral unity and their self-concept. They were proud of the Torah and what it meant to them.

---

1. John Bright, *Covenant and Promise*, Philadelphia: The Westminster Press, 1967, p. 31.

You yourselves have seen what I did to Egypt and how I carried you on eagles' wings and brought you to myself. Now if you obey me fully and keep my covenant then out of all nations you will be my treasured possession. Although the whole earth is mine, you will be for me a kingdom and a holy nation (Exod. 19:4ff.).

Maintaining their true national identity became increasingly difficult. The united monarchy dissolved into two separate kingdoms, Israel and Judah. The temple was in Judah, and in times of war or administration tension between the two states, travel by Israelites to Zion was often dangerous. The annual covenant renewal services were postponed, sometimes for years and years. Alternative locations were substituted for Jerusalem. Covenant loyalty weakened. Since the Levites and the men from the schools of the prophets (I Sam. 10:5-12) constituted a power bloc that sometimes rivaled the crown, little was done by the king and the treasurer to insure their support. All too often the king was Baalite, or permissive in religion and he wanted peace. Trouble over religion, usually from the prophets, disrupted an otherwise peaceful land. Baalite leaders were usually generous with money and women. As long as the people paid taxes and did what they were told in terms of public works, the king left Baalite chapels alone. Recruits for learning Torah dwindled. It seems likely they had few men who had studied the Torah and could speak about it with clarity and conviction. If the people were not coming to sacrifice, and if the tithe paid to the Levites was not enforced by the crown, the educational and religious administration had difficulty refilling the ranks with competent men. God intervened in history several times to save the situation. He often did so through the prophets (Heb. 1:1).

132

What is History?

The collection of prophetic documents broadly called The Prophets was divided into the Former and the Latter Prophets. The former were the books that followed the Pentateuch. They were the history books of the early Hebrew nation. The prophets were therefore more than simply men who were visited by God from time to time. They were historians. No one can write a history without being a philosopher.

What is history? It can not be simply a record of the past. If that were true, everything that happened in every place and at every moment of every month of the past would have to be written down. That is impossible. So history is the recording, for some reason or other, of events that seem important. But what events are worth remembering? And for that matter, different men may prefer events not be recorded and remembered. Two different men will choose different happenings to record for the future. The authors of the Bible were united about one basic concept; history really began with Abraham; and whatever happened prior to that was important only to show the absolute chaos of man and society. The tracing of contributions to covenant fulfillment was the unifying principle of the Old Testament writers.

The Substance of History

History is made up of three things. First, it has a philosophy lying behind it. There is no real history without some unifying basis for selecting the events to be recorded. Second, there must be the selection of an event itself for inclusion in the record. An event is by definition an occurrence that has unusual value and meaning. All happenings are potential events, but an event is an occurrence that has been raised in rank. Third, there must be the meaning of the event. A happening is just a happening until some extra meaning is assigned to it. So history is a rather complicated thing made up of various elements.

The naturalist has no such view of history. For him the endless cycle of nature is all there is to life. Man is part of nature and runs his course as all things do. Why record the falling of each leaf? What is the point of endlessly listing kings and boundaries? All is but an endless and meaningless cycle. Nietzche said it well of this view:

> Everything goeth, everything returneth; eternally rolleth the wheel of existence. Everything dieth, everything blossometh forth again; eternally runneth on the year of existence. Everything breaketh, everything is integrated anew; eternally buildeth itself the house of existence. All things separate, all things again greet one another; eternally true to itself remaineth the ring (nature cycle) of existence.[2]

That exact philosophy was found to lie at the base of Baalism. But more of that later. What is significant is there is no need for history unless there is some goal or point to it. Covenant broke the eternal cycle-of-nature philosophy and put history on a lineal track. History measured the distance from promise to fulfillment! Specifically, history for the Israelite was tracing God's covenanted promise through to its fulfillment. Whatever affected the movement toward covenanted promise was important. If an occurrence had significant effect on the success of the covenant it was immediately elevated to the status of an event. Events were, for the Hebrew, anything that hurt or helped the covenant. They were equally interested in both.

---

2. Hendrikus Berkhoff, *Christ the Meaning of History,* Richmond, Virginia: John Knox Press, 1966, p. 27.

Modern historians also record matters they feel are important. The rich and powerful are admired. What made them rich or powerful is recorded. Whatever brought about their downfall is recorded. Nations and kings, boundaries and treaties, wars and wealth are matters of record. That is called political history.

Other historians record social movements. They are more interested in the waves that roll beneath the boats of the kings and the wealthy. They trace the ebb and flow of national and international trends. That is social history.

The Marxists have their own philosophy of history. It is decidedly naturalistic. Marxists believe they have discovered the "scientifically fixed" laws of production and consumption, of technology and cycles of class evolution. The class stuggle drives on, as a law of nature, until capitalism collapses and power, the means of production, falls into the hands of the common man. When that happens the struggle between man and men will stop, peace will come, nature and society will continue on smoothly. Whatever aids that natural process is important. Whatever worked against that process was judged bad. Whatever supported communism was good. Whatever worked against it was bad. It sounds a bit like Hebrew philosophy. Communism had its roots in Christianity.

Some have rightly pointed out the prophetic-messianic strain in the thought of the Protestant-educated Jew, Marx. Communism received its astounding and recruiting power from the Judeo-Christian heritage coupled with the naturalistic conformity to the law of economic process.[3]

The difference between a communist and a prophet is that communists believe it is natural law driving them to

3. Berkhoff, *ibid.*, p. 34.

135

eventual success. The prophets said it was Jehovah who was in charge of history.

The prophets judged events. That is why there is a Book of Judges in the Bible. These leaders kept Israel on course. Historians judge events and assign importance to some and not others. The prophets spoke for God showing the people what kinds of behaviors were consistent with the Torah. Acts consistent with the Law of Moses were judged to be moral as well as legal. Acts contrary to the Code were identified and judged not merely illegal, but also immoral. A prophet judged all events on the continuing basis of the Treaty with God. He was not merely a bystander recording happenings and then denouncing the offender. He was not a disinterested and neutral journalist observing the flow of events. He directed the flow. He both made and recorded history. Since the history-of-salvation measured progress from promise to fulfillment, he had a vital stake in aiding Israel's achievement of the promises. He did not always thunder down judgments, for he loved his people. His judgments were announcements that such and such a deed was contrary to the Torah or was counterproductive for Israel's hope.

Since God's promises were sure, and the God of history was working out His will, and since the will of God was that man cooperate and work along with God toward goal fulfillment, the prophet had another job. He was God's advocate. He interpreted events and put them into proper perspective —related to the promises. He worked toward encouraging the people to keep the covenant and thus bring in the promises. He became, in a real sense, God's covenant lawyer.

Baalism and the Covenant

Baalism was a very sophisticated and well organized religion. It was based on what many modern philosophers regard as sound presupposition. They were naturalists. Their system was an integrated whole. For that reason, the prophets could give it no quarter. It was a battle to the death. Israelite faith and Baalite naturalism could not both be true and both survive side by side. Each had an integrated view of society. It was all or nothing for both. Both had religion mixed with politics and shrines, with agricultural and private life. There were two different priesthoods, two ideas about what sacrifice meant, and two different philosophies about dealing with other faiths. In short, Baalism was based upon the assumption nature was all of reality. They believed what happened in nature was a reflection of what the gods were doing. Thus to be religious one must accept nature as it is and replicate in his life and religion, just as nature did, the productive acts of the gods. That was totally unacceptable to the Hebrew. YHWH was the only true God. Anyone worshipping any other god or failing to keep the law in direct regard to God's honor was to die. That was what Torah stated and that is what they intended to do. No quarter. If an Israelite became a Baalite it was an offense of the greatest magnitude. He must die at once.

There was more at stake than simply the name of God. Confidence in the nature cycle as ultimate reality meant the death of any concept of covenant. Covenant meant God acted in special ways for His people. God's people were to live as lords of nature. They obeyed not nature but covenant. Each religion was deeply and soundly rooted in opposing philosophies.

To be sure, there were good moments for both. And bad. King Ahab had married a Baalite princess. She was a bitter enemy of the Jehovahite sect. She killed thousands of the leaders. Elijah, God's chief prophet at the time, was terrified. All Israel was intimidated by her and the Baal administration. Elijah said,

> I have been zealous for the Lord God almighty. The Israelites have rejected your covenant, broken down your altars, and put your prophets to death with the sword. I am the only one left and they are trying to kill me too (I Kgs. 19:14ff.).

The Baalites had their problems too. One time, Elijah confronted the entire assembled nation. He walked through the crowd to the grand pavilion of the king. Ahab saw him coming, perhaps surprised, as a warrant had been issued by the queen. The king said,

"Is that you, you troubler of Israel?"

"I have not made trouble for Israel," Elijah replied, "but you and your father's family have. You have abandoned the Lord's commands and have followed the Baals."

A contest of power proceeded. Fire from heaven was sought, first by the Baalites, then by Elijah according to the agreement. In vain the priests of Baal appealed to all their lords. Elijah confronted the population.

"How long will you waver between the two opinions? If YHWH is God follow him. But if a Baal is god follow him."

The sacrifice of Elijah was ignited into flames by God, in spite of the fact it had been soaked thoroughly with tubs of water. After the contest, Elijah's position before the people was so strengthened he ordered the four hundred priests of Baal who attended the royal chapel and ate at the queen's table, to be taken captive. He then took them all to the Kishon valley and slaughtered them (I Kgs. 18:40).

The real battle between YHWH and Baal was spiritual, that is, moral, intellectual, philosophical. Was nature the ultimate reality or was God eternal? Both could not be true. In the books of the prophets the reflection of the battle can be seen.

The root meaning of *baal* in Hebrew was simply "lord" and also "husband." A play on words was made by some prophets.

> "In that day," declares the Lord, "you will call ME husband. You will no longer call me, my master. I will remove the names of the Baals from her lips; No longer will their names be invoked" (Hos. 2:16).

When a Baalite said, "Baal," he may have reference to "a lord," i.e., any god of any name. He may have meant the one Thunder God whose given name was Baal. When using the name in the plural, "baalim," he meant a group of gods of any name. The play on names allowed baalism to be adopted by many Hebrews and hide the fact from Jehovahite authorities. They could sound very much like a true covenanter.

"Do you worship the Lord?" one may be asked, meaning YHWH.

"Yes, all my family believes in the lord," the Baalite replied (Lord Baal).

"I mean the one true Lord," insisted the Jehovahite. "Yes, indeed, we believe in the Lord ('Baal') of the heavens."

As long as Baalite philosophy allowed YHWH to take his place as a valid baal, the lord of the mountain, Hebrews were tempted to "get along."

An analysis of Baalism is advisable to indicate the serious threat it posed to the Covenant. The description will give valuable background for reading and understanding the Old Testament.

Philosophic Assumption

Baalites believed that nature was a reflection of the activity of the gods. They held the analogy-of-the-gods theology.

139

They were in the last analysis naturalists. Nature was all there was to reality, as the gods and nature were actually one thing. They celebrated the nature cycle. Peace or happiness was living with nature, learning her ways, adjusting to her patterns and accepting it as the sum of life. Since nature provided for reproduction, and no life was possible without reproductive continuity, and no truly good life was possible without reproduction of domestic animals and planted crops, fertility celebration (worship) was emphasized. It was the most important thing about nature. Sex was not something sinful or wrong for them. It was the one true aspect of life worthy of celebration. It was participation in eternal-life as life was passed on to the next generation by sexual activity in man and animals.

Theological Description

In the pantheon of the Canaanites, the high god was El. He was as close as they could come to a creator God. Except for being a sort of father to the gods, he played little part in religion. The most powerful of the active gods was young Baal. He was usually pictured as a bull or the god of thunder. Both were symbols of power and fertility. He raged, roamed and made love to his mistress sister, Aneth. El had a son called "death." "Death" and Baal were bitter enemies.[4] The story of all life was the story of the struggles between Baal and death. One represented the end and the other the beginning of the reproductive cycle. That cycle alone was understood as eternal.

The earth was something of a mother-earth. She lay exposed as a woman before her lord and husband, Baal.

---

4. William F. Albright, *Yahweh and the Gods of Canaan*, Winona Lake, Indiana: Eisenbrauns, 1965, p. 115.

When Baal came in a storm, like a raging bull to a heifer, he made love to earth and impregnated her with the semen of life: rain.

The "high places of Baal" (Amos 6:9) were chapels located atop rolling hills of the land. Thus each day all were reminded of the awaiting breasts of mother earth. Sex was essential for life and therefore something to be celebrated in religion.

The life cycle of man was inseparably bound up with that of grain. Baal was the son of Dagon. Dagon was the word for wheat. It was an agricultural society who held grain to be the source of life for man and animals. The Hebrews were a shepherding and wandering type people. Their God was the one who spoke from the mountain. When the Hebrews moved into the rich valleys of Samaria and Galilee, it would only seem natural for the Baalites to suggest they now honor the god of grain and no longer the god of the mountain.

The happy and secure life cycle was also inseparably bound up with animals; cattle, sheep, and goats. It was necessary to picture and celebrate in their religion that relationship. To show solidarity with animals and to symbolize their interdependence, expressions were provided in part of the religious cultic forms.

The Cultic Practices

From both the Ras Shamra texts and passages from the prophetic books a clear picture of their actual practices can be obtained. They had weekly services, special days, regional celebrations and national annual celebrations. The Baalite crier would go through the valley crying, "Go to Bethel and worship. Go to Gilgal and participate (in sex). Sacrifice

141

at the high place. On the day after tomorrow, go to Gilgal."
Amos mocked their cry.

> Go to Bethel—and SIN!
> Go to Gilgal and SIN yet more.
> Bring your sacrifices every morning,
> your tithes every three years.
> Burn leavened bread as a thank offering . . .
> and boast about them, you Israelites,
> for this is what you love to do,
> declares the Sovereign Lord (Amos. 4:4ff.).

They had beautiful services. Harps played and people
sang lovely songs. They had children present little dramas
about the coming of spring or of "Thanksgiving Day" at
harvest time. At the change of season the new benefits of
life would be gratefully celebrated. The processions came
with ceremony to the high place. The wooden statue of
Moloch (Amos 5:26) would be honored. It represented
some splendid idea about natural law. A sacrifice as gift to
the gods would be made.

The prophet thundered it was not YHWH they were
worshipping at all, regardless of the name "lord" used there.

> I hate, I despise your feasts;
> I cannot stand your assemblies.
> Even though you bring me burnt offerings
> and grain offerings,
> I will not accept them.
>
> Away with the noise of your songs!
> I will not listen to the music of your harps.
> But let justice roll on like a river,
> And righteousness as a mighty stream (Amos 5:21).

You will recall justice meant "making decisions according
to the Torah." That was why the laws were sometimes called

the "judgments" and the statutes. "Righteousness" was clearly defined by the Law.

> And if we are careful to obey all this law before the Lord our God, as He has commanded us, THAT will be our righteousness (Deut. 6:25).

The people of the lands dominated by Baal were expected to participate in a sort of brotherhood ceremony. Once a year, or once a month, or as each sect or chapel eldership might suggest, every man and woman of mature age was expected to participate in sex at the chapel or temple. Anyone wanting sex could find it, in a religious atmosphere, at the chapel, if he were a member. He and she were to make themselves available in turn. Temple prayer associates, prostitutes, were there at all times, of course. For them, sex was neither shameful nor private. It was private for married couples, of course, and it is likely the ideal was for married people to have sex only with the partner except when at the temple and in an attitude of humanity-solidarity. The king and an equivalent of a modern "Miss Canaan of Bethel" mated in public to picture the necessary relationship between Baal and Aneth, men with men, and men with animals. It showed all happily sharing in nature.

> The cultic drama of a dying and rising fertility god clearly played an essential role in the cultus. In addition there was temple prostitution, considered very important because it was felt to promote fertility. A sacred "marriage" which combined those two aspects was a part of the cultic drama.[5]

The prophets were appalled at the practices. Man was to have solidarity with God. Hebrews were to obey not nature

---

5. Helmer Ringgren, *Israelite Religion*, tr. David E. Green, Philadelphia: Fortress Press, 1966, p. 43.

but the Torah. Religion was the Covenant, the Torah, the Passover, the Psalms, the Exodus, the overcoming of nature. Israel was married to Jehovah not Baal (Ezek. 16:8).

A Baalite child was taught it was right to go to the temple and have sex, as her mother did. Her father, a respected man of the community and a good family man did so. If intercourse had been presented as a kind of prayer and dedication of life to God, and the proof of Baal's acceptance of the offering was a feeling of satisfaction after the act was over, it would have been very difficult to have told a Baalite worshiper he was not approved of God. He had inner assurance. He had, he would claim, explosive personal proof that the gods had accepted that sex as prayer and offering. And what did the Jehovahite offer as proof of the validity of his narrow-minded religion—an alleged event that took place five or six hundred years ago!

Both sides appealed to experience as proof of the validity of their respective faiths. One appealed to personal experience. The other appealed to the experience of the covenanted people of God. God's prophets condemned Baalism.

In the house of their god, . . . the father and son use the same girl (Amos 2:7).

They were unfaithful to the Lord, they gave birth to illegitimate children (Hos. 5:7).

She burnt incense to the Baals, she decked herself with rings and jewelry and went after her lovers (Hos. 2:13).

They sacrifice on the mountain tops and burn offerings on the hills, under oak, poplar and terebinth where the shade is pleasant. Therefore your daughters turn to prostitution and your daughters-in-law to adultery (Hos. 4:13).

144

They ridiculed the divination practices.

They consult a wooden idol, and are answered by a stick!
(Hos. 4:12).

Because the men themselves consort with harlots and sacrifice with temple prostitutes—a people without understanding
will come to ruin (Hos. 4:14).

In addition to prostitution at the temple, the Baalites had
a kind of unity with animals ceremony. A man was mated to
a sheep and a woman with a goat. It was not only at Sodom
this kind of thing was done. The practice was so odious to
the Israelite the prophets hesitated to write of it. It was as
terrible in their minds as child burning at Moloch.

There is fleeting reference to each.

It is said of these people "they offer human sacrifice and
kiss the sacred calves" (Hos. 13:1-3).

The Economic and Social Establishment

The frequent references to economic warfare against
Israelites indicated another aspect of the religion. The temples
and chapels collected the tithes. Temple prostitution may
have also rendered an income for the cult, although there is
scant evidence for this in the Bible. As late as the time of
Paul the Greeks at Corinth had a temple with a thousand
temple prostitutes in service. These plied their trade at night
in the streets of the city.[6] The temples were wealthy. They
made loans and advanced funds to the king and citizens—
if they were members in good standing.

It created a serious hardship for the Israelite. If he had
a crop failure it would be blamed on his failure to honor

---

6. Will Durant, *A History of Greece,* New York: Simon and Schuster,
1939, Vol. IV, p. 39.

Dagon, god of grain and the father of lord Baal. If his sheep died or became infertile, it was said he had not paid honor at the temple replication-of-nature rite. If he needed money he had to go to fellow Jehovahites. He did not have access to the Baalite treasuries. Or he got the money at crippling interest rates. The Jehovahites were hated as being self-righteous, narrow-minded separatists who criticized all religions but their own. Consequently, whenever the Jehovahite defaulted on a loan, the Baalite chapel treasurers were quick to fore-close. Amos listed sins in connection with Baalism, and started with the selling of people, i.e., debtors for silver, and "the righteous" for a pair of sandals. He used "the righteous" to mean true Jehovahites. Even though a debt were only the price of a pair of shoes, the Baalite judges sentenced the Jehovahite into slavery for it.

> They sell the righteous for silver and the needy for a pair of sandals. They trample on the heads of the poor . . . and deny justice to the oppressed. Father and son use the same girl . . . they lie down beside every altar on garments taken in pledge and in the house of their god they drink wine taken as fines (Amos 2:6).

In the Baalite courts, presided over by Baalite judges and rendering verdicts happy to the local population, the Jehovahite was hard pressed to hold his own.

> They set up kings without my consent, they choose princes without my approval . . . they make idols for themselves. They sow the wind and reap the whirlwind!
>
> Israel is swallowed up. Now she is among the nations as a worthless thing. . . . The prophet is considered a fool, the inspired man a maniac . . . snares await him on all his paths and hostility in the house of his God (Hos. 8:3—9:7).

146

In every way pressure was put on the Israelite to become more open minded about religion. The least they could do, claimed the Baalites, was to allow freedom of religion. Who is that god of the mountain, they asked, who thinks there is no other god but him? Let him come off that hill and see there is land and sea and fields as well as his mountain. What a petty deity! What a petty and narrow-minded and rationalistic people to follow such a god. Away with them! The prophets of God tell how it went.

> But you made the Nazarites drink wine and commanded the prophets not to prophesy (Amos 2:12).

> You hate the one who reproves in court, you despise the one who tells the truth (Amos 5:10).

> You oppress the righteous and take bribes, you deprive the poor of justice in the courts (Amos 5:12).

> Therefore the prudent man keeps quiet in such times, for the times are evil (Amos 5:13).

When the prophets of God preached the curses of the covenant for covenant breakers, they were silenced.

> "Do not prophesy," their prophets say, "do not prophesy about such things, disgrace will not overtake us" (Mic. 2:6).

> If a liar and a deceiver comes and says, "I will prophesy for you plenty of wine and beer," he would be just the prophet for this people! (Mic. 2:11).

> As for the prophets who lead my people astray, if one feeds them, they will prophesy, "Peace!" (Mic. 3:5).

> Her leaders judge for a bribe, her priests teach for a price, and her prophets tell fortunes for money (Mic. 3:11).

> The godly (Jehovahites) are swept from the land (Mic. 7:2).

How little did the common population understand the snare of naturalistic philosophy! Only in the grace of God could any kind of revealed religion have survived. New leaders were chosen by God from time to time. A Jehovahite general named Jehu was one. He at first pretended to be an ardent Baalite.

"Ahab served Baal a little. Jehu will serve him much."

He called an assembly in honor of Baal. The text says, "All the ministers of Baal came. Not one stayed away" (II Kgs. 9:20ff.). When they were sacrificing, Jehu closed the doors and surrounded the hall with some eighty warriors.

"If any of you lets any of the men I am placing in your hands escape, it will be your life for his life."

So they cut them down with the sword. The guards and the officers threw the bodies out and then entered the inner part of the temple of Baal. They destroyed it all. The text adds, "and the people have used it as a latrine to this day."

The entire Baal confrontation moved through several stages. First there was settlement of the lands by invading Israelites, and the effort to wipe out Baalism. It failed. Stage two was an effort to allow Baalites to worship quietly for the sake of a united and peaceful era. Solomon was the one who allowed, as the third stage, Baalite chapels to be erected on temple property. A period of live and let live developed. It was hoped the prosperity brought by covenant obedience would establish the validity of the Jehovahite claims and thus peacefully end the strife. It failed. Stage four arrived when Baalism became strong enough to challenge Covenant as the official state religion. Baalism won. Manasseh adopted Baalism as the official Israelite religion. The prophets found themselves spokesmen for a hated minority. They became outlaws. During this era the Jehovahites were barely able to survive.

The respective points of view between the Baalite religion and the People of the Covenant are contrasted below.

Baalism	*Covenanters*
1. Philosophy: Natural law, the nature cycle, and the analogy-of-the-gods. Reproduction is the essence of life. Nature is god.	1. Philosophy: God is in charge of history and the covenant tells what God wants. Fellowship is the essence of life.
2. Religion: Replication of the nature cycle in ceremony. Chapels, sacrifices, sex as worship, adoration of nature and reproduction. Acts picturing solidarity as one family of mankind (sex) and interdependence of man with animals (sex).	2. Religion: Administration of the Torah, as civil law, and morals and worship as specified in Torah. The nation and the religion are one and the same thing. Sin is treason as well as evil. All is related to the Law of Moses.
3. Society: All citizens ought to live in unity with nature and as one family on earth. Each city or society may define Baal as it wishes but all are under the same system. Each family participates in the worship and sex as part of the whole.	3. Society: Israel is the kingdom of YHWH and should live in harmony with Torah. No one may break the Law without punishment by the law. All society exists to do what God has said he wants.
4. Toleration: Toleration for any who are willing to cooperate with the idea any god is a good Baal. No toleration for narrow-minded bigots who think they have a private way with God.	4. Toleration: Absolutely no toleration for any religion except that of the Torah.

5. Sacrifices: For replication of the nature cycle myth. Also for divination. Thank offerings, with music. Human sacrifice of infants in isolated cases.

5. Sacrifices: Gifts, and atonement for sins. Covenant renewal. Intercession, confession, rededication. No divination.

6. Guidance: By divination and "seeing." By prophets supporting the harmonization of life with nature.

6. Guidance: By the Torah and the prophet who supported the Torah. By periodic visitations from God.

The Discovery of the Scroll

One of the very bright spots in Israel's history came after a most difficult era. Manasseh had been unusually destructive to Israel even though his reign brought in great prosperity for the land. His son ruled for a few years and was a Baalite also. When he was murdered, the grandson of Manasseh, Josiah, a young child, was saved by a loyal military officer. The boy must have had strong Jehovahite influence, for he became, in spite of his father and grandfather, a devout Hebrew. At the age of sixteen, he undertook in earnest "to seek after the God of David, his father" (II Chron. 34:3).

While repairing the temple a priest named Hilkiah found a copy of "the Book of the Law of Jehovah by the hand of Moses" (II Chron. 34:14). It is generally assumed Manasseh had all known copies of the Law destroyed. When the Law was read to the young king, reforms began in earnest. He repaired the temple completely, the Law was read to all the population, all foreign cult objects were removed from the temple, the city of Jerusalem and the entire land. Child sacrifice in Hinnom was outlawed, and all Baalite "high places" were razed (II Kgs. 23:4-14).

150

The worship site in Samaria, which served as an alternative place of sacrifice was destroyed, but not before the priests were slain and their bones burned on the altar. A prophet had said over three hundred years before just such an event would take place here and even named the king who would do it—by name: Josiah! (I Kgs. 13:1-3 and II Kgs. 23:15, 16).

Perhaps the most significant aspect of reform undertaken by Josiah was the reestablishment of the Passover. The texts stated not since the days of Samuel the prophet had the Passover been so carefully observed (II Chron. 35:1-14).

It was the discovery of the "Book of the Law" that accelerated the reform movement. That time in Hebrew history was surely the greatest since David. Both men, from rival dynasties, were united in devotion to their God and to the Torah. They were both brothers in flesh, as descendants of Abraham and brothers in spirit. They both loved and supported God's holy covenant. Their names have honored place in the history of the covenant. Kings most honored were David and Josiah.

Before his death, Josiah had consulted a prophetess named Huldah. She told him the reforms he proposed were needed. But she gave bad news. God had all but decided to punish Israel by invoking the curses of the covenant. Punishment for the nation was coming in spite of the reforms. She added they would be postponed until after his death.

During the administration of Josiah the land again was filled with prophets. Many of them wrote books which are in the Old Testament. The great Jeremiah began to minister in the thirteenth year of Josiah's reign (Jer. 1:2). That was

151

about the year 627 B.C.[7] Zephaniah also dated his work in Josiah's time (Zeph. 1:1). Apparently it took some time for the reforms to be administered in the local provinces. Even then, so perverse were many of the population, local high places continued to be attended and supported, according to Zephaniah. Nahum did not date his book, but since its main theme is the impending fall of Nineveh, it must be during Josiah's reign. Nineveh fell three years before Josiah's death in 615 B.C. Habakkuk very likely preached at this same time, for he tells of the Babylonian invasion being at hand (Hab. 1:1-11). Something important was about to happen in Israel's history.

Two Episodes in Covenant

Recorded by the former prophets were two episodes illustrating how thoroughly the philosophy of covenant permeated prophetic thinking. They showed both negative consequences and positive benefits related to *hesed* or the keeping of obligations as a way of life. Both episodes were true, of course, and knowing the basis upon which those ancient historians chose from hundreds of happenings there for the permanent record, we have a clue to why these cases are in the Bible.

Episode One. This circumstance concerned a "young prophet," and an "old prophet." Both proved to be unfortunate men. They seemed to the prophetic writers, perhaps, to mirror what was wrong with Israel's leadership. A young prophet was instructed by YHWH to make a declaration from God to the king. He was commanded, for reasons not

---

7. Leon Wood, *A Survey of Israel's History*, Grand Rapids: Zondervan, 1970, p. 370.

152

disclosed, to neither eat nor drink until he had returned from his mission. He went, declared the word of the Lord as instructed, and set out for home. While in route, but before completing the mission as stipulated, he passed the dwelling of the "old prophet." The elder hailed him, invited him to rest and take refreshment in food and drink. Courtesy demanded it. The youth demurred citing the stipulations placed upon him by the Lord. The old prophet said,

> I too am a prophet as you are and an angel said to me by the word of the Lord, "Bring him back with you to your house as that he may eat bread and drink water." But he was lying (I Kgs. 13:18).

To his doom the young man believed the lie. He sat at refreshment as guest of the family of the prophet. As the younger prophet continued on his way, a wild animal sprang out and slew him in the road. The editorial comment of the old prophet was simply,

> It is the man of God who defied the word of the Lord (I Kgs. 13:26).

This case illustrated the wide range of responses God may make in cases of disobedience. The ancestors of this man went into the desert with Moses. His fathers disobeyed God and some died on the spot—the ten spies. The rest of the people struggled in the desert for years and years and died without obtaining the promised land. Sometimes the reaction of God was gradual and prolonged. David ate the sacred bread and was forgiven. He sinned with Bathsheba and was punished but forgiven. There were a variety of reactions by God when he was faced with disobedience.

Episode Two. The second illustration concerned a military commander of the Syrian army named Naaman. He discovered he had leprosy. Leprosy was regarded, right or wrong, as symbolic of sin. What sin did to the soul leprosy did to the body. Both had unknown beginnings. Both progressed slowly. Neither was painful. Both brought disfigurement and loathing. Both disrupted relationships and eventually caused death. One brought death of the body. The other brought moral death.

An Israelite slave girl of Naaman's house suggested Naaman visit a famous prophet in Israel and be healed. With letters of introduction and gifts, he arrived at the Israelite court and then the Jordan River where Elisha the prophet was living.

> So Naaman went with his horses and chariots and stopped at the door of Elisha's house. Elisha sent a messenger to him and said, "Go wash yourself seven times in the Jordan and your flesh will be restored" (II Kgs. 5:9, 10).

Naaman was livid. He had been twice insulted. He was not received in state as befitted his position. He was commanded through a servant as any slave might have been commanded, to go and wash! He stormed away. He refused to believe the Jordan was curative. He had expected typical Canaanite religious rites to have been performed.

> I thought he surely would come out to me and stand and call on the name of his god and wave his hand over the spot and cure me of my leprosy. Are not the Abana and Phaphar, the rivers of Damascus better than all the waters of Israel? (II Kgs. 5:12ff.).

His counselors advised calm compliance. They asked, "If the prophet had commanded you to do some great thing would you not have done it?" With additional talk he was persuaded. He might have felt foolish as he was aided in removing his armor, and laid aside the robes indicating rank, and in full view of all entered the water. He lowered himself until submerged. He came up. Number one was over. Encouraged from the shore, he proceeded to dip himself another five times. The last plunging was the hard one. He would either come up out of the water, dripping like a wet hound and still a leper, and become the laughing stock of the Near East, or he would come up clean. He lowered himself into the water for the last time,

> . . . as the man of God had told him and his flesh was restored, and became clean like that of a young child (II Kgs. 5:14).

It was a covenant. Parties: God, by the prophet, and Naaman
Terms: Dip seven times in the Jordan River
Promises: Be cleansed of leprosy

The implication was all too clear. Men of God were men of their word. God was good at His word. Mankind, whether Israelite or pagan, could trust God when He spoke. Obedience to God brought life. Disobedience brought death. Centuries later the Apostles of Christ, and prophets of the New Covenant, used such cases as these to remind their people of the consequences of disobedience and arrogance (II Pet. 2:1-22) and the blessings of being faithful (II Pet. 3:11-18).

The Latter Prophets

The latter prophets were those who wrote prophetic books for the Bible. They were not, strictly speaking, historians. They were making history. Isaiah, Jeremiah, Daniel, Hosea, Joel, Amos, and others are representatives. It is fair to identify these men as lawyers of the covenant as well as preachers of the hour with a message from God for that hour.

We will examine the relationship of the message of the prophets to the covenant. They shared with the former prophets the same philosophy of history. Everything was measured by the norm: the Torah. When God spoke to them it was also in reference to the Torah.

The Lawsuit Motif

In the latter prophets a new and ominous development took place. Men of God placed their prophecies in a lawsuit model. That is, they called upon the witnesses of the covenant. When one party had felt neglected by or abused because of the failure of his partner, he sent him a message of inquiry. If that did not bring about better compliance, he sent an official legate. There are several examples in the Old Testament scriptures where this was done. Prophets were acting as legates from the King. If the partner did not recover and perform his obligation according to his oath, the last resort before force was applied was summoning the offender before the original witnesses to the treaty. If the errant partner, the covenant-breaker, did not appear to answer the charge, the witnesses were summoned to hear the grievances of the offended party without him. It was a serious matter to have any major prophet place his statements within the motif of the courtroom or the hearing chamber. It implied God was all but finished talking. He was, in fact, all finished trying to persuade and was laying the foundation for the use of force. He was showing to all the justification he had in inflicting on the partner what both had agreed was just. When each partner had at the oath-swearing walked between the halves of the oath animal and touched blood, each gave to the other permission to shed his blood upon breach of the covenant. Until the latter prophets, the lawsuit motif was not employed.

The original witnesses to the Sinai Treaty were identified.

This day I call heaven and earth as witnesses against you that I have set before you life and death, blessings and curses (Deut. 30:19).

I call heaven and earth as witnesses against you this day that you will quickly perish from the land that you are crossing the Jordan to possess (Deut. 4:26).

This was standard practice in ancient treaty making. For example:

Witnesses in other Ancient Near Eastern treaties include heaven and earth as well as other gods. But since Israel's God was involved in the treaty, he couldn't very well be a witness. Therefore he summoned his creation to be His witness.[8]

Micah used law court imagery in his prophecy. He denounced Israel before the witnesses.

Listen to what the Lord says. Stand up and plead your case before the mountains; let the hills hear what you have to say (Mic. 6:1).

He was God's attorney-at-law pleading God's lawsuit before the court of original witnesses to the Treaty.

Hear, O mountains, the Lord's accusation; Listen you everlasting foundations of the earth. For the Lord has a case against his people. He is lodging a charge against Israel (Mic. 6:2).

The prophet Micah reviewed the past relationship of God and Israel. He began with the Exodus, the great event

---

8. Donald B. Allen, *Deuteronomy: An Expression of Covenant and Responsibility,* unpublished thesis for Master of Arts, Lincoln Christian Seminary, Lincoln, Illinois, 1980, p. 83.

leading to the covenant at Sinai making the Hebrews a nation. And now, the prophet was saying the covenant was breaking down. The word "case" was the word *ryv* in Hebrew and was the term used for civil actions at law.[9]

Hosea did not use the word *b'rth* (covenant) in the text, but all his key terms and metaphors were covenant related.

> Hear the word of the Lord, you Israelites, because the Lord has a charge to bring against you who live in the land. There is no faithfulness, no love, no acknowledgment of God in the land (Hos. 4:1-3).

The terms used to identify Israel's sins were parallelisms. They all meant the same basic thing. They all rooted in covenant. For instance, there can be no "faithfulness" to God where there had been no commitment. Love (Hebrew *'ahav*) was a general term for covenant support with a genuine heart (Deut. 6:4). Note its use in parallelism in the Torah. The parallel meanings will be placed below each other to indicate the author meant to repeat himself.

> Now choose life . . . and that
> you may love the Lord your God,
>> listen to His voice, and
>> hold fast to Him (Deut. 30:20).

These three words mean the same thing. They carry identical concepts. Again:

> For I command you today to love the Lord your God,
>> to walk in His ways, and
>> to keep his commands, decrees
>> and laws (Deut. 30:16).

---

9. J. Limburg, "The Root *RYB* and the Prophetic Lawsuit Speeches," in *Society of Biblical Literature*, 88, 1969, p. 291-304.

Frank Moore Cross, *Canaanite Myth and Hebrew Epic*, Cambridge: Harvard University Press, 1973, p. 188.

Yada' was a covenant-related term. Hebrew *yada'* was usually translated "know." A careful examination of the texts will show it was a significant treaty term.

The most obvious technical use of "know" is that in reference to mutual legal recognition on the part of Suzerain and vassal. In the treaty between the Hittite King Suppiliumas and Huqqamanas of western Asia Minor, Suppiliumas says to his vassal, "And you Huqqanas, know only The Sun (UTU 'pat . . .sak) regarding lordship.[10]

The negative use of *yada'* in "do not know" or "did not know" when used in treaty context meant either "not in a formal relationship," or "not doing what the relationship required."

A similar usage is found in a letter to Esarhadden in which it was said of the Cimmerians, "They are nomads, they know neither an oath by the gods nor a sworn treaty." The most recent translations favor "they do not care for" or "they do not respect" but the specifically technical sense "they recognize as binding neither an oath sworn by the gods nor a sworn treaty" may be prefered.[11]

Hosea understood the context of the term, for he used it in connection with Israel's election by God.

But I am the Lord your God who brought you out of Egypt. You shall acknowledge no God but me, no Savior except me (13:4).

Compare Amos's similar statement:

Only you have I known of all the families on the earth, therefore I will punish you for all your iniquities (Amos 3:2).

And Moses' complaint of Israel:

---

10. Herbert B. Huffman, "The Treaty Background of Hebrew YADA," *Bulletin of American School of Oriental Research*, 181:31, 1966.
11. *Ibid.*, p. 32.

You have been in rebellion against YHWH from the day he knew you (Deut. 9:7 MT).

The context indicated Moses referred to the "day of the assembly" (Deut. 9:9) or the giving of the Law at Horeb-Sinai. Thus the meaning of *yada'* used by Moses was, "You have been violating the covenant from the very day I brought it off the mountain to you!" It is obvious God knew Israel in the usual sense of "have some information about" from the beginning, and thus *yada'* in that context must refer to "entered into covenant with."

In the scripture *yada'* was used of private relationship, such as sexual intimacy.

Cain knew his wife and she conceived and bore Enoch (Gen. 4:17).
As yet she had known no man (Judg. 11:39).
But the king knew her not (I Kgs. 1:4).
But Joseph knew her not (Matt. 1:25).

When the prophets say, "There is no faithfulness, no *yada'*, no justice," they were saying the same thing: no keeping faith with.

Micah spoke of the fundamental and basic failure. They failed to develop into men and women of integrity. They lacked integrity with God and they lacked integrity in dealings with men.

"He has showed you, O man, what is good" (Mic. 6:8). Micah was simply quoting the text of the Book of the Covenant. His entire passage was a paraphrase of Deuteronomy Ten.

And now Israel what does the Lord your God ask of you but to fear the Lord your God
to walk in all His ways,
to love Him, and
to serve the Lord your God

with all your heart, and
   all your soul,
      to observe the Lord's commands and decrees . . .
that I am giving you for your own *good*? (Deut. 10:1-13).

Micah repeated these same concepts in a little different way. There should have been no misunderstanding by Israel.

He has showed you O man what is good; and what does the Lord require of you?
To act justly,
To love mercy,
To walk humbly with your God (Mic. 6:8).

All these words have the context of covenant keeping with steady integrity. It was the fundamental moral breakdown of Israel that caused God to foreclose on them. All the words he selected indicate duty to covenant partner as a way of life.

The term "justice" is a noun form of the root that produced the word "judgment." The execution of the "judgments" of God declared in the Torah was "justice." Justice was doing just as God had said! (Deut. 33:21b). It was a lifestyle of integrity, not simply ill-willed statute keeping, though apart from law there is no justice, whether in Israel or any other place on earth.

The term "mercy" has been shown to mean "support of the covenanted partner with a sincere heart." It did not simply mean a feeling of pity. It was not an emotion. It was, as Gleuck demonstrated conclusively, an attitude of covenant keeping with affection. Israel lacked that good will and the keeping of covenant. The two concepts were bound together in one single category for the Hebrews.

The next phrase he used was "to walk humbly with" your God. The phrase was without definition until the Law of Moses was given. We must not assume it was a "spiritual"

161

intercourse. We have no idea of what that meant in Moses' day. We must not assume it meant a deep prayer life. We simply have no definition of the words other than their use in parallelism: to keep the Law of Moses (Deut. 30:16, 17). Micah was not a universal moralist. He was a covenant lawyer showing Israel had utterly failed to maintain the agreed upon behaviors and thus was immoral. Morality for the Hebrew was keeping the Law of God.

Micah stated to the court that God intended to impose the penalty for breach of the oath at Sinai. He also showed God to be a covenant keeper in planning to restore Israel from exile as he had agreed (Lev. 26:40). But the restoration depended upon the return to covenant, said the Lord. When Israel again turned to the Lord, then God, on his part, would also

be true to Jacob,
show mercy to Abraham as pledged on oath to our fathers
(Mic. 7:10).

"Being true to" meant what the parallels show it to mean. One must have a commitment to be true to anything or anyone. Commitment meant "oath" as pledged. The prophets did not always use the term covenant, but their vocabulary abounds with covenant-keeping terminology. It is unfortunate the Greek language had no single word to carry the dual concepts in those now rather moralistic terms. The charge in the court of all the world was: Israel deserved punishment as a Treaty breaker.

Isaiah also began his document with the court scene. He followed the lawsuit motif.

Hear, O heavens, and Listen , O Earth!
I reared children and brought them up,
but they have rebelled against me. . . .

162

Now hear the word of the Lord . . .
Listen to the lawsuit of your God (Isa. 1:1-10).

The same three reoccurring covenant-related words were used by Isaiah.

See how the *faithful* city has become a harlot. She was once full of *justice.*
Righteousness used to dwell in her (Isa. 1:21).

Faithfulness was full parallel to covenant keeping in their literature. Justice was *mishpat.* The plural was *mishpatim.* *Mishpatim* were the stipulated commands of the Lord. "No justice" meant "no keeping of the Law of Moses."

Jeremiah, somewhat optimistic in the beginning of his service, became the chief spokesman for the view Israel was heading for utter ruin. He preached at the command of God; the days of talk of reconciliation were almost over. Except that Josiah had come upon the scene and made marvelous efforts to reform the land, disaster already would have fallen upon them. The kingdom of the North, Israel, went into captivity while Jeremiah was alive. It was swept away into the sheol of forgotten history and never recovered. Samaria was never a capital of any nation again.

The presentation of YHWH's case against Judah was similar to other prophets of that age. His opening statement to the court used the same type of language.

Therefore I bring charges against you again, declares the Lord, . . . observe closely, Has a nation ever changed its gods? But my people have exchanged their Glory for worthless idols. Be appalled at this O heavens! Shudder with great horror! (Jer. 2:9-12).

If an opposing lawyer had asked the following question, Jeremiah told the answer of God in advance.

163

Why do you bring charges against me? You have rebelled against me, declares the Lord (2:29).

The other prophet, Micah, had asked before the court the reason the defendant had not kept the pact. "My people, what have I done to you? How have I burdened you?" (Mic. 6:3). Jeremiah asked the same question.

What fault did your fathers find in me that they strayed so far from me? (Jer. 2:5).

Listen to the terms of this covenant . . .

"Cursed is the man who does not obey the terms of this covenant."
From the time I brought you up from Egypt until today, I have warned them again and again saying, "Obey me" . . . So I have brought on them all the curses of the covenant . . . (Jer. 11:7, 8).

Later in the document Jeremiah enumerated how God had sought conferences and reconciliation only to be ignored by Israel.

Daniel represented the same theology of covenant. He evaluated Israel's conduct against the Treaty at Sinai. All the tragic events prophesied against Israel had come to pass because of covenant violation. That was most explicitly confessed in Daniel's magnificent intercessory prayer.

O Lord, the great and terrible God who keepest covenant and steadfast love (hesed) to those who love him and keep his commandments, we have sinned and done wrong and acted wickedly, and rebelled, turning aside from thy commandments and ordinances . . . and the curse and oath which are written in the Law of Moses . . . has been poured out upon us. . . . We have not obeyed the voice of the Lord our God by following his laws . . . as written in the Law of Moses.

164

We do not present our supplications before thee on the ground our righteousness, but on the ground of thy great mercy. O Lord, hear. O Lord forgive. O Lord, give heed and act . . . (Dan. 9:4-19, RSV).

Prior to the exile the prophets painted vivid and terrible pictures of the doom awaiting a faithless nation. Their pictures were but echoes of the Code of Moses. The Treaty had described their doom.

If you reject my statutes, and break my covenant, then I will send among you wild animals, who will make you bereft of children and destroy your cattle, and make you few in number, and your ways desolate (Lev. 26:15-20).

Jeremiah:

A lion from the forest will smite them, a desert wolf will ravage them. A panther is watching over your cities. Everybody who leaves them will be torn to pieces (5:6).

The Code:

And if you do not obey all these curses will come upon you . . . cursed in the city . . . in the country . . . in your kneeding trough . . . the fruit of your womb, the crops of your land, the calves of your herds . . . with scorching heat and drought (Deut. 28:16).

Jeremiah:

My anger and my wrath will be poured out on this place, on man and beast, on the fruit of the ground. It will burn and not be quenched (7:18ff.).

The Code:

I will send against them the fangs of wild animals, and the venom of vipers that glide in the dust (Deut. 32:24).

Jeremiah:

See, I will send venemous snakes among you, vipers that cannot be charmed and they will bite you (8:17).

165

The prophet was only reminding all of the curses of the covenant Israel had agreed were fitting for a faithless nation so recently saved from bondage.

> The prophets were not arbitrary in choosing the vivid and lurid figures in which they depicted the wrath to come. They were not indulging in morbid imagination but were fundamentally like lawyers quoting the law.
>
> This is what the covenant had said would happen.[12]

The sins and the crimes listed by the prophets were those prohibited in the Law of Moses. Their failures were failures to do what the Law had required. We may speak of both sins and crimes in the same way. In a theocracy a sin was also a crime against the state. In the following charts some indication is given of the close connection between the message of the prophet and the Treaty at Sinai.

Hosea:

Passage	Terminology	The Code
1:3	"Departing from the Lord"	Exod. 20:1-3
1:5, 5:7	"Children conceived in sin"	Exod. 20:14
2:8	"Used for Baal"	Exod. 20:1
4:11	"to prostitution"	Deut. 5:18
4:6	"rejected knowledge"	Deut. 30:1-10
	"no faithfulness of love of God"	
4:17ff.	"rulers love shameful ways"	Deut. 17:14ff.
10:4, 5	"false oaths . . . lawsuits"	Deut. 23:21
12:7, 8	"dishonest scales"	Deut. 25:15
13:1-3	"sacrificing babies, kissing calves"	Deut. 18:9ff.
9:7, 8	"the prophet considered a fool"	Deut. 18:14ff.

---

12. Delbert Hillars, *Covenant: The History of a Biblical Idea*, p. 134.

Micah:

Passage	Terminology	The Code
1:7	"Idols, temple gifts, prostitutes"	Exod. 20:1-20
2:6	"Do not prophesy. Doom will not overtake us"	Deut. 28:15ff.
3:7	"Seers and diviners"	Deut. 18:10,11
3:11	"bribes, money . . ."	Deut. 1:16-18
3:11	"prophets tell fortunes for money"	Deut. 24:17
		Deut. 18:20
2:2	"covet and defraud"	Exod. 20:17
		Deut. 15:7ff.

Amos:

Passage	Terminology	The Code
2:6, 7	"trample the poor, sell people for silver, deny justice to oppressed"	Deut. 15:1ff. Deut. 24:10ff.
2:12	"made Nazarites drink wine"	Num. 6:1-8
3:14	"of Baal"	Exod. 20:1ff.
6:19	"make high places,	Deut. 12:2ff.
4:4	Bethel, Gilgal. . . ."	Deut. 12:2ff.
5:26	Moloch,	Deut. 12:2ff.
8:4	"trample the needy"	Deut. 15:11
5:13	"the prudent keep still"	Lev. 5:1
	"despise who tell the truth"	Lev. 5:1
2:7, 8	"temple of their gods, lie with same girl"	Exod. 20:1-15

The prophets used both specific and general terms to describe the sins of the population. It is important to understand the category system of the Hebrews. The following terms and phrases were general categories. They were almost synonyms used to measure total breach of faith with a sworn partner. They describe the total response expected by God. "Love of God," "justice," "hearing His voice," "faithfulness," "*hesed* or mercy," "walking in His way," "obeying the voice of God," and such. Those words all covered the same category: ethical covenant keeping. They did not refer to different categories. They all meant to describe separately the same matters.

Curses and the Prophecies

The prophets were not "hellfire and brimstone" preachers as much as lawyers quoting to the jury the terms of the broken contract. Their descriptions of the coming tragedies for Israel were framed in terms obtained from the Treaty text.

Prophetic Vision	Echoing	The Torah
Jer. 8:17	"terror, fever, drain away your life"	Lev. 26:15
Jer. 5:6	"wild animals against you"	Lev. 26:22
Ezek. 5:10	"eating one's own children"	Lev. 26:29
Isa. 29:3	"besieged in cities . . . etc."	Deut. 28:53
Isa. 29:9	"stunned, staggering, but not from beer!"	Deut. 28:29
Amos 6:7	"You noblemen, you shall be first"	Deut. 28:56f.
Mic. 1:15	"I will bring a conqueror"	Deut. 28:49
Nahum 3:13	"Look at your troops. They are all (like) women!"	Lev. 26:36
Mic. 6:16b	"The scorn of the nations"	Deut. 28:37

The prophets were not ecstatic visionaries but lawyers of the covenant with their feet on the ground. They frame their oracles of woe in terms echoing the curses associated with the covenant.[13]

---

13. Brinsmead, "Covenant," *Present Truth*, November 1976, p. 33.

Grace and the Torah

Why could the prophets hail Jehovah's grace and patience while uttering such awful predictions? Where was the grace of God? Why was there so much attention on the Torah of God and not on His grace? How could the Psalmist sing so frequently of God's kindnesses? Entire houses of theology have been built on the failure of law and the victory of grace. The fact is, however, the matter is not that clear cut. One must hold a theology of law and grace compatible with the Biblical explanation of them both. The Law was grace in many ways. And the Gospel is called law (Rom. 8:2ff.).

Let us bring things into perspective by reviewing key concepts in this chapter. All prophecies in the Old Testament scriptures were related to the Old Covenant in some vital way. The histories of the former prophets were records of the God of the covenant, the people of the covenant and the ups and downs of their relationship. The latter prophets, those pre-exile eighth and seventh century B.C. prophets overtly called upon the witnesses of the treaty. That was a signal the patience of God was almost exhausted.

Some matters about covenants themselves may be reviewed. Covenants were conditional. There were two kinds of covenant failure. Utter failure to perform freed the other party from any obligation. Simple error or failure to keep the stipulations in exact detail was sin and was wrong, but it was not sufficient reason for one party to abandon the agreement. In such cases, the *hesed* of one party required him to step in and come to the aid of the faltering partner. Honorable men understood this and acted accordingly. The very existence of the sacrificial system as a part of the covenant implied God expected some minor and individual failure. That was taken into account in the Treaty. God could not have abandoned the people for the errors of a few. The failure of one entire generation came close to being utter abandonment of the treaty. Yet for an eternal God one generation of failure was not sufficient to consider the relationship abandoned completely. God obligated Himself to come to the aid of Israel when she needed it the most: when she was in danger of utter abandonment. He came to her aid in five vital ways. God's grace and love are here demonstrated.

1. He gave the Torah. He entered covenant. That in itself was very substantial grace of God. He gave man the basis for confidence in Him. He made promises and limited His anger. He eliminated guessing about Him.

> God entered history and tied himself to particular events which He promises will have everlasting consequences . . . there is a new security to life. The covenant as it is filled in by the law, helps man to know where he stands. He can count on things because a stable element has been added to his life and to history. Trust is possible. The paralyzing capriciousness of Near Eastern gods is totally excluded.[14]

Man could at last move out into the world with some degree of confidence. He had an anchor. He had obligated himself, and God had signed a legally binding Treaty. He would not act contrary to it. God became predictable! No relationship can endure unless predictability is established for the other person. Covenant IS the grace of God in action.

2. God showed grace to Israel by bringing her out of captivity when she by her own admission was a wicked, corrupt and uncircumcised people. He was not obligated by any act of goodness or honor on their part. He gave them

---

14. William Dyrness, *Themes in Old Testament Theology*, Downer's Grove, Illinois: InterVarsity Press, 1979, p. 125.

170

the Law. That was grace also. The Torah described in both general and detailed ways what conduct God expected of His people. No friend can grow in spirit unless each knows what the other friend considers honorable. There can be no fellowship without communication. The Torah was God's greatest communication since the creation of the world. He told Israel what He had to have to be able to work with her. That was grace also.

3. God showed grace to man in a third way. He taught Israel by experience over hundreds of years that obedience brought blessings, and disobedience, rebellion, and breach of honor brought punishment. God demonstrated to them the stability of nature, of His concern, and of His demands. He gave them an existential and historical basis of evaluation of conduct. Planning is not possible unless the variables are stable. At least the important variables must be stable. God was a variable that had to be considered. Steady covenant punishments for sin and blessings for faithfulness was a grace of God.

4. God intervened historically on several occasions to support the leader, the army, individuals and the nation. That was grace. Admittedly the balance between self-reliance and resting on God is delicate. For God to constantly intervene in history was to destroy the reliability of nature. Nonetheless, God intervened to Israel's benefit sufficiently to preserve her. He refrained from intervention enough to maintain the usefulness of miracle.

5. God sent prophets who understood His own point of view and who also were given the "Spirit of YHWH." They spoke for God. It was a conversation with the nation. Their chief cry was, "Jehovah's Word!" The regular review of the situation by God for the people was vital to the success

171

of the relationship. God sent prophets aplenty. That was His *hesed*, His covenant loyalty. *Hesed* was not an emotion. It was HELP. It was help when needed most. This patience of God in reminding each generation of the covenant, the appointment of priests to aid in the corporate worship, the reading of the Law each year, the ceremonies reminding Israel of her status, the high ethical demands of the Covenant toward neighbors, and the like, were all expressions of God's grace and care down through the years.

One could not accuse YHWH of acting in haste when He concluded the covenant was ruined. He did what He did gradually and with patience. He was not quick to anger. Five hundred years is not too short a time for God to draw conclusions. He was full of covenant support and patience: grace. But God is just what He is. Experience had shown that He could get fed up with man's unfaithfulness. YHWH was long-suffering, but His patience was not inexhaustible.

The imposing of sanctions promised by Jeremiah and the others was another example of God's mercy to the coming generations. They could be sure he was serious when he spoke about sin and faithfulness. The lesson was not missed on Daniel.

> You have fulfilled the words spoken against us and our rulers by bringing on us this great disaster. . . . Just as it is written in the Law of Moses. . . . The Lord did not hesitate to bring disaster upon us for the Lord, our God is righteous in everything he does (Dan. 9:11).

The Crisis of Conditionality

During the time of the latter prophets there arose a great tension regarding which way God would deal with His covenant people. All the pre-exile prophets reflected this

172

tension. Would God allow Israel to suffer defeat by her enemies, or did Israel's status as God's "elect" guarantee her permanent security? In other words, how would the conditionality of the covenant be worked out?

The central theme of the latter prophets was the invocation of the promises of the pact in a formal way. The promises of the treaty were divided into two kinds, however. There were both blessings and curses.

In the original code of Moses the curses and blessings were contrasted. It was one or the other. The eighth and seventh century B.C. prophets united them. There would be both the curses and the blessings. One prophet, Isaiah, cited the Davidic covenant as example of the unconditional election by God of David's dynasty and Jerusalem as His "son" and His holy city. Jeremiah appealed to the Sinai Covenant and emphasized conditionality. Jeremiah knew no unconditional promises. For him, "eternal" when used in covenant context meant simply "in perpetuity." The covenant was everlasting only in the sense there was no termination date as part of the stipulations of the Treaty itself. Jerusalem was to be the eternal city of David just as long as the Davidic covenant lasted. Jeremiah understood conditionality. Israel's eternal election was also "open ended." It could last forever, but was limited to the mutuality of the covenant. Forever meant, as far as Israel was concerned, "as long as the covenant stands."

All the major prophets pictured the curses of the covenant and then a restoration. Both events were pictured in the extreme. Overstatement was used, particularly in regard to the restoration. They were so overdrawn some theologians believe them yet to be fulfilled. The fact that the exile was the end of the Davidic dynasty put a strain upon Old Testament theology from which it never recovered. Prophets who had declared God would intervene and save Israel from captivity were stunned when Josiah went forth to war in confidence of God and was slain in battle. Prophets who had been saying, "It can't happen to us. We are elect of God," were stunned when Samaria fell and its king sent into captivity. Jeremiah was not surprised. He saw election as conditional. His opponents saw it as unconditional. They had been saying all would be well: trust in God; He will not allow His elect Israel to be destroyed.

> Do not listen to what the prophets are prophesying to you;
> They fill you with false hopes. They speak visions from their own minds not the mouth of the Lord. They keep saying to those who despise me, "We will have peace." And to all . . . they say, "No harm will come to you" (Jer. 23:16, 17).

and

> How can you say, "We are wise. We have the Law of the Lord" . . . (Jer. 8:8).

> Prophet and priest alike all practice deceit. They dress the wound of my people as though it were not serious. "Peace, peace," they say, when there is no peace. (Jer. 6:14).

> They say, "He will do nothing. No harm will come to us. We will never see the sword or famine. The prophets are but wind. And the Word is not in them, so what they say, let it be done to them!" (Jer. 5:12ff.).

To this Jeremiah replied they could not simply depend on their status as the Elect of God. Covenants are conditional, and not only for individuals. Take care Israel!

> If at any time I announce that a nation or a kingdom is to be uprooted, torn down, and destroyed, and if that nation I warned repents of its evil, then I will relent and not inflict on it the disaster I had planned.

174

And if at another time I announce that a nation or kingdom is to be built up and planted, and if it does evil in my sight, and does not obey me, then I will reconsider the good I had intended to do for it (Jer. 18:7-10).

Jeremiah foresaw the restoration of Israel after the captivity. His pictures of it were gentle and moving. But he did not see the return to the same kind of Theocracy. To him, it was an utter failure. He understood YHWH was to bring them back into the land, but he saw a new and better covenant in store.

> The time is coming, declares the Lord,
> When I will make a new covenant with the house of Israel
> and the house of Jacob.
> It will not be like the covenant
> I make with their forefathers
> when I took them by the hand
> to lead them out of Egypt,
> because they broke my covenant,
> although I was a husband to them.
> This is the covenant I will make with the house of Israel
> after that time, declares the Lord.
> I will put my law in their minds,
> and write it on their hearts.
> I will be their God and they will be my people.
> No longer will a man teach his neighbor, saying,
> "Know the Lord."
> Because they will all know me,
> from the least to the greatest,
> declares the Lord,
> And I will forgive their wickedness
> and will remember their sins no more (Jer. 31:31ff.).

Neither the Jews at that age nor those in the land after the captivity would have believed what kind of a covenant it would come to be! For the time being, that covenant age was postponed. The former covenant was yet in force, if on sinking sand. It was about to be enforced to such an extent Ezekiel called it the "death" of Israel. There was to be a resurrection of sorts, to be sure. But the Mosaic Theocratic covenant was not to last. This passage recalled the original oath of covenant, what each party had said, and it pictured what was in store for Israel.

The men who have violated my covenant and have not fulfilled the terms of the covenant they made before me,

I will treat like the calf they cut in two and then walked between its pieces. The leaders of Judah, and Jerusalem, the court officials and priests, and all the people of the land who walked between the pieces of the calf, I will hand over to their enemies who seek their lives (Jer. 34:18-20).

All of the prophecies of the pre-exile prophets were seen within the context of the Old Covenant. The "restoration" was to be a restoration of the Davidic kingdom. Ezekiel pictured it as a marvelous new kingdom, with a wonderful new temple, a splendid new city of Jerusalem, and a mighty new David on the throne. That was what the Torah had said. As it happened God intervened in an unexpected and startling way, and the prophets saw that, if dimly. They did not and indeed could not have seen anything apart from the "eternal" covenant of Moses and David. Their glorious pictures of the rebuilt Israel were to happen, and in a way more glorious than they ever expected. But when it did come, the people of Israel were to be bitterly disappointed by it.

The Covenant in the Psalms

The Psalms contain a complete history of the Israelite nation. A theological history of Israel could be reconstructed

176

by a careful examination of the Psalms. It is not our purpose to do this in the present study of covenant. The Psalms arose among the people of the covenant and were closely related to Israel's faith and her Election as People of God.

The purpose of the Psalms was to help the people stay true to the covenant and praise the God of Israel and the whole earth. They celebrated the covenant with Abraham.

> Give thanks to the Lord, call on His name;
>   make known among the nations what he has done.
> Sing to him, sing praise to him;
>   tell of his wonderful acts.
>
> Remember the wonders he has done, his miracles,
>   the judgments he has pronounced.
> O descendants of Abraham his servant,
>   O sons of Jacob, his chosen ones.
>
> He is the Lord our God;
>   His judgments are in all the earth.
> He remembers his covenant forever,
>   the word he commanded for a thousand generations.
> The covenant he made with Abraham,
>   the oath he swore to Isaac.
> He confirmed it to Jacob as a decree;
>   to Israel as an everlasting covenant;
> To you I will give the land of Canaan
>   as the portion you will inherit (Ps. 105:1ff.).

In this song the early history of Israel was recalled. It was a rather good account of the Genesis and Exodus events. It mentions the shepherding days, the removal of Joseph to Egypt, the oppression, the ten plagues, and "He brought out Israel, laden with silver and gold."

> He brought out his people . . . that they might keep his precepts and observe his laws (Ps. 105:43, 45).

177

There were songs of the Torah.

> Blessed are they whose ways are blameless,
>   who walk according to the law of the Lord.
> Blessed are they who keep his statutes,
>   and seek him with all their hearts.
> They do nothing wrong; they walk in his ways . . .
>   O that my ways were steadfast
> In observing your decrees.
>
> How can a young man keep his way pure?
>   By living according to your word.
> I seek you with all my heart;
>   do not let me stray from your commands.
> I have hidden your word in my heart
>   that I might not sin against you (Ps. 119:1ff.).

They sang of the Holy City Jerusalem which God had chosen as the resting place of the Ark of the Covenant.

> The Lord has chosen Zion,
>   He has chosen it as his dwelling (Ps. 132:13).
>
> I rejoiced with those who said to me,
>   "Let us go to the house of the Lord."
> Our feet are standing
>   in your gates O Jerusalem.
>
> Jerusalem is like a city . . .
>   Pray for the peace of Jerusalem (Ps. 122:ff.).
>
> As we have heard,
>   as we have seen,
> in the city of the Lord Almighty,
>   in the city of our God
> God makes her secure forever (Ps. 48:8).

They sang of their great King David and of his election by God to establish an everlasting dynasty in Jerusalem.

They gloried in that covenant and sang of the faithfulness
of God to David.

I will sing of the *hesed* of the Lord forever,
   with my mouth I will make your faithfulness known
   through all generations.

You said, "I have made a covenant with my chosen one.
   I have sworn to David my servant,
I will establish your line forever,
   and make your throne firm throughout all generations
   (Ps. 89:1-4).

I will crush his foes before him,
   and strike down his adversaries.
My faithful love (*hesed*) will be with him,
If his sons forsake my laws . . .
   I will punish their sin with a rod,
and their iniquity with flogging;
   But I will not take my love (*hesed*) from him,
nor will I ever betray my faithfulness,
   I will not violate my covenant,
Nor alter what my lips have uttered,
   That his line will continue forever,
And his throne endure before me like the sun (Ps. 89:30-37).

There are songs of personal fear. They all appeal to YHWH
for succor (Ps. 69). There are songs of abject repentance
and beggings for pardon, as after the incident with Bathsheba
(Ps. 51). There were songs sung when in exile (Ps. 106:40ff.),
and when they returned (Ps. 116).

And they sang of the *hesed*, the covenant faithfulness
of God.

Give thanks unto the Lord, his *hesed* endures for ever.
   Let Israel say, "His *hesed* endures for ever."
Let Aaron say, "His *hesed* endures forever."
   In anguish I cried to the Lord,
And he answered by setting me free. . . .

179

It is better to take refuge in the Lord
    than to trust in man.
It is better to take refuge in the Lord
    than to trust in princes. . . .
Give thanks to the Lord for He is good.
    His *hesed* endures for ever (Ps. 118).

Several songs came to have special meaning for the Hebrews later, when the new era had begun. They particularly saw this Psalm in a new light.

The Lord said to my Lord,
    "Sit at my right hand
until I make all your enemies
    your footstool.
The Lord will extend your mighty sceptre from Zion;
    Your troops will be willing on your day of battle.
The Lord has sworn, and will not change his mind,
    "You are a priest forever,
in the order of Melchizedek . . . " (Ps. 110:1-7).

Conclusion

There are many aspects of the prophetic messages not reviewed in this brief examination. The key message of the prophets was the Covenant must be taken seriously. For instance, all religions pray so prayer was not itself true religion. Covenant keeping is true religion. Many religions offered sacrifices to gods at great personal expense. That was not the essence of religion. Men everywhere are faithful. They are faithful to their culture, or family, or false god, or peer group, or nation, or their own personal welfare, or their own personal whims. Ethics was not simply being faithful. It was being faithful to God as defined by the covenant. All men love. They love something: their families, their wives, their clan, their gods. Love is a meaningless ethic without a better definition and a correct object. Love without covenant is empty sentimentalism. Faith is not true ethic. All men trust something: other men, their gods, their chariots, their minds, their bankers. Trust without a covenant is empty and meaningless as ethic or religion. The Baalites believed in something very strongly. It is the OBJECT of love, the faith, the faithfulness that made a way of life meaningful life. Doing what is right must be defined. God must say what is ultimately right. In short, there must be a norm, a standard, a fixed point of reference to have true ethics or religion. That norm was the Torah.

The early prophets, the "former prophets" wrote histories. They chose data that illustrated the essence of the covenant: what it was, how it worked, what its effects would be. It put into history all who affected the success of the promises of covenant. Those who touched it adversely were evil men. Those who aided the success of Israel and the covenant were heroes.

All prophets who lived before the great exile had difficulty with a religion called Baalism. Much of their Biblical data was directed at the elimination of Baalism as a cult. The battle was long and very difficult. It was because Baalism was a rather sophisticated philosophy integrated into a complete religious, economic and social system. Since this was also true of the covenant, mutual forbearance was impossible. It was a struggle to the death.

The eighth and seventh century B.C. prophets were called the latter prophets. Their chief concern was saving Israel from doom. Her doom was provided for by covenant upon utter breach of faith. At last God invoked the witnesses. He called Israel into court. He announced to all she had

181

utterly failed to be true to her commitments made so eagerly at Sinai. Her doom was sealed, the prophets said.

The prophets also announced the return of a remnant to Canaan after the punishment was over. At that time a new people was seen. A new covenant was described. A new land and new heaven was pictured. A new Jerusalem was to be built. A new temple was to be erected on Zion. All nations would flow into it. From Jerusalem the Law of the Lord would go as far as the islands of the sea. The return would show God to be true to His covenanted promises.

God was full of patience, but His patience was not inexhaustible. He had shown marvelous grace to Israel. He gave them the Torah to provide a basis of faith in Him. He gave them the Law to define what was right and wrong. He helped them time and again in history. He sent the prophets to guide them at critical moments. He had been longsuffering. But enough was enough. He was sending her into punishment as the agreement stipulated.

The Psalms were also related to the covenant. There were relatively few Psalms that did not reflect the feeling that Israel was the chosen people of the only true God. Her history and philosophy were restated in song. Human reactions to those facts were exhibited in the Psalms. The covenants were frequently mentioned. Covenant-keeping terms were used frequently. We may say, in short, all the literature of the Old Testament came into existence because the Covenant came into existence. Canon scripture of every sort is implied in the very notion of Treaty. All Old Testament scriptures assume the limitations placed upon the thinking of the author by the covenant. That is not to say they were limited in receiving revelation. It is to say revelation from God came in covenant form and harmonized with and related to the covenant under which the prophets preached or the writers of scripture were inspired to write.

Questions on Chapter Four

1. The "former prophets" were
   a) ecstatic visionaries   c) anti-king
   b) historians   d) anti-social
2. The "latter prophets" were
   a) lawyers of covenant   c) anti-Israel
   b) ecstatic visionaries   d) anti-king
3. Any written history needs three things for coherent understanding.
   a) _____
   b) _____
   c) _____
4. Explain why "love" and "faith" and "loyalty" can work against a person.
5. An "event" is an occurrence that has been _____.
6. The prophets used the _____ as the norm of good ethics.
7. The prophets appealed to the _____ for proof they were right.
8. The pictures of woe painted by prophets were echoes of the _____.
9. Daniel confessed the sin of Israel had been _____.
10. T F The sins listed by prophets were found prohibited by the Law.
11. T F In a Theocracy, sin was one thing and treason another.
12. T F Baalites had a loose, illogical and disjointed religion.

13. T F Baalism assumed the laws of nature were the laws of gods.
14. T F Jehovahites treated the Baalites with gentle persuasion.
15. T F God exercised great patience with Israel.
16. Tell four ways Jehovah showed great grace to Israel.
    a) _____
    b) _____
    c) _____
    d) _____
17. The prophets foretold both _____ and _____ for Israel.
18. Explain the tension between faith and "conditionality."
19. Baalism based itself on _____ experience. (present or past)
20. Jehovahites based their faith on _____ history. (present or past)

PLEASE TURN THE BOOK OVER FOR ANSWERS.

8. Curses and promises found in the covenant.
7. Covenant
6. Covenant
5. "elevated to the rank of Event"
4. If love is directed at the wrong thing, or expressed in a wrong way, then love or faith or hope or faithfulness can destroy a person. It is the OBJECT of faith that makes it valuable.
3. Written histories must have a) A philosophy of selection of data. b) Actual selection of Event. c) An explanation of the connections.
2. a) Lawyers of covenant
1. b) Historians. They wrote the early histories of Israel.

9. Breach of the Mosaic Covenant
10. T
11. F   In a theocracy sin is treason, sin is breach of the peace, etc.
12. F   Baalism was a very well integrated social system.
13. T   Such a philosophy is also called "naturalism."
14. F   They killed them.
15. T
16. God showed grace to Israel in five ways
    a) Making a covenant to stabilize their views of God.
    b) Setting out in some detail what God liked and did not like.
    c) Intervening in strategic times to save Israel.
    d) Allowing Israel to see the consequences of error and benefits of law.
    e) Sending the prophets to guide the nation.
17. Judgment and restoration (allow any words meaning the same thing).
18. God's promises are to a group. We can trust God about that. Our benefit as individuals is conditional.
19. Present: In the recurring nature cycle. That was reality, they said.
20. Past: the Exodus, the call of Abraham, the saving of the nation in history.

185

Chapter Five

THE END OF THE OLD COVENANT

The people of the Covenant went into the Babylonian captivity as the prophets had said. They were scattered from Western Europe to Southern India to Eastern China.[1] Many became high-ranking officials in the Babylonian and Persian empires. Others were threatened from several sources. They were sold into slavery. Enslaved women produced children from men representing many races. For this reason Jewish descent was changed from male to female. If a child's mother were Jewish the child was Jewish. Through the years many gained their freedom and became productive citizens of the host country. Some became very successful merchants and traders. As the curses of the covenant had said they were scattered among "every nation under heaven."

A small but determined band was finally allowed by the Persian government to return to Jerusalem and begin to rebuild the fortunes of the nation. They came back in three groups, but leadership finally fell to Nehemiah, a Jewish official in the Persian Empire. The people cooperated and worked. By pleading, demanding, threatening, Nehemiah held them together until they were strong. They rebuilt Jerusalem. Eventually they rebuilt the Temple. Baalism was gone forever. It was swept away in the series of conquests by the Great Empires. The faith in God of the Jehovahites finally won over Baalism's natural religion. Those who returned were absolutely determined to do everything the Lord wanted. They never again had any interest in any religion or god but Jehovah and His Holy Torah. They all renewed the covenant in a moving and far-reaching covenant renewal ceremony. There was a long confessional prayer. It was addressed to God, "who keeps his covenant and *hesed*"

---

1. W. C. White, *The Chinese Jews*, Toronto: Toronto University Press, 1966.

(Neh. 9:32). The previous relationship with God was reviewed. The prayer ended with a statement of national covenant renewal.

> In view of all this we are making a binding agreement (*b'rth*), putting it in writing, and our leaders, our Levites, and our priests are affixing their seals to it . . . and the rest of the people . . . and all who separate themselves together from the neighboring peoples for the sake of the Law of God, together with their wives and all their sons and daughters who are able to understand, all these now join their brothers the nobles and bind themselves with a curse and an oath to follow the Law of God given through Moses the servant of God and to obey carefully all the commands, regulations, and decrees of the Lord our God.
>
> We promise not to give our daughters in marriage. . . .
> We will not buy . . . on the Sabbath. . . .
> We assume the responsibility for. . . .
> We have cast lots to . . . bring wood . . . altar. . . .
> We assume the responsibility for . . . firstfruits. . . .
> We will not neglect the house of our God (Neh. 10:1-39).

An ingredient appeared in that prayer that was to be the cutting issue in theology in the New Testament, beginning with John, continuing with Jesus and his Apostles and dividing the church thereafter. The covenant was sworn and signed only by those "who are able to understand." The idea that everyone born of Abraham, regardless of his personal faith and covenant keeping as a proper member of Israel, was being strained.

Some Jews chose to come home. Others chose to remain abroad where they had houses and lands. Since choosing had more to do with covenant keeping than blood, the emphasis of being Jews by blood weakened. It finally destroyed the

Old Covenant completely. Another factor contributed to the shattering of the dream of a restored Davidic Kingdom. Only about one-tenth of all Jews returned to their promised land to live. What was the status of those who could have returned but chose not to? Were the promises of covenant only for those living on their inheritance? What about the Hebrew language? Could a man be a Jew and not speak the language of the Torah? How could his sin be atoned apart from the Temple Sacrifices as prescribed by Law?

Ezra was very strict. Even Jews who came home at some expense and in devotion to the Law were not enrolled if they could not prove pure descent by documentary evidence (Neh. 7:64). Those who had married foreign women were required by the leadership to divorce them (Ezra 10:19). This strict accounting of blood left many who loved the Lord but who, by no fault of their own had foreign blood, outside the central power structure of emerging Judaism. Things were very confused. They had a city and a temple and Levites. But they had no king with Davidic blood. Delegates from Ezra and Nehemiah to Jewish communities abroad collected money from wealthy exiles and brought that to the Temple. The delegates tried to convince the remaining Jews to come home. The delegates were called in Greek *apostolos*. It meant messenger, but actually was one having official power to speak for the leadership in Jerusalem. We will hear more of this kind of man later.

The faith of the exiles was in danger. Many had simply given up being Israelites. Others remembered vaguely their uncles speak of a place called Canaan, but that was, they said, long ago, in their grandfathers' time. Or was it great-grandfathers' time? Well, anyway. . . . The *apostolos* organized families of exiles who could not come home and who had some link, in faith or in blood, to the covenant, into assemblies called synagogues. It took ten families to make an official synagogue. They became a little Jewish outpost where the Torah was studied, prayers said, and offerings for Jerusalem and the poor taken. They provided hospitality to Jewish travelers and purchased Jewish slaves if they heard of any. The slaves they set free. In Paul's time there was an entire synagogue of ex-slaves in Jerusalem (Acts 6:9). For the diaspora Jew, the Jew living abroad, the synagogue became his local temple.[2] From then until long after the time of Jesus, the dispersed Jew would play a very significant role in covenant story of the Bible.

Events in New Canaan

The returned people did not fare well, at least when compared with the prophetic visions of "multitudes" returning to Zion. Those who did return did so with joy and real exultation. They wept. They loved their God and their homeland. But, they hardly had begun to get matters under control when Alexander the Great conquered all of the Near East, including Canaan.[3] When he died his empire was divided between three generals. They each ruled a third of the former empire. The middle Greek empire ruled Palestine. They tried to Hellenize it. They introduced the Greek language, order and religion. Their new lords imitated Alexander and announced themselves to be gods.[4]

---

2. Isaac Levi, *The Synagogue: Its History and Functions*, London: Vallentine, 1964, p. 1.

3. William H. McNeil, *History of Western Civilization*, Chicago: University of Chicago Press, 1969, p. 567ff.

4. William W. Tarn, *Hellenistic Civilization*, Chicago: Meridian Books, 1961, p. 60.

It galled the Jew to submit to yet another conqueror. Worse yet, his very status as elect was in danger. His land was polluted by foreign gods as bad as Baal. Greek games undermined humility and modesty. Greek administration threatened the return of the Kingdom. Greek religion was of a higher type than Baalism, but was naturalism all over again.

There was one great period in Jewish post-exile politics. Under a family of priests who came to be known as Maccabees, "the hammers," the Jews threw off the yoke of Asia-Greece and became an independent nation for one hundred years. The descendants of the Maccabees provided both the high priests and the kings during most of that time. Their line continued until Herod the Great. The descendants of the Maccabees were, as a group, no better than the descendants of David. Nonetheless, during their dynasty the Jews achieved the independence and statehood declared by the pre-exile prophets. They had their temple, and the *apostolos* continued to direct a steady flow of returnees to Jerusalem. They brought with them the "wealth of the nations." At the Passover the numbers of exiles swelled the city. The Ezra-Nehemiah pure-bloods could take justified pride in much their children did as covenanters.[5]

The Greek Old Testament

During the exile a very large Jewish community gathered in Alexandria. The city had been built by orders of the conqueror and took his name (as with a dozen other cities). They had a very impressive museum and a famous library of over 500,000 volumes.[6] It was here the Hebrew Old

---

5. Moshe Pearlman, *The Maccabees*, London: Weidenfeld and Nicolson, 1973, p. 55ff.

6. McNeil, *op cit.*, p. 115.

Testament Scriptures were translated into Greek. That translation was both a benefit and a danger to Judaism. It was beneficial in that it allowed the exiled Jews access to scriptures in the *lingua franca*. It was a danger because it weakened the concept of covenant, replacing covenant-related words with individualistic and moralistic Greek terms. The tension between Greek ideas and Hebrew ideas as they met in that translation (and sometimes reinterpretation) is still reflected in theological systems today, and still contributes to division in the Christian movement.

The problem was the Greeks had definitions to words which were, at least in the philosophical arena, understood to harmonize with Platonic presuppositions and world-view, whereas the Hebrew mindset was covenantal. The temptation when reading the Greek version of the Old Testament was to give Greek definitions to the words. The proper understanding of the scriptures required the Hebrew definitions be assigned to the Greek words. If this were not the case, (and it appears it sometimes was not) there was not merely translation but redefinition of previous Hebrew concepts. When the Septuagint, the Greek Old Testament, used the word sacrifice, it must have the Hebrew definition, not that of Athens. When "hearing" was used, the Greeks would understand it to mean simply "listening to." The Hebrew meant "hear and do" (Mt. 7:24). When the word "flesh" was used in a philosophic sense, it meant to Greeks the sinful, earthy, and unworthy part of man's nature. The Hebrews would understand it as Paul redefined it: a sinful and wicked way of life (Gal. 5:19), or a lifestyle dominated by meeting the needs of the body (Gal. 6:7). The Hebrew would never have agreed the flesh of man was sinful in and of itself or by its very nature. The Hebrew idea of covenant was absent in Greek mythology and religion. Indeed it was completely out of place in Greek religious thought. Their gods used POWER not mutuality to gain ends. The typical Greek understanding of covenant was that of testament, or a will by which one party gave to another a benefit. Their idea of covenant is reflected only once in the entire New Testament scriptures (Heb. 9:16).

Covenant in the Maccabees

In the literature reporting the era of the Maccabees, two Greek words were used to carry the concepts of the one Hebrew *b'rth*. Several times the Maccabees were negotiating treaties with the Syrian-Greek authorities. Those treaties were carried by the word *suntheke*. When a treaty was signed it produced *eirene* (peace), *philia* (friendship), and *adelphotes* (brotherhood). Those are terms that abound in the theology of the New Testament. Their "cause" was the treaty relationship. In the Maccabees the word *diatheke* was used only when refering to the Biblical "covenants of promise" (Eph. 2:12). The only exception to that practice was in I Macc. 1:11 and 2:9. The exception indicated the view that both *diatheke* and *sunatheke* meant treaty of some sort. New Testament writers did not employ *suntheke*, or a "negotiated treaty" at all. They used only the *diatheke* a "handed down treaty," refering to a relationship with God.

The first glow of success with the Maccabees was wonderful. After the death of Mattathias, the father, each son in turn assumed the leadership of the freedom movement. They began as rebels, fleeing the wrath of the Seleucid Greeks whose headquarters were in Jerusalem, practically on the temple grounds! They developed into a guerrilla force and gained effective control of the entire countryside. Their ranks swelled until they were able to ambush a Greek army, defeating it so badly it fled far into the north. Again and again the Jewish military forces defeated well organized armies sent from Damascus to subdue that troublesome province— Judah. At last peace was achieved when a *suntheke* was signed.[7] But the dream was shattered when various elements in Judaism competed for power. At last Rome was asked to protect the land from both Egypt and Asia Minor. The Maccabee dynasty called the Hasmonean House was replaced by a new set whose founder was an Edomite, Antipas. The Jews had recently conquered Edom and forcibly converted the population to Judaism. It is a bit ironic one of the sons of the "convert" Antipas would soon become King and be known in history as Herod the Great, the one who rebuilt the third and last temple in Jerusalem. It was that edifice Jesus and the Apostles knew.

Various Sects Shatter the Dream

The dream of the restored kingdom grew dimmer. Sects multiplied in the land. Each group had its program. Each blamed others for the loss of the ideal.

The legacy of the Maccabees was carried on by the "Zealots," men who dreamed of the reestablishment of the royal house of David. Their men attempted several times to lead rebellions but failed.

The Pharisees were the spiritual heirs of the Ezra-Nehemiah pure-bloods. They grew less interested in a political state as

---

7. Pearlman, *op. cit.*, p. 234.

time went on. They concentrated efforts at ceremonial and personal religion, not national restoration. The Sadducees were political in orientation. They wanted to preserve the freedom of Judah at all costs. They were not very interested in the ceremonial and religious aspects of the state of New Judah. Another group was the Samaritans. They were outcasts to the pure-bloods of Judah and Galilee.[8] Samaritans followed only the Torah, the Pentateuch. Forbidden by Ezra and Nehemiah to come to Zion, they worshipped at their own mountain (John 4:24f.).

The other group, whose identity has only recently been defined, though not conclusively, was the Essenes. They were similar, if not a branch of the Dead Sea Scroll people. They used the word covenant frequently. They understood themselves to be the people of the "new covenant" of Jeremiah. Their members were *hasidim,* the "faithful," or "the covenanters." They had given up entirely any hope for Israel as a reestablished Theocracy.[9] They looked only for a smashing coming of Messiah who would sweep away all the wicked pretense of Jerusalem and the pseudo-temple worship practiced there. At that time, by the overt interruption of God, the mighty Kingdom of David would be restored and the prophecies of Isaiah and the others come to pass. They looked for a very literal restoration of David's throne, ushered in by such an earth-shaking revelation from heaven one could say there was a "new heaven and a new earth" (Isa. 65:17).

The sects of Israel illustrate the trauma felt in the land when the prophecies, as they understood them, did not

---

8. Hasanein W. Kahen, *The Samaritans: Their History, Religion, and Customs,* 1974, p. 70ff.

9. Josephus, *Wars,* ii, 8.

happen. There was no Davidic throne. An Edomite sat there. At times there were two high priests—both of the wrong bloodline. Most of Israel was still scattered across the face of the known earth. The Ark of the Covenant had disappeared. No one knew where the stone tablets were. The nation was in a shambles. Groups formed—each with its own idea as the solution to Canaan's problems.

The Messianic Dream

The pre-exile prophecies were the source of much of the theological difficulty. The concept of Messiah grew by fusing several concepts. The cord of messianic hope was woven with four strands. "The one to come" (Dan. 7:13) was to restore Israel. He would be a true "son of David" (Isa. 11:ff.). He would be "anointed" (literally "messiahed") by God, as was his father David (I Sam. 16:13). The second strand was that of prophet (Deut. 18:15-18). He was to be a "suffering servant" (Isa. 53:1ff.) prophet. He would speak from God. He would lead the people as Moses and Elijah had. He was a "messenger" and "covenant for the peoples" (Isa. 42:1-6). He would be all that Israel as a nation should have been before God: a servant of God (Isa. 49:1-9). All true servants of God seem to have suffered for it. As Elijah anointed Elisha when making him a true prophet (I Kgs. 19:16), so the coming prophet would be God's anointed, God's "messiahed" (Isa. 61:1-6).

> The Spirit of the Sovereign Lord is on me
> because the Lord has anointed me to preach good news
> to the poor.
> He sent me to bind up the brokenhearted,
> to proclaim freedom to the captives and release to the
> prisoners,
> To proclaim the year of the Lord's favor.

195

The third strand was that of priest (Isa. 53:12b), for "he made intercession for many." The Psalmist had said of the Lord,

> The Lord has sworn
> and will not change his mind;
> You are a priest forever,
> after the order of Melchizedek (Ps. 110:4).

As Aaron had been anointed by Moses to his high office as priest and intercessor (Exod. 29:7) so the coming priest would be called "the Messiah, the Lord's Anointed."

The fourth strand of the messianic cord was the "son of man." The figure can be found in Psalm 8:4. The more frequent use of the phrase is to be found in Ezekiel. God addressed the prophet as "son of man." The "son of man" was to be a watchman for the city of Israel warning the inhabitants to flee should an enemy approach.

> Son of man, I have made you a watchman for the house of Israel. So hear the word I speak and give them warning from me (Ezek. 33:7).

There seems little doubt this was Jesus' self-image, for it was his most frequently employed Old Testament description of himself. Another idea is contained in the phrase son of man. It is obtained from the prophet Daniel. He saw the "Son of Man" as an eschatological redeemer, a future man from heaven come to bring judgment from God and usher in the new age. After the four empires had run their courses, Daniel said, another figure in history would come.

> In my vision at night I looked and there before me was one like the son of man, coming with the clouds of heaven. He approached the Ancient of Days and was led into His presence. He was given glory, authority and sovereign

196

power. All peoples, nations, and men of every language worshipped him. His dominion is an everlasting dominion that will not pass away, and his kingdom is one that will never end (Dan. 7:13, 14).

There are currently several ideas about what the passage in Daniel meant. Of one thing we can be sure. It was understood by some in the age of the Apostles to have referred to a supernatural figure, one who came from heaven to earth to set up His own eternal kingdom.

> . . . we know from contemporary sources that certain circles in Judaism interpreted this figure in individualistic terms. The Son of Man became a heavenly, preexistant, supernatural figure who has been preserved in the presence of God. In God's time he will come to earth to raise the dead, judge the wicked, to redeem God's people and gather them into a glorious everlasting kingdom.[10]

It was difficult then as it is today to hold together all the strands of Old Testament visions weaving them into a complete whole. The four strands were woven together in various ways. Contradictions in imagery were smoothed away as each group saw fit. Messianic hopes were almost at a fever pitch by the time Jesus came on the scene. What is important to a study of covenant is that whatever the future brought, it implied the One to come was to have all authority to set things right. He would combine in Himself the authority of prophet, priest, king, and divine redeemer. When He came, Israel's problems would be over.

The Last Promise to Abraham

What of the last promise given to Abraham? "And in your seed shall all the nations of the earth be blessed" (Gen.

---

10. George Eldon Ladd, *The Last Things*, Grand Rapids: Baker, 1971, p. 93.

197

12:1-3). The latter prophets, Joel, Isaiah, and Jeremiah began speaking of the "gentiles." The word was *ta ethne* in Greek. It was used in parallelism with "peoples, nations and tongues" in several passages. How were the "nations" of the earth to be blessed by the "seed" of Abraham? How, indeed, could they be as blessed as the Jews, heirs of the Abrahamic promises and holders of the land of Israel? There was not enough land in Canaan for all the gentiles pictured as returning with the Jews in the restoration. Yet, the gentiles had increasingly high profile in the latter prophets. They "wait for His law" (Isa. 42:4). They will come back to Zion with Israel and will "carry your sons in their arms, and your daughters on their shoulders" (Isa. 49:22). The gentiles would be listed along with Jews as they returned to the land of promise.

> After this I will return
>> and rebuild David's fallen tent.
> Its ruins I will rebuild
>> and I will restore it,
> that the remnant of men may seek the Lord,
>> and all the gentiles that bear my name,
> says the Lord, who does these things,
>> that I have known for ages (Amos 9:11, 12; Cf. Acts 15:16, 17).

The Psalms also expected the gentiles some day to share in the knowledge and worship of the Lord.

> Therefore I will praise you among the Gentiles, I will sing hymns to your name (Ps. 18:49),

and

> Rejoice, O Gentiles, with His people (Deut. 32:43),

and again

> Praise the Lord, all you Gentiles, and sing praises to him all you peoples (Ps. 117:1).

198

Isaiah said,

> A root of Jesse will spring up,
>   one who will arise to rule over the nations,
> the Gentiles will hope in him (Isa. 11:10).

The blessing of *ta ethne* was to come through the "seed" of Abraham. It was God's intention to have created a devout and loyal people on earth—the Hebrews. When the nations saw what a fine, pure, and honorable people they were, they would say,

> Surely this nation is a wise and understanding people. What other nation is so great as to have their gods near them as the Lord our God is near us when we pray to him.
>
> And what other nation is so great as to have such righteous decrees and laws as this body of laws I am setting before you this day? (Deut. 4:6ff.).

God's plan was to develop an intensely loyal people who would come when he commanded, "Come," and would go up when He commanded, "Go up." Because one day He was to issue the command all heaven had been awaiting,

> Go into all the world and preach the good news to all creation (Mark 16:15).
>
> Therefore go and make disciples of all *ta ethne*, baptizing them in the name of the Father and the Son, and the Holy Spirit, and teaching them to obey everything I have commanded you (Matt. 28:18).

Hints of the Coming End of the Old Covenant

There were several ideas in the Old Testament scriptures giving hint of a time when the Old Covenant would be ended or re-structured, or corrected.

199

1. The very early statement by God to the serpent in the garden, hinted at something in the future which would strike at the very life of the serpent for all mankind's sake.

> And I will put enmity between you and the woman, between your offspring and hers, he will crush your head, and you will strike his heel (Gen. 3:15).

It was understood in Christ's time the serpent was crushed at the cross but he indeed did "strike" the son of woman who died there. Mary saw at the cross both the striking and the crushing. Paul wrote to the church, "The God of peace will soon crush Satan under your feet" (Rom. 16:20). He understood the church to finish the crushing of Satan and his power through the gospel message. Since the gospel was God's power to save, said Paul, for both Jew and Greek, there must be an end to the Covenant of Moses in order for the Greeks to share with Jews. The Torah of Moses was the one thing standing between their becoming one people, as mankind was in the garden of Eden.

2. The promise given to Abraham implied an end of the first or Sinai Covenant. If the nations of the world were to be blessed, and the definition of blessing remained the same: either spiritual (atonement) or physical (lands and cattle), there had to be some revision of the Old Covenant. The parties had to be expanded to include all peoples; in which case a new covenant would have to be drawn up so specifying. If the terms were expanded to apply to all the earth it meant the end of central worship in Jerusalem. All mankind can neither live in Canaan nor come to Jerusalem to sacrifice. If the promises were expanded to include all mankind, what was unique about the Law of the Jews? Mankind would, without the burden of the Law, get all the blessing of it while Israel would still be shackled to it. One

way or the other, the Jews should have understood that last promise to Abraham hinted at a time in the future when the Old Testament would be revised.

3. The prophecy of Moses about one who was to come after him is another indication the Jews should have expected a new covenant some day (Deut. 18:15-18). Peter reminded his Jewish listeners of it.

> The Lord your God will raise up a prophet like me from among your own people; you must listen to everything he tells you. Anyone who does not listen to him will be completely cut off from among his people (Acts 3:22).

The passage implied a new leader with a new law, for Moses was first and foremost the Israelite lawgiver. The passage would have no unusual meaning if the coming prophet merely urged the people to keep the old covenant law. All prophets did that. When he said, "a prophet like unto me," he was lifting that prophet above the common lot and very strongly implying he would be bringing a new law or new covenant.

4. The prophetic passage in Jeremiah was a clear indication the Old Covenant one day was to be rewritten. "It will not be like the covenant I made with their forefathers . . ." (Jer. 31:31ff.). It would be a new covenant. It would be not written on stone, but "on their hearts." Children, strangers, and brothers will not have to be exhorted to "know the Lord." There would be none in the New Covenant who had not already come to "know the Lord." None would be in the new kingdom who had not already sworn allegiance to the new king. Indeed, swearing allegiance to Messiah would be the very way one became a member of the New Covenant people of God. The writer of Hebrews, in a simple, but masterful bit of logic ended all argument.

201

If there had been nothing wrong with that first covenant, no place would have been sought for another. . . .

But God found fault with the people and said . . . "I will make a new covenant." By calling this covenant "new," he has made the first one "old," and what is obsolete and aging will soon disappear (Heb. 8:7-13).

Joining the Old Covenant

There was no provision in the Code of Moses for conversion to or initiation by a Gentile into Israel. Ezra and Nehemiah were very strict about it. The rule began to break down among the exiles who remained outside their jurisdiction. They felt somewhat justified in remaining abroad for perhaps two reasons. The wealthy were able to use their business to produce income for Jerusalem. The prophet Jeremiah had suggested they live peacefully in the foreign lands.

Thus says the Lord God of hosts, the God of Israel, to all the exiles whom I have sent into exile from Jerusalem to Babylon: build houses and live in them, plant gardens and eat their produce. Take wives and have sons and daughters. . . . multiply there and do not decrease. But seek the welfare of the city where I have sent you into exile, and pray to the Lord on its behalf, for in its welfare you will find your welfare (Jer. 29:4-7).

That did not imply they were not to return to Judah, but it urged each to settle down and prosper as best he could. When the Septuagint had been translated, it became a respected and well known document (Acts 15:21). The Jews convinced many that naturalism and the analogy of the gods was false. They pointed out the elementary nature of idolatry. Their religion had very lofty morals. In short, there arose a desire for admission into the Jewish community. Those admitted were identified as proselytes or "the ones who come forward."

Becoming a Jew by faith in Jehovah was possible for a Jew by birth. Many had lost their Baalite faith in captivity. They were Israelites by descent and had married within the people of Israel, but were themselves not practicing any religion, perhaps. These needed instruction, or in a sense, converting to Judiasm. The *apostolos* and the synagogues engaged in this.

It was hard for a proselyte to be a Jew entirely. The ceremonial aspects were discomforting and, it undoubtedly would seem to a non-Jew, had considerably less philosophic foundation and support than the moral aspects of the Law. On the other hand, the ceremonial laws forced constant attention on the fact the Jews were a separate people for God's own use. The Jews in diaspora were eager to receive converts.[11]

A non-Jew could become a Jew by three acts, if done in good faith and without hidden motive. Anyone, for instance, who became a Jew simply for the purpose of marrying an Israelite was "not a proper Jew."[12] One who came to believe in God and wanted some kind of a covenanted relationship with Him could become Jewish by three acts.

1) *circumcision.* It was said, "A few drops of the blood of the covenant must be made to flow from him."[13]

---

11. Richard R. DeRitter, *Discipling the Nations*, Grand Rapids: Baker, 1971, p. 93.

12. Yeb. 147-8.

13. Shab. 367.

2) *baptism.*

> One does not become a proselyte until he has been circumcised and has performed ablution; and so long as he has not performed ablution he is still a gentile.[14]

And again, Epictetus left this remark,

> When we see a man playing half one part and half another, we are accustomed to saying, "He is not a Jew, but he is playing the Jew." It is only when he has the experience of the baptized and the chosen that he really is and is called a Jew.[15]

And,

> Circumcised but not immersed proselytes and their children render things ceremonially unclean.[16]

And,

> One who has become a proselyte is like one newly born.[17]

This longer quotation from the Jewish scholar and father, Maimonides, will show both the practice and the theology of baptism for proselytes.

> By three things did Israel enter into the covenant, by circumcision, and baptism, and sacrifice . . . and at this time when there is no sacrificing, they must be circumcised and be baptized. And when the Temple shall be built, they are to bring the sacrifice. A stranger that is circumcised and not baptized, or baptized and not circumcised is not a proselyte until he be both circumcised and baptized: and he must be baptized in the presence of three. . . .

---

14. Ber. 288.

15. Dissertations of Epictetus, II.9:19:20 (Also F. Derwacter, *Preparing the Way of Paul*, New York: Macmillan, 1930, p. 28.

16. A.Z. 287.

17. San. 562, (See also DeRitter, *op. cit.*, p. 90.)

The Gentile that is made proselyte and the slave that is made free, behold he is like a child new born.[18]

It should also be noted that:

Entrance into the commonwealth of Israel was more than naturalization. It was essentially admission to full covenant status.[19]

And,

When he comes up from the waters of baptism, he has entered the covenant.[20]

3) *sacrifice.* The initiate was to offer a sacrifice. A small animal, even a dove would be sufficient. If at all possible, the sacrifice or a sacrifice ought to be made in Jerusalem. Some rabbis did not regard a proselyte as fully sincere who did not participate in the Passover in Jerusalem.[21]

The pressures on the Old Covenant were more than it could bear. In Canaan itself, the idea of a gradual return of the Davidic Theocracy through the efforts of the faithful was all but dead. In the diaspora, the *parties* aspect of the Law was being subverted by a wave of proselytes. The cultus of the Torah, the endless ceremonies, the worship at Mount Zion by all once a year, along with inheritance regulations were not being observed. A new diaspora Judaism was in the making. The Old Covenant was "spiritualized" by Talmud type reinterpretations. In short, the end of the Law was at hand. Its demise would not be resented by most Jews if only

18. Maimonides, *Isure Biah*, XIII and XIV, (See also T. F. Torrence, "Proselyte Baptism," *New Testament Studies*, 1945, p. 150-154.

19. DeRitter, *op. cit.*, p. 104.

20. T. M. Taylor, "The Beginnings of Jewish Proselyte Baptism," in *New Testament Studies*, Feb., 1956, p. 193-198.

21. Joachim Jeremias, *Jerusalem in the Time of Jesus*, London: SCM Press, 1969, p. 320.

there were Divine authority for its withdrawal. That did not seem possible, however, for it was described in a dozen places in the scriptures as an "eternal covenant."

There has recently been a shift by scholarship away from the previous belief that proselyte baptism originated after John's baptism and was the practice among Jews of the second century A.D. Such a view was held by Joseph Crehan.[22] More recently A. Oepke supported the view of a pre-Christian origin of the practice. H. H. Rowley supported the same conclusion. Richard DeRitter, the splendid scholar from Holland, after reviewing the data, quoted Oepke with approval.[23]

It is hardly conceivable that the Jewish ritual should be adopted at a time when baptism had become an established religious practice in Christianity. After 70 A.D. at least the opposition to Christianity was too sharp to allow for the rise of a Christian custom among the Jews. Proselyte baptism must have preceded Christian baptism.[24]

John the Baptist

The end was approaching. The last of the Hebrew prophets came. His name was that of David's gentle, brave and honest friend. They called him John. Jesus said there was none greater. The Jewish people regarded him as a true prophet. He had a simple message. He was to prepare the way for

---

22. Joseph Crehan, *Early Christian Baptism and Creed*, London, 1950, p. 2-4.

23. DeRitter, *op. cit.*, p. 105.

24. A. Oepke, "Jewish Proselyte Baptism," *Theological Dictionary of the New Testament*, I, Grand Rapids: Eerdmans, 1964, p. 535.

H. H. Rowley, "Jewish Proselyte Baptism and John's Baptism," *Hebrew Union College Annual*, 1940, p. 313-334.

the soon to come Son of David, the true Messiah. "Let all Israel repent and be prepared to follow him," was John's message. They came to be baptized by him. Perhaps some who came were honest proselytes wishing to be doubly sure they were properly introduced into Judaism. John apparently held the diaspora Jew and the proselyte in higher esteem than the Jerusalem establishment. When the latter came to him to be baptized, he attacked them in sermon. He said they needed to repent and join Israel in heart as well as flesh. He might have said,

You blue-bloods from Jerusalem who boast of pure descent from Abraham, you need to repent too. You need to become a convert yourself. And don't shout at me, "We have Abraham and Moses. We live in Zion!" Your brothers in the diaspora are better Jews than you are. At least they took it seriously enough to repent and return to God. They chose their relationship. You merely inherited yours. Hypocrites! Who warned you? Who got you out of your soft chairs to come to the river? Not that you don't need it. You need it worse than all the others. The proselytes are better Jews than you are! Yes, it's true. Abraham can't save you! Repentance can. You need to choose into the covenant of Abraham as he did. You need to be circumcised—in heart and mind. You need to be immersed as a new convert. At least they chose to be Jews! And they will make it into the coming kingdom before any of you will. Do not shout, "Moses, Moses, We have Moses" at me, you snakes, you sons of your father the snake! Go back to your city. Go back to die. Who told you to come here anyway? Those coming here have chosen God as their savior. You could use that too! I tell you the Messiah is coming and I am your last chance to get yourselves ready. God has asked me to prepare this people for the King. Who will come and surrender to God and promise to follow Messiah when he comes?

Those who came he baptized in the Jordan.

John was God's last prophet under the Old Covenant. His chief duty was to testify about Jesus. He was to identify Him to all. He was to provide a seedbed of loyal disciples for Messiah's use. He was to decrease while Messiah increased. He did his job well. Messiah said of Him, "There was none greater" (Matt. 11:11). John's baptism was of repentance, not a real joining of the Old Covenant by birth, but an adult kind of joining. It was very like the oath signing of Nehemiah 10. Those who heard him were "choosing in" with all who promised to follow Messiah.

Jesus came to the Jordan to be baptized by His cousin. John did not care to baptize Jesus. It ought to be the other way around, he said. Jesus insisted and John baptized Him. God testified from heaven Jesus was favored and upon Him rested the Holy Spirit.

Why did Jesus receive baptism? He was indicating His own choice. He was saying to the people,

> Even if I were not born the Son of God, as I am, I would choose to be one—with all of you. In this act I am saying I want to be part of the Kingdom. Were I the least in Israel I would choose God and his new covenant.

John identified Jesus to some of his closer disciples. They left John and followed Jesus, as it had been planned by God. Jesus received His first followers from the band prepared for Him by John. They proved to be the most productive, at least as far as the records show, of all His disciples.

Jesus and the End of the Law

Jesus came. Had that event been merely part of nature, the stars would have fallen, volcanoes erupted fire and smoke, the sun gone dark, the moon turned to blood, the

208

hills would have prostrated themselves before Him, the valleys made a flat path for Him, clouds would have made His clothing and lightning His crown. Streams would have leaped for joy and deserts bloomed as a garden. Shout the good news! Messiah has come.

The coming of Christ in cosmic meaning was explosive and decisive. It meant the end of one age and the beginning of another. He was the greatest human in history. He was more than human, of course, but in space and time Jesus Christ stands above all others.

Christ had several tasks relating to the Law. His career revolved around the resolution of these needs. They sometimes came into conflict with each other. The achieving of one goal disrupted another.

1. Christ demonstrated what God wanted in man. He was what God wanted when He made Adam. Christ was therefore spoken as the second Adam (I Cor. 15:22). He was the "image" in which man had been cast (Heb. 1:1-3). What God wanted in the Law of Moses was someone like Christ (Rom. 8:1-3). He fulfilled the law as God had wanted when it was given at Sinai (Matt. 5:17). What God wanted in the remnant He demonstrated in Christ, God's true suffering Servant (Matt. 12:17). He was what God wanted of the church Christ was to establish (Eph. 4:12-16). He is the model for the new "humanity" God intended to create in Christ (Eph. 2:15f.). In short, a humanity having the personality and character of Jesus Christ was what God intended for man from the very beginning (Rom. 8:29).

Because of this, Jesus needed to demonstrate the Law was just and right, and man could and should have kept it. He kept it as God intended it be kept.

2. Christ needed to reinterpret the Law for men, placing things in proper perspective. The Law was never intended

209

to be a rule for all mankind. It was for the "house of Israel." To be fit for all mankind, the specific ceremonies and a one-location Temple were not appropriate. Christ needed to set out with some authority what ethics and duty would be when the kingdom came. For that reason He often contrasted what had been written with what He would bring (Matt. 5:21ff.).

> You have heard that it was said, "Do not commit adultery." But I say to you that anyone who looks at a woman lustfully has already committed adultery in his heart.

Many of the teachings of Jesus were efforts to separate principles of the Law from the specific statutes. In that former age, when Israel was a child (Hos. 11:1ff.), he needed the specific regulations to remain faithful. When he had grown up, and no longer needed that kind of tutor, the Law ended (Gal. 4:1, 2). Two principles of the Law constituted its very heart and soul, Jesus said. One was taken from the ancient Hebrew *shema* (Deut. 6:5).

> "Teacher, which is the greatest commandment of the Law?" Jesus replied, "Love the Lord your God with all your heart, and with all your soul, and with all your mind. And the second is like it: Love your neighbor as yourself" (Matt. 22:36ff.).

Jesus understood the concept of priority in matters of faith and order. All commands have their respective values. There will always be cases of conflict of law and even of principle. Jesus' complaint against the Pharisees was they held no sane priority system in the Law of Moses. Worse yet, when there was an apparent conflict of law, they chose to enforce the one that made them look better, and which made the other person look worse (Mark 7:1ff.).

3. Christ came to put an end to the entire Mosaic system. He was to be its last sacrifice (Heb. 1:3). The Law was to remain in force until "all be accomplished" (Matt. 5:18). Jesus was put to death as a law breaker. Although He appeared to be quite human to His enemies, He told them He was the Son of God, "thus making himself equal with God" (John 5:18). In their eyes He was a lawbreaker. For that He ought to die, they said at His trial (Matt. 26:65). From their human and legal point of view they were right. For that reason, Jesus declared, they could indeed insult or "blaspheme" Him at that time, and it would be forgiven them. They would yet see the resurrection and perhaps believe. But, He said, whoever blasphemes the Holy Spirit (attributes to the Devil His message) would never be forgiven (Mark 12:37ff.).

When He died upon the cross, the last sacrifice was finished. It was for that reason He had come into the world (John 12:27, 28). When that goal was won, Jesus ended the Law.

> It is finished (John 19:28). In that moment the curtain of the Temple was torn in two from top to bottom (Matt. 27:51).

Paul interpreted the meaning of the event.

> . . . having cancelled the written code with its regulations that was against us and that opposed us; he took it away, nailing it to the cross. And having disarmed the powers, he made a public spectacle of them, triumphing over them by the cross (Col. 2:14, 15).

In a sense, Jesus was put to death by the Law. He did good, but the law still condemned Him. That was why Paul later used such references as "against which there is no Law" (Gal. 5:22). The Law had outgrown its usefulness and had actually been used to crucify the Son of God. As

211

always, if anything adversely touched the success of God's mission, and the people of the covenant, and the success of the relationship, it was considered a vile thing. The very Torah had been used to slay Messiah. God nailed it to a tree. As the Law said, "Cursed be everyone that hangeth on a tree!" (Deut. 21:23).

From that time forward, the Torah was seen as an enemy of the people of God. Jesus and Torah, both servants of God were nailed to the cross together. One died for the sins listed by the other. When Jesus died, the Law died with Him. He was without sin, but died for sins identified in the Torah.

4. Jesus was related to the Law in another special way. He was Jehovah in a body (John 1:1, 14). He gave Abraham the covenant and spoke of grand things to come with him (John 8:56). He was the other party of the Mosaic Treaty. He wrote the Law of Moses, but kept hearing from the Jews, "We have Moses and the prophets. What do we need of you?" In the parable of the rich man and Lazarus we see the irritation reflected. When the rich man died and wanted someone to be sent back to warn his brothers, Jesus had Abraham hurl these words back at them: "They have Moses and the Prophets. Let them listen to them" (Luke 16:29). Jesus faced the same attack again and again. "We know Moses, and we know Abraham, and we know the Torah. But who do you think you are?" (John 8:53).

"Abraham is our father," they would say.

"If he were, you would do what he did: believe in and 'know' me."

"The only father we have is God Himself. We are chosen people," they replied. Jesus, exasperated with them, used the word "know." "I 'know' the Father, whom you claim as your God, though you do not 'know' Him." "Know" (Heb.

yada) was the intimate covenant-related word in the prophets. Keeping the word of the Lord was true *yada'*. Jesus told them they must now keep His—Jesus' word. If they did they would live forever, He said. Jesus said, in effect, Abraham was glad to have known Him even if the Jews were not. They understood the implication.

> "You are not yet fifty years old," the Jews said to him, "and have you seen Abraham?"
>
> "I tell you the truth," Jesus answered, "before Abraham was born, I am" (John 8:57).

The Voice speaking to Moses from the burning bush had said, "I am. . . ." The word *YHWH* was a form of the words, "I am." Jesus irritated the Jews by constantly referring to himself with the same sound. "I am the door," "I am the bread of life," "I am the good shepherd," etc.

The fact was, Jesus was the party of the first part of the covenants. He was the Suzerain who offered a vassal relationship to Abraham, Israel and David. The descendants of those men didn't know Him when they met Him. Christ spent a lot of time establishing His authority. He stilled the sea. "Even the winds and the sea obey him" (Matt. 8:27ff.). He raised the dead (Mark 5:35ff.). He changed the water into wine (John 2:11). He commanded demons and they obeyed, acknowledging His authority (Luke 9:28). He healed the leper and the infirm (Luke 5:12-18). In short, He demonstrated He controlled nature as God controlled it.

He made startling claims of which the following list is but an example. He claimed He had power to forgive sin (Mark 2:10), was God's Son (John 5:17), was to raise the dead (John 5:21f.), was to be judge of mankind (John 5:21ff.), was the very picture of God, (John 14:6-9), was the only source of salvation (John 14:6), was sent by God into the

213

world (John 17:17), spoke the true words of God (John 8:23ff.), and He was coming again (John 14:1-4).

The point is, the demand of the Torah to observe what Moses had said was so deeply ingrained in them they could not give any credibility to their own Suzerain when He came to them in person.

Jesus stated He was lord of the Sabbath (Mark 2:28). He told a parable such as the prodigal son. It was His intent to show the father of the two sons was God, the younger son the gentiles—the "pig eaters," and the older boy the Jewish nation sulking because God loved all mankind.

In another parable He told of the vineyard owner who rented it to vinedressers. He sent men to collect his due. They treated them shamefully. He sent his son. They killed him. Jesus then asked what the owner ought to do.

"He will bring those wretches to a wretched end," they replied, "and he will rent the vineyard to other tenants. . . ."

Jesus said to them, "Have you never read the scripture,

The stone the builders rejected has become the capstone;

the Lord has done this,
and it is marvelous in our eyes?

Therefore I tell you that the kingdom of God will be taken away from you and given to a people who will produce its fruit. Who falls on the stone will be broken to pieces, but he on whom it falls will be crushed" (Matt. 21:43).

He was not talking merely about the particular administrators of the Torah in His own time. He was speaking of the end of the entire system. "It will be given to a *people*," Jesus said. It was the same word He used in the third promise to Abraham, "and in your 'seed' will all *people* of the world

214

be blessed." That same word appeared in the great commission, "Go and make disciples of all the *people* . . ."

One time a military officer asked Jesus to help his servant who was at home in great distress. Jesus agreed to come. The centurian said,

> I do not deserve to have you come under my roof, but just say the word and my servant will be healed. For I myself am a man under authority with soldiers under me. I tell this one, "Go," and he goes; and that one, "Come," and he comes. . . .
>
> Jesus heard this and was astonished and said to those following him, "I have not found anyone in Israel with such great faith. I say to you that many will come from the east and the west, and take their places at the feast with Abraham, Isaac, and Jacob in the kingdom of heaven. But the subjects of the kingdom will be thrown outside, into the darkness, where there will be weeping and grinding of teeth (Matt. 8:8ff.).

Jesus understood the centurian to represent the gentiles who would accept the authority of Christ, and enter His service with a good heart. He saw the "subjects of the kingdom," to be the Jewish nation, the entire old economy, the Mosaic Treaty people. The former faithful Hebrews who were true to YHWH (and thus to Jesus) would, of course, be at the great celebration. They were represented by Abraham, Isaac, and Jacob. Jesus was One with the Jehovah of the Old Covenant. He had the authority to do what He wanted with it. In fact, the entire Old Covenant was in such disarray Jehovah was almost obligated to step in and save the situation. He did so in Christ. He swept it all away, proclaiming grace to all who would have been condemned by that Law. Only those who loved the covenant more than the Lord of the covenant were excluded from the new era.

Jesus made it clear He was not merely another prophet. "If you knew who it was who was speaking to you, you would ask from him living water," he told the Samaritan woman (John 4:10). He was not the "best man" at a wedding, He was the bridegroom.

> How can the guests of the bridegroom mourn while he is with them? The time will come when the bridegroom will be taken from them; then they will fast. No one sews a patch of unshrunk cloth on an old garment. . . . Neither do men pour new wine into old wineskins. If they do the skins will burst (Matt. 9:14-17).

The principle may be applied in any number of ways, but the immediate context of the passage was in direct reference to an observance held in high regard by the Pharisees, keepers of the Old Covenant. The Old Covenant could not hold the new wine of Christ's coming kingdom and covenant. He was not planning to patch up, as a prophet might, the old robe of the Law. A new garment for a new age was the plan.

The "teachers of the Law" held a view Elijah must come before the Son of Man came. Jesus agreed that Elijah must come before the Messiah would come. He identified John the Baptist as Elijah and Himself as the Son of Man.

> Elijah has already come, and they did not recognize him, and have done to him everything they wished. In the same way the Son of Man is going to suffer at their hands. Then the disciples understood he was talking to them about John the Baptist (Matt. 17:10ff.).

And,

> The Law and the prophets were proclaimed until John. Since that time the good news of the kingdom of God is being preached . . . (Luke 16:16).

216

The greatest example of the abiding authority of Christ compared to the authority of the Old Covenant was at the transfiguration. He was pictured as white as snow and glowing. His entire body was transfigured. Years before Moses came off the mountain with only his face aglow. At the side of Jesus appeared Moses the Lawgiver. He represented the Old Covenant. On the other side was Elijah. (He had come after all!) He represented the best of the old Prophets. There the three stood before the Apostles talking to each other.

> . . . a voice from the cloud said, "This is my Son whom I love; with him I am well pleased. Listen to Him."
>
> When they looked up they saw no one except Jesus (Matt. 17:1ff.).

The meaning was clear. God commanded men to listen to Jesus. They were not to listen to Moses. They were not to listen to Elijah. Christ was the Son of God. He had authority to do anything He wanted. The prophet Jeremiah in the passage declaring the coming new covenant (31:31) referred to the forgiveness of sin. Jesus was God and had the authority to forgive sin.

> When Jesus saw their faith he said to the paralytic, "Take heart, son, your sins are forgiven."
>
> At this, some of the teachers of the Law said to themselves, "This fellow is blaspheming!"
>
> Knowing their thoughts, Jesus said, "Why do you entertain evil thoughts in your hearts?
>
> Which is easier: to say, 'Your sins are forgiven,' or 'Get up and walk?' But so that you may know the Son of Man has authority on earth to forgive sins," then he said to the paralytic, "Get up, take your mat and go home" (Matt. 9:3ff.).

217

The confrontations Jesus had with people were always over the issue of the authority of the Old Covenant as opposed to his authority. If Jesus had been no threat to that entire system, he would not have encountered such bitter opposition.

The Covenant Orientation of Jesus

The word covenant is found infrequently in the bio-graphical-theological records about Christ.

The infrequent use of the word covenant is explained by understanding there was no real problem with the concept of covenant. Both sides agreed it was the frame-of-reference of all religious discussion. On that point Jesus and his enemies were agreed.

The reason for tension over religion was Jesus set about laying the foundation for changes in covenant. He spent much of His time, as we just saw, establishing the fact He had authority to do whatever He wanted to do with covenant or anything else. Every idea of Jesus, every sentence and every plea was related to a discussion of the three aspects of a Treaty: parties, terms or promises.

He intended to make significant changes in each. He planned to change the *parties* to the relationship. The original parties had been the blood descendants of Abraham through Isaac, and so forth. Jesus planned to sweep all that away.

> He came to his own but his own did not receive him; yet to all who received him to those who believe in his name, he gave the right to become children of God—children not born of natural descent . . . but of God (John 1:11ff.).

The Jews understood what "disciple" meant: the party to a covenant, at least in the minds of the Israelite. This exchange with a man showed it.

He answered, "I have told you already and you do not listen. Why do you want to hear it again? Do you want to become his disciples too?"

Then they hurled insults at him and said,

"You are this fellow's disciple! We are disciples of Moses! We know what God spoke to Moses, but as for this fellow, we don't even know where he comes from" (John 9:28, 29).

Jesus said to Nicodemus,

"I tell you the truth, unless a man is born of water and the Spirit, he cannot enter the kingdom of God. Flesh gives birth to flesh, but the Spirit gives birth to spirit" (John 3:5).

Christ's philosophy of covenant was similar in some ways to the old Covenant and different in some ways. Covenant implied mutuality. Jesus held all men to be responsible for evidence. Words opened the hearts of men. Men must be born of the Spirit to be sons of God, He said (John 3:1-5). Words opened men's hearts, and by words they are born of the Spirit.

The Spirit gives life; the flesh counts for nothing. The words I have spoken to you are spirit and they are life (John 6:63).

The code of Moses had said, "Now choose life that you and your children may live, and that you may love the Lord your God, listening to his voice . . ." (Deut. 30:19). Men who do not believe refuse to do so because they would rather have the praise of their peers than the good will of God. Jesus did not believe men were depraved. He held them responsible.

How can you believe if you accept praise from one another, yet make no effort to obtain the praise that comes from the only God? (John 5:44).

Jesus changed *stipulations* not only in the specifics of obligation but also in the nature of the Torah. Jesus' code was psychologically sound. It was positive. It focused attention on the goals and not on the punishments of covenant. The former covenant had said, "Cursed be. . . ." Jesus' covenant said, "Blessed are ye. . . ." As regarded the psychological stance of covenant, the contrasts were striking.

The Moses Code	*The New Code*
"Cursed is the man who carves an image."	"Blessed are the poor in spirit, for theirs is the kingdom."
"Cursed is the man who moves a boundry stone."	"Blessed are the meek, for they shall inherit the earth."
"Cursed is the man who dishonors. . . .'"	"Blessed are the merciful. . . ."
"Cursed is the man who withholds justice."	"Blessed are those who hunger and thirst after righteousness."
"Cursed is the man who accepts a bribe to kill an innocent person."	"Blessed are the peacemakers, for they shall be called sons of God."
"Cursed is the man who does not uphold the words of this law" (Deut. 27:15ff.).	"Blessed are you when people insult you, persecute you, and falsely say all kinds of evil against you because of me" (Matt. 5: 1ff.).

Jesus summed up all his ethical principles into one definition. Godliness was the sum of ethic, He said.

Be perfect as your heavenly father is perfect (Matt. 5:48). The command is without real value, however, without an adequate description of what God is and does. God was described by Jesus as similar to an earthly father. He loved His children and did good for them (Matt. 7:7). He allowed them to seek their own way (Luke 15:11ff.) and learn from experience. He was willing to throw off all dignity and status and run weeping for joy toward a lost son who was returning home. He threw His arms around him, restored him to the family and declared a holiday with wonderful celebration. The best definition of God-like thinking, feeling, decision making, and behavior was Jesus. He was one with the Father (John 10:30). To be like Christ was to be like God. Christlikeness was Godliness.

A student is not above his teacher, but everyone who is fully trained will be like his teacher (Luke 6:40).

The word "student" in this passage was the Greek word "disciple." And the word "teacher" the word "master." Consequently another version of the same passage might read,

No disciple is greater than his master, but when every disciple is perfected, fully taught, he will be like his master.

Later, when the New Covenant was officially inaugurated, the Apostles of Christ used Christ as the example of all good things. "Ye must be holy as I am holy," now read, "Ye must be like Christ."

Christlikeness as Covenant Ethic

The ethics of the Old Covenant were bound up in the administration of the stipulations of the Theocratic Law. A diagram (on page 222) will show the essential relationship and priority system. They key ethical terms employed in the Torah and the prophets will be shown.

God's relationship with Israel was in covenant, identified by the large circle. Then there was the entire matter of attitude toward the relationship. The attitude of covenant support, or covenant faithfulness with a good and cordial heart was called *hesed* and is carried by the middle-sized circle.

WHAT THE BIBLE SAYS ABOUT COVENANT

Ethical Generalities

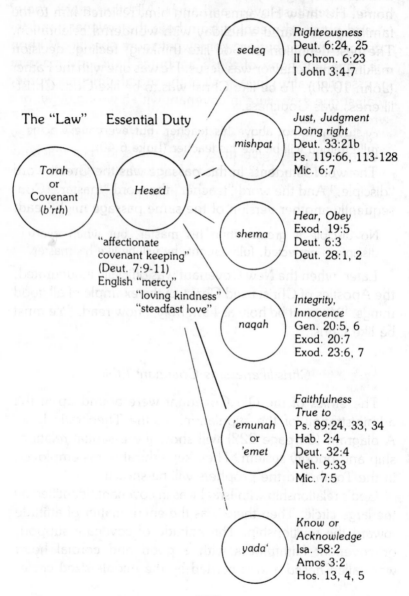

Righteousness
Deut. 6:24, 25
II Chron. 6:23
I John 3:4-7

sedeq

The "Law"   Essential Duty

Torah
or
Covenant
(*b'rth*)

— *Hesed*

Just, Judgment
Doing right
Deut. 33:21b
Ps. 119:66, 113-128
Mic. 6:7

mishpat

"affectionate
covenant keeping"
(Deut. 7:9-11)
English "mercy"
"loving kindness"
"steadfast love"

Hear, Obey
Exod. 19:5
Deut. 6:3
Deut. 28:1, 2

shema

Integrity,
Innocence
Gen. 20:5, 6
Exod. 20:7
Exod. 23:6, 7

naqah

Faithfulness
True to
Ps. 89:24, 33, 34
Hab. 2:4
Deut. 32:4
Neh. 9:33
Mic. 7:5

'emunah
or
'emet

Know or
Acknowledge
Isa. 58:2
Amos 3:2
Hos. 13, 4, 5

yada'

222

Hesed is weakly rendered in English: "mercy," "loving kind-ness," "steadfast love," and such. All other ethics rooted in and obtained meaning from both the covenant and the support-attitude but are somewhat more specific. Without the covenant none of these attributes have any meaning or essential value. In fact, all of the moral attributes worked against one if he were in covenant with a wrong deity, or a wrong person.

Jesus taught that His words were the new Torah. A "New Commandment I give unto you," He said. His teachings were to become the standard of all future judgment.

Ethical Generalities

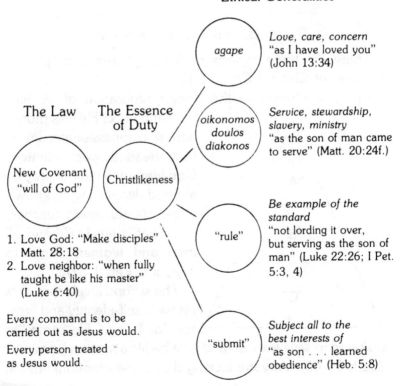

agape — Love, care, concern "as I have loved you" (John 13:34)

The Law — The Essence of Duty

oikonomos doulos diakonos — Service, stewardship, slavery, ministry "as the son of man came to serve" (Matt. 20:24f.)

New Covenant "will of God" — Christlikeness

"rule" — Be example of the standard "not lording it over, but serving as the son of man" (Luke 22:26; I Pet. 5:3, 4)

1. Love God: "Make disciples" Matt. 28:18
2. Love neighbor: "when fully taught be like his master" (Luke 6:40)

Every command is to be carried out as Jesus would.

Every person treated as Jesus would.

"submit" — Subject all to the best interests of "as son . . . learned obedience" (Heb. 5:8)

As for the person who hears my words and does not keep them, I do not judge him. . . .

There is a judge for the one who rejects me, and does not accept my words, the very word that I speak will condemn him on the last day (John 12:47).

The word of Christ is the Torah of the New Covenant. Above is a drawing showing the key words as defined by Jesus.

Christlikeness was the ethical demand of the coming kingdom. Jesus was the "Word become flesh." Not only were His instructions the new law of righteousness, but His example was equally instruction.

The A, B, and C of Christlikeness

There are three aspects or levels of true and spiritual imitation of Christ (I Cor. 11:1).

Level one refers to the honest replication of his life-

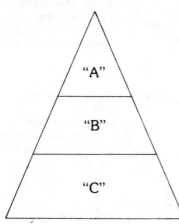

style and ethic. He was moral, honest, compassionate, direct, clear headed, goal oriented, God fearing, a man of prayer, a good leader, with knowledge, steady, good teacher, etc. That is level "C" and all men and women ought to copy it (I Pet. 1:21).

The second level represents his basic self-identity and "reason for living." He came "to seek and to save the lost, and give his life a ransom for many" (Mark 10:45). Anyone lacking that same emotional-moral commitment, the same longing is unlike Christ in his most definitive self-perception. "As I have been sent, so send I you" (John 20:21). Sharing Christ's same purpose for living is Christlikeness "B."

The third level is the replication of his method: equiping others to carry on with us and after us. That is Level "A." He taught and asked His disciples to teach. He left heaven and commanded His disciples to go into all the world. He showed them how, turned it over to them, and returned to heaven. It is unlike Christ to serve well but neglect to educate, train, equip and commission others (II Tim. 2:2). Insuring the success of the mission after we are gone by converting, enlisting to service, equipping, and helping others get started in some kind of church/mission service is like Christ and therefore high Biblical ethic. It is what the chart identifies as Level "A."

Jesus changed the *promises* of the covenant radically. He was not interested in appealing to men by physical promises, though He gave some. His covenant resulted in eternal life. Whoever drank the water He had to give drank to eternal life (John 4:13). Whoever ate the manna He brought would never die (John 6:30ff.). The sheep hearing His voice would be led both in and out.

My sheep listen to my voice, I know them and they follow me, and I give them eternal life (John 10:17ff.).

Whoever listened to the voice of Christ will live forever.

"Your brother will rise again."
"I know he will rise again in the resurrection at the last day."
Jesus said to her, "I am the resurrection and the life. He who believes in me will live even though he dies . . ." (John 11:25).

225

The promises of the former covenant were all physical, national and more or less immediate. They were immediate in that they were limited to earthly blessings. It was in regard to the matter of defective promise the writer of Hebrews said,

> But the ministry is as superior to theirs as the covenant of which he is mediator is superior to the old one, and it is founded on better promises (Heb. 8:6).

Even if a Jew had lived in a time when both he and his neighbors kept the Law of Moses perfectly, and received all the blessings of the land, yet there was something missing. Jesus said,

> For whoever wants to save his life shall lose it but whoever loses his life for me and the gospel will save it. What good is it for a man to gain the whole world, yet forfeit his soul? Or what can a man give in exchange for his soul? (Mark 8:35-37).

Jesus continued the teaching by placing the promises within the context of stipulation. Promises, in covenant, were conditional.

> If anyone is ashamed of me and my words in this adulterous generation, the Son of Man will be ashamed of him when he comes in his Father's glory with the holy angels (Mark 8:38).

The Death and Resurrection of Christ

All essential matters in the new covenant had an Apostolic linkup to the death and resurrection of Christ.

> What shall I say? "Father save me from this hour?" No, it was for this very reason I came to this hour (John 12:28).

In the section of this study dealing with Paul's theology of the new covenant we shall follow some implications of the above statement by Jesus. It is sufficient here to show Christ understood his death as formal covenant ratification.

This cup is the new covenant in my blood (Luke 22:20).

This is my blood of the covenant which is poured out for many for the forgiveness of sins (Matt. 26:28).

The words "this is the blood of the covenant" were technical terms for formal covenant oath taking (Exod. 24:8). God was promising in the oath remission of sin through Christ. God signed, as it were, the New Covenant at Calvary. He signed it in blood. He pledged the same effort to save mankind as it cost in agony to lose His only begotten Son. As surely as Christ shed His blood at the cross so shall God save to the uttermost all who draw near to Him through Christ (Heb. 10:19-23).

Man has a tendency to doubt. He has a short memory of good things done for him. He is stubborn. The cross was meant to convince him of God's love. It was meant to attract him to grace.

But I when I am lifted up from the earth will draw all men to myself (John 12:32).

And Paul wrote,

Or do you show contempt for the riches of his kindness and patience, not realizing that God's kindness should lead you to repentance? (Rom. 2:4).

And,

If God is for us, who can be against us? He who did not spare his own son, but gave him up for us all—how will he not also along with him, graciously give us all things? (Rom. 8:31).

In the cross God's essential nature and character won. The more man sinned the more grace and love God showed.

227

Man pressed it to the very end. God did not flinch. What the promises of lands and houses, flocks and national power, promised in the Law could not do, God did at Calvary. He broke men's hearts and got their allegiance. It says something for God's image in man!

The cross assured all men of God's good will toward them.

But God demonstrated his love for us in this: while we were yet sinners Christ died for us (Rom. 5:8).

God raised Jesus from the dead, the first of millions! (I Cor. 15:20). God kept his commitment to Christ,

You will not abandon me to the grave, nor will you let your holy one see decay. You have made known to me the paths of life, you will fill me with joy in your presence (Ps. 28:10).

Paul called the resurrection a "guarantee offering." The sacrificial system provided Paul a frame-of-reference for the death and also the resurrection.

In the past God overlooked such ignorance, But now he commands all people everywhere to repent, For he has set a day when he will judge the world with justice by a man whom he has appointed. He has given assurance to all men by raising him from the dead (Acts 17:30, 31).

Abraham died without seeing the great promises. His bones lay in the purchased tomb. Moses lay in trans-Jordan. Aaron's dry bones slowly returned to dust in Canaan. David's tomb could be seen in Peter's time. The Son of David, the "seed" of Abraham, the prophet like unto Moses, does not lie in the snug earth.

He ever lives to make intercession for us (Heb. 7:25).

The resurrection authenticated the promises made at the cross. Without the resurrection, men prone to doubt would likely have termed the gifts at the cross empty promises and its hope just empty dreams.

> Jesus Christ, a son of David according to the flesh, but declared the Son of God with power by the resurrection (Rom. 1:1-4).

The Great Commission

When Christ died and was buried, the confused and dispirited disciples waited. On that resurrection morning the women found the tomb empty. They believed at first someone had taken the body away. They asked a man, supposedly the gardener, where the body had been taken. Jesus revealed Himself to them instructing them to tell the leaders of the disciples what they had seen. He walked through a wall into the room where they were meeting and greeted them. Some were terrified. Some doubted their own senses. A week later, when Thomas was present, he was asked by Christ to place his hand in the wound in the side and to touch the nail holes in the Lord's hands. Thomas was convinced at last.

> "My Lord and my God!"
> Then Jesus told him, "Because you have seen me you have believed. Blessed are those who have not seen me and believed."
> Jesus did many other miraculous signs in the presence of the disciples which are not recorded in this book. But these are written that you may believe that Jesus is the Christ, the Son of God, and by believing you may have life in his name (John 20:28-31).

He appeared to several during the next forty days (I Cor. 15:3-15). The forty days were significant. It was forty years before Israel entered Canaan after their salvation from Egyptian bondage. The events of the exodus were the foundation on which the Torah of Moses was built. The death and resurrection of Christ was the foundation of the entire Christian system. All mankind was freed from the bondage of sin at Calvary. Forty days after the resurrection the New Covenant was proclaimed at Pentecost. At that time the first members of that New Creation passed into New Canaan, the church (Heb. 12:18-23).

When it came time for Jesus to return to heaven to be seated at the right hand of God (Acts 2:25), He gathered His disciples and commanded them. He was on a mountain. Moses got the Law on a mountain. Christ gave the commission to the Apostles and to all future disciples. Here is an example of many concise summaries of the New Covenant to be found in the writing of the ancient church. Christ invoked His authority and said:

All authority in heaven and earth has been given to me. Therefore go and make disciples of all the nations, baptizing them in the name of the Father, and of the Son, and of the Holy Spirit, and teaching them to obey everything I have commanded you. And surely I will be with you always, to the very end of the age (Matt. 28:18-20).

Whenever one invokes authority he means what he is about to say has unusual significance. Christ said, in effect, "What I am about to say will never be contradicted by anyone in heaven or on the earth. You may utterly depend upon what I shall say. I have the authority to say it, the complete authority of heaven and earth." Do you remember the invocation to the witnesses to the first covenant?

Hear O heavens and give ear O earth to what the Lord says . . . (Deut. 32:1; Isa. 1:2).

Jesus was not invoking witnesses; he was through with that kind of thing. He just stated it plainly. It was above

230

contradiction. There are in the English version of the command four verbs: go, make disciples, baptizing, and teaching. In the Greek there was only one verb in the imperative mood. The other three were participles. Participles modify verbs, telling when and how the command was to be accomplished.

He said, "having gone, MAKE DISCIPLES, baptizing them . . . and teaching them." Success or obedience was to be measured not merely by going, teaching or baptizing, but by making converts. To paraphrase the commission, what Jesus said was this:

> Go everywhere and carry out your covenanted duty—to make converts to me. Obtain from them a pledge of allegiance to me, explaining they must do whatever I have commanded you. My covenant promise is this: I will be going with you, suffering with you, glorying with you, and if you should die for it, I will be there dying with you. I will never forsake you.

Parties: God and the disciples of Christ

Terms: Go, MAKE DISCIPLES, baptizing, teaching to obey Christ.

Promises: "I will be with you always."

The Radical Reinterpretation of Scripture

There is no doubt the Apostles had a new and radical use of the Old Testament scriptures. At first glance it seems almost lawless. They seemed to take "out of context" many Old Testament passages. I think they got their basic principle of interpretation from Jesus himself. No other source accounts for their uniform departure from usual use of documents. Jesus explained after His resurrection how the prophecies of Old Canon applied to Him (Luke 24:44, 45). He taught

231

them to use the concept of parallelism. They were familiar with it as a Hebrew literary form: the repeating of a concept in the second word or phrase.

> The second line of a couplet need not be a separate statement from that of the first line, but may be, in the spirit of parallelism, a saying over again of what has been said.[25]

Now, Jesus would have said, "Apply the same principle to Israel as the 'son' of God and me as the Son of God. My career paralleled the career of Israel: Born into a covenant, fled into Egypt, came out of Egypt, was tempted forty *yom*, came home to Canaan, organized the twelve, gave new "commandments" on a mountain, lived and worked among men teaching them to be good servants of God, suffered "death" and was raised again, and ushered in a new era having a "new" covenant with Messiah as the new Son of David."

This will help explain the somewhat odd selection of scriptures from the Old Testament, such as "Out of Egypt have I called my son." The original context was quite different in tone from Matthew's use of it.

The Original	*The Parallelism*
When Israel was a child I loved him, and out of Egypt I called my son.	"Out of Egypt I have called my son" (Matt. 2:15).
But the more I called him, the further they went from me (Hos. 11:1).	"The child became strong; he was filled with wisdom and the grace of God was upon him" (Luke 2:40).

---

25. R. G. Moulton, *Hebrew Literary Forms,* Boston: D. C. Heath Co., 1899, p. 65.

Apart from seeing parallels, the use of the scripture was "out of context." The passage in Hosea was not meant as predictive prophecy when written, but could be used, according to Jesus, as parallel prophecy.

The principle seemed to be: whatever in the experience of Israel or David paralleled the life of Christ was understood as a type of prophecy. The Apostles understood the age of the "Kingdom of God" or the "Kingdom of heaven" (they are one and the same), to be the age of Messiah's reign. The era of the church was the fulfillment of the passages describing the glories of the returned remnant. They became the "gathered" of the New Testament. They saw the church as the only "Israel of God" (Gal. 6:14-16). Although there are limited studies available, it seems likely the basic eschatology of the Apostles was rooted in a continued parallelism with the life of Israel-Christ. The church would have its entry into Canaan, its preaching of the New Messiah and his Torah, its trauma toward the end of history, i.e., its cross, and its glorious resurrection and the reign of God in the "eternal kingdom." The details of the career of the church are no easier to harmonize with the details of the life of Christ than it was to harmonize the details of the life of Christ with that of Israel. There can be no doubt the Apostles held the philosophy of parallelism however.

So Christ came and ended the age of Moses and the prophets. When Moses came, it was as moonlight on the darkened earth. When Messiah came the daybreak came, bringing salvation and warmth to all mankind.

I would not discredit Moses for he was faithful in his day and faithful in his generation. No other mortal man was ever honored in life and death as he was honored, for on the height of Pisgah he viewed the land that God promised

to Abraham, Isaac and Jacob. He died and He who made
and governs the world buried and left him there and I say,
"Noble man of God, noble toiler, self-sacrificing, self-forget-
ing, servant of God, rest! Thy labor is done, thy laurels are
won. I will not detract from thy glory." But he to whom I
pay this tribute said that the day would come when God
would raise up one whom men should revere in all things
(Deut. 18:15, 18). He has come and the angels from the
mighty hosts of heaven came down to earth to sing the
sweetest of lullabies in the records of time over the cradle in
the manger of Bethlehem. He lived and walked and taught
among men and finally the shadows of death settled down
upon His pathway. He was our pilot toward the promised
land; He who forgot Himself and unselfishly labored for
others came down to the lowest depths that men might
live. He died for them. The weight of the world's woe broke
His tender heart; the sun went out in darkness and the very
earth that He made by His own Omnipotent power reeled
like a drunken man or like a storm-tossed ship. But He
came up again and He has gone to be with God: He has
entered heaven by His own blood. Sleep on Moses! Reign
on Messiah! On thy brow, O Moses, I press the chaplet thou
didst so well and honestly win. Reign on Messiah! I press on
Thy noble brow the combined diadems, the combined crowns
of all the kings, of all the emperors, and of all the rulers of
earth! Reign on Messiah until all the hearts of earth and
heaven shall be attuned to Thy praise! Reign on Messiah
until all the kingdoms of this world shall be swallowed up in
Thy kingdom! Reign on Messiah until every knee shall bow
and every tongue confess! Reign on Messiah until earth rises
to Thee and heaven comes down to us and in Thy glory we
shall behold Thy face and join with all the sanctified in every
age in singing the song of Him who slept near Pisgah's height
and to the Lamb that was slain! Reign on Messiah until there

shall not be any rebellion, any sin, any sorrow, any graves, any funerals in all Thy vast domain, when the kingdom shall be Thine and the glory shall be Thine, and when the New Jerusalem shall come down and we shall see Thy face and go out no more. Amen and amen.[26]

Conclusion

This chapter continued the story of the covenant and the people of the covenant from their captivity until the resurrection of Christ. The exile split the study of Israel into two parts: the Ezra-Nehemiah remnant of returnees to Judah and the Diaspora. The remnant rebuilt the nation. Under leadership who were very strict Covenanters, the nation recovered. They were then conquered by the Greek-Persian civilization. The Maccabees threw off the yoke and Israel enjoyed one hundred years of self-rule. Their dream of the Davidic Theocracy died as the Romans came (64 B.C.). Sects of the Jews quarreled. Division within the nation put a severe strain on any consensus about what the true covenanter was to do.

The Diaspora Jew needed to be converted all over again. The Jerusalem leadership led in this by sending delegates called *apostolos*. Synagogues sprang up and a new type of Judaism grew: Talmudic Judaism. The Diaspora Jew accepted into its ranks converts from among the Gentiles. They required them to honestly believe in Jehovah God, be circumcised, be baptized and offer a sacrifice. This allowing of converts and the widening rift in theology that practice introduced threatened the nature of the Old Covenant itself. Both groups were in disarray.

---

26. Ashley Johnson, *Sermons on the Two Covenants*, Delight, Arkansas: Gospel Light Publishing Company, reprint 1899, p. 165, 166.

In short, the idea of covenant, at least as administrated by the Israelites was under more pressure than it could bear.

At that point in history the Lord Jesus Christ was born and lived. He intended to renew the covenant with Israel along radically new lines. He had in mind to change the parties, and the terms, and the promises. To do that He established His authority as God's Son. His opposition came from the Jewish establishment who held their grip on Moses too tightly to see it was Jehovah Himself who was speaking with them. Jesus gave a clear idea of what the New Covenant would be.

God signed the New Covenant at Calvary in the blood of Christ. He established Christ's authority in the resurrection. God showed good will to man at the cross. He demonstrated His power to do what He promised in the resurrection. Before Christ ascended He commissioned His disciples to make disciples of all the nations based upon His eternal authority.

Parties: Christ's disciples
Terms: Make Disciples of all Peoples
Promises: "I will be with you always"

Questions on Chapter Five

1. T   F   The pre-exile prophets pictured a glorious return to Canaan.
2. T   F   Most of the Exiles came home with Ezra and others.
3. T   F   Most of the Exiles stayed and lived in the land of the exile.
4. T   F   Israel never became a real independent nation after the return.
5. T   F   Ezra and Nehemiah accepted converts to Judaism.

236

6. T   F   The Jews of the Diaspora accepted gentile converts as Jews.

7. T   F   Several of the post-exile kings were of David's line.

8. T   F   Jesus understood it was He who met and talked to Abraham.

9. T   F   The exiles sent money to and sometimes visited Jerusalem.

10. A person sent from Ezra to the exiles as delegate was called   a) Jews   c) Diaspora
       b) Servants   d) Apostolos

11. Jesus' greatest theological and personal battle was over
    a) Authority   c) His teaching on the Law
    b) His parentage   d) His refusal to fast

12. Name the three aspects of a covenant.
    a) _____
    b) _____
    c) _____

13. What three things did a Gentile have to do to become a Jew?
    a) _____ b) _____ c) _____

14. John's baptism was kind of
    a) foolish way of doing a "works righteousness."
    b) "choosing into" the coming Messiah's group in advance
    c) act that pictured the death and resurrection of Christ
    d) ritual the Jews liked to do.

15. The various groups in Israel were
    a) friendly rivals
    b) very critical of each other
    c) tried to stamp others out

16. Jesus intended to alter the old covenant as to
    a) parties but not stipulations
    b) promises but not parties
    c) stipulations but not promises
    d) the parties and stipulations and the promises.

17. Jesus said the two greatest commandments were
    a) _____
    b) _____

PLEASE TURN THE BOOK OVER FOR ANSWERS.

17. "love God"; "love neighbor"
16. d)
15. b)
14. b) "choose in"
13. Circumcision if a male; Immersion in water; Sacrifice
12. Parties; Terms or stipulations; Promises
11. a)
10. d)
9. T
8. T Jesus was the "Word of God," and the same God as spoke to Moses in the bush and gave the covenant to Abraham. Do not attempt to define too sharply the "trinity" but understand the Father, Son, and Holy Spirit are One God. Jesus' point was that He had been directing Israel's destiny all along.
7. F
6. T
5. F
4. F
3. T
2. F
1. T

Chapter Six

THE APOSTOLIC THEOLOGY OF TWO COVENANTS

Jesus issued the marching orders of the church. The last promise given to Abraham was about to be fulfilled. The plan of the ages was now being fully revealed (Rom. 16:26).

Go and make disciples of all the nations, baptizing them in the name of the Father, and the Son and the Holy Spirit, teaching them to observe all that I have commanded you . . . (Matt. 28:18-20).

The Apostles waited in Jerusalem as told by Jesus until they received "power from on high." God wanted it clear the Apostles spoke for Christ. When they spoke, it was the Lord Jesus speaking.

I have given them your word and the world has hated them, for they are not of the world any more than I am of the world. My prayer is not that you take them out of the world, but that you protect them from the evil one. . . . Sanctify them by the truth; your word is truth. As you sent me into the world I have sent them into the world.

My prayer is not for them only. I pray for those who will believe on me through their message (John 17:14ff.).

All of the Apostles understood they had the authority to speak for Christ. To lie to them was to lie to the Holy Spirit. To disobey them was to disobey the Spirit. To listen to them was to hear what the Spirit was saying.

"And after it was sold, was not the money at your disposal? What made you think of doing such a thing? You have not lied to men but to God" (Acts 5:4).

But God has revealed it to us by his Spirit. . . . This is what we speak, not in words taught us by human wisdom, but in words taught by the Spirit, expressing spiritual truths in spiritual words (I Cor. 2:10ff.).

239

When you received the word of God, which you heard from us, you accepted it not as the word of men, but as it actually is, the word of God (I Thess. 2:13).

Dear friends, do not believe every spirit, but test the spirits to see whether they are of God, for many false prophets have gone out into the world. This is how you recognize the Spirit of God: every spirit that acknowledges that Jesus Christ has come in the flesh is from God. . . . We are from God, and whoever knows God listens to us; but whoever is not of God does not listen to us (I John 4:1-6).

Therefore he who rejects this instruction, does not reject man, but God, who gave us his Holy Spirit (I Thess. 4:8). So then, brothers, stand firm and hold to the teachings we passed on to you, whether by word of mouth of by letter (II Thess. 2:15).

He chose to give us birth through the word of truth, . . . humbly accept the word planted in you which can save you. Do not merely listen to the word, . . . but doing it—he will be blessed in what he does (James 1:18-25).

It was a fundamental assumption the Apostles spoke with authority. This was another basic assumption of the ancient church: the apostles both understood what Jesus wanted, and they were faithful in doing it. The acceptance of that assumption allows us to understand the purpose of the message, the church and the great commission. That is, we can look at the activities of the Apostles and know what Jesus wanted. We see they did two basic things: they established local churches, and they nurtured those congregations so they would become like Christ, and start other churches. They understood the great commission.

Acts and the New Covenant People

Jesus returned to heaven and the "last age" (Acts 2:17) commenced. The Spirit reversed the tragedy of the Tower of Babel and again had all men speaking and hearing one language: the gospel (Acts 2:1-13ff.). The Apostles under the guidance of the Holy Spirit, exercised their mandate and announced the new "election" of God: "All men who appeal to God in Christ will be saved" (2:21). They declared the Lord Jesus, risen from the dead, was indeed the very Lord and the long awaited Messiah—Christ. Christ was the Greek word for "anointed one."

When they heard this they were cut to the heart and said to Peter and the other Apostles,

"Men and brothers, what shall we do?"

Peter replied, "Repent and be baptized, every one of you, in the name of Jesus Christ, so that your sins may be forgiven and you will receive the gift of the Holy Spirit" (Acts 2:37, 38).

Jesus had given to the Apostles authority to set the terms of entry.

I will give you keys of the kingdom of heaven, and whatever you bind on earth will be bound in heaven, and whatever you loose on earth will be loosed in heaven (Matt. 16:19).

The reference surely was in regard to the church, as Jesus had elicited from them a clear statement of His identity and authority. He then declared His intention to establish a church, "and the gates of Hades will not overcome it." He used the terms kingdom and church interchangeably (Matt. 16:18 and 19), as did the other New Testament writers (Heb. 12:23 and 28).

The new Israel was organized into synagogue type assemblies who "devoted themselves to the Apostles' teaching, and to the fellowship (collections), to the breaking of bread and to prayer" (Acts 2:42), and "the Lord added to their number daily those who were being saved" (2:47).

Two Philosophies of Mission

In the Book of Acts there were two philosophies of mission, or rather, two ways of executing the one great mission. Both had far reaching theological implications. The Apostles represented the one procedure. The Apostle Paul the other. The two were not in conflict, certainly, yet the implications were so staggering each method ought to be identified more fully.

1. The *centripetal* theology of mission. The Apostles remained in Jerusalem as the Lord had commanded. As far as the book of Acts indicated they more or less remained there, leaving for special reasons only. The church did not engage in full scale mission to the Gentiles for many years, and then at the express demand of the Spirit (Acts 10:19, 20). Even then Peter was called to account for his actions by the Jerusalem church (Acts 11:1-4). This problem arose because of their "centripetal" theology. Centripetal means "thrown inward."[1] In A.D. 70 when Jerusalem fell and with it national Israel, this theology disappeared. The other theory, represented by Paul continued down through the centuries. Both were highly successful. Both fulfilled what the prophets had foretold.

In the days to come, the mountain of the Lord's house shall be set over all other mountains, . . . All nations shall come streaming to it, many peoples will say, "Come, let us climb

---

1. David W. Wead, "The Centripetal Philosophy of Mission," *Scripture, Tradition, and Interpretation*, W. Ward Gasque and William Sanford LaSor, ed., Grand Rapids: Eerdmans, 1978, p. 176-189.

242

up . . . to the house of the God of Jacob, that He may teach
us his ways, and we may walk in his paths."
For instruction issues from Zion, and out of Jerusalem comes
the word of the Lord;
He will be judge between nations, arbiter among many
peoples (Isa. 2:2 and Micah 4:1ff., NEB).

The Apostles went daily to the Temple to instruct the
diaspora Jews and proselytes who came to Jerusalem from
every nation. Acts chapter two listed over a dozen nations
sending representatives to Zion. They received instruction
from the Lord of the new era.

I am coming to gather all nations and tongues;
    and they shall come and see my glory.
And I will set a sign among them. And from them I will send
    survivors to the nations, to Tarshish,
Put, and Lud, who draw the bow, to Tubal and Javan, to
the coastlands far off, that have not heard my fame and
    seen my glory and they shall declare my glory among
the nations (Isa. 66:18, 19, RSV).

The Septuagint Greek text rendered the word "survivors"
or "fugitives" as *sesòsmenous*, "those who have been saved"!
It was understood by the Apostles they were the representatives of the King, ruling in Jerusalem. They taught the
visitors from all lands who came to the city and temple.
Those converted were not absorbed into the Jewish church
community, but returned to their own lands bearing to their
families and friends the glad tidings.

This is the first sure and certain mention of mission as we
today employ the term—the sending of individuals to distant
peoples to proclaim God's glory among them. This completely corresponds to the mission of the Apostles when
the church first began. One is amazed at it: here, just as the

243

Old Testament is coming to an end, God is already seen as leading from the narrow confines of the chosen people out into the whole, wide world . . . it is not that they all journey to Zion and are absorbed into the community there. The final thing is the way taken by the word borne by the messengers of His glory to the peoples who are not Israel to the nations of the world.[2]

Luke took great pains to record examples of specific parallels between the picture of the glorious reign of Messiah recorded in the prophets and what was happening in the church in Israel.

Isaiah 65:25	"the wolf and the lamb will feed together"	Acts 6:1-7
Isaiah 66:12	"I will extend peace to her . . ."	Acts 9:31
Isaiah 66:12	"and the wealth of nations like a flowing stream"	I Cor. 16:1-4
Jer. 31:19	"And I will add to her numbers"	Acts 2:47
Jer. 33:17	"David will never fail to have . . ."	Acts 7:56
Isaiah 49:6b	"I will make you a light to the Gentiles"	Acts 10-11
Isaiah 42:7	"Free captives from prison"	Acts 5:19
	"to release from the dungeon . . . darkness"	Acts 16:26
Isaiah 42:6	"to be a covenant to the people"	Acts 3:25
Isaiah 42:1	"I will put my Spirit on Him . . ."	Acts 7:55
Isaiah 42:7	"To open the eyes of the blind . . ."	Acts 9:18
Isaiah 44:18	"Forget the former things, do not dwell on the past . . ."	Acts 17:34
Isaiah 44:25	"and remember your sin no more"	Acts 3:19-21
Isaiah 44:56:4	"to the eunuchs who keep my Sabbaths . . ."	Acts 8:38

---

2. C. Westerman, *Isaiah 40-66*, 1969, p. 356.

Amos 9:11,12 "and Gentiles that bear my name" Acts 11:26
Amos 9:11,12 "I will rebuild the fallen house   Acts 15:14-16
of David"
Isaiah 2:4   "and settle disputes for many   Acts 15:1-8
peoples"
Isaiah 2:17   "Ananias heard this he fell down   Acts 5:5
and died"

There are almost endless examples from the various texts. These are sufficient to establish Apostolic thinking. The nations did flow into Jerusalem, the wealth gained from Gentiles came with them, "and they laid them at the Apostles' feet." The "Law of the Spirit" did go forth from the Temple to the ends of the earth. Former captives carried it back to their lands. What Isaiah had foretold came true.

Because their minds were blinded and carnal, the Jews thought the glory of David, or Babylon, or Rome was superior to the lowly prince of heaven, riding on the foal of an ass. They boasted in the blood of Abraham, but failed to honor Abraham's Suzerain. Similarly it is a carnal-minded man and a true descendant of the blinded Jews, who sees the church, Christ's body, as less glorious than Solomon's empire.

2. The other view of Mission was *centrifugal.* It went out from Jerusalem to the ends of the earth. Paul and Barnabas, Mark and Luke, Timothy, Titus, Aristarchus, Priscilla and Aquila are all examples. Whether in good times or bad, the church spread over all the earth, "as the waters cover the sea" (Isa. 11:9b).

> On that day a great persecution broke out against the church at Jerusalem, and all except the Apostles were scattered throughout Judea and Samaria.
> Those who had been scattered preached the word wherever they went (Acts 8:1ff.).

While they were worshipping and fasting, the Holy Spirit said, "Set apart for me Barnabas and Saul for the work to which I have called them" (Acts 13:2).

Both theologies of mission merged at last, as the age of the old National Theocracy ended in great trauma in 70 A.D., and as the Israel of God began to mature in her new role.

The Conversion of Saul

A most bitter enemy of the ancient movement was Saul of Tarsus. He was a Jew from the diaspora, but he was a blue-blood (Phil. 3:5ff.). He had the confidence of the Jewish establishment at Jerusalem (Acts 9:1f.), and was their agent to stamp out the "new sect." He struck fear into the hearts of the church. On his way to Damascus Christ appeared to him. He learned it was Jesus whom he had been persecuting.

"Saul, Saul, why do you persecute me?" the voice said to him.

"Who are you, Lord?" Saul asked.

"I am Jesus whom you are persecuting" (Acts 9:5).

He had been as blind as the other Pharisees. His blindness, whether by psychological reason, or an act of God, or both, helped contribute to his views of the Law of Moses, which had blinded his eyes. He later said he acted in all good conscience.

I have lived in good conscience all my life (Acts 23:1) so much so I persecuted the church (Phil. 3:6) and I did it in ignorance and unbelief (I Tim. 1:13).

A man named Ananias was sent to help Saul. He was told that Saul was a chosen vessel. Ananias asked Saul why he was waiting. He said, "Get up, be baptized, and wash away your sins calling upon the name of the Lord" (Acts 22:16). Saul became a great worker in the church. His companions became leaders in many churches. He contributed more documents to the New Testament Canon than any other author. He understood his duty to win the Gentiles to Christ (I Cor. 9:16-23). The first half of the Book of Acts dealt with the centripetal idea of mission, focusing on Peter and Jerusalem. The last half of Acts evidenced the centrifugal thrust of mission, as Paul and his helpers took the gospel to the ends of the earth. In my opinion there was none greater than Paul. He served his Lord faithfully until his death.

Clash of Covenant: First Jerusalem Conference

There was a very moral soldier named Cornelius. He was "God-fearing," generous, competent, a centurion of the Italian Band. Although not a proselyte, he had a good reputation among the Jews. He was a Gentile who believed in YHWH. While at prayer an angel told him to go to Joppa and find Simon Peter, Jesus' disciple. Cornelius sent for him at once. Although Cornelius was a very good man, had a vision, was complimented by God, well respected by all, and obedient to the angel by sending for Peter, he was not saved. Saved became the synonym for "knowing God," or having a covenanted relationship with God. The angel said to him,

Send to Joppa for Simon who is called Peter. He will give you a message through which you and all your household will be saved (Acts 11:14).

We see a reflection of the essential "conditionality" of the New Era. Regardless of the morality of a man, when

247

he was not in a relationship with Christ, he was not saved. We may say confidently the parties to the New Covenant were only those "in Christ" (Rom. 8:1).

God had somewhat more difficulty with the preacher than with the convert in this case. God prepared Peter for the event by lowering on a sheet, in a vision, all kinds of meat listed as unclean in the Torah. Peter was revolted at the thought of eating pig or snake, magpie, buzzard, cat, or lizard, because the Law did not approve eating these. Although the Law was long since dead on the cross Peter apparently needed the instruction again. He was told to kill and eat. He refused. He assured God,

> I have never eaten anything common or unclean. The voice came to him a second time, "Do not call anything impure that God has made clean." This happened three times . . . (Acts 10:13ff.).

Peter went with the delegates sent by Cornelius. He apparently protected himself by taking witnesses, because "some of the brothers" from Joppa went with him. In the Book of Acts, "brothers" quite frequently meant Jewish Christians, as in this case. They came to be witnesses for Peter, and he needed them at the conference later.

Peter preached to Cornelius' assembled group. He centered his message in the death, resurrection and authority of Christ. The Holy Spirit ratified his sermon: Gentile believers could become full members of Christ apart from any conversion to Judaism.

> The circumcised believers who came with Peter were astonished that the gift of the Holy Spirit had been poured out *even on the Gentiles* (Acts 10:45).

Peter then commanded them to be baptized. There would have been no problem with Cornelius. He had given every indication he was prepared to do whatever God wanted. But what about the "circumcised believers"? Peter challenged them to forbid water to baptize these Gentile believers. Then Cornelius and his household were introduced into the church as the Jews had been. The act was to cause great difficulty at Jerusalem.

When Peter went up to Jerusalem, the "circumcised believers criticized him," because he had gone into the house of uncircumcised men and ate with them. The real objection was the baptism of the Gentiles into the church without their having become Jewish proselytes first. The issue was clear. Was the new covenant the old covenant spiritualized? Was the new covenant added to the former one? Did a Christian have to become a Jew to become a member of the church? Peter explained that the Lord had asked him specifically to do what he had done, and the matter was closed—for the time being. What we have seen here is a contest of wills and a defining of the nature of the Christian oath. Is the believer in Christ pledging his loyalty to Christ or is it an oath to the Law of Moses and Christ? That is, to what extent was the believer in Christ obligated to the Law of Moses?

Clash of Covenant: Second Jerusalem Conference

The matter was not settled. Barnabas and Saul, now called Paul, had been making good progress in the Eastern Mediterranean area. Antioch was a key location from which the message spread to the Diaspora synagogues, and Gentile cities. The news of their success reached Jerusalem. Barnabas had been an *Apostolos* from Jerusalem to Antioch, and had been well received (Acts 11:22-25). Some men from

Jerusalem, not *Apostolos*, came to Antioch teaching the converts of Paul and Barnabas, "Unless you are circumcised according to the custom taught by Moses, you cannot be saved" (Acts 15:1). There arose a "sharp dispute and debate" over the issue. Several believers, including Barnabas and Paul, were sent by the churches to Jerusalem to put the question before the Apostles. There was a cordial reception. The glowing reports of the mission in Asia Minor were received with joy. Then the matter of the Covenant was brought up.

> Then some of the believers who belonged to the party of the Pharisees stood up and said,
>
> "The Gentiles must be circumcised and required to obey the Law of Moses" (Acts 15:5).

Jesus had been correct about the Pharisees. After the resurrection many came to believe He was exactly what He claimed. They became part of the church at Jerusalem. Their distinctive traits were yet exhibited in the church and they continued to support the Torah as Christian Law and Christ as Lord. They saw Him as Lord of a continuing national Israel.

Peter spoke at the beginning of the meeting. He reviewed the Pentecost event and his message there, and he called attention to Cornelius.

> He made no distinction between us and them, for he purified their hearts by faith.
>
> And now, why do we try to test God by putting on the necks of the disciples a yoke that neither we nor our fathers have been able to bear? No, we believe that it is through the grace of the Lord Jesus that we are saved, just as they are (Acts 15:9ff.).

250

The issue here was: do the Gentiles need to keep the Law of Moses, or at least agree to keep it to the same extent Jesus did, or to the best of their ability? Jesus had kept the Law in many ways, so we can see how the Pharisees (now Christian) might suggest being like Christ meant keeping the Law of Moses. There may have been a deeper issue at the bottom of the reasoning. If Christ were divorced from Law completely, what would come of the Hebrew philosophy of man, angels, heaven, ethics, the future of man, life after death, etc.? In short, they may have feared the loss of the entire Old Testament scriptures to the church.

Peter did not back away from the issue. He went further than he had ever gone to that point. Not only were the Gentiles saved by faith in Christ, as opposed to the Law of Moses, but so were the Jews! The Cornelius model of conversion was declared as the official model for all the church, Jew and Gentile! That was revolutionary at the time. It is apparent not all the believers accepted the judgment of the Apostle, for to his death Paul was followed about by Christian Jews subverting his theology of salvation by faith in Christ apart from the Law.

James spoke. He agreed the Gentiles were prophesied to be part of the church equally with Jews. He quoted Amos:

> After this I will return and rebuild David's tent. Its ruins I will rebuild . . . that the remnant of men may seek the Lord and all the Gentiles who bear my name . . . (Acts 15:16).

James understood the church to be the rebuilt fallen house of David. He understood the Gentiles to join the Jews in it. There could be only one Lord, one faith, one baptism for all (Eph. 4:1, 2). He realized the Law or covenant of Moses constituted a serious stumbling block to the average Gentile. He said,

251

It is my judgment, therefore, that we should not make it
difficult for the Gentiles who are turning to God . . . (15:19).

In saying this, he realized there might be a serious problem for the Jews of the Diaspora. Many Gentiles had been
studying the Torah, and held Moses in high respect. Genesis
contained a very radical, if reasonable, philosophy of God,
nature, and man. It would not do for the church to be understood as repudiating Moses. In other words, nothing ought
to be done to alienate the Jew or proselyte who loved Moses.
A Jew could keep the holidays as a Jewish patriot, and
refuse pork and read the Torah, but it had no authority
where the Apostles had spoken to the contrary. It was not
necessary for the Gentile either to know of Moses, or agree
to anything about the Torah when accepting the message
of grace in Christ. All men and women must declare allegiance to Christ, and Christ alone, in order to be saved.

A letter was sent to all the churches under the signature
of the elders and the Apostles. It effectively ended the
opposition to the gospel except for a few who dogged Paul
to his dying day. It was very difficult for a Jew, even knowing in his mind eating pork was all right, to sit at table with
those who did. The Torah was deeply engrained in the
Jew (Gal. 2:11ff.).

Two Covenants

The Apostles understood that every Book of the Old
Testament Canon was related in presupposition to the Torah.
Wisdom was keeping the Torah. Job was about suffering in
a righteous man, something the Torah had implied was not
to happen. The songs were in connection with the worship
of Israel, which, of course, was rooted in the Old Covenant at Sinai.

252

As a result, the Apostles uniformly separated the covenants of the Old Testament from Christ's covenant. They treated the religion of the Old Testament as a completely different covenant from that of Christ. They had a simple, rather clean-cut theology of the Two Covenants.

Passages that indicate the two covenant orientation of the Apostles will be numbered for easy reference. Some ideas will be taken from the Book of Hebrews, but an analysis of that document will be assigned another place.

1. Romans Seven

In Romans chapter seven, Paul tried to make it clear the Law was dead and gone. He used the illustration of marriage. When a husband, such as the Law, died, the woman was free to marry another. She was not free as long as the husband was alive. The Law of Moses was dead.

> So, my brothers, you also died to the Law through the body of Christ, that you might belong to another, to him who was raised from the dead, that you might bear fruit to God (Rom. 7:4).
>
> . . . we have been released from the Law, so we serve in the new way of the Spirit, not in the old way of the written code (Rom. 7:6).

What did Paul mean by the word law? As he usually used it, he meant Pentateuch: the Torah, the Old Covenant. In this passage he identified it as containing at least the Ten Commandments.

> I would not have known what it was to covet if the Law had not said, "Do not covet" (Rom. 7:7 from Deut. 5:21).

2. Romans Ten

Paul insisted the Jew was in grave difficulty if the Law was still in force against him. He was obliged to keep it perfectly, or risk the curses of the covenant. He was trying to be righteous by his own way of behaving. Paul believed in joining Christ one participated in all Christ was and had. He was as righteous as Christ, when "in Christ."

On the other hand, if the Law were done away, it no longer defined righteousness. God had brought a different and superior definition of what the word "righteous" meant. The definition was Christ, and being like Christ was the "law of the Spirit."

> Since they did not know the righteousness that comes from God, and sought to establish their own, they did not submit to God's righteousness.
>
> Christ is the end of the Law, so there may be righteousness for all that believe (Rom. 10:3, 4).

3. *Second Corinthians Three*

In this wonderful passage, Paul compared and contrasted the covenants. The descriptive words will be placed in the appropriate column. Certain translations use stronger words than others. The New International Version of II Cor. 3:6-18 is used here.

"Old Covenant"	*"New Covenant"*
"tables of stone"	"new covenant"
"in letter"	"in Spirit"
"kills"	"gives life"
"glory"	"greater glory"
"fading"	"permanent"
"brings condemnation"	"brings righteousness"
"Israelites look . . .	"we behold . . .
at Moses' face . . .	glory of the Lord . . .
which is veiled"	with unveiled face"
"veil lies over their minds"	"veil is taken away"
"mind hardened"	"we are being transformed"
	"the Lord is the Spirit"
	"there is freedom"

254

There seems to be no middle ground. It is all or nothing. Moses mediated a covenant dimming in value, as the glory of his face dimmed. The Ten Commandments were listed among the parts of the Old Covenant. If parts of the Ten Commandments were reinstated or approved by the Apostles, they were to be kept. They were to be kept, however, not because they were in the Old Testament, but because they were again authorized by Christ.

4. *Galatians Two*

> We who are Jews by birth and not "Gentile sinners," know that a man is not justified by observing the Law, but by faith in Jesus Christ . . . not by observing the Law because by observing the Law no man will be justified (Gal. 2:15, 16).

Justified meant, within the context of the Old Testament Law of Moses, the standard had been met. No one could be justified by that standard any longer (if indeed they ever could) because that standard was done away at the cross. The new standard was joining with Christ, becoming part of His very body, the church, and possessing the Holy Spirit, sharing in all Christ was and is. He was therefore justified by Christ, the new standard. When one lived as Christ wanted, not as the Law had demanded, it was no longer he that lived, but Christ lived again in him. A man could not keep the Law correctly anyway. His conscience was always troubling him. No one could ever feel freed from sin under the old way.

5. *Galatians Three*

One of the strongest presentations of the gospel as superior to the Code of Moses was Paul's treatment of Jesus as the "seed" of Abraham.

The gospel was preached in advance to Abraham: "All nations will be blessed through you" (Gal. 3:8).

Paul reminded all that Abraham had several sons by several wives. He had but one son given to him supernaturally, as it were: Isaac. Isaac was a son of promise and covenant blessings passed through him and only him.

The scripture does not say, "and to seeds," meaning many people, but, "and to your seed," meaning one person, who is Christ (Gal. 3:16).

Jesus stands where Isaac stood: covenant blessings flow through Him and only Him. Having the blood of Isaac was essential to be an heir of the promises. Having the blood of Christ now became equally essential, said Paul. Once it was Isaac's blood. Now it is Christ's blood that passed the covenant blessing along. One touched the blood when one declared his allegiance to Christ as Abraham did. Abraham entered into the covenant for himself, he personally "believed God," and that was his righteousness. That was all God asked. Now, all men must be like Abraham. They must also trust God, in Christ. They must believe that the promises made in Christ are as good as those made to Abraham. There is no way out: As Abraham risked all in belief of God's honor, so all men, personally must trust God's promises made at Calvary.

In the strongest statement Paul made about the matter he ended any hope of recovery for the Law.

You are all sons of God through Jesus Christ, for all of you who were baptized into Christ have been clothed with Christ. There is neither Jew nor Greek, slave nor free, male nor female, for you are all one in Jesus Christ.

If you belong to Christ, then you are Abraham's seed, and heirs according to the promise (Gal. 3:26ff.).

256

Paul followed the lead of Peter at the second Jerusalem conference: he reversed the argument. Peter said the Jews were saved by faith in Christ apart from the Law just as Gentiles were! Now Paul took away the last shred of pride in being a descendant of Abraham based on physical inheritance. Paul declared the Gentiles to be Israelites!

If you belong to Christ, then you are Abraham's seed and heirs of the promises.

A Jew not in Christ was "not my people" (Rom. 9:25). A Gentile in Christ was part of "all Israel" (Rom. 11:26). The "all Israel" of which Paul spoke was related to the covenant of the "deliverer from Zion,"

The deliverer will come from Zion; he will turn Godlessness away from Jacob,

And this is my covenant with them when I take away their sins (Rom. 11:26).

No one's sins can ever be taken away but through the blood of the second Isaac, Paul argued.

6. *Galatians Four*

Abraham had at least two sons, one by a slave woman named Hagar. Her boy was Ishmael. The son of a promise was Sarah's boy, Isaac. In the metaphor Paul joined the Covenant of Abraham and the Mosaic saying the latter was "added to" the former "until the Seed to whom the promise referred had come." One woman, Hagar, represented both the Law of Moses and the covenant of Abraham, except for the last unfulfilled promise. The other woman, Sarah, was the New Covenant. Her son was to inherit. Hagar's son would not inherit the covenant. Abraham sent Hagar and Ishmael away!

257

These things may be taken figuratively, for the women represent two covenants. One covenant is from Mount Sinai and
bears children who are to be slaves: this is Hagar. Now
Hagar stands for Mount Sinai in Arabia and corresponds
to the present city of Jerusalem, because she is in slavery
with her children. But the Jerusalem that is above is our
mother. . . .

Now you, brothers, like Isaac, are children of promise. . . .
But what does the scripture say, "Get rid of the slave woman
and her son, for the slave woman's son will never share in
the inheritance with the freed woman's son" (Gal. 4:24ff.).

Jerusalem is another name for the church when so modified.

But you have come to Mount Zion, to the heavenly Jerusalem, the city of the Living God . . . to the church of the
firstborn, whose names are written in heaven (Heb. 12:22f.).

When Paul said, "Cast out Hagar," he was only echoing
the parable of Jesus about the "sons of the Kingdom." He
meant "cast out the Covenant." In a real sense he meant,
"Cast out of any peace with God" based upon the Old Covenant. And as it referred to the Jerusalem of the New David,
it meant "Cast out of the city all non-Israelites-by-faith."
For Paul there was no possibility of two covenants existing
side-by-side in history, one for the Jews and one for the
Christian. There were two covenants but one replaced the
other completely. "Cast out Hagar."

7. *Ephesians Two*

Paul addressed the same problem in the epistle to Ephesus.
Once, he said, there were two kinds of people on earth:
Jews and Gentiles. The wall that created the division was
the Covenant of Moses (2:15). In Christ God destroyed the

barrier, "the dividing wall of hostility." He took it out of the way. Now all mankind is one and is freed from the Law.

> His purpose was to create in himself one new man out of the two, thus making peace, and in this one body to reconcile them both to God through the cross, by which he put to death their hostility. He came and preached peace to you who were "far away," and peace to those who were near. For through him we have access to God in one Spirit (Eph. 2:15b-18).

The former covenant, usually identified by Paul as the Law, was "destroyed," "abolished," "put to death." He used the word "covenant" in the previous passage (2:12) so we may understand Paul to mean the Old Covenant when he said, "the Law." There was a new people of God, a new commonwealth, a new "family of God." All men were equal before it. There was no more law of Moses. It was dead. The circumcised and the uncircumcised must "call" for grace.

> Consequently, you are no longer foreigners and aliens, but fellow citizens with God's people and members of God's household, built upon the foundation of the Apostles and the prophets, with Christ Jesus himself as the chief corner-stone (Eph. 2:19ff.).

The Apostles had authority to relate the two covenants in the way learned from Jesus. In these selected passages they reflect their orientation. The Old Law was gone, but the people of God continued on in Christ. The history of redemption carried on. The bringing men back to God continued. According to the Apostles, then, God's covenant history continued without interruption. It is vitally important that we allow the Apostles to state what continued and what did not. The lines they have drawn are normative for all ages, for all believers.

259

8. *Hebrews Seven*

> The Lord has sworn and will not change his mind, you are
> a priest forever,
> in the order of Melchizedek (Heb. 7:17 and Ps. 110:4).

The Law of Moses provided for a priesthood. It descended
from the house of Aaron. Levi also provided a priesthood,
the administrators of the Torah in key matters. The Law of
Moses said nothing about any other priesthoods. They were
illegal. But Jesus was a priest. The scripture called Him a
priest "forever." He was a priest like Melchizedek. That
amounted to an illegal priesthood. Undoubtedly the Jews
argued that very point. One could have a Levitical priesthood or an illegal priesthood! After all, wasn't Jesus from
the tribe of Judah? There was no priesthood from Judah.

The choice was between the Law and Christ. The Law
provided the priesthood, and the Levitical priesthood
administrated and taught the Law.

> For when there is a change of priesthood, there must also
> be a change of the Law (Heb. 7:12).

Abraham bowed to Melchizedek and paid tithes to him.
Aaron and Levi did the same. If one will push physical
descent to its conclusion, Levi bowed to Melchizedek when
Abraham did—at least genetic Levi did. Melchizedek was
superior to Abraham, Aaron and Levi. Christ was therefore
superior to Israel and all its priesthoods. As Abraham bowed
and paid tithes to Melchizedek, so the sons of Abraham
ought to bow before Christ, giving Him what they owe.

How Much of the Law was "Dead"?

Paul and the Apostles used the Old Canon to prove
Christ was Lord. They held it in honor. They taught from it.

260

You have known the Holy Scriptures which are able to make you wise for salvation through faith in Jesus Christ. All scripture is God-breathed and is useful for teaching, rebuking, correcting, and training in righteousness, so that the man of God may be thoroughly equipped for every good work (II Tim. 3:15ff.).

In a later section the value of the Torah will be examined. It is sufficient here to observe the Old Testament scriptures and the Old Covenant are two different things. They are related, of course. The relationship they properly hold is the way the Apostles related them. Briefly summarized, the principles of covenanted relationships with God did not change when the covenant Treaty changed. Loyalty to commitments did not change, although what was committed changed. Help for the covenanted partner did not change, but the definition of true help, depending as it did on each Treaty, changed.

In Apostolic theology the Law, and in a real sense, all the Canon of the Old Covenant passed from Law into History with Christ. It once was Divine Law. It became Divine history. It provides a background for understanding how God dealt with peoples in the past. Unless, however, the Apostles specifically made an aspect of the Torah binding on the new Israel, the old Law was for the old Israel. Understood that way, the rather strong statement by Ashley Johnson seems true.

It could not be the ceremonial law simply that they were contending had passed away. It could not mean the statutes of Israel simply, it could not mean the ten commandments merely, because Paul says if a man is circumcised he is in debt to the whole Law. That means every word in the ritualistic or ceremonial law if you are bound to put it that way, and also the ten commandments and the statutes. There is no way out of it. All or none. Every word, every jot, every tittle, every sentence, every statute or none!. . . . Where is the man since Pentecost who has had the authority Peter had? He had the keys to the kingdom. Where is the man since Paul who had the authority that he had? He was the last man on earth to have beheld and heard Jesus. They agree the First Covenant is no part of the New.[3]

It was clear from the study of the Old Covenant itself, the Treaty, there was no distinction between aspects of the Law. Western Civilizations have massive codes of Law. They are divided for convenience' sake into Administrative Law, Judicial Law, Contracts, Torts, Criminal Law, and the like. It would be a serious mistake to impose upon the Hebrew Law an alien system; and, based upon western categories, attempt to divide the Torah. It ought to be taken first as given in the original and then as understood by the Apostles, who shared Jesus' views. Such distinctions as "ceremonial," "moral," "judicial," "administrative," are imposed upon the text, and do not reflect either the prophets' or the Apostles' view. That procedure does, however, allow theologians to pick and choose what elements in the Law they would like to impose on others. They announce that list as "moral," and the rest ceremonial. The entire procedure is unwarranted because it imposes a category system upon the text. The presuppositions of that new system warp the conclusion, producing meanings unknown to Apostles, or an emphasis not pressed by New Testament writers.

---

3. Ashley Johnson, *Sermons on the Two Covenants,* Delight, Arkansas: Gospel Light, 1899 (reprinted), p. 118.

Weaknesses of the Old Covenant

The Apostles, on the authority of its Author, announced the end of the Law. It had been good for its purposes, they said, but had far too many handicaps to be a rule for all mankind.

1. The Law was preoccupied with the outward man.

This is an illustration for the present time . . . they are only a matter of food and drink and various ceremonial washings —external regulations applying until the time of the new order (Heb. 9:9).

Therefore do not let anyone judge you by what you eat or drink, or with regard to a religious festival, a New Moon celebration or a Sabbath day. These were a shadow of the things that were to come. The reality, however is found in Christ . . . "Do not handle," "Do not touch," "Do not taste," . . . such regulations have an appearance of wisdom, . . . but lack any real value in restraining sensual indulgence (Col. 2:16ff.).

Nothing outside a man can make him "unclean" by going into him. Rather it is what comes out of a man that makes him "unclean." For from within, out of men's hearts, come evil thoughts, sexual immorality, theft . . . arrogance and folly. All these evils come from inside a man and make him "unclean" (Mark 7:14ff.).

2. It was filled with curses and death.

He has made us competent as ministers of a new covenant —not of the letter but of the Spirit; for the letter kills but the spirit gives life. Now if the ministry that brought death, which was engraved in letters on stone . . . (II Cor. 3:6ff.).

Those who rely on observing the Law are under a curse, for it is written: "Cursed is everyone who does not continue to do everything written in the Book of the Law" (Gal. 3:10).

3. There was no Christ in it.

Before faith came we were held prisoners of the law, locked up until faith should be revealed. So the law was put in charge to lead us to Christ, . . . as long as the heir is a child, he is no different from a slave, although he owns the whole estate. He is subject to guardians and trustees until the time set by his father. . . . But when the time was fully come, God sent his Son, born of a woman, born under Law, to redeem those under Law that we might receive the full rights as sons (Gal. 3:23ff. and 4:1ff.).

I am the way, the truth, and the life, and no man comes to the Father except by me (John 14:6).

All three words Jesus used get meaning from their use in the Old Testament. The "way" was the Law of Moses. The new way is Christ. The "truth" was a life corresponding to the demands of the Torah. Now, meeting the demands of Christ is walking in truth. The "Life" was keeping the Law, "for the Lord is your life, and He will give you . . . (Deut. 30:20). Now, Jesus is the only way to life. The Torah was deficient because Christ was not in it.

4. It taught men the very sins it prohibited.

I would not have known what it was to covet if the Law had not said, "Do not covet" (Rom. 7:7).

A person tends to become what he has his mind on. "As a man thinketh in his heart, so is he" (Prov. 23:7; cf. Matt. 12:34). When a person thought of all the sins listed, his mind was filled with evil ideas. When the Great Example came, He modeled the perfect life. The more men think of Him the more they become like Him (II Cor. 3:18).

5. It had no Holy Spirit in it.

In the last days, God says, I will pour out my Spirit on all people; your sons and daughters will prophesy, your young men will see visions and your old men will dream dreams (Joel 2:28 and Acts 2:17).

Paul asked the question of the Galatians.

You foolish Galatians! I would like to learn one thing from you: Did you receive the Spirit by observing the Law, or by believing what you heard? (Gal. 3:2ff.).

In the former era a few prophets and kings (I Sam. 16:13) received the Spirit and were enabled to do mighty things. In the era of Messiah, the Spirit would dwell in every covenanter's heart. Paul called the new covenant the covenant of the Spirit (II Cor. 6:3). The manifestation of the Spirit may differ in individuals (I Cor. 12:15), but each and every one baptized into Christ (Acts 2:38) has received the Holy Spirit (I Cor. 12:13). The Spirit enabled all to aid the church as the prophets aided Israel (I Cor. 14:5). The best aid in any church is to act like Christ and treat others as if they were Christ. The one most like Christ, who loved and aided, manifests the Spirit in His highest way (I Cor. 13:1).

6. It had no living Mediator in God's Presence.

We have a great high priest, one who has gone into heaven, Jesus the Son of God. Let us hold firmly to the faith we profess. For we do not have a high priest who is unable to sympathize with our weaknesses, but we have one who has been tempted in every way just as we are, yet without sin. (Heb. 4:14f.).

Because of this oath Jesus has become the guarantee of the better covenant. Now there were many of those priests, since death prevented them from continuing in office, but because he lives for ever, he has a permanent priesthood. Therefore he is able to save completely those who come to God through him, because he always lives to intercede for them (Heb. 7:22-25).

7. It could not take away sin.

This is the covenant I will make with them after that time, says the Lord, . . . "their sins and lawless acts I will remember no more" (Jer. 31:31ff.).

And where these have been forgiven, there is no longer any sacrifice for sin (Heb. 10:15ff.).

The sins under the first covenant were "covered" in a way foreshadowing the last full remission. Since the atonement of bulls and goats was annual, there was never a full pardon. The people returned each year to sacrifice again. The old covenant rite merely rolled the sin ahead, as it were, year after year, as they grew higher and heavier, until at last they were laid on Christ, God's perfect lamb.

Sacrifice and offerings you did not desire, but a body you prepared for me; . . . Then I said, Here I am—it is written about me in the scroll—I have come to do your will, O God (Heb. 10:5 and Ps. 40:6-8).

When he said, "Here I am, I have come to do your will," He sets aside the first to establish the second, and by that will we have been made holy through the sacrifice of the body of Christ once for all (Heb. 10:5ff.).

The blood of bulls and goats were but a shadow of the real sacrifice to come. They were to provide the essential definition of Hebrew sacrifices. The word *will* in the above passage was the Greek *thelema*. Its root was *thelo*: will, intent or purpose. It was used in this passage as a synonym for the usual word covenant, *diatheke*. For that reason the words *testament, covenant* and *will* of God, may be used interchangeably. At any rate, the former will did not provide for full pardon, just the bare shadow of good conscience. In Christ there was full and absolute forgivenesss of sin.

266

Because it is impossible for the blood of bulls and goats to take away sin (Heb. 10:1-4).

He did not enter by means of the blood of goats and calves, but he entered the Most Holy Place by his own blood, having obtained eternal redemption. . . . The Law was only a shadow of the good things that are coming . . . (Heb. 9:25—10:1).

7. It could not impart righteousness.

The life I live in the body I live in faith in the Son of God, who loved me and gave himself up for me. I do not set aside the grace of God, for if righteousness could have been gained through the Law, Christ died for nothing (Gal. 2:21f.).

For if a law had been given that could impart life, then righteousness would certainly have come by a law (Gal. 3:21).

Paul discussed "righteousness" or "justification" in two ways, in two contexts. The two words were the same in Hebrew (*sedeq*) and therefore mean the same thing in the Greek and English. In the Old Testment the keeping of the Law was their *sedeq* (Deut. 6:24). No one could ever have complete (*sedeq*) under the Law. Everyone broke the law. Since the breaking of one was the breaking of all, no one ever had (*sedeq*), was truly righteous or justified by his behavior.

Paul used the term in the New Testament documents to refer to the new norm or standard or righteousness: Christlike behavior (Phil. 3:7ff.). John also defined righteousness as Christlike attitudes and conduct.

He who does what is right is righteous, just as He is righteous (I John 3:7).

When one used the standard of Christ to judge an act, he was justified. An act done to be like Christ or to further the cause of Christ was a righteous act, and a justified act.

267

Paul used the term in a mystical or covenantal sense. When one joined Christ, he shared all Christ was. He was hidden in Christ. When God looked at Paul, He saw only Christ, and Paul was justified by his faith in Christ. We do not mean a mystical faith, apart from the body of Christ, or apart from obedience to Christ, but a covenanted faith in Christ. God agreed (covenanted) to see Christ when He looked at one in Christ. Thus Paul could say he was justified only by the blood of Christ; that he was only ultimately righteous because he participated in the perfection found in Christ Jesus the Lord. Only when in the church, Christ's body, did one share the "fulness of Him who fills all in all" (Eph. 1:23). It made little difference which way the term was being used by Paul or John. Apart from Christ's righteousness one's own justification was not possible. One was righteous because forgiven.

Jesus said,

This is my blood of the covenant, which is poured out for many for the forgiveness of sin (Matt. 26:29).

John said,

Behold the lamb of God who takes away the sin of the world (John 1:29).

The justifying blood of Christ was available to those in former times. Because Christ was the last sacrifice of the Old System, those under it had full atonement, if they had sacrificed in good faith as part of it, or in the case of the Patriarchs, if they had "walked with God" according to the light He revealed to them.

For this reason Jesus is the mediator of a new covenant, that those who are called may receive the promised eternal inheritance—now that he has died as a ransom to set them free from the sins committed under the first covenant (Heb. 9:15).

8. The Torah could not give eternal life.

You diligently study the scriptures because you think that by them you possess eternal life. Yet you refuse to come to me that you may have life (John 5:39ff.).

Jesus was a type of Adam. In contrast to first Adam, whose sin and disobedience brought death, the second Adam's obedience (Phil. 2:8) brought life to all men (I Cor. 15:22):

For as in Adam all die, so also in Christ are all made alive.

All men live eternally, but not all men will live eternally with God. Some will be "excluded from his presence," after the judgment. All whose names were found in the book of life will forever live in fellowship with God (Rev. 21:27).

Summary of the Negative View of Torah

The Apostolic view of the specific covenant of Moses was negative. The total Old Testament, however, linked in a most vital way to the message of Christ. To put it another way, the total frame of reference of the Old Testament was accepted by the Apostles. But the specific stipulations of the Treaty of Moses were not understood as binding on the believer in Christ. There was an overt and sometimes abrupt, if not hostile demand for dis-continuity between the covenants. The negative terms and phrases used by the Apostles will be summarized.

"taken from you and given to another"	(Matt. 21:42f)
"until all be accomplished"	(Matt. 5:18)
"thrown outside"	(Matt. 8:11)
"until John"	(Luke 16:16)

"saw Jesus only" ("hear ye him")	(Matt. 17:5)
"died to the law"	(Rom. 7:4ff.)
"released from"	
"set free from"	(Rom. 8:1, 2)
"not my people"	(Rom. 9:24)
"broken off"	(Rom. 11:17)
"Christ is the end of the law"	(Rom. 10:4)
"the Law of sin and death"	(Rom. 8:2)
"ministry of death"	(II Cor. 3:7ff.)
"Fading"	
"No glory"	
"Veiled"	
"cursed"	(Gal. 3:13)
"enslaved"	(Gal. 4:1,7,24)
"cast out" ("get rid of")	(Gal. 4:30)
"wall of hostility"	(Eph. 2:14)
"abolished"	(Eph. 2:15)
"weak and miserable principles"	(Gal. 4:9)
"canceled" "opposed to us"	(Col. 2:14)
"against us"	
"disarmed"	(Col. 2:15)
"lack any value in"	(Col. 2:23)
"fallen from grace'	(Gal. 5:4)
"alienated from Christ"	(Gal. 5:4)
"for lawbreakers and rebels"	(I Tim. 1:9)
"lesser"	(Heb. 7:7)
"change of the law"	(Heb. 7:12)
"former"	(Heb. 7:18)
"set aside"	(Heb. 7:18)
"weak and useless"	(Heb. 7:18)
"made nothing perfect"	(Heb. 7:18)
"something wrong with"	(Heb. 8:7)
"inferior"	
"poorer"	
"a shadow"	

"obsolete"	(Heb. 8:13)
"aging"	
"soon to disappear"	
"less perfect"	(Heb. 9:11)
"part of this creation"	(Heb. 9:11)
"outwardly clean"	(Heb. 9:13)
"impossible to take away sins"	(Heb. 10:4)
"sets aside"	(Heb. 10:9)
"no longer any"	(Heb. 10:18)
"burdened with"	(Acts 15:10)
"unbearable yoke upon"	(Acts 15:10)
"yoke of slavery"	(Gal. 5:3)

Shadow and Substance

God taught in several ways (Heb. 1:1) by direct revelation (Isa. 55:3), by example (I Cor. 11:1), and by a special kind of model, example or figure called a "type" (I Cor. 10:6). The Greek word was *typos* and was used as imprint of a nail (John 20:25), model of the real thing (Acts 7:44), of a mold or imprint (Rom. 6:17) and of an image formed from an original design or dye-casting, as in a printer's type putting on the paper the "anti-type" or later-type. The principle of type and anti-type was parallelism. The two figures paralleled each other in some significant way. Some element of the original type was repeated and fulfilled in the later anti-type.

There were several kinds of "types"! They were usually identified by the writer at the time of their use. Thus, Adam was described as "one who was a pattern (*typos*) of the one to come" (Rom. 5:14). The Law contained "a shadow of the good things that are coming" (Heb. 10:1). The Hebrew nation was used "as example" (*typikos*) for us (I Cor. 10:6). *Typikos* was an adverbial form of *typos* found in verse six

271

of the same passage. There was to be a "prophet like Moses" (Deut. 18:18), and a priest "like Melchizedek" (Ps. 110:4), and a king like David (Isa. 9:6, 7). Baptism was an anti-type of the waters of Noah (I Pet. 3:21).

There was another kind of typology involving the transfer of names. The former name was simply applied to the anti-type without much indication of meaning. The aspects of the similarity between the two being pointed out by the writer were not identified further. Messiah was called "David" (Ezek. 34:24), also "our Passover," (I Cor. 5:7) and "the firstfruits" (I Cor. 15:23). The church was called "Israel" (Gal. 6:16) as well as "the Jerusalem that is above" (Gal. 4:26). Circumcision was used to mean the cutting off of all sinful unholy living (Rom. 2:28-29). The death of Christ on the cross was called the "circumcision of Christ" (Col. 2:11).

Abraham was a type of men of faith (Gen. 13:7-9; cf. Rom. 4:14-16). Isaac was a fore-type of one born as the result of a promise (Gen. 17:16-19; cf. Gal. 4:28) all Christians are born of a promise made to Abraham in Christ. The cities of refuge (Num. 35:9ff.) were for accidental man-slaying as Christ is "refuge" for those fleeing the wrath of sin's judgment (Heb. 6:18-20).

We have already seen in this chapter Israel was a type of Christ, (Hos. 11:1). Events may also be seen as type and anti-type.

> . . . the idea that a new and definitive exodus had been accomplished in Christ Jesus appears as a fundamental institution in almost all of the New Testament writers. It seems clear that Jesus Himself understood his mission in terms of a new exodus.[4]

---

4. James Plastraras, *Creation and Covenant*, Milwaukee: Bruce Publishing, 1968, p. 119.

It seems to me there may be other examples of deliberate forecasting in "types," by the Lord but which are not identified as such in the New Testament. It is interesting to find potential parallels in private study of the Bible. It is not wise, however, to go much beyond what the Apostles have written and identified as type and anti-type. The danger is the use of alleged types to support a theological system in a way not intended or approved by the Apostles. This is not to say the Apostles legislated in the New Testament all legitimate cases of prototyping. The history of Biblical interpretation is filled with the most unusual and almost insane selections of matters in the Old Testament to give meaning to the New. That is not good typology. The Apostles identified the anti-types they felt were helpful and appropriate. The New Testament is the judge of the Old, not the reverse. The potential types in the Old Testament ought not be identified as true types in the absence of Apostolic identification. To have good Biblical theology regarding typology, one *always*, I repeat, *always* begins with the New Testament. One must find the anti-type before looking for the type. Any other procedure will put the Biblical scholar exactly where the pre-incarnation Jew was: expecting something far removed from what God had planned. To put it another way, the tree casts the shadow. One does not look at the shadow to describe the tree. One looks at the tree. When the shadow falls on the traveler passing through the Old Testament, he must not assume Christ cast the shadow. He must wait until he sees which tree cast it. The tree casts the shadow and only the Apostles were authorized to identify the tree. We are asked to teach what the Apostles have already identified as substance casting its shadow back into the Old Testament. We are not obligated to teach innovative speculations on other potential types. Much harm has come to the unity of the church by interpreting the New Testament by the Old. The New Testament interprets the Old Testament. The Apostles revealed all we need to know about essential typology. Typology involved not merely the Code itself, but united the entire Old Testament as a complete pre-Christian system. *There are a variety of ways of teaching typology, for instance.*

As Adam brought sin and death to all, Christ brings righteousness and life.

As Isaac had covenant blood so Christ alone possesses covenant blood.

As Abraham believed God's unseen promise so Christians believe Christ.

As Jehovah brought Israel out of Egypt, so Christ brings mankind from sin.

As an animal's blood covered sins for a year, Christ's covers eternally.

As those looking on the serpent were healed, so all seeing Jesus are saved.

As Israel was the people of God, so the church is the people of God.

As David's enemies mocked him, so Christ was mocked.

As Abraham respected Melchizedek, so Israel should honor Christ.

As the waters of Noah killed, so the waters of Christ save.

The longer I study the Bible, the more persuaded I am of the value of the parallelism. It provided the basis for defining Old Testament words. It provided the means of understanding both Israel and Christ as God's suffering servant. It opened the door of understanding of the Apostolic use of the Old Testament in its foreshadowing of Christ's life, death and resurrection. It provided the basis of typology, a most helpful way of using the Old Testament in Christian doctrine. While I do not agree with all Berkhof has written, I believe he is correct in his appreciation of typology.

When I wrote down my insights on repetition and typology, I was not yet acquainted with the discussion which had already begun at that time in Protestant theology about the meaning and extent of typology. . . . This discussion has confirmed my ideas about the essential role of typology in the Bible. . . . A study of the mutual relations of the christological, ecclesiological, and eschatological types would deepen our insight into the basic function of typology and its limits.[5]

The Book of Hebrews and Covenant

The Hebrew writer engaged the idea of covenant in the most overt way of any New Testament author. For him, Christianity apart from covenant was unthinkable. Indeed, for the Jew, without covenant there was no real philosophy, ethic, national identity, or hope. The question germane to this study is whether he was writing to Jews and using covenant to persuade them, or whether he was a Christian placing before the church the assumptions of Christ; and providing the gospel with its everlasting, supra-cultural frame-of-reference. Did the Gospel come in its own self-explanatory package: covenant? That is the essential question. Or, to put it another way, did the Hebrew writer make explicit what the other writers assumed was true? Was *Hebrews*

---

5. Hendrikus Berkhof, *Christ, the Meaning of History*, Richmond: John Knox Press, 1966, p. 212.

attempting to show all men the philosophic background of Christ, so there would be no need to recast him as harmonious with their own philosophic frame-of-reference? All cultures have some kind of Treaty idea or mutuality with attendant obligation. Is covenant the only real frame of the picture of the story of Jesus? I believe that to be the case. The gospel carried with it its own set of assumptions: the Old Testament history and philosophy: "God was in Christ reconciling the world to himself" (II Cor. 5:18f.).

All three aspects of normal Treaties were discussed by the writer of Hebrews. PARTIES were contrasted. The writer treated this by the basic structuring of the book. He established the superiority of Christ in every aspect of Hebrew religion. Parties as a concept was carried by the word *called* or *elect*; or the process of becoming a party to a covenant—*election*. God chose with whom He would be in covenant. Elected meant chosen for a relationship, that is, chosen for Suzerainty-Vassal relationship, or, as the prophets put it frequently, chosen for marriage.

> Therefore, holy brothers, who share in the heavenly calling, fix your thoughts on Jesus the Apostle and high priest whom we confess (Heb. 3:1).

Anyone who could "confess with your mouth Jesus is Lord, and believe in your heart that God has raised him from the dead" (Rom. 10:9f.), was elect of God. Being saved was called election by Hebrews. We will go into some detail about this in the chapters which follow. It is enough here to note the Hebrew discussed the *parties* to a covenant. In chapter ten, he warned about treating Christ, the very source of one's election, with contempt or neglect.

> Anyone who rejected the Law of Moses died without mercy on the testimony of two or three witnesses. How much more

severely do you think a man deserves to be punished who has trampled the Son of God under foot, who has treated as an unholy thing the blood of the covenant that sanctified him? (Heb. 10:29).

He was contrasting those who followed Moses as guide and mediator with those following Christ as *party* to a covenant. When discussing the prophecy of Jeremiah, he identified the party to the covenant as the reason God intended a new covenant.

If there had been nothing wrong with that first covenant, no place would have been sought for another, but God found fault with the People and said, "The time is coming . . ." (Heb. 8:7).

The entire notion one could be born of flesh and blood and be heir to Christ's blessing as a result, upon the faith of the parent or the blood of the parent was under discussion. None would be in Messiah's covenant who had not been sanctified by the "blood of the covenant."

The TERMS, the law or stipulations of the covenants were contrasted.

. . . another priest to arise in the order of Melchizedek and not Aaron. For when there is a change of priesthood there must also be a change in the law (Heb. 7:12).

The new law or duty of covenant was to be like Christ.

In fact, though by this time you ought to be teachers, you need someone to teach you the elementary truths of God's word all over again. . . . Therefore let us leave the elementary teachings about Christ, and go on to maturity (Heb. 11ff.).

Let us fix our eyes on Jesus, the author and perfector of our faith, who for the joy set before him endured the cross, scorning its shame, and sat down at the right hand of the throne of God. Consider him who endured such opposition from sinful men, so that you will not grow weary and lose heart (Heb. 12:2ff.).

The PROMISES of the new covenant were contrasted with those of Moses.

But the ministry Jesus has received is as superior to theirs as the covenant of which he is mediator is superior to the old one, and is founded on better promises (Heb. 8:6).

The distinctive element in the definition and illustration of true faith, in Hebrews, was its link to promise. Faith was faith in the promise made. That was true of Abraham's faith. God had said, "So shall your offspring be," and Abraham believed God, "and it was credited to him as righteousness" (Gen. 15:5, 6; cf. Heb. 11:12). The concept of reward or fulfilled promise, if you will, was what one believed as faith in God. Faith in God was the confidence the unseen promise was real, was sure.

Now faith is being sure of what we hoped for, and certain of what we do not see. This was what the ancients were commended for (Heb. 11:1).

To paraphrase the passage, using the word promise for hope (they are one in concept) the passage was saying,

Now faith means having complete confidence that what God has promised will happen, and being certain He will do what He has said. Acting in confidence of God is what the ancient righteous were commended for.

Great stress was laid on the fact God had consistently both blessed (Rahab) and condemned (in the exodus) in harmony with what He had said He would do. One can utterly depend upon God and what He has said.

He is faithful who promised! (Heb. 10:23).

Conditionality in Hebrews

When speaking of conditionality one faces the ultimate issue in both ancient and modern soteriology (doctrine of salvation). The Hebrew followed the theology of the prophets: a continued relationship to God was as conditional as the initial oath was meaningful. In other words, if the pledge the believer made to God was not "held firmly to the end," the promises of God would be voided (Jer. 34:18).

> "So I declared an oath in my anger, they shall never enter my rest."
>
> See to it brothers, that none of you has a sinful unbelieving heart that none turns away from the living God . . . but encourage one another daily, as long as it is called 'today.' . . .
>
> We have come to share in Christ if we hold firmly to the end the confidence we had at first (Heb. 3:12ff.).

Those who have "once been enlightened, who have tasted the heavenly gift, who have shared in the Holy Spirit" (Heb. 6:4), and then repudiated it, "if they fall away," for them it is impossible to be saved.

> If we deliberately keep on sinning after we have received the knowledge of the truth, no sacrifice for sins is left, only the fearful expectation of judgment . . . do you think a man deserves to be punished who has trampled the Son of God under foot, and has treated as an unholy thing the blood of the covenant by which he was sanctified. . . . For we know him who said, "It is mine to avenge, I will repay" (Heb. 10:26ff.).
>
> Do not throw away your confidence, it will be richly rewarded. You need to persevere so that when you have done

279

the will of God, you will receive what is promised (Heb. 10:35).

Covenants were by their very nature mutual. Both parties made commitments, promises. Treaty meant conditionality if it meant anything at all. One ought to remember, however, it was the basic *confidence* in what God had promised that needed to be kept firm.

We have come to share in Christ if we hold firmly to the end the confidence we had at first (Heb. 3:14).

He became the source of eternal salvation for all who obey him (Heb. 5:8).

One ought not be surprised at that kind of thinking. It was thoroughly Hebraic. It was exactly how Jesus spoke. Note the parallelism in the passage that follows. It illustrates the Hebraic orientation of Jesus.

Whoever believes on the Son has life, but whoever does not obey the Son shall not see life, for the wrath of God remains on him (John 3:36).

The passage has a "front-and-back" parallelism. When paralleled out it would look like this:

Whoever "believes" on the Son has life.
Whoever "not believes" on the Son not has life.

In the Greek passage two different words were used: *pisteuo*, almost always rendered "believe" or "have faith," and the negative *apeitheo* usually translated "be disobedient," as Paul speaking to Agrippa, "I was not disobedient (apeitheo) to that heavenly vision" (Acts 26:19). The true negative parallelism would properly be,

Whoever *believes* on the son has life, but whoever does *not obey* the son shall not see life (RSV).

280

In the mind of Christ, as with any Jew, to believe-on and to obey were essentially the same idea. One did not lead to the other, as with the Greeks. One was the other. "Shema" meant to the Hebew a blending of "hear and do." Shema was a combination of three Greek categories—hear, believe, obey. In Hebrew they were one. Thus to believe God and to do what He said was the same thing. Jesus was a Hebrew.

Faith in its New Testament sense is never mere intellectual assent. . . . "Salvation by faith alone" must inevitably be rejected if faith is defined as intellectual assent (James 2:14-26). In the New Testament generally, faith is closely associated with hearing, and in Biblical language, hearing is almost synonymous with obeying.[6]

If, however, faith alone means without faith no obedience is valid, any Biblical scholar must agree. In the book of Hebrews, the standard was not "by faith alone," but was rather, "not without faith."

For without faith it is impossible to please God, because anyone who comes to him must believe that he exists and that he rewards those that earnestly seek him (Heb. 11:6).

There was a world of difference, philosophically speaking, between "not without faith," and "by faith only," with its incipient Gnosticism. In other words, the two covenants have both similar and differing aspects. The definition of faith did not change. The promises changed. What the Apostles identified as similar and what the Apostles state as different was by definition "sound doctrine" in the New Testament.

---

6. Alan Richardson, *An Introduction to New Testament Theology*, New York: Harper-Row, 1958, p. 30.

The basic purpose of the Hebrew writer was both to encourage faithfulness and to warn of neglect or repudiation of covenant. In doing so he compared the covenant of Christ with that of Moses. Christ, he said, was superior to anything in the Old Testament. He was superior to angels (1:5), to Moses (3:2), to Joshua (4:8), to the Sabbath rest in Canaan (4:9), to the Aaronic High Priesthood (5:4) or the Levitical priesthood (7:6), to the law of Moses (7:12), to the Old Covenant (8:6), to the promises of that covenant (8:6), to the entire Tabernacle system of worship (9:10), to the blood of sacrificial animals (9:11, 12), to the sacrifice's benefit (10:3), to the judgment upon the unfaithful (10:16f.) and to the intercession of priesthood (10:19ff.). Being faithful to Christ and the new Mount Zion (12:22) put all Christians in the best company in all human history: with men of faith (11:1ff.). All believers ought to cooperate with their leaders to the mutual benefit and salvation of all (13:7). Christians ought to bear suffering "outside the camp" i.e., while in this world, knowing we have an enduring city to come (13:13).

The Value of the Law

The negative view of the Law expressed by the Apostles was counter balanced by explanations of its value for Christians. All scripture was inspired of God and suitable for teaching, rebuking and training in righteousness (II Tim. 3:16). It must be correctly used (I Tim. 1:8).

1. Schoolmaster

Before this faith came, we were held prisoner by the law, locked up until faith should be revealed. So the law was put in charge to lead us to Christ. Now that faith has come, we are no longer under the supervision of the law (Gal. 3:23f.).

In Hebrew a guardian was not a mere babysitter. He was a teacher. One guarded a young man by instruction (Ps. 119:9). The Law was a tutor as one version has it in Gal. 3:24.[7] The Authorized Version rendered it schoolmaster. An instructor, tutor, or schoolmaster assigned to guard the boy until he can become the manager of his estate had as first task instruction. The Law taught language to the Hebrews. God defined terms for them. They learned what "love" meant. They learned what "take heed" meant. They learned what *hesed* or covenant faithfulness meant. They understood Law as both the Torah and the events of history. They learned what faithfulness meant, what sacrifice, redeemed, atonement, elected, priesthood, obedience, grace, good judgment, true praise, love of neighbor and the like really meant.

> The New Testament language has at its base the vernacular first century Greek, but the idiom expounding the New Testament revelation must be studied against its Semitic background since it is employed in expounding the meaning of the redemptive history moving from the revelation in the Old Testament to the redemptive event in Jesus Christ.[8]

The above quotation from George Eldon Ladd was the same understanding expressed by another theologian who lived and wrote 150 years earlier. Alexander Campbell had written,

> All the leading terms and phrases of the New Testament are to be understood and explained by the history of the Jewish nation and God's government of them.[9]

---

7. Revised Challoner-Rheims Version (Roman Catholic) Patterson, N.J.: St. Anthony Press Guild, 1947.

8. George Eldon Ladd, *The New Testament and Criticism*, Grand Rapids: Eerdmans, 1967, p. 103.

9. Alexander Campbell, *The Christian System*, Cincinnati: Standard Publishing Company, 1835, reprinted, p. 119.

The Old Testament was a good school teacher, using all good methods: history, law, example, "typology," prophecy, and by insisting on definition.

2. *Show Man's Incapactiy*

Are you foolish? After beginning with the Spirit are you now trying to attain your goal by human effort? No man is justified before God by the law. . . . The law was not based on faith, on the contrary, "the man who does these things shall live by them," . . . For if a law had been given that could impart life, then righteousness certainly would have come through the law (Gal. 3:3, 21).

Man was lost in his own self interest. God "gave them up" to do whatever they wanted (Rom. 1:24). Men wrote their own laws. Even then they broke them (Rom. 2:14). No one has ever been able to live up to what good men everywhere held to be right. "All have sinned and fallen short of the glory of God" (Rom. 3:23). God holds all men accountable whether by the Law of Moses or the law of conscience (Rom. 3:19). If any man thinks that life could be attained by the Law, he was mistaken. "The man that does these things shall gain his life by them," offered the Jew an opportunity to build his own road to heaven. The Law was to demonstrate man could not find life by measuring himself against a standard and then demanding God pay him with eternal life. All men know they have failed morally.

3. *History of Salvation*

The Old Testament scriptures trace the progress of God's plans for mankind.

When the time had fully come, God sent his Son, born of a woman, born under law, to redeem those under law that we may receive full rights as sons (Gal. 4:4).

284

Without the Old Testament, the letters of the New Testament would have little context. "Had fully come," implied there was a time not appropriate for the coming. We would know nothing of such appropriateness without the promises and the previous experiences of the ones to whom they were given. "Born under law," would be left to every man's speculation had not there been a record of the instituting of the Law and the experience of those under it. "To redeem those," would be potentially twisted a dozen ways without the definition of redeemed and the context of redemption under the old Law.

When Paul defined the gospel, he mentioned, "according to the scriptures" twice. Without the scriptures it would be anybody's guess as to the context of the message.

> Now I make known to you the gospel, . . . that Christ died for our sins according to the scriptures, that he was buried, and that he was raised on the third day, according to the scriptures (I Cor. 15:1-3).

He did not define "according to the scriptures." He may have meant, "As was foretold in the prophets," or perhaps, "within the context of covenant promise," or "as a demonstration of God's power previously shown in the Bible." Whatever the specifics intended by Paul, the Old Testament scripture provide the only context for understanding the New Testament history and scripture.

Paul told Timothy the Law was good if used correctly.

> They want to be teachers of the law, but they do not know what they are talking about, or what they so confidently affirm. We know that the law is good if a man uses it properly (I Tim. 1:7ff.).

Paul gave his basic philosophy of what made the teaching of the Law good, and how it can be correctly understood.

Anything that supported the gospel from the Old Testament was good for instruction. It would be

> . . . sound doctrine that conforms to the glorious gospel of the blessed God, which he entrusted to me (I Tim. 1:11).

4. Identify Sin

The value of the Law could be seen in identifying sin and describing its results.

> Just as through the disobedience of one man the many were made sinners, so also through the obedience of the one man the many will be made righteous. The law was added so that the trespass might increase (Rom. 5:19f.).

The Law was added to make plain what trespasses were. "To increase the trespass," meant to make it plainer, more obvious and more specific.

> What shall we say then? Is the law sin? Far from it. Indeed I would not have known what sin was except through the law. For I would not have known what it was to covet had not the law said, "Do not covet" (Rom. 7:7).

The Law was, according to Paul, "holy, just and good," and yet it caused one to be clearly identified as a sinner.

> Did that which is good, then, become death to me? By no means! But in order that sin might be recognized as sin, it produced death in me through what was good, so that through the commandment sin might become utterly sinful (Rom. 7:12ff.).

In some cases, the man was a sinner when breaking the universal covenant of Noah, "Do not kill a man." With or without the Law of Moses he was a sinner. On the other hand, one became a lawbreaker only after the Law was passed. So the coming of the Law of Moses with its 613

286

stipulations, created lawbreakers right and left. This was especially true in a national theocracy.

At the time the Law was given it was a helpful and necessary instrument, meant for the good of Israel. It was very beneficial—at one time. The covenant showed God's respect for human freedom.[10] It openly declared what God needed to make and keep them a true Theocracy.[11] It prohibited men from being justified by doing "what was right in his own eyes" (Judg. 17:6). It provided for a maximum of personal freedoms even counting the 613 stipulations.[12]

The Use of the Law in Conversion

The Law of Moses was not used in conversion. It was not preached by the Apostles. There is not one case of conversion where the Law was preached to produce a guilt in the prospective convert. The Law was not part of the gospel. The gospel about Jesus Christ was preached on the merits of the eyewitnesses (Acts 10:39-42) and demonstrations of the Holy Spirit (Heb. 2:1-3). It produced belief (Rom. 10:17).

The apostles did not attempt to create guilt in their converts. They tried to draw them toward Jesus Christ. The state of their guilt was of little concern to the Apostles, apparently. The confession asked by the Apostles was not a confession of sins, but of belief in Christ as Lord (Rom. 10:9, 10; cf. Acts 8:36-38).

Jesus believed the "golden rule" was stamped on the hearts and minds of every man and woman born in the image

---

10. D. R. Hillers, *Covenant: The History of a Biblical Idea*, Baltimore: Johns Hopkins, 1969, p. 49, 65.

11. J. M. Myers, *Grace and Torah*, Philadelphia: Fortress Press, 1975, p. 18.

12. Hillers, *ibid.*, p. 95.

of God. He understood every human, every angel, every creature of the rational universe had stamped on his heart and soul: "Thou shalt love the Lord thy God," and "Thou shalt love thy neighbor as thyself." God would hold all men accountable for that, at least (Rom. 1:18-24). When the cross was preached, the enormity of the error, the injustice, the wrong of it, the sin of it became apparent. Seeing Jesus, the prince of heaven, dying because of man's corruption showed sin's power and ugliness (Gal. 3:1). The edicts of the Law of Moses paled against the convicting power of the cross. The mighty "word of the cross" (I Cor. 1:18) broke men's hearts, and caused them to come home to the God of Eden.

After conversion, when the converts need stability, the Old Testament was taught. It could strengthen one's faith. The law was schoolmaster, but should teach what the Apostles taught from it, and for the same reasons.

Ad olam: Hebrew Forever

The most common word in Hebrew for everlasting, forever, eternally, never ending, and such was *olam*—ever. When prefixed with *ad* to become *ad olam* the word was translated as forever, or everlasting. There was no evidence in the writings of the Apostles of any problem over the word. There are considerable problems over it now. The *promises* of the Abrahamic covenant were said to be *ad olam*.

The whole land of Canaan . . . I will give as an everlasting (*olam*) possession (Gen. 17:8).

The *stipulations* of covenants were said to be forever. Circumcision leads the rather long list.

288

They must be circumcised. My covenant in your flesh is to be an everlasting covenant. Any uncircumcised male . . . is to be cut off from his people; he has broken my covenant (Gen. 17:13).

The *parties* were spoken as participants in the covenant forever.

I will establish my covenant with him as an everlasting covenant for his descendants after him (Gen. 17:19).

Many aspects of the Mosaic covenant were spoken of as *ad olam*. The Sabbath (Exod. 12:24), the nation of Israel (Jer. 18:9, 10), David's throne (II Sam. 7:12) the scapegoat ceremony (Lev. 16:29), the Passover (Lev. 16:31), an ear-pierced slave (Exod. 21:6), the Aaronic Priesthood, (Exod. 40:15), the house of Levi as priests (I Sam. 2:30ff.), sacrificial meat to Levite families (Num. 18:19), Jerusalem as the capital city (Ps. 132:13, 14), all serve as example.

What did the Apostles say about such things? They said little in a direct way. The reason was clear: *ad olam* meant in perpetuity when used in a Treaty context. Treaties could be either for a specified number of years, or they could be open-ended. They would last as long as both parties continued according to agreement. It was in perpetuity— forever. When the treaty ended all parts of it ended. Since all the promises of the Old Testament were part of the Old Treaty, when the treaty ended so did the *ad olam* promises. The same would be true of parties and obligations. Conditionality was so fundamental the Hebrews found little objection to ending specifics of a covenant if the entire covenant was ended.

Conclusion

The Lord gave to the Apostles authority to speak for Him in all matters of faith and order. He insured their ability by giving them the Holy Spirit. After the ascension of Jesus the Apostles first preached the full gospel message to the common public on Pentecost. They made converts with the message of the death and resurrection of Christ as it proved His Lordship. Those who accepted the message were organized into churches and taught the Apostles' doctrine.

Two different although not incompatible approaches to mission were evident in the ancient church. One method, called centripetal, employed the Apostles in the temple and in the Holy City to teach the visiting diaspora Jews and proselytes. When they were converted they carried the message of salvation in Christ as far as "the islands of the sea." The other method was overt centrifugal. It spun outward by direct command of the Spirit and sent evangelists seeking the lost, as Jesus had commanded. It did not wait for the lost to come to them.

There was a clash of theology over the place and use of the Law of Moses in the ancient church. Two conferences were held over the issue. The first was rather local and involved Peter's receiving into the church non-Jews. He was approved in his actions by the conference. The other conference involved Paul and Barnabas, accused of the same error. They were also approved by the church. The conclusion was no Gentile need become a Jew in order to become a Christian.

The Apostles held a two covenant theology. The specific Torah of Moses, the very Treaty at Sinai was held to be canceled, dead and gone. The philosophy of the Torah, the notion of mutual covenant making and keeping was not abandoned. The scriptures themselves, called the Old Testament, were instructive and helpful as history, philosophy and example, but not as law. The word of the Apostles was the law of Christ.

The importance of parallelism in the thinking of the Apostles was stressed in this chapter. It provided the key for a good many difficult problems in relating the two covenants properly. The way the Apostles used the two covenants sometimes emphasized dis-continuity; but, sometimes continuity remains the standard view for all Christian people.

Questions on Chapter Six

1. Everything we know about Jesus came through
   a) the Apostles   c) the prophets
   b) a Book that fell from heaven d) the Law of Moses
2. Break the Great Commission into its Covenant parts.
   _____ : _____
   _____ : _____
   _____ : _____
3. There were _____ methods of mission in the New Testament.
4. T F The Apostles understood the church age as the Messianic age.
5. T F David's throne is still empty of its king.
6. T F The gospel was understood as rebuilding David's broken city.
7. T F The word church and the word kingdom were used interchangeably.
8. T F "Going" was the main idea of the Great Commission.
9. The first Gentile convert in the New Testament was
   a) Peter   c) Paul
   b) The Ethiopian d) Cornelius

10. What was the burning theological issue within the ancient church?
    a) Is Christ Lord?
    b) Is baptism essential?
    c) Must a Gentile become a Jewish Christian?
    d) Will Jerusalem be rebuilt?
11. T   F   There was a Treaty within the Old Testament scriptures.
12. T   F   All books in the Old Testament were related to the Old Treaty.
13. T   F   The Old Testament is not inspired of God.
14. T   F   It is wrong to teach Christians from the Old Testament.
15. T   F   The Ten Commandments were done away at the cross.
16. Isaac was a type of _____ (Paul, Jesus, Moses, the NT).
17. Define parallelism and give two examples.
18. The Covenant of Moses was _____ the Abrahamic covenant.
19. The "dividing wall of hostility" was _____.
20. "And if you be Christ's then you are Abraham's _____ and _____."
21. "Where there is a change in priesthood there must be a change in _____."
22. Eternal life was part of the _____ (new, old) covenant.
23. The author of Hebrews supported the idea of
    a) Once saved always saved
    b) No assurance of salvation
    c) conditionality
    d) unconditionality
24. At the cross of Christ, the Old Testament changed from _____ to _____.
25. The Old Testament is a history of _____.

292

1. a) Jesus Himself wrote nothing.
2. Parties: God and all "in Christ"
   Terms: Make disciples ("going, baptizing, teaching")
   Promises: I will be with you always.
3. Two
4. T
5. F
6. T
7. T   Hebrews twelve.
8. F   Going was a participle, MAKE DISCIPLES was the verb.
9. d) Cornelius (The Ethiopian was reading the Old Testament. A Jew.)
10. c)
11. T
12. T
13. F   The Old Testament is inspired of God as history not law.
14. F   It is right, but must be viewed as the Apostles viewed it.
15. T   However, nine of them were reinstituted on Christ's authority.
16. Jesus was "seed" of Abraham as was Isaac.
17. A parallelism is a literary devise wherein a concept is repeated or defined by a following word or phrase.
    "Repent and turn again." (Acts 3:19)
    "A just and blameless man" (Job 12:4)
    "I have slain a man to my wounding, and a young man to my hurt." (Gen. 4:23)

PLEASE TURN THE PAGE OVER FOR ANSWERS.

PLEASE TURN THE BOOK OVER FOR ANSWERS.

25. Salvation or redemption or God's reconciliation with mankind.
24. Law to History
23. c) conditionality
22. New
21. Law
20. seed and heir
19. The Law of Moses
18. Added to

Chapter Seven

THE NEW COVENANT

In keeping with the command of Christ, the Apostles and leaders of the early church went to "the Jews first, then to the Gentiles" (Rom. 1:16). It was essential to have a clear covenant orientation when presenting Christ to Jews. The prophet had said, "The time is coming when I will make a new covenant with the house of Israel and the house of Judah" (Jer. 31:31f.). Even then, the message was not centered in covenant itself. The central message of the Apostles was summed up in the good confession, "Jesus is Lord" (Rom. 10:9). He was Messiah, and He brought the new covenant. The term "good news" was an expression prefered to covenant in their vocabulary. The good news announced God was prepared to give salvation to all men, regardless of their past, whether they were Jews or Greeks, slaves, free, male, female, king or peasant. Messiah brought a new law: do what is best for all men in every situation (Mark 10:44). What was best for all was being reconciled to God and then reconciled to each other. God intended to unite men in Christ. He intended to bring peace between heaven and earth through Christ (Eph. 1:9, 10). The core of the message about Christ was His death and resurrection. Every essential idea of the new age was related in some way to Christ's death and resurrection.

The message was so simple common men could speak accurately about it. Three prepositional phrases summarized the message when in covenant context; "in Christ," "like Christ," and "with Christ." The *parties* to the new kingdom were all those "in Christ." The essence of the *stipulations* of covenant was to be "like Christ." And the *promises* were summarized by simply stating all the faithful were to share "with Christ" all He was and had. That simple formula united the ancient church as the Old Covenant united the tribes of Israel. We can trace in the New Testament Canon how the new movement took shape around Christ as the New Covenant.

From B'rth to Diatheke

In the absence of clear evidence to the contrary, New Testament words must have the Old Testament meanings. That is a fundamental assumption when reading the Bible as a whole. The first century church was Jewish. They understood the church as the continuation of the people of God from the Old Testament age. They were Messianic Jews. Their first scriptures were the Old Testament documents. The LXX, Greek Old Testament, used the word *diatheke* to translate the word treaty.

> The LXX assumes that *diatheke* expresses the essential content of *b'rth*, and . . . the only other occasional renderings are *suntheke* (4Bas.) and *entole* (3Bas. 11:11). It may thus be assumed that where the LXX uses *diatheke* the intention is to mediate the sense and usage of *b'rth*.[1]

The word *diatheke* was used in the more ancient Greek texts meaning "to come to an arrangement or to order things with others."[2] Jesus used forms of the verb to mean "to appoint" (Luke 22:29), and "to determine." The prefix *dia* did not mean "fully" or "consistently" as in some cases, but rather, "arranging apart from one another."[3]

---

1. Gottfried Quell, *"diatheke,"* *Theological Dictionary of the New Testament,* Vol. II, ed. Gerhard Kittel, Grand Rapids: Eerdmans, 1964, p. 107.
2. Johannes Behm, *"diatheke,"* *TDNT,* Vol. II, p. 105.
3. A. Debrunner, as quoted by Johannes Behm, *TDNT,* Vol. II, p. 105.

In other words, *diatheke* meant an imposed rather than a negotiated treaty or arrangement.

As far as the sense of the Greek goes, the New Testament word covenant meant "the arrangement God had made." The arrangement God made was once the Treaty of Moses; now it was the Treaty of Christ. God's offer was not something man earned or deserved. Hence the entire new system was called "grace" (Titus 2:11).

One technical use of *diatheke* was reflected in the Book of Hebrews. The legal context of covenant in the Greek world was indicated by the Latin *testamentum* and the English testament, meaning the disposition of an estate, the document of a "last will and testament." The word was used that way only once (Heb. 9:16f.) in the entire New Testament Canon. Its use there was in a closely reasoned passage, and ought not be generalized. That is, *diatheke* ought not be understood as a disposition of property by God upon His death. Properly understood, the word "testament" is acceptable. Its relationships to "testimonies," and "documents of attestation," are closer to the meanings of the ancient church.

From Diatheke to PURPOSE

Was there a redefinition of the word covenant between the time of Abraham/Sinai and its use by the Lord and His Apostles? To that question we must answer a qualified, "Yes." There was no change in essence, formulary, or meaning. There was a significant, radical and revolutionary shift of emphasis. The emphasis changed from *form* to *purpose*.

When Christ came into the world, he said,

"Sacrifice and offering you did not desire, but a body

you prepared for me; with burnt offerings and sin offerings you were not pleased. Then I said, "Here I am—it is written about me in the scroll—I have come to do your will, O God." . . .

He sets aside the first to establish the second. And by that will we have been made holy through the sacrifice of Jesus Christ once for all (Heb. 10:5-10).

He used the word *will* as a synonym for covenant (v. 16). The Greek word for will, intent, or purpose was from *thelo*. In most places in the New Testament, the concept of God's will parallels the meaning of covenant duty. The emphasis changed from minute statute keeping to accomplishing what God wanted: not sacrifice, but advancing God's will or purpose. The attention was off WHAT I was to do and focused on WHY God was in a peace treaty with me. To put it another way, a new covenanter was not preoccupied with his status. He focused on getting done what God wanted done in the world. He was not forever trying to earn the good life by keeping endless regulations. He was interested in seeing the program of world reconciliation succeed. He measured success not by how closely he conformed to ceremonial or legal standards, but how any given act contributed to the success of God's purpose, will, or intent.

Categories and their Names

Apart from the covenant frame of reference, it is difficult to trace a given theme from Christ to the Apostles. For instance, Jesus used the figure of a kingdom to organize and relate various ideas in his teachings. The Apostles did not follow that lead. There was no effort to use the idea of kingdom to unify their teachings. Jesus used the term disciple frequently. It was occasionally used in Acts and rarely in the epistles. "Discipling" did not become the one integrative idea in ancient theology. Grace was assumed to be the basic core element of Biblical theology for many years. Paul used the term and its relatives quite frequently. Jesus himself never spoke the word, at least as far as the record goes. It is to be found but four times in all the gospels; three in John and always about Christ. The word covenant was not used very much. But its synonym was used most frequently. The Apostles used *thelema* (noun form of *thelo*) to bear all the ideas of covenant. When *thelema* was heard, covenant was understood.

> Thy kingdom come,
> thy will (*thelema*) be done on earth,
> as it is in heaven.

Kittel, the acknowledged international authority on Biblical terms, when discussing *thelo* showed it to have the same content as *diatheke,* when used in that context.

Thelein as commanding will, a) Expressly of God and His purposes and rule. In the LXX (it) is used of God's sovereign rule in creation and history. . . .

b) There is a human analogy to the authorative utterances of God's will in the rule of princes and administrators, in the directions of the royal will, also in the desires of officials, in military commands, and in the promulgation of law.[4]

There was no will of God expressed in ancient times, for God's people, which was not in specific form, i.e., in Treaty form. Thus when the term will of God was used in the New Testament, it referred to the revealed will of God

---

4. Gottlab Schrenk, *"thelo,"* TDNT, Vol. III, 1965, p. 47.

for mankind, and was always related to purpose: reconciliation. As Ashley Johnson said:

> In the passage here (Heb. 8:13) we have the word "covenant." In other passages we have the word "testament." We have also the phrase, "everlasting covenant." Indeed they are translated from the same Greek word. . . .
>
> When I say "covenant," therefore I mean "testament," and when I say "testament," I shall mean "covenant." When I use covenant and testament, I shall mean in every day usage, "will." God's testament. God's covenant, God's will concerning us.[5]

In this present study I shall follow the same procedure as Ashley Johnson. The New Covenant was to accomplish the stated purposes of God, not regarding Israel, but regarding all mankind.

Christ the Covenant

Messiah was described as a covenant Himself.

> I will keep you and make you a covenant for the peoples, to open eyes that are blind, to free captives from prison, and to release from the dungeon those who sit in darkness (Isa. 42:6ff.).

The passage was quoted by Jesus. He was a covenant (Matt. 12:14ff.). Christ stood between God and man as covenant did. He was helpless mankind's link to God. God would accept reconciliation with man through Christ. He was the only access to God.

---

5. Ashley Johnson, *Sermons on the Two Covenants*, Delight, Arkansas: Gospel Light (reprint), 1899, p. 8.

No one comes to the Father but through me. If you really knew me you would know my Father as well. From now on you know him and have seen him (John 14:6f.).

Such an announcement immediately separated mankind into two categories: those "in Christ," and those not in Christ. The people not in Christ were regarded as hostile aliens, as "dead" in sins and trespasses regardless of their moral conduct (Acts 11:14). In Ephesians Paul carried to its conclusion the stated premise of Christ. He identified all men not in Christ as "dead, culture led, philosophy led, Satan led, disobedient, separated, excluded, without God, without hope, hostile, far off, foreigners and aliens (Eph. 2:1ff.). When "in Christ," one was raised up, saved, recreated, brought near, at peace with, fellow-citizens with God's people, and members of God's household (Eph. 2:14ff.). The church of Christ was the continuation of the covenanted people of God. One was "elect" in Christ (v. 4) having been adopted, redeemed, and forgiven "through the blood." There can be no doubt of the covenant orientation of Paul. He used covenant terminology in the discussion.

The Second Birth

One came into the first kingdom of Israel (Deut. 19:5ff.) by birth into the covenanted people. One came into the second kingdom, the kingdom of Messiah, by the second birth. "Made alive" (Eph. 2:1) probably had reference to a resurrection from the dead lot of humanity, but the metaphor paralleled the concept of being born again (John 3:3). Jesus' language of new birth was followed by Paul (Philemon 1:10), Peter (I Pet. 1:21ff.), John (I John 2:29). The terminology was covenantal (John 3:1ff.) referring to the *parties*.

301

One's new birth began when the gospel was "planted" in his mind (James 1:18-22). The "seed" was the message of Christ (I Pet. 1:21f.). The embryo was created when the evidence of the death and resurrection was presented and belief began (I Cor. 4:15). Gestation was short or long, depending on each convert. Gestation was "coming to one's self" (Luke 15:17), for "a godly sorrow for sin leadeth a man to repentance" (II Cor. 7:10). The actual birth occurred in water (Titus 3:5). Baptism was the pledge of loyalty from a good conscience to God (I Pet. 3:21). The covenant bound when the birth took place or when the oath was taken (Heb. 9:18). No other view was represented in any writings of the ancient church during the first four hundred years.[6] Only a small, if vocal, minority of Christian scholars published a different view. It is the consensus of informed scholarship that baptism was the water of regeneration.

Prior to the execution of a single stipulation of the New Covenant Messiah granted to the believer citizenship (Gal. 3:27), remission of sin (Acts 2:38), the gift of the Holy Spirit (Acts 2:38), and participation in all future promises (Rom. 8:17ff.). It may be correctly stated that no Christian had his sins remitted by any stipulation or work of the New Covenant. He received that grace as a gift of God upon his surrender and pledge to God.

The entire process of new birth was under the supervision of the Holy Spirit. The Spirit of Christ revealed the message (I Cor. 2:13f.), sent out the preachers (Acts 13:1-3), often found the prospects (Acts 16:9ff.), got the parties together (Acts 8:26f.), sometimes overcame language barriers (Acts 2:4ff.), and demonstrated his own satisfaction with

---

6. Alexander Campbell, *Christian System*, 1835, Cincinnati: Standard Publishing Co., Reprinted, p. 189.

the message by sign and miracles (Heb. 2:2ff.). Accordingly anyone thus converted was regarded as born of the Spirit (John 3:5). We might say the Spirit was ultimate cause (John 3:5), the Spirit's preacher the efficient cause (I Cor. 4:15), the message of the Spirit the immediate cause (James 1:18), and the heart of faith the submissive cause (Acts 2:40). The new birth was by divine initiation, but was accomplished by mutual participation. After all, it does take two to make a baby!

Paul discussed the same process in Romans Ten, but in reverse order.

> Everyone who calls upon the name of the Lord shall be saved. How, then, can they call on the one they have not believed in? And how can they believe in the one of whom they have not heard? And how can they hear without someone preaching to them? And how can they preach unless they are sent? (Rom. 10:13-15).

The only description we have in Acts of "calling on His name," was in reference to Paul himself. He had been praying for several days, presumably asking for God's forgiveness. Ananias told him,

> And now, what are you waiting for? Get up, be baptized and wash away your sins, calling on his name (Acts 22:16).

Baptism as Covenant Pledge

The waters of Noah brought death to the sinners in his time. The same water saved Noah, by God's grace. Water was judgment and water separated the living from the dead. The water of Christ was also a kind of judgment.[7] It was a judgment on

---

7. Merideth Kline, *By Oath Consigned*, Grand Rapids: Eerdmans, 1968, p. 65ff.

sin. It was both God's judgment and the convert's. One's old life was sinful; they agreed on that judgment. The soul that sinneth, it shall die—was agreed upon by each. The water was also a pledge by both. The sinner pledged to God his life and God pledged admission to the covenant.

> In it, only a few people were saved through water, and this water symbolizes baptism that now saves you also—not the removal of dirt from the body, but the pledge of a good conscience toward God. It saves you by the resurrection of Christ (I Pet. 3:21).

Some former translations used the word "answer." The gospel offered to a sinsick civilization a cleansing of conscience. The sinner had God's assurance of forgiveness if he but said, "Yes." Baptism was man's answer to God. The word endings in Greek allowed for either the initiative or the responsive rendering. Some translators preferred the initiative form: pledge or an asking, while others the responsive form: an answer.

"the prayer for a clear conscience before God" — Moffatt
"the answer of a good conscience" — KJV
"the craving for a clear conscience" — Williams

"the appeal made to God" — NEB
"the request to God for" — Schonfield

"the interrogation of a good conscience" — ASV
"the asking God for a clear conscience" — Beck

"because in being baptized we are turning to God and asking him to cleanse our hearts from sin" — Living Bible
"the pledge of a good conscience" — NIV

When one entered the waters of baptism he was testifying to his faith in the death and resurrection. Actually he was speaking of three deaths and resurrections. He was saying, "I believe Jesus Christ was buried and raised from the dead, just as I am going under this water, cut off from life, and will come up again." He was also saying, "As Jesus died and rose again, so my old way of life is dead and buried; and as He rose from death, so I shall be a new person and live as He directs." And in a sense he was saying, "Some day I shall die and be buried in the earth. But I believe, as surely as He rose again, and as surely as this one brings me up out of the water, I shall come up out of the grave, because of His own resurrection" (Rom. 6:4-6).

The witnesses to a baptism saw the believer alive and in view, as people once saw Jesus. Then the candidate disappeared from sight in the water as Jesus did in the tomb. They saw him once again as Jesus was seen once again after His resurrection. From the perspective of the candidate, he was alive and breathing once. Now he was under the water, cut off from life-support systems, as Jesus was cut off. If the one baptizing did not bring him up, he would stay there and die, so to speak. But God, through the church, brought him up to air and life, as Jesus was raised to live forever.

> Blessed and holy are those who have part in the first resurrection, The second death has no power over them (Rev. 20:6).

Baptism was, in addition to the beautiful symbolism of death and resurrection, a statement being made to God. This is somewhat the pledge every seeker made to God at baptism.

> "My feet go into the water, into death. Never again will my feet walk to evil. My genitals are buried to sin. Never will they be allowed to serve evil. My hands are immersed. They will not steal, strike in anger, oppress the poor, or attack

the weak. My hands are pledged to Christ. My mind, ambition, ability, imagination, are all immersed. Never again will I use my head for wrong goals, improper gain, or inappropriate dreams or fantasy. My head, heart, and soul are all pledged to God.

The person I once was is now dead and buried. I make that pledge. The person I am to be is alive for Christ's use. I make that pledge. I am all Christ's. My answer, Lord, is "Yes." I give this act as my most sacred oath."

Baptism now saves you, . . . as a pledge of a good conscience toward God. It saves you by the resurrection of Jesus Christ (I Pet. 3:21).

Prayer was never used as an oath or answer in the New Testament. It lacked essential ingredients to be a Hebrew oath. It had no death in it. And it was too gnostic. Prayer involved the mind, certainly, and the emotions, and some of the will, but only one part of the will. And prayer lacked the body—essential for Hebrew personhood. A person's body sinned. In their minds it was a "body of sin," a dead weight of years of defilement. It needed cleansing. Baptism involved all of man's nature. Prayer only promised to deliver the body of God. Baptism delivered it.

Water was associated with oath taking from the time of Moses. At the oath swearing at Sinai, Moses mixed the blood with water, to extend its use. By the time the 600,000 had passed, there might have been a thin mixture left! The Syrian, Naaman was cleansed by dipping himself in water. The proselytes dipped themselves in the waters of baptism as an initiation or a "choosing into" the brotherhood of Israel. When the Lord Jesus was slain—in God's oath taking, blood and water flowed from his side. Paul linked the death of Jesus, i.e., the blood, with a believer's baptism. It recalled a commitment made there.

We died to sin, how can we live in it any longer? Or don't you know that all of us who were baptized into Jesus Christ were baptized into his death? We were therefore buried with him through baptism, into death, in order that, just as Christ was raised from the dead through the glory of the Father, we too may live a new life. If we have been united with him in his death, we shall certainly be united with him in his resurrection. For we know that our old self was crucified with him, so that the body of sin might be rendered powerless, that we should no longer be slaves to sin—because anyone who has died has been freed from sin (Rom. 6:2-7).

The conscience would be cleansed at baptism only if the candidate believed two things. He must truly believe with a good conscience, "in his heart," that Jesus rose from the dead. Without that, it would be mere ceremonial game playing. And, he must believe God has promised him remission of sin and admission to covenanted peace when that oath is sworn. If the candidate felt relief and joy when he arose (Acts 8:39) he believed God. If he had no relief, he was either mistaught, and thus cheated of his birthright, or he did not believe the scriptures. The linking of baptism with remission of sin is illustrated by this parallel. Both involved a pledging. God pledged in a very physical way at Calvary. He expects man to do the same.

This is my blood of the covenant which is poured out for many . . . for the forgiveness of sins (Matt. 26:28).

Repent and be baptized . . . for the forgiveness of your sins (Acts 2:38).

Of course, there was no eternal or magical link of remission of sin to baptism. The link was covenantal. It was parallel to the cleansing of Naaman.

307

There was nothing about water as opposed to sand or sawdust as an element making baptism function as intended. God made things valuable by His selection of them for a purpose. He could have used any number of ways for man to respond. He chose baptism. It had value only because it was covenanted. If one were unable to be baptized, perhaps God would consider an alternative, although we have no examples of that being done. The point is baptism was neither legalistic nor mechanical. It was moral. After all, how can one mean, "Yes," to God while saying no to baptism? Nor is it satisfactory to identify physical acts of faith as "works" and mental acts as "faith." Works, in the theology of Paul, were never identified as the execution of a command of Christ or the Apostles. Works were, for Paul, doing what the law had required (Gal. 3:2) or a self-announced definition of good deed (Eph. 2:9). God's free gift can be unmerited, not earned, not deserved and yet be conditional or mutual. God gave (graced) Joshua Jericho, but Joshua was required to participate in the work of faith. Naaman was freely given cleansing, but he had to obey.

The basic and root theological error resulting in the low view of baptism came from the adoption of Greek presupposition about matter and spirit. For the Greeks, matter was wrong and unspiritual. Spirit had no form, color, substance, and was pure "spirit." When that assumption was carried into Christian thought, it came to be expressed by the statement: "No physical act can have anything to do with a man's salvation." Thus mental processes came to be identified as faith and physical processes works. That two-category explanation can be of little use in Bible study, for the Bible is Covenant. Covenants were mutual and conditional in nature. The above stated Greek type principle, if carried to its logical conclusion would also eliminate the cross, the church and the incarnation. Each was quite physical. Such an assumption is a revival of gnosticism, although in a much milder form. Its revival was carried by certain strains of European protestantism. The reformation was part of the renaissance. The renaissance was produced by the Greek revival.[8]

In covenant, the *forms* taken had no value in and of themselves (as with the water in baptism). Their value came by inclusion as part of a covenant.

That is why Moses was warned when he was about to build the tabernacle, "See to it that you make everything according to the pattern shown you on the mountain" (Exod. 25:40). The ministry Jesus has . . . is superior to the old one . . . (Heb. 8:24, 25).

Baptism and Circumcision

There is a difference between the oath or pledge of a covenant and the "sign" of a covenant. The Hebrew for oath was *alah*. It also was used for "the curse of covenant," because an oath was both a commitment and a self-curse. The sign of a covenant was *'ot*. The oath was walking between a halves of the slain animals, touching "the blood of the covenant." A sign was a visible representation or memorial to that ceremony. It may have been a pile of rocks (Gen. 31:44f.), or a rainbow (Gen. 9:13), or others. The oath swearing of God and Abraham was passing between the halves (Gen. 15:17, 18). The sign of the covenant signed that night was circumcision (17:11). The sign of the

---

8. Edward M. Hulme, *Renaissance and Reformation*, New York: Century Publishing Co., 1917, p. 88-91.

Mosaic covenant was the Sabbath (Exod. 31:13). The sign of the Christian covenant was possessing the Holy Spirit, or living the kind of life Jesus did (Eph. 1:13).

A passage in Colossians used the words, circumcision, sinful nature, the circumcision of Christ, and baptism as burial together in a discussion. Paul did not equate circumcision with baptism. He did not use them in parallel. The "circumcision not done with hands," that is, "the circumcision of Christ," was his death. He was cut off. His entire body on the cross was "circumcised." The Christian joined Christ at baptism when he participated in that death and resurrection.

> What happened at Calvary was not a symbolic oath-cursing but the actual carrying out of the curse in the circumcision of God in the crucifixion of his only begotten son. There "the body of [Jesus'] flesh by his death" (Col. 1:22) was actually cut off (apekdusis) (Col. 2:11) so that "we [Jew and Gentile] might be presented holy and blameless and irreproachable," who once were "estranged and hostile in mind, doing evil deeds" (Col. 1:21, 22) . . . Paul used apekdusis. . . .
>
> To catch the sense of the word, we should translate it "fully put off" expressing the exclusion of every possibility of returning again to the former state or condition. Paul means therefore, that Jesus' death was HIS circumcision.[9]

The Christian took the initial oath at his own death and resurrection at baptism. Paul did not mean baptism as Christian circumcision. The death of Christ, as he paid the "curses" of the covenant, symbolized by the cutting off in circumcision, was the cutting off of the entire Old System. Paul's

---

9. Paul Jewett, *Infant Baptism and the Covenant of Grace*, Grand Rapids: Eerdmans, 1978, p. 89.

point was that a Jew need for fear any "cutting off" from God because he abandoned the Old Covenant. Yes, he said, God would curse anyone not circumcised. But all indeed were circumcised when Christ suffered the penalty in his being "cut off" for all mankind. And, he added, all participated in the benefits found at the cross when baptized into Christ's death.

> The use of the aorist passive throughout the passage, makes it evident that to experience the circumcision of Christ in putting off the body of flesh, is the same thing as being buried and raised with him in baptism through faith.[10]

This is not to say, however, that baptism and circumcision are equated as signs. The Apostolic parallels were these:

	Jewish	Christian
Base of Covenant:	In the flesh of Abraham	By choice, i.e., by the spirit, of Christ.
Entry into:	By birth as a blood descendant of Abraham.	By rebirth culminated at baptism.
The sign or seal:	Circumcision at eight days.	Walking by the Spirit.

The danger of equating the signs, of making baptism and circumcision both "seals," serving the same purpose, is to raise contradiction in Paul's experience and theology. It was but a short step from "neither circumcision nor uncircumcision has any value" (Gal. 5:6), to "neither baptism nor unbaptism has any value." That would, of course, contradict Christ (Mark 16:15, 16). Paul could indeed say circumcision meant nothing. That was true. It was "dead works"; but it was dead works because the Law of which

---

10. Jewett, *ibid.*, p. 89.

it was a part was "dead" (Rom. 7:1ff.). Paul would never have said such a thing had the Law been still in force.

One thing is clear, water apart from pledge and belief in the gospel by the candidate was works righteousness. It was meaningless. Faith was what made baptism do what was intended. The purpose of baptism was to give an unforgetable pledge demonstrating to God the will and the ability to bring Him that "body of sin," for cleansing. God demonstrated His intentions at Calvary in a very real and physical way. God honored man by graciously allowing him to reciprocate as covenant partner.

Since man's sins were moral, infants were not regarded as sinners (Isa. 7:15, 16). Jesus used the innocence of children as examples of the innocence found in the new kingdom (Matt. 19:14). When entire "households" became Christian (Acts 11:14), it must not be assumed infants were included. Baptism was oath taking, and a covenant could be entered only by those able to understand the moral commitment being made there (Neh. 10:28, 29). Covenant allowed for both God's part in salvation and man's responsibility for evidence and his responsibility to exhibit his battered but valid image of God. God initiated covenants; they were written by Him, handed down to mankind, and man was saved by accepting God's offer. The entire New Covenant was a covenant of grace. It was God's kiss of love to estranged and lonely man. The praise belonged to Him and Him alone (Eph. 1:14).

The Stipulations of New Covenant

Stipulations referred to obligations assumed in the oath. They did not refer to the entry requirements. Election was one thing. Covenant keeping another. God elected Christ

312

(I Pet. 1:20), Abraham and his descendants (Deut. 7:6ff.) and He chose all who were "in Christ" (Eph. 1:4). In the Old Covenant man's promises were the stipulations, or the Law, or the obligation he assumed. To what was the believer commited in the New Covenant? In this study, no effort will be made to identify details. The broad understanding of key category-bearing words is sufficient.

Method of Analysis

In the New Testament no passage stated to the effect, "This is the new covenant list of stipulations," as was found in the Torah. It was equally clear every passage of the Canon was not meant as stipulation of covenant. There was a covenant functioning long before the documents were written. In other words, the New Testament was not the covenant itself. The New Testament was the Canon of the New Covenant, the writings of it, the bearer of it, and the explanation of how the covenant itself ought to be executed. It was inspired, certainly, but according to its purpose. The New Testament scripture was not a legal code book. It was not exactly a "constitution," although it served similar functions. It certainly was not a manual of regulations. The gospel created the church and the church, through its Apostles and others, wrote many documents. The church, who had both heard the message and seen the documents, judged those in the canon to bear best the ancient message. They collected these over some time and finally ratified a given number. Every generation of churches that followed declared the books of the canon inspired, as they certainly were when first written. The New Testament did not represent a code of stipulations. It stated clearly the mandate,

313

the commission. It defined the message and gave broad guidelines for execution of the mission. It was therefore more valuable, in a sense, than the covenant itself. For the New Testament scriptures contained not only the covenant, but also a brief history of how it was administrated by the Apostles and ancient church, together with letters illustrating *problem solving* in harmony with the covenant. It showed how the Apostles used the new philosophy of *means-to-end* to administer the will of God.

One can identify the covenant itself from passages where the subject was clearly under discussion. One such passage will be used as example. Another method is to separate the words of the Apostles into category terms and specific terms. Taken together, they would naturally render a description of the covenant stipulations. A third method is to use parallel data identified as obligation, and assign it the word stipulation. To put the same thing another way, one can sort out all passages in the New Testament that speak of some kind of obligation, organize them under correct Apostolic terminology and summarize obligations in a means-to-end way. All three methods reach identically the same conclusions. We know very well what the stipulations of the New Covenant were.

The methods I have described, particularly that of summarizing demands as the stipulations of covenant, was the method employed by Klaus Baltzer, professor of Old Testament at the University of Munich in his book, *Covenant Formulary*. His categories were: *parties, ethical demands,* and *blessings and curses*.[11] His categories parallel the ones

---

11. Klaus Baltzer, *The Covenant Formulary*, Philadelphia: Fortress Press, 1971, pp. vi-vii.

used in this book, but bear slightly different names. The data under each category is the same, however.

Category Terms

The Lord Jesus Christ used one word to summarize all the demands of the new covenant church: "disciples." He described in some detail what a true disciple was, how to make an unbeliever one, and what the goal or standard was. In "disciple" were found parties, terms, and promises.

Going, MAKE DISCIPLES, baptizing them . . . teaching them to observe all that I have commanded (Matt. 28:18f.).

Making disciples had reference to making converts. This was evident from Luke's frequent statements.

In those days when the number of disciples was increasing . . . (Acts 6:1).

So the word of God spread and the number of disciples increased rapidly and a large number of priests became obedient to the faith (Acts 6:7).

But the word of God continued to grow and spread (Acts 12:24).

There they spoke so effectively that a great number of Jews and Gentiles believed (Acts 14:1).

So the church was strengthened in the faith and grew daily in numbers (Acts 16:5).

Perfecting of disciples, or the equipping of them for service, or the continued teaching of them so they could become increasingly like their master was not called "making disciples," or "discipling." The description of a good disciple was best demonstrated by Jesus Himself. One must forsake all other goals as primary and seek to be like Jesus

315

(Luke 14:26), follow the word of Christ (John 15:7-12), be willing to suffer for the same reasons He suffered (John 15:20), do the kind of thing Jesus did, and thus become perfected, equipped, matured, fully taught—like Christ.

A disciple is not above his master, but every disciple when perfected will be like his master (Luke 6:40, AV).

You will note Jesus later interchanged the word "disciple" with "servant."

Remember the words I spoke to you, "No servant is greater than his master," if they persecuted me they will persecute you . . . (John 15:20).

The exchange of terms by Jesus, servant for disciple, is the key to unlock Paul's thinking and vocabulary of covenant obligation. He did not use disciple, preferring servant or steward. Making disciples was a parallel concept with election. Perfecting them was parallel with stipulations of covenant. Becoming perfected was the summation of the promises (Rom. 8:28f.).

Dear Friends, now we are children of God, and what we will be has not yet been made known. But we know that when he appears we shall be like him, for we shall see him as he is (I John 3:2).

Paul and the "Mystery" of God

The word "mystery" of God, when used in context of ministry, meant what others called covenant. Paul's "mystery" was the New Covenant. Jesus was the "mystery" revealed (Matt. 12:28). The spreading of the gospel was the mystery being revealed, Jesus said (Mark 4:11). Paul clearly indicated the "mystery" was no longer hidden (Rom. 16:25f.)

316

but was now "revealed," and "made known." The mystery was the command of the eternal God. It was the proclamation of Jesus Christ, the gospel, "so that all nations might believe and obey him." In the Ephesian letter, Paul defined "mystery" several times.

The administration of God's grace that was given to me for you. That is, the mystery made known to me by revelation, as I have already written briefly.

This mystery is that thru the gospel the Gentiles are heirs together with Israel, members together in one body, and sharers together in the promise in Christ Jesus.

This grace was given to me: to preach to the Gentiles the unsearchable riches of Christ, and to make plain to everyone my administration of this mystery . . . hidden . . . His intent was now, through the church, the manifold wisdom of God should be made known . . . according to his eternal PURPOSE which he accomplished in Christ Jesus our Lord (Eph. 3:2-12).

Parties: Israel and Gentiles "in one body"
Stipulation: "The administration of this mystery"
Promises: "in the promises in Christ Jesus . . . unsearchable riches"

The Ministry of Reconciliation

In a very instructive passage, the vocabulary patterns of Paul were revealed with startling clarity. He did not use the term covenant often. When referring to the Old Covenant he preferred the term Law. He knew it was part of a covenant. When discussing the New Covenant he preferred the name of Christ. He knew Christ was the covenant in person. In the following passage, he indicated his thinking with a type

317

of parallel vocabulary. He began with the word *covenant*, it became the word *ministry*, that in turn became *the ministry of reconciliation.*

New Covenant stipulation is ministry (II Cor. 3:6).
Ministry is ministry of reconciliation (II Cor. 5:18, 20).
New Covenant stipulation is the ministry of reconciliation.

In the third chapter there was an extensive discussion of the two covenants. In chapter four, the style, hazards, goals, and glories of ministry were discussed. "Your servants for Christ's sake," "being given over to death for Christ's sake," "for your benefit," "we make it our goal to please Him," "it is for the sake of God," and

That those who live should no longer live to themselves but for him who died for them and was raised from the dead (II Cor. 4:1—5:15),

reflected Christ's definition of servant. A servant advanced the best interests of his Master. The best interests of Christ was for all men to "believe and obey" the gospel, become reconciled to God, and live like Christ.

All this is from God who reconciled us to himself through Christ and gave us the ministry of reconciliation: that God was reconciling the world to Himself in Christ, not counting men's sins against them. And He has committed to us the ministry of reconciliation. We are therefore Christ's ambassadors, as though God was making his appeal through us.

We implore you on Christ's behalf, "Be reconciled to God."

God made him who knew no sin to be sin on our behalf, so that in him we might become the righteousness of God" (II Cor. 5:18-22).

There was, in a sense, a separation of the moral and the ceremonial aspects of the Law of Moses. It was not a formal separation, certainly, and I know of no scholar who has been able to satisfactorily separate them on any agreed principle. Nonetheless, the quality of life called ethics, is different from specific duty. They are certainly related, but the latter may change. The former does not. The ethic of the Torah was summed up in Christ, according to Paul. The new covenant was the covenant of the Spirit (II Cor. 3:3 and 6). In other words, being led of the Spirit was being led to be like Christ. Christlikeness was true spirituality.

Now the Lord (Jesus) is the Spirit and where the Spirit of the Lord is there is freedom. And we, who with unveiled faces all reflect the Lord's glory, are being transformed into his likeness with ever increasing glory, which comes from the Lord, who is the Spirit (II Cor. 3:17f.).

Becoming like Christ was the "law of liberty." Being part of the ministry of reconciliation in a Christlike manner was fulfillment of the stipulation of the New Covenant. To put the two duties another way "speaking the truth in love" (Eph. 4:15, 16).

The Two Category Analysis

There were two kinds of people created by Christ's mediatorship: the lost and the redeemed. God had a purpose for each. For the lost, the purpose was reconciliation. That summed up almost all the ceremonial aspects of covenant keeping, according to Paul. There was also a purpose for the saved. It was to become like Christ: in one's soul (Phil. 3:12-15), as a church body (Eph. 4:12-16), in suffering (I Pet. 1:21), and in society (Eph. 5:1). Whatever contributed to those ends was covenant keeping.

So men ought to regard us as servants of Christ and as those entrusted with the secret things (*mysterion*) of God. Now it is required that those who have been given a trust must prove faithful (I Cor. 4:1).

The two categories of the *stipulations* of the covenant have been given several other names. Evangelism is parallel to reconciliation because it is the means to that end. Nurture is parallel to Christlikeness, because it is means to end. "Inside orientation" means preoccupation with duties of the church where Christians were being built up and served. "Outside orientation" is used when referring to activities aimed at reaching the lost for Christ. A "missionary" is usually one who is making new Christians in an old land. "Minister" is a word used when a pastor or minister is staying in his own country. The use of the terms in the above ways is not Biblically accurate, but they indicate a correct understanding of "lost" and "saved."

God was reconciling the world to himself, and gave to us the ministry of reconciliation (II Cor. 5:18).

From Him the whole body joined and held together by every supporting ligament, grows and upbuilds itself in love (Eph. 4:16).

Two separate words were used by Paul in the Ephesian passage. *Auxasin* usually referred to growth in size (Acts 7:17). *Oikodomen* was translated by "upbuilds itself" and was usually associated with ministry to the church itself (I Cor. 14:3, 4). It is an example of the two categories being assumed in the ancient church.

And the church . . . enjoyed a time of peace. It was strengthened; and encouraged by the Holy Spirit, it grew in numbers (Acts 6:31).

320

So the churches were encouraged in the faith, and grew daily in numbers (Acts 16:5).

The stipulations of the New Covenant were two, when speaking in general terms. One was to win the world to Christ, called *reconciliation*. The other was to change the world by each convert becoming more like Christ, called *Christlikeness*. The same idea was reflected in many ways, providing valuable clues to ancient category systems.

> Tongues then are a sign, not for believers, but unbelievers; prophecy, however is for believers, not for unbelievers (I Cor. 14:22).

> I have written to you in my letter not to associate with sexually immoral people—not at all meaning the people of this world. In that case you would have to leave this world. But . . . not to associate with anyone who calls himself a brother who is immoral . . . (I Cor. 5:9ff.).

Category Terms for Election

Election referred to *parties*. The church was the family of the elect (Eph. 2:12-22), "a royal priesthood, holy nation, a people belonging to God" as old Israel was (I Pet. 2:9). Disciple, steward, minister, servant, slave of Christ, God's plot, Christ's body, the brethren, the holy, Jerusalem, Israel, the kingdom, Zion, the church, and others were all words referring to parties of covenant. The process of conversion was described as calling and election (II Pet. 1:10), salvation, justification, new birth, redemption, santification, enlightenment, adoption, and the like. Each of these terms separately referred to the entire process. One was not first redeemed, then enlightened, then called, then new born, then saved, and later sanctified. These terms were most frequently used as synedoche, "the part represents the whole," and conversely, "the whole is represented by the part." The Hebrews made quite frequent use of the figure. It could help the Bible student understand generalizations expressed by different words. For instance, *hearing* was said to save (Gal. 3:5). Obviously it represented the other aspects of becoming Christian. *Belief* was frequently used to represent the entire process of justification (John 3:16). At times *repentance* was the part representing the whole (II Pet. 3:9). *Confession* was employed as the summation of all aspects of coming to God (Matt. 10:32, 33). *Baptism* was employed as the part for the whole (I Pet. 3:21).

Category Terms for Stipulation

"Led of the Spirit" (Gal. 5:25), "filled with the Spirit" (Eph. 5:18), "walking in his steps," (I Pet. 3:21), being edified, built up or builded-into (Eph. 2:2), living for him (II Cor. 5:15), "being transformed into his image" (II Cor. 3:18), preaching the gospel (I Cor. 9:16-18), "administration of this mystery" (Eph. 3:9), serving, ministering (II Tim. 4:5), "shepherding God's flock" (I Pet. 5:2), "holding forth the word of life" (Phil. 2:16) being examples of Christ (I Pet. 5:3) and others, represented summaries of the stipulations of the New Covenant. When one was baptized he made a lifetime commitment to advance the cause of his Lord. He became a slave of Christ. He gave his life away, assuming the role of Christ's steward. His duty was to help win to God all mankind by all Christlike means (I Cor. 9:16-27).

The Promises of the New Covenant

Promises of the covenant were carried by the same two words employed in the Old Testament: blessings and woes.

Each had a set of blessings (Matt. 5:1ff.) and a set of woes (Matt. 23:13-29). The reader can examine the details for himself. The dual concept of blessing and woe was carried throughout the Bible.

> Yet when I preach the gospel, I cannot boast, for I am compelled to preach. Woe to me if I do not preach the gospel. If I preach voluntarily I have a reward, but if not voluntarily I am simply discharging a trust committed to me. . . .
>
> I have become all things to all men so that by all possible means I might save some. I do all for the sake of the gospel, that I might share in its blessings. . . . I beat my body and make it my slave, so that after I have preached to others I myself will not be disqualified for the prize (I Cor. 9:16-27).

The blessings of the covenant must be separated into two basic categories to fully understand them. Paul summarized them by one simple phrase, *with Christ* (Rom. 8:32) . . . Jesus indicated there were two types of blessings.

> No one who left home and brothers . . . sisters . . . mothers . . . children . . . or fields for me and the gospel will fail to receive a hundred times as much in this present age, (homes, brothers, . . . and with them, persecutions) and in the age to come, eternal life (Mark 10:29, 30).

1. Universal Covenanted blessings.

One kind of promise was universal for all in Christ. One received these whether he knew they existed or not, simply because he joined Christ: Remission of Sin (Acts 2:38), the gift of the Holy Spirit (I Cor. 12:7), Christ as intercessor and advocate with the Father (I John 2:1ff.). We all have part in the common ministry, a matter angels sought (I Pet. 1:12). Peter considered the sharing in the church and the stabilizing influence of its godliness as a very great blessing.

He has given us his very great and precious promises, so that through them you might participate in the divine nature, and escape the corruption of the world caused by evil desires (I Pet. 1:4).

All future things belonged without measure to all believers in Christ: the resurrection from the dead (I Cor. 15:20ff.), passing through the judgment (Rev. 21:27), being confessed as Christ's disciple (Matt. 10:33, 34), a new spiritual-substantial body (I Cor. 15:49), a home "in heaven" (John 14:1-4), and seeing "a new heaven and a new earth" (II Pet. 3:10-13). All the above mentioned were summarized by Christ as "eternal life" (John 3:16).

2. Potential Covenanted Blessings.

I do not care for the term "potential." Perhaps the word personal would be better. Or even personal/conditional. What is being referred to is the entire class of earthly blessings or benefits as answered prayer, matters related to illness, or genetic defect, the extent and degree of individual suffering, the having or not having mothers, sisters, houses, land, wife or husband, and the like. These came to individuals in differing measure. One thing was certain. Christ was the model. No disciple could expect anything different in the way of treatment than Jesus received. But every disciple could expect to receive all Jesus had to give: peace with God (John 14:27).

The New Covenant and Suffering

Jesus denied all suffering came from sins, whether of the parent or the individual (John 9:1ff.). Some suffered because they were in the wrong place at the wrong time

(Luke 13:4). Some suffered because of incompetence and poor personal judgment (Luke 14:28ff.). Some suffered because aid did not come to them in time (John 5:1ff.), or because of the sinfulness of others (Matt. 21:33). Pain, at least in this body, was not necessarily a bad thing. Pain in the foot was better than no signal the foot was cut. Pain in the foot was better than infection in the foot. Some caused themselves pain in order to serve faithfully (Matt. 19:12). Others caused themselves pain by neglect of duty (Matt. 25:1ff.). A few brought ill upon themselves by breaking civil laws (Rom. 13:4-7). Many suffered simply because they were servants of Christ:

> Blessed are you when people insult you, persecute you, and falsely say all manner of evil against you because of me. Rejoice and be glad, for in the same way they persecuted the prophets that were before you (Matt. 5:11, 12).

Some Christians suffered because of justice (I Pet. 2:20), and some unjustly. Slaves suffered because of the wickedness of "menstealers" (I Tim. 1:10). Masters who were "harsh" were to be served well by believers (I Pet. 2:18ff.). Men suffered from enemies, nature, and regretably from "false brothers" (II Cor. 11:26). God had not promised daily bread as a matter of covenant (II Cor. 11:27). God asked men to die for him; and saw a good many die while the wicked watched with satisfaction (Acts 7:57ff.).

The Apostles did not emphasize physical blessings. To have done so would have disarmed the believer facing hard times. It would have left the one falsely taught hating God for not intervening when called upon. Paul asked God for relief from some "thorn in the flesh." God's reply was what Christ had promised.

325

My grace is sufficient for you, for my power is made perfect
in weakness (II Cor. 12:8).

It simply was not true that uncontaminated faith would
protect the believer from suffering. God asked the believer
to pray within the framework of Christ's norms. Prayer
could move mountains. That was true, but it is a rare case
where mountains ought to be moved. It caused less in-
convenience to many to just walk over it or go around it.
God did not exempt His true disciples from natural or social
processes.

He causes His sun to shine on the evil and the good, and
sends rain on the righteous and the unrighteous (Matt. 5:45).

Suffering was not believed to be the result of lack of faith
or an unconfessed sin. Accidents and illnesses were like the
wind and rain. In some cases God healed (James 5:14ff.),
but He also said "to take as an example of patience in the
face of suffering, the prophets who spoke in the name of
the Lord" (5:10). God could and did interfere with nature
but He preferred His people to employ their abilities in nature
and society for His good (Luke 16:2ff.). Paul suffered for
his Lord out of deep covenant-loyalty. It was never assumed
to have been caused by lack of faith or as punishment for
sins committed and unconfessed.

Are they servants of Christ? (I am out of my head to talk like
this.) I am more. I have worked much harder, been in prison
more frequently, been flogged more severely, and been
exposed to death again and again. Five times I received of
the Jews the forty lashes minus one. Three times I was
beaten with rods, once I was stoned, three times I was ship-
wrecked, I spent a day and a night in the open sea, I have
been constantly on the move. I have been in danger from

bandits, in danger from my own countrymen, in danger from Gentiles; in danger in the city, in danger in the country, in danger at sea; and in danger from false brothers. I have labored and toiled and often gone without sleep. I have known hunger and thirst, and often gone without food; I have been cold and naked. Besides everything else, I face daily the pressure of my concern for all the churches (II Cor. 11:22-28).

Circumstances whether good or ill must be used for Christ. Even failure could be used for Christ. It warned of repeating the procedure. All things could work together for good. They did work together for good for those using them to aid God's purposes. They did not just naturally turn out for good.

We know that in all things God works for the good of those who love him, who have been called according to his purpose (Rom. 8:28).

James forbade the believer to say God had sent a trial to test him.

No one should say when tempted, God is tempting me (James 1:13).

Because the word "trials" and "temptations" were the same word in Greek, it was further wrong to say, "God sent me a difficulty." What God did was see how the believer reacted. In every event God evaluated how a man reacted. God was not understood to send trials to provide evaluative circumstances.

The attitude of the new covenant toward suffering was found in Christ. He was "made perfect through suffering" (Heb. 5:8). Paul sought to make up what lacked in suffering by Christ for the sake of the church (Col. 1:24). Unjust suffering in doing God's will was why Christ came and was to be the example for the people of God (I Pet. 2:21). The momentary suffering on earth was not to be compared with the future glory (Rom. 8:18). Suffering could cause reversions to the loss of one's salvation (Heb. 10:32-39). To avoid suffering some had accepted circumcision and endangered their salvation (Gal. 6:12-16). Workers for God should expect to both labor and suffer (I Tim. 4:10). Christians were specifically told they were going to suffer (I Thess. 3:4). The ability to suffer, if need be, to promote Christ's purposes was related to salvation.

> Now if we are his children we are his heirs, heirs of God, and co-heirs with Christ, if indeed we share in his sufferings in order that we may also share in his glory (Rom. 8:17).

The Matthew Six Passage

The passage most frequently misunderstood as promising physical blessings for righteousness was a statement by Jesus.

> But seek first his kingdom and his righteousness and all these things will be given to you as well (Matt. 6:33).

It sounded very much as a typical conditional promise. However, the context provided an alternative understanding. Jesus was not promising "these things," meaning food, drink, and clothing if one were sufficiently righteous. On the contrary, God provided for all things in nature. He mentioned the lilies and sparrows. Lilies burned up in the summer sun. Sparrows fell. God knew that, and did not frequently interfere. Nor did He interfere when the sun and rain fell on the good and the bad. What was important for

328

the citizen of the new kingdom of heaven was to live in nature without being dominated by it. "Who of you by worrying can add a single hour to his life" Jesus asked (Matt. 6:27). Seeking to do God's will, seeking as first priority God's righteousness was the lifestyle of the kingdom citizen. To paraphrase the passage,

> You are to seek to build up the church, the kingdom of Christ and harmonize your life with the example of Christ as your first and highest priority. People from the beginning have had food, drink and shelter. These things will come to you as well as others. Do not be preoccupied with obtaining them.

The Tabernacle and the Church

The Tabernacle was a large tent, the center of Hebrew worship. The Hebrew writer referred to it in connection with Christ, but did not go into detail about its anti-types. He referred to the items of furniture in it. His main application in typology was Christ, who, as the high priest, carried His own blood into the Holy Place, and through the curtain, "his own flesh," into the Most Holy Place, heaven (Heb. 9:1-14). Christ was understood as an altar (Heb. 13:10). Only Christians were allowed to eat from that sacrifice. The Laver was understood by some to be baptism (Titus 3:5). The Holy Place was taken as the Church, for inside it were to be found the Candlestick, representing the Holy Spirit or perhaps the word of God (Ps. 119:105). The Table of Consecrated Bread was perhaps a type of the Lord's Table. The golden altar of incense represented prayer (Rev. 5:9) although the contexts of the passages were not parallel. The Ark was the most sacred object. Beside it was the covenant or perhaps the salvation history of the world held in

329

heaven, or the dwelling place of God.[12] Scholars differ on it. The text did not say what its anti-type was. He simply said, "But we can not discuss these things in detail now" (9:5). The Most Holy Place itself was heaven or the presence of God (9:24). The high priest sprinkled the blood of atonement on the Mercy Seat of the Ark seven times. He then returned to announce to the people the act of atonement had been carried out. He blessed them. Jesus went into the presence of God with His own blood and shall come again to bless His own (9:28).

The People of God: the Church

Christ separated the people of God from any national government. That was a very radical departure from the old covenant. Events during the diaspora pointed in that direction. The Old Theocracy was dead forever. The church, new Israel, was to go into every land. It was a kingdom "not of this world" (John 18:36). That must not be understood as meaning his kingdom was individualistic. It was not. It was an organized body, a very physical body. It was a corporate body. The church was the continuation of Christ in history. To attack it was to attack Christ (Acts 9:5). It was called Christ (I Cor. 12:12). While it was one body around the world, it was manifested in local assemblies, similar to synagogues (James 2:2). There was local leadership (Phil. 1:1) called elders, leaders, overseers, bishops, or shepherds. Another class of workers were called "ministers," or deacons and deaconesses (I Tim. 3:12ff.). Members

---

12. Victor E. Hoven, *Shadow and Substance*, St. Louis: Bethany, 1934, p. 163ff.

were admitted to the assembly upon their pledge to Christ. Baptism was a pledge of loyalty to Christ and to the church, His body. Paul said in the church dwelled the "fulness of Him who fills all in all" (Eph. 1:23).

The church met on the first day of the week (Acts 20:7). The practice was related to the resurrection. Sunday came to be known as the Lord's Day. It was called the Lord's Day because the Lord's Supper was celebrated at that time by all members of the church.[13]

The Lord's supper was initiated by Christ (Matt. 26:26ff.). It was a ceremony having bread and wine (I Cor. 11:20, 21). Eating a common meal together, during which a special time was devoted to the "Lord's Supper" itself was a common early practice. It helped integrate all elements in the church into one new humanity planned by God (Eph. 2:15). The Table of the Lord was the covenant renewal service. It was a time to remember Christ's death and resurrection (I Cor. 11:23ff.). It was a meal to indicate a) Christ's presence with them in the millennial kingdom (Matt. 26:29). b) The oneness of the members of the church. They were "one body" (I Cor. 12:20), just as Israel was one kingdom of tribes. When a member repeated the sacred words, "This is my body," he meant two things: a) "This act recalls Christ's body on the tree," and also, "This group is my body, my life, my soul—because it is His body."

The ancient church called the Lord's Table the "Thanksgiving," and saw it as a sacrament. It served the same function as the Passover Feast in Israel. The Lord's Supper was meant as a sacrifice, hence the word "sacrament." When one came to the table of Christ he was to confess his sins, as done in the old system. He was then to renew his pledge to Christ.

---

13. Paul Jewett, *The Lord's Day*, Grand Rapids, Michigan: Eerdmans, 1971.

The eating and the drinking was oath renewal. A person said to God and all the church brethren, "I am part of Israel, the church. I renew the covenant with you. I will serve and love you." There was a self-curse in every Hebrew oath. The believer was understood by God to be saying, "You may regard me as one who killed the Master and who counted his blood an unholy thing if I do not keep this pledge." That was why Paul said,

> For whoever eats the bread or drinks the cup of the Lord in an unworthy manner will be guilty of sinning against the body and blood of the Lord. . . . For anyone who eats and drinks without recognizing the Body of the Lord, eats and drinks judgment on himself. That is why many among you are sick, and a number of you have fallen asleep (I Cor. 11:27-31).

In sacrament, what was being pictured was also happening. For instance, when an animal was sacrificed in Israel it pictured a death, and it was a death—the death of the sheep. It was also the death of the worshipper if he came with a good heart. God agreed the sheep could stand in his place. So when the sheep died, the man died, at least in God's eyes. It was possible only by covenanted agreement with God.

In the same way, the Eucharist ("the Thanksgiving") was sacramental. What it pictured was happening. The service was not merely a memorial. It was a participation in the blood of Christ. It was a joining with, or a touching the blood of Christ. The blood cleansed from all sin (I John 1:7-10). The contents of the cup was not changed into Christ's blood as a physical element. But in result, it was as if one had made Christ's redeeming blood part of his body. At the old Israelite sacrifices God acted in heaven when man acted on earth. Man sacrificed in good faith and God acted, in good faith, to cover his sins for a year. In the same way, God acted at baptism to cover our sins when we acted in good faith in our pledge. That was covenant at work. At the Lord's Table, God acted in heaven to further remit sins done by the believer as the Christian partook of His blood and body as a pledge renewal. The Lord's Table was much more than a mere memorial service. It was covenant renewal. Jesus used the formal oath taking terms when He instituted the practice.

Drink from it all of you. "This is my blood of the covenant . . ." (Matt. 26:28).

Paul asked,

The cup of blessing that we bless, is it not a participation in the blood (I Cor. 10:15)?

The oath pledged to administrate the church to the best interests of Christ and its members, to do nothing to humiliate the church (I Cor. 11:22), to discipline wayward members (I Cor. 5:13), to help the weak in the faith (Gal. 6:1), to care for the poor (Acts 6:1ff.), to support its mission effort (Phil. 4:10ff.), care for widows and orphans (James 1:27), and to maintain the "unity of the Spirit" (Eph. 4:1ff.). The chief duty was to carry on the mission: reconciliation and Christlikeness (II Tim. 4:1-5). The church was to have the same loyalty old Israel received from the faithful. The church was to insure the next generation of ministers by choosing out men of good report and commissioning them (II Tim. 2:2). In short, the church was to continue the world mission of Christ, to be administrators of the new covenant (II Cor. 3:6).

Paul's Sacrificial System

Paul viewed the Church as having a kind of sacrificial system. He was not using a formal "typology" model. His was a way of thinking about service to God in the new covenant as the priesthood. He linked world mission to priest and sacrifice. It showed Paul's clear-headed concentration on purpose.

1. The life lived as Christ's servant was a "living sacrifice" and was the worship in the new kingdom of the Spirit of God.

> I urge you, brothers in view of God's mercy, to offer your-selves as living sacrifices, holy and pleasing to God—which is your spiritual worship. Do not conform any longer to the pattern of this world, but be transformed by the renewing of your mind. Then you will be able to test and approve what God's will is—his good, pleasing and perfect will (Rom. 12:1, 2).

There were three Greek words representing "worship" in the New Testament: *proskuneo, sebomai,* and *latreia.* The last was used by Paul in the passage. It was an officially appointed priestly or delegated service. Christian worship, reflecting the sacrifices, offerings and ministries carried on in the tabernacle, was being like Christ. Being conformed to "that good and perfect will of God" was true New Covenant worship. In the former system, a sinner gave a sheep or dove or other offering to God as worship. The priest took it and sacrificed it. In the new order, every believer was a priest. His offering was a living body, a life lived in conformity to God's new pattern, Christ. The assembly was not exclusively where New Covenant worship happened. The assembly was for hearing the word of God, for fellowship, prayer, mutual edification, and the Lord's table. An individual was to worship everywhere. Activities at the assembly were limited to those which edified all. The word of God always edified, as did singing, giving, and renewing covenant with the church and its Lord. What a Christian did all week long was true New Covenant worship as it advanced the will of God.

2. The second kind of sacrifice to God was a convert. A Gentile who accepted Christ as Lord was the kind of offering sought by God in the new era.

> Because of the grace God gave me to be a minister of Christ Jesus with the priestly duty of proclaiming the gospel of God so that the Gentiles might become an offering acceptable to God, sanctified by the Holy Spirit (Rom. 15:16).

The priests of the former covenant offered a lamb or goat to God in thanksgiving, surrender and worship. In the new era, a person won to God was a sacrifice by the new priesthood. The implication was too obvious. One who did not participate in the winning of the Gentiles was not offering acceptable sacrifices to God and was in breach of covenant.

3. The kind of sacrifice and offering God sought from New Israel was support of the spreading of the gospel message. Paul wrote to the church at Philippi thanking them for their recently arrived gift.

> I am amply supplied now that I have received from Epaphroditus the gifts you sent. They are a fragrant offering, an acceptable sacrifice, pleasing to God. And my God will meet all your needs according to his glorious riches in Christ Jesus (Phil. 4:18).

Money, clothing, moral support, or books—in short, whatever was needed by an evangelist of Christ was the kind of offering God sought. It was not simply a "glass of cold water" to which Paul was referring. He made that clear when he replied it was not the money itself he wanted. The offering represented to Paul participation in new covenant stewardship by that church. That kind of sacrifice was "credited to your account" (Phil. 4:17). When one did not take an active part in the ministry of reconciliation with what was he to appear before God? How much did he hold the "blood of the covenant by which he was sanctified" in honor? What had he pledged at the Lord's Table?

4. A life given to God's mission was understood as Paul's sacrifice to God. A life lost, used up, killed, or exhausted for the sake of the success of Christ was true worship before God.

> I am already being poured out as a drink offering, and the time of my departure has come. I have fought the good fight, I have finished the course, I have kept the faith (II Tim. 4:6).

5. The confession by a Gentile that "Jesus is Lord," was held to be the "sacrifice of Praise" to God. The passage is worded in such a way it may be understood to refer to singing or shouting praise to God. The preferred understanding; a confession of faith by a new convert, fits the context. In the broadest sense the passage meant any praise of God by lips which have already confessed Christ. The narrow meaning is to be preferred, however, since it harmonizes with parallel passages.

> Through Jesus therefore, let us continually offer to God a sacrifice of praise—the fruit of the lips that confess his name and do not forget to do good and share with others, for with such sacrifices God is pleased (Heb. 13:15, 16).

336

The sharing mentioned was probably in reference to support of the church leaders, since the writer calls to their minds, immediately after his requests for sharing, the leadership of the churches. "Sharing" was the other word Paul used in Philippians 4:14 following which he identified such sharing as "sacrifice." Of course, it was far more important in that day, if not in all ages, to see vital believers (preachers) have their physical needs met prior to meeting the needs of the community at large. The eternal salvation of all men depended upon Christian leadership.

This review shows the thinking of the leadership in the early church. The covenant context was unmistakable. The church as God's Israel to the world acting in a priestly way, mediating reconciliation through the word, provided support for consistent thinking among writers in the ancient church.

> As you come to Him, the Living Stone, rejected by men, but chosen by God and precious to him—you also like living stones are being built into a spiritual house to be a holy priesthood, offering spiritual sacrifices acceptable to God through Jesus Christ. . . .
>
> But you are a chosen race, a royal priesthood, a holy nation, a people belonging to God, that you might declare the praise of Him who called you out of darkness into his wonderful light (I Pet. 2:4-10).

They learned it from Jesus.

> I have glorified you on earth, having accomplished the work you gave me to do (John 17:4).

Church and State

The Christian was to be part of the civil governments where he lived. He was to obey as a matter of conscience the civil authorities as the Israelite obeyed the Theocracy. Governments were God's servants to keep order (Rom. 13:1ff.). The church could go about its business without having to administrate civil codes. Its duty was to save lost souls. Sometimes the "law of the Spirit" brought a believer into conflict with civil authorities. In such cases, depending upon its impact on the long-range goals of Christ, a decision must be made. Where there was clear conflict and no possibility of negotiation, the will of Christ was to prevail.

> Judge for yourselves whether it is right in God's sight to obey you rather than God, for we cannot help speaking about what we have seen and heard (Acts 4:19).

The church was not to be anti-government as a religious position. It was to pray for rulers and men in high places (I Tim. 2:1ff.). No ethnic was required to give up his language (I Cor. 14:18) or his customs as long as they were compatible with Christ's program (I Cor. 9:16ff.). The unity of the church was not in political agreements, nor social compatibility, but in Christ, and in his mission.

> There is one body, and one Spirit, just as you were called to one hope when you were called—one Lord, one faith, one baptism; one God and Father of all (Eph. 4:1-4).

This program released the church from the restrictive confines of the Mediterranean and launched it throughout the world. Now, one did not have to choose between his own group, but could bring his group to Christ, living the kind of life in that group Jesus would have lived had he been born there. The church was of many different tongues, but it spoke but one language: the word of the cross. It dressed many different ways, but could always be recognized—each looked like Christ, talked as He did and carried

338

on His mission as if it were one's very own. A redeemed culture was a marvelous gift to give Christ.

Conclusion

The Hebrew word for covenant, b'rth, became in the New Testament Canon diatheke. The meaning was the same, for the LXX selected it for use in the passages where b'rth had been. Diatheke referred to a Treaty or accord not negotiated, but rather handed down. God did not negotiate with man about the terms of the New Covenant any more than he had the Old. Salvation was by God's own initiative. Apart from God's own grace and His initiative in Christ, there was no salvation for mankind.

Christ was Himself the covenant. All normal aspects of the Treaty with Him were defined by reference to Him. That is, the parties were all "in Christ," the stipulations were to be "like Christ," and the promises were to share all things "with Christ."

The parties of the New Treaty were those who were born into it by the second or the new birth. The new birth was contrasted with natural birth, whether by Abraham or the Gentiles. The seed or sperm was the word of God. The father was either God or the Holy Spirit, as the source of the birth. The preacher delivering the word to the prospect was also referred to as their "father" in the faith. The gestation was "coming to one's self," and the birth was regarded as one's baptism. In that metaphor, the Spirit or the word was the first act or the initiation of the birth, and baptism the last. One was, of course, born of water and the Spirit. Faith prepared one for owning allegiance to God. The actual pledge of eternal loyalty was baptism. It pictured the death and resurrection of both Christ and the candidate. In that act the whole man was being surrendered to God. Upon one's oath, and prior to meeting any stipulation, remission of sin, the Holy Spirit, admission to Christ's body and other future promises were given by God. The convert was saved not by any of his own acts of righteousness, but by being "in Christ."

The stipulations of the New Covenant were, when discussed in one category, to be "like Christ." The Apostles, armed with authority from Christ, usually discussed the obligation of covenant in two categories: regarding the unbeliever and the believer. The covenant emphasis shifted from statutory covenant keeping to accomplishing the purposes of God in Christ. The purpose of God for the lost was summed best by "reconciliation." The purpose of the church, the saved, the believer, was to grow up in all ways into Christ's image. The church, the message, the stewardship of one's life were all related to goal achievement regarding the two kinds of humanity.

The promises of the New Covenant were also in two categories. There was a class of immediate, universal (for the kingdom citizen) and uncomplicated promises. Examples of those were remission of sin, the gift of the Holy Spirit, a ministry in the church, the hope of the resurrection, a new body, and heaven. All such promises were often summed up by "eternal life." The second type of promises was limited, highly conditional, individual and more earthy. Examples of those were the degree of suffering one could expect, the kind and amount of food, clothing, shelter and the like. God had not promised exemption from suffering, or to meet any specific standard of "need." The believer was expected to suffer for Christ and the church, using every circumstance to advance the purposes and will of God.

The church was the main instrument God chose to use to win the world. It was separated from civil governments to allow it true international access. Unity in the body was found in the Apostles' doctrine, and not in any aspect of cultural conformity. God intended in the church to create a new kind of humanity, refashioned after the original model, Christ. The New Covenant was the revealed "mystery" of God. True spiritual sacrifices and offerings were aid to the mission and souls won for Christ, and being conformed to Christ's image.

Questions on Chapter Seven

1. "Diatheke" meant _____.
2. The change of emphasis between the two covenants was about
    a) sin   c) God's grace
    b) circumcision   d) purpose
3. "God's will" was
    a) God's still small voice   c) a mystery
    b) the new covenant   d) known by prayer
4. The essence of the New Covenant was
    a) Paul's doctrine   c) Christ Himself
    b) baptism   d) goodness
5. "In Christ" referred to the _____ of a covenant.
6. T F Election meant God choosing for salvation.
7. T F God chose who was to be saved.
8. T F God chose to save all who pledge allegiance to Christ.
9. T F Baptism was a sign that one was already saved.

10. T F   Hebrew oath taking was limited to persons having reached understanding.
11. T F   The "stipulations" of the New Covenant were listed in Code Law.
12. T F   How one entered a covenant was by meeting the "stipulations."
13. Name the two kinds of mankind: _____ and the _____.
14. Comment on this statement: "If I love God, pray always, do no wrong, walk by the Spirit and tithe, God has assured he will take care of me and no harm will come to me."
15. Name God's will for lost mankind. _____
16. Name God's will for each Christian and the Church.
    _____
17. Explain why Christ separated the People of God from civil government.
18. What two names were applied to the categories "Inside" and "Outside?"
19. New Covenant worship was basically:
    a) How I lived all week   c) Our own secret times with God
    b) What we did on Sunday d) Listening to God's voice
20. Making a convert was
    a) unnecessary   c) a good thing for some
    b) a priestly duty   d) God's business
21. T F   Only the ordained ministers can baptize someone.
22. T F   The entire church is the "priesthood of God."
23. Explain what a "sacrament" was and how it differed from simple "memorial."
24. "When one sins as a Christian he is automatically out of covenant." Is that sentence true? How do we know?

1. A non-negotiated Treaty, the same as *B'rth*.
2. d) Purpose. The synonym "will" or intent or purpose showed that to be true.
3. b) the New Testament. God's secret will is also His revealed will.
4. c) Christ is the New Covenant
5. Parties
6. T   God had always selected those whom He would use or bless.
7. T   God chooses by stipulation in the New Covenant.
8. T   God did not decide who would respond. He wants all to respond.
9. F   Baptism was the pledge itself.
10. T   Children not of an accountable age were not sinners.
11. F   The Law of the Spirit was to be like Christ.
12. F   Stipulations were the duty AFTER entering a covenant.
13. The lost and those "in Christ."
14. That is simply not the case. Jesus did all that, so did Steven, so did Paul, yet all suffered. We will get what Christ got.
15. Reconciliation or any other Biblical name for it.
16. To be like Christ
17. To allow the church to save the souls of people, not direct their nation.
18. Growth in size, or reconciliation; and growth in love or Christlikeness.
19. a) Livng a life all week for Christ.
20. b)

PLEASE TURN THE BOOK OVER FOR ANSWERS.

21. F If by "ordained" is meant "clergy."

22. T

23. In true sacrament, what is being pictured is happening. In Greek type "memorial," the thing done is only an emblem of the real thing.

24. No, unless he repudiated Christ. The fact there is a Lord's Table implies the remission of sins done after becoming a Christian was possible. God expected immature Christians to grow, thus implying they would be sinning as they grew. They are to sin less and less as they get older in Christ.

Chapter Eight

NEW TESTAMENT *HESED*

Do you remember the word *hesed*? It was the most frequently used word to describe YHWH in the Old Testament. It was, therefore, the chief word describing godliness. If the reader will forgive me, I shall continue to use the original because no English word combined the two elements found in *hesed*. A language can not be faulted for that. God spoke to the prophets in another language. Do you recall the two elements making up *hesed*?

One element in *hesed* was covenant keeping. Its closest parallel was faithfulness.

> But I will not take my *hesed* from him
>   nor will I ever betray my faithfulness.
> I will not violate my covenant,
>   or alter what my lips have uttered,
> Once for all I have sworn by my holiness . . . (Ps. 89:34ff.).

Using parallels the meaning of *hesed* was clear. It was not the motive for action, nor the attitude itself, it was the performance of the agreed stipulations. It was faithfulness to an oath. It was the very doing of the covenant. That was the first half of the word.

The second element in *hesed* was acting as partner in such a way the other was benefited. The support of the covenant was support of an individual in the covenant. The covenant was made for a reason. It was to provide a sure and steady help in time of trouble. The help provided went beyond the written stipulations. Covenants were to link *people* together. Attention was upon the benefit to the parties, and *hesed* was aid in the best interests of the other. There was an element of loving concern for his welfare which went beyond what was stipulated. *Hesed* required each party to

345

treat the other as father and son, or as brothers in a bond as strong as flesh and blood. When the partner suffered, aid was to be given. If the partner was in danger of default on the agreement, all possible aid was to be offered. In that way, each set of promises had both parties working for their success. Such was the second half of the word. Unite the two and you have *hesed*: "Promoting the best interest of the other, according to the covenant."

Hesed Became "Service."

Jesus filled four words with the meaning of *hesed*: service, love, rule, and submit. While each of the words presented a slightly different angle, they all meant the same thing: take care of the best interests of the other person. Paul's favorite expression carrying exactly the same idea was "one another." The mutuality expressed was *hesed*. What was best for "one another" depended upon the exact relationship, i.e., their covenant. The agreement may have been formal or informal. Measuring up to legitimate expectations was the notion in both *hesed* and "one another."

Jesus told the same story dozens of times, we suppose. It came to us in a couple of different forms. The structure of the story and the point remained the same. A certain wealthy man delivered to his slaves, managers, or servants a certain sum of money according to their abilities. He charged each, "Put this money to work until I come back." Then he went on a long journey. The first two traded well and doubled the investment for the master. The master returned and was pleased with the increase of his wealth. He rewarded each. He called them "good," "faithful," and "trustworthy" servants. The other fellow did not care apparently for the rough and tumble life of the marketplace. He disliked responsibility. He thought the master a bit hard to deal with. He did not want to be found in the wrong when he returned. He took the money, wrapped it carefully in his "sweat band," and buried it safely in his yard. He also rendered account. Christ's definition of that type of service: "wicked" and "lazy." The master had him killed (Luke 19:11ff.). A servant was one who cared for the interest of another.

Initiative and Stewardship

Jesus told another parable to illustrate the role human initiative was to play in service to God. A certain master suspected his accountant of dishonesty. He decided to replace him so he called him in, asked for an accounting, and gave him notice. The accountant was shocked. His livelihood was threatened. He must care for his future somehow. He used good initiative. He came up with a solution. He knew how to "land on his feet," in this dog-eat-dog world. He called in certain heavy debtors. He asked to see the receipts held by the master's debtor. He then marked huge sums paid on both the debtor's receipt and on the master's books. Of course each debtor was pleased at such generosity. He liked the accountant more all the time. The accountant ought to come over for dinner some evening. The steward undoubtedly responded that he may be needing a favor himself one day. "Well, I certainly will not forget this generosity," was the creditor's reply. After the servant had secured sufficient friendships, through them his own future, he submitted the books and left the master's service (Luke 16:1ff.).

Christ commended the unjust steward. He was, of course, not commending the crookedness. He was commending

347

the clever way the man used his initiative to care for his own best interest. That same kind of initiative, less the dishonesty, of course, was to be employed in Christ's service. One must know the world, know what the master wanted, and use his good judgment and common sense to get it.

In a related case Jesus told of an owner and a servant who worked side by side in a field all day. Both were equally tired. Upon reaching the house, the master reclined at table. He ordered the same servant to fix a meal as usual, bring it to him, and wait on him as he ate supper. Jesus asked, "Will he thank his servant?" No, he replied, the servant was doing his stated duty. One did not get thanked for that. One got thanked for going beyond duty. One was a profitable servant who did more than expected. A simple trade off of service for food and shelter was no profit to a man. One must use his initiative, going beyond mere duty to be pleasing to God, Jesus claimed. One could not simply meet the stated demands of a master. He must advance the master's interests in ways not specified, and in the absence of the master. True *hesed* did what was best for the master in harmony with agreements and going beyond them in support (Luke 17:7ff.).

God expected men to carry on his business in good faith. Men of God could not simply be rote rule keepers any longer. They must assume the responsibility to initiate ways of succeeding for God's benefit. The measure of accountability demanded by God went beyond the sterile statute keeping and legal enforcements. God's goals must be achieved, productive means selected, and procedures evaluated in terms of priority management.

> Who is the faithful and wise manager whom the master puts in charge of his servants . . .? It will be good for that servant the master finds doing so when he returns (Luke 12:42).

348

The servant who knows his master's will and does not get ready or does not do what his master wants will be beaten with many blows.

From everyone who has been given much, much will be demanded, and the man who has been entrusted with much, much more will be asked (Luke 12:47f.).

Whoever can be trusted with little can be trusted with much, and whoever is dishonest with very little will be dishonest with much. If you have not been trustworthy in handling worldly wealth, who will trust you with true riches (Luke 16:10).

Christ was not talking about worldliness or speaking against the wealthy. He was illustrating the demand for competent management for Him. Paul identified the true wealth with which the servant of God had been entrusted.

We have this treasure in earthen vessels to show the all surpassing power is from God and not ourselves (II Cor. 4:7).

The treasure was defined in the sentence above, "the light of the knowledge of the glory of God in the face of Christ." In other words, the true stewardship was the mission as a whole, not mere obedience in its parts.

So men ought to regard us as servants of Christ, and as those entrusted with the secret things of God. Now it is required that those who have been given a trust must prove faithful (I Cor. 4:1).

Advancing the best interests of Christ was stewardship. Stewardship was not paying the tithe in order to go to heaven. That was Old Testament mentality. Stewardship was not enforcing rules on people in the church as proof of faithfulness. Stewardship was goal achievement. The goal was to reconcile the world to God and help those be like Christ. The entire discussion by Christ of stewardship was really a discussion of true *hesed*. "The Faith" was the covenant will of God. *Hesed* was being a "faithful and true" servant, advancing the best interests of the mission (will) of Christ.

Rule and Serve

Leadership was important to the disciples of Jesus. One day they were walking along together, talking of the future kingdom. Each pictured himself having a vital place in it. To them, at that time, a vital place meant a powerful position. One might have preferred to be Minister of War, another Minister of Agriculture or Trade. Judas had an advantage for the position of Minister of Finance. The top position was unassigned, the Chief Executive, the Prime Minister. To whom would that position go? Jesus heard them arguing. He redefined the word "rule."

> You know that the rulers of the Gentiles lord it over them, and their high officials exercise authority over them. Not so with you. Instead, whoever wants to become great among you must become your servant, and whoever wants to become first must be your slave—just as the Son of Man did not come to be served, but to serve, and to give his life a ransom for many (Matt. 20:25ff.).

There were two possible definitions of rule, Jesus said. One was possessing the power to command. It was the power of position, of coercion, the power to make people regret it if they did not agree. It was the right or power to "lord it over" people. That kind of rule was not what Jesus had in mind. His was far too revolutionary for mere exercise of power. He said, in effect, the one who was able to help others achieve goals was the best ruler. He defined "rule" as "serve." The power base of Jesus' rule was the ability to contribute to one's need so vitally they submitted to the help. Rule was helping others. That was the sort of things slaves did. That was why Jesus came—to help the covenant partner of God, mankind. He was to give the kind of help they really needed: His own death for sin on the cross. Anyone who wanted a place of honor or position in the Kingdom of God must gain it by one's expertise, aid, or help in promoting the best interests of Christ: reconciliation.

In English there are two definitions of "rule." One means "lord it over." The other means be the measure of the rule. It is called a "ruler," in classes at school. It is used to mark progress or measure a distance. That kind of idea was obtained from Christ's use of the word. The person who best exemplified the rule, Christlikeness, was obviously the best ruler. The one able to persuade others to live according to the rule of Christ was a good ruler. One ruled in the kingdom of God by persuasion and example. To be a good ruler one must be able to do three things: know the rule, be an example of the rule, and persuade others to abide by the rule. Peter wrote to the rulers in the church and used the same language. He did not call them rulers, although others did (Heb. 13:17). Peter called them "elders," "overseers," and "shepherds."

> To the elders among you I appeal as a fellow elder, a witness of the suffering of Christ and one who will share in the glory to be revealed. Be shepherds of God's flock under your care, serving as overseers, not because you must, but because you are willing . . . eager to serve, not lording it over those entrusted to you, but being examples to your flock. And when the chief shepherd appears, you will receive a crown of glory that will never fade away.

His ideas were straight from Christ: "not lording it over," "I appeal to you," "a fellow," "being examples to" and the reference to Christ as the supreme example. Persuasion by reference to the life of Christ, and by being an example of Christ's rules in action, was Christian persuasion. That was the way Christ ruled the ancient Church. The revolutionary new concept of rule was to challenge the entire ancient world. God expected that rule to one day be the universal law in all the earth.

In faithfulness he will bring forth justice,
   he will not falter or be discouraged
til he establishes justice on earth.
In his law the islands will put their hopes (Isa. 42:3).

Rule and Love

The Lord Jesus defined "serve" as advancing the best interests of the other. He redefined rule to mean the exact same thing. He defined love in the same way. "If you love me, you will keep my commandments," he said (John 14:15). Love was the kind of behavior Jesus did: "A new commandment I give to you, that you love one another as I have loved you" (John 15:12). One was told to serve as Jesus had served, to rule as Jesus had ruled, and to love as Jesus had loved. Love, rule, and serve were in parallel. Paul linked the two concepts of love and serve just as Jesus had.

Do not use your freedom to indulge your sinful nature;
rather, serve one another in love (Gal. 5:13).

In the New Testament, love was not an emotion. It was a way of behaving. It included emotions, but *agape* was a total response, a way of doing good for someone. Again Jesus was the standard of what was good for someone. Jesus said, "As I have loved you." John repeated the definition.

352

This is how we know what love is: Jesus Christ laid down his life for us (I John 3:16).

Anyone who does not do what is right is not a child of God; neither is anyone who does not love his brother (I John 3:10).

If anyone obeys his word, God's love is truly made complete in him. This is how we know we are in him: whoever claims to live in him must walk as Jesus walked (I John 2:6).

Walking as Jesus walked, being an example of aid, support, encouragement was love toward one. Paul defined love by a series of words in a letter to Corinth.

Love is patient, love is kind. It does not envy, it does not boast, it is not proud. It is not rude, it is not self-seeking, it is not easily angered, it keeps no record of wrongs. Love does not delight in evil, but rejoices in the truth. It always protects, always trusts, always hopes, always perseveres (I Cor. 13:4-6).

Doing what was right for the other person was love. What is truly "right" for all people was to be reconciled to God and choosing to be like Christ. Love was helping the other person achieve. Jesus defined three words with the same meaning as *hesed*: serving, ruling, and loving. In each case the true definition was keeping covenant—like Christ. Serve like Christ. Rule like Christ. Love like Christ. One other term was redefined by Christ.

Love and Submit

Obedience or submission was also redefined by Christ. At one time obedience meant do as told without questioning. That part was not changed except submission must be in such a way the best interests of the other were truly served. Rote obedience to anyone or any thing was out! Jesus claimed He went to the cross by His own choice, "of my own accord.

No one takes it from me" (John 10:17). He was said to have become "obedient unto death" (Phil. 2:5ff.). Obedience partook of the same redefinition as rule. Obedience was being persuaded. Obedience on Christ's part was keeping faith, doing duty . . . unto death.

A Christian was to do what was best for the other person. Jesus went to the cross compelled by what mankind needed. He was obedient to the real need of the other covenant partner. He did what was best for Adam's race. Paul asked the church to be mutually submissive.

Submit to one another out of reverence to Christ (Eph. 5:21).

It is written in Hebrews,

Obey your rulers and submit to their authority. They keep watch over you as men who must give account. Obey them so that their work will be a joy, not a burden, for that would be no advantage to you (Heb. 13:17).

When one took off the glasses of Greek culture, and with it the idea that rule meant raw power to command, he would see what was being said in harmony with Jesus' concept of rule. A paraphrase might well be,

Help make your leaders successful. Submit your own wills to what is best for the church and the leaders. They are attempting to model what Christ wants from us all. They will have to give account of their example to you, so aid them to be good stewards of God. Cooperate with them to build the church. Do not give them trouble, subject your own opinions to their experience, do not make them carry you on their backs. Take the initiative. Do what they are trying to do—be like the Lord Jesus. What advantage is it to you if they fail? If they succeed you also succeed. They are teaching the truth. When you succeed, they are successful. Be mutually supportive. They have the truth and you need it. Submit to one another, and meet the other person's need.

354

An elder, leader, ruler in the church had only as much authority as he could gain and keep by the aid he provided. The way to rule in the church was through the rule: do as Jesus did. Teaching, persuading, doing the work as example, and helping the other be successful in his efforts, was New Covenant authority and was New Covenant obedience. Christ intended to conquer the world with *hesed*. It was to be the universal standard of behavior. Helping other people succeed in living as Christ would live, was the new Torah of the Spirit.

Jesus as the Standard

The definition of steward, servant, or slave when used by the Apostles in Christian context, was one who provided aid to the other as Jesus would. Christ was the standard for everything. One was to treat the other person as if he were Jesus, with all courtesy. "Show perfect courtesy to all men" (I Pet. 3:8). Jesus was the standard of what was right. "He who does what is right is righteous, just as He is righteous" (I John 3:7). Christ was the example of walking in the light,"as He is in the light," (I John 1:7), of knowing God (I John 2:3), of "living in Him" (I John 2:6), of possessing the true light (I John 2:8), of what one would be when perfected at his appearing (I John 3:2), of personal purity, (I John 3:3), of the sinless life (I John 3:4-6), of love of brothers (I John 3:16), of assurance His Spirit was in each (I John 3:24, 25), of assurance God loved each (I John 4:7-11), of being born again (I John 5:1-5). The criterion of the believer's judgment was if one treated others by the Christian standard: as if he were Christ (Matt. 25:40). The standard of suffering was Jesus (I Pet. 2:21). The standard of giving was Jesus (II Cor. 8:9). The example leaders were to pass on was Jesus.

355

Follow my example as I follow the example of Christ (I Cor. 11:1).

True *hesed,* true covenant morality, what was best for all men, was to be like Christ, the model of creation. *Hesed* was Christlikeness.

Be imitators of God therefore, as dearly beloved children, and live a life of love, as Christ loved us and gave himself up for us as a fragrant offering and sacrifice to God (Eph. 5:1).

Christlikeness and Covenant Righteousness

Proposition: When "in Christ" one is regarded as sharing the status and ethic of Christ. God sees Jesus when He looks at us if we are performing the covenant.

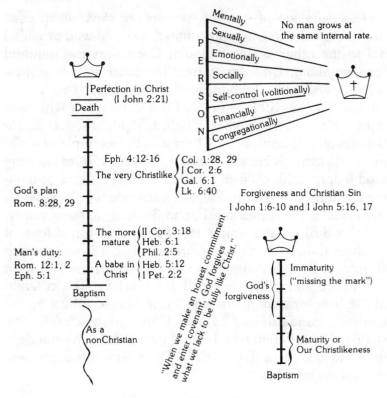

356

The Range of Service

There were many words in the New Testament translated service or servant. Each had the noun and verb form. The implication of such fact raised to highest profile the concept of service. Each of the terms came from a slightly different background and had slightly different shades of meaning. At the heart of each lay the same idea: aiding the other person succeed. 1. *Doulos.* The word for slave was *doulos*. It was very frequently used by Jesus to describe the accountability demanded by God of his stewards (Matt. 25:14). Christ was so described (Phil. 2:7). Paul described himself as one (Phil. 1:1). All Christians were slaves of Christ (I Cor. 6:20). 2. *Diakonos* was a common word for servant in the New Testament (II Cor. 4:5). The same word was rendered deacon (I Tim. 3:8), deaconess (Rom. 16:1), and minister (II Cor. 3:6). One lexiographer defined the term,

> One who advances his master's interests even at the sacrifice of his own interests.[1]

3. *Oikonomos* was chosen by Paul when he wanted to link service to a total system of responsibility. It was rendered "manager" in the NIV. A stewardship was oversight of the master's entire business. Business manager was a synonym. Christ regarded his people as stewards (Luke 16:1-13). Every Christian was to manage the church to Christ's best interest (I Pet. 4:10). The management of the covenant, the revealed "mystery" of God was a stewardship (Eph. 3:3, 9). 4. *Leitourgos.* The official agent for another in priestly or official capacity was minister-priest. The word liturgical came

---

1. J. H. Thayer, *Greek-English Lexicon,* New York: American Book Company, 1886, p. 138.

from it.[2] One charged with a kingly duty, a holy duty, or a high religious duty was a *leitourgos*. 5. *Pais* was a relatively undefined household word for a servant (Acts 12:13). Such a person was often a younger member of the family, or a young hired helper, or a young slave boy or girl. 6. *Hyperetes.* David was said to have "served" his own generation by the will of God (Acts 13:36). In the most ancient times the slaves who rowed the ships were this kind of servants: unsung, in unseen position, committed to die in action. Mark was described as having served Paul and Barnabas in that way (Acts 13:5). 7. *Oiketes* was a household servant. The root word was the same as steward. A steward differed from an *oiketes* in matters of oversight as opposed to menial service. Any one who served the master of a house was called a "household servant."

The fact there were many different terms employed for service suggested the lifestyle of the ancient church.

Christlikeness: Words and Gospel

The message preached by the Apostles resulting in conversion centered in the fact of Christ's Lordship. The death and resurrection was the chief proof offered. When many converts began coming, especially among peoples who had no Hebrew background, nurture was difficult. While the Jewish people were rather stable in their morals, the Gentiles were not stable apparently. Moreover, it was not possible for the eyewitnesses to give each convert a description of the entire lifestyle and ethic of Jesus. As a result, the Apostles

---

2. See any Greek Lexicon. *Webster's Seventh New Collegiate Dictionary,* Springfield, Massachusetts: Merriam-Webster, 1976, p. 494.

described Christ in terms of behaviors and attitudes. The procedure became one of the earliest expressions of the theology of culture. One was not to imitate the cultural or social style of Jesus, but rather His attitudes and purposes. When the gospels began to circulate, the generalities gave way to biographic style.

Behaviors that Were Never Like Christ

The letters of the Apostles reflected the procedure. Paul often generalized the kind of life never like Christ as "the works of the flesh." He did not mean the body was evil in itself, but rather, any life dominated by attention to the body was evil.

> The acts of the sinful nature are obvious: sexual immorality, impurity, and debauchery, idolatry, and witchcraft, hatred, discord, jealousy, fits of rage, selfish ambition, dissentions, factions, and envy, drunkenness, orgies and the like . . . (Gal. 5:19ff.).

When Paul spoke of liberty, it was understood not to extend to these kinds of behaviors. They were never like Christ and therefore always sinful.

Behaviors Always Like Christ

There were several attitudes and behaviors that were always like Christ, subject, of course, to good motive. Paul's usual term for such was some form of the word "Spirit" (Eph. 5:18ff.). Tenderness, compassion, comfort, love, fellowship, single-mindedness, unselfish caring, cooperativeness and an attitude of service were also descriptions (Phil. 2:1-9).

359

Whatever is true, whatever is noble, whatever is right, whatever is pure, whatever is lovely, whatever is admirable, if anything is excellent or praiseworthy—think about such things (Phil. 4:8).

The Doctrine of Implied Powers

In any legal or moral system appeared a concept of principal and agent. The acts of the agent were the acts of the principal. A person who sent another to commit a crime shared the guilt on that basis. The owner of an ox known to gore was slain along with the ox on that principle. One who heard Jesus heard the Father who sent Him (John 8:42ff.). An extension of that principle was the law of implied powers. When one was commanded to do a thing, in the absence of specific instructions to the contrary, it was assumed he also was authorized to do whatever was necessary to accomplish the command. If one were, for instance, told to go to such and such place, he was by implication also empowered to choose the route, the means of travel and get protection, if necessary. The idea was reflected in Paul's statement.

Everything is permissible for me,
    but not everything is beneficial.
Everything is permissible for me,
    but I will not be mastered by anything (I Cor. 6:12).

Based upon the doctrine of implied powers the church had met in homes, used synagogues, the Temple, later built buildings, created benevolent agencies, controlled printing presses, owned and operated broadcasting stations, and the like. There were two limitations. The means employed must be functional, "beneficial," and must not nullify the word of God (Mark 7:8). The expediency must not work against the command itself. The churches had great discretionary power. They were God's international Israel. On the basis of implied power the very New Testament Canon was bound. Institutions created by the church ought not work against the mission as a whole. The love feast at Corinth was an example of an institution of the church working against the church's own best interests.

On the same basis, freedoms were curtailed, for temporary reasons, "because of the present crisis" (I Cor. 7:26), social reasons (I Cor. 8:9), or administrative reasons (I Cor. 14:34). When the crisis was over, and no such problem existed requiring limitations, the rule of Christlikeness and freedom in Christ ought to prevail (Col. 2:16-23). Nothing was to be done which did not edify all the church (I Cor. 14:12). Personal expressions, while valid for an individual, might be forbidden at church by the doctrine of implied power (I Cor. 14:32, 33). What was being said was similar to discussing the end justifying the means. Certainly not every end justified every means in the Apostolic church. It was equally certain that no means was justified which did not serve the end.

Christlikeness: Individuals

Individuals differed in the degree of Christlikeness exhibited when converted. Cornelius needed to change allegiance and and perhaps a few other matters of emphasis after he became a Christian. Some at Corinth were rather thoroughly perverted when they came to Christ (I Cor. 6:11). The needs of those were different from Cornelius' needs. Few grew into Christlikeness at the same rate. Judging the progress of others by their overt conduct was a risky thing,

361

Paul said (Rom. 14:1-5). Babes grew at different rates. Individuals grew in different aspects of Christlikeness at differing rates. One was more like Christ for example, in his social relationships, and less like Him in financial matters. Another may have been very competent in money matters but weaker in private prayer. Some may have been very advanced in knowledge but immature in mutual respect. For that reason, the church was not to impose a list of rules on everybody. There was one basic rule: "Love the Lord thy God," and "love thy neighbor as thyself" (Gal. 5:14).

Furthermore, each individual was to add some ministry to the church. Each was to give some gift to build up the body. For some that meant giving considerable money, for others, teaching, for some, administration, for others preaching or translating in a variety of languages. For some it was healing, helping, showing hospitality, or encouragements and the like (Rom. 12:3ff.). A person was "normal" in a given culture when he/she lived as Christ would have lived had He been born in that society in that time. "Abnormal" behavior for a believer was behaving unlike Christ.

The individual Christian was to be like Christ all week long. He was to be what Jesus would have been had He held that job. By aiding co-workers succeed, the believer was doing what Jesus would have done. Such behavior was "right in the sight of everybody" (Rom. 12:17). When God had people well placed in society who were "as wise as serpents and as harmless as doves" (Matt. 10:16) the explosive leaven of God could work in society (Matt. 13:33f.).

Christlikeness: The Church

The church was an end in itself in that it was the very arena of eternal reconciliation. The church was the "one new

362

humanity" created out of all classes and tongues on earth in Christ (Eph. 2:15, 16). Relationships in the church were to reflect Christ so the corporate image presented to the community would be as attractive as if Christ were living there. Indeed He was there. The church was the body of Christ as much as the flesh that hung on the cross was Christ's.[3]

The rule for all relationships in the church reflected *hesed*. As Christ aided the church to the point of dying for it so it would be glorious, respected, loved and supported, so a husband was to love his wife. The wife was to be submissive, to respect, and to support the success of the husband as the church supported and advanced Christ (Eph. 5:32, 33). Husbands ought to understand their duty was to help the wife be like Christ. A woman bossed about, treated as an employee, and made to agree with foolish ideas, was not being treated as Christ treated the church. Husbands were to understand they were to rule the household as Christ did the church—by example and persuasion. The church (parallel to the wife) set the hours of the meeting, chose the preacher, collected money, sent it here and there, disciplined wayward members, and exercised great discretionary powers. Christ gave her that right. Husbands were to do the same for the wife.

Women and men were equal in the church in the sight of God.[4] Men ought to protect and honor women (Phil. 4:2ff.) as Christ did.[5] Women ought to advance the best interests of men before their own best interests as a class

---

3. John A. T. Robinson, *The Body: A Study in Pauline Theology*, London: SCM Press, 1966.

4. Paul Jewett, *Man as Male and Female*. Grand Rapids: Eerdmans, 1975, p. 142ff.

5. Dorothy R. Pape, *In Search of God's Ideal Woman*, Downer's Grove, Illinois: InterVarsity Press, 1976, p. 51ff.

in society. Men were to work for the best of women.

The married ought to aid the single. Being married was not necessarily the ideal (I Cor. 7:27). Jesus was single. Younger widows should remarry (I Tim. 5:14). The single helped the married be honorable. The married aided singles to live for Christ.

The young were to aid the older be like Christ. The younger were not allowed to rebuke the older person, but rather were instructed to treat them as parents in the Lord (I Tim. 5:1). The church was to care for older widows (I Tim. 5:3). The younger were to be submissive to those who were older, Peter instructed (I Pet. 5:5). The older were to be examples of godliness, nor greedy, nor domineering, liberal to all, serving God with clear conscience. In short, each set was to care for the best interests of the other.

Children were to obey their parents (Col. 3:20). The child was to advance the best interests of the parent. In this case the best interest of the parent was to be respected as having well behaved, well disciplined, and devout children. No man was permitted to be a leader in the church who did not have the respect of his household (I Tim. 3:4, 5). He, in turn was to care for his own. The father was to nurture the children in the faith, avoid being too harsh with them, leading them all to Christlikeness (Col. 3:21). A parent was a success in the Lord when the child did what Christ wanted, on his/her own initiative, in the absence of the parent. A parent who can strike a good balance between guidance and freedom for the child could likely lead the church well. A child who was badly abused by parents ought not allow such a thing. To be abused in silence was not acting in the best interests of the parent. An abusive and cruel parent was a failure, one who would give answer to the law and to God. Common sense required the child to render real aid to those unhappy adults. Obedience against the best interests of the parent was abuse of the intention of submission.

Leaders in the church were to work for the best interests of the body. The best interest of the body was to grow (Eph. 4:16). A static ingrown church was a failure. The church was to work for the best interest of the leadership. A bucking and quarrelsome church was unlike Christ.

The stronger members of the church were to care for the weaker members. Paul said two things perfectly consistent with covenant thinking.

Carry each other's burdens, and in this way you will fulfill the law of Christ . . . for each man should carry his own load (Gal. 6:2, 5).

Those who were "weak in the faith," presented a difficult problem. There were two kinds. One set were those recently converted who were emotionally linked to many aspects of the former way of life. They wrote for themselves very restrictive rules to help avoid temptations. They were acting in all good faith and with good judgment. A stronger believer, not attracted to potential sin-traps, could eat or drink or go to festivals and the like without troubling his faith. His freedom, however, may lead another into trouble.

When you sin against your weak brother in this way, and wound their weak consciences you sin against Christ. Therefore if what I eat causes my brother to fall into sin, I will never eat meat again, so that I will not make him fall (I Cor. 8:12, 13).

365

Another kind of person weak in the faith was the one who was personally attracted to certain sins and wanted to avoid them. He generalized his weaknesses to everyone and laid on others the rules created for himself. He was a vocal, emphatic, domineering purist, the "touch not," "taste not," and "handle not," abstainer (Rom. 14:2). Even then Paul said to understand his difficulty. On the other hand, the weaker one must not destroy Christian liberty and dominate another's life (Rom. 14:3). The abstainer must not be allowed to rewrite the covenant (Gal. 5:1). One was very free as a Christian for nothing was unclean in itself (Rom. 14:14), but freedom in Christ did not extend to the destruction of the faith of the honestly weak (I Cor. 8:9-13).

The revolutionary standard of Christ struck the ancient world like a whirlwind. At last a program had come which made sense, and had an objective standard. The standard was Christ. Christ was the covenant. To be like Christ was covenant with compassion: *hesed*. The ancient prayer of the Jew was overridden by God.

> I thank God I was not born a Gentile,
> I thank God I was not born a slave,
> I thank God I was not born a woman.[6]

It really made little difference whether one was born a man. As a man he was charged to advance the best interests of women. What difference did it make if one were born a master? He was charged to work for the best interests of the slave. He was to aid the slave be like Christ. What difference if one were a Greek? He must aid the Jew. If born a

---

6. Scott Bartchy, *Slavery in the First Century*, SLB Dissertation Series #11, University of Montana, 1973.

Jew, he must support the best interests of, the success of, the legitimate ambitions of the Greek. It was true what they were saying,

These men who have turned the world upside down have arrived here also! (Acts 17:6).

The Hebrew church deferred to the Greek in a dispute (Acts 6:1ff.) and the offering Paul was collecting among the Gentile churches was for a Hebrew people (I Cor. 16:1ff.). In every human relationship in the church, the rule of Christ was to prevail. Christ and the church was the model, not only for husband and wife, but for all situations where there were socially superior/inferior relationships. The socially superior was to be superior as Christ; and the socially inferior was to remember Jesus as a servant. Each was to behave as Jesus would.

Christlikeness: The World

A Christian's true worship was done in the world (Rom. 12:1, 2). His worship was his service to the other. As he aided all men to succeed he was worshipping in spirit and truth, as Jesus commanded (John 4:24).

The slave was not to demand his freedom, although he was to take it if possible (I Cor. 7:21). The slave was to treat the master as if he were Christ (Col. 3:22ff.). Conversely, the masters were to treat the slaves the same way they would treat Christ had He been their slave. "You have a master in heaven," they were warned (Eph. 6:9).

Paul sent an escaped slave named Useful back to his Christian master. He charged the master to receive him as a brother and a slave now that Useful had become Christian

367

(Philemon 1:16). Of course, Christianity meant the end of certain kinds of slavery. When the church obtained social power, it was to treat, by law, all citizens as it wished to be treated. A Christian master was to treat slaves, be they Christian or not, as he would like to be treated had he been a slave.

The creditor was to work for the best interests of the debtor, to the extent of forgiving the debt entirely if it came to that (Matt. 18:23-25). Of course it was not good for a debtor to default. It hurt him in all future matters. The best interest of the debtor was for the creditor to help him find ways of paying off the debt. The debtor, on the other hand, was commanded to pay his just debts. Paul said, "Owe no man anything" (Rom. 13:8). He had a responsibility to creditors.

The political magistrate was to work for the best interests of the citizenry. He was to be a terror to evil. His duty was to provide social order for the good of all (Rom. 13:4-7). The citizen was to work to make the government a success. He was to pay taxes (Rom. 13:6), pray for the success of rulers (I Tim. 2:1), and honor those whose position required it even if the individual were not worthy personally (Acts 26:25). The best ruler was one who created a climate of peace and good order in which the citizenry could thrive as they did God's work and "lived peaceful and tranquil lives" (I Tim. 2:2). The citizenry was to insure the success of the government. It was no benefit to government to tolerate gross violations of its mandate from God. To close an eye to injustice was wrong under the Old Covenant and under the New. Government was itself a Treaty with the people. Both government and citizenry had obligations and benefits in the relationship.

HESED: Christlikeness

Proposition: "Those who act like Christ and help others to attain Christlikeness are showing New Covenant *hesed*."

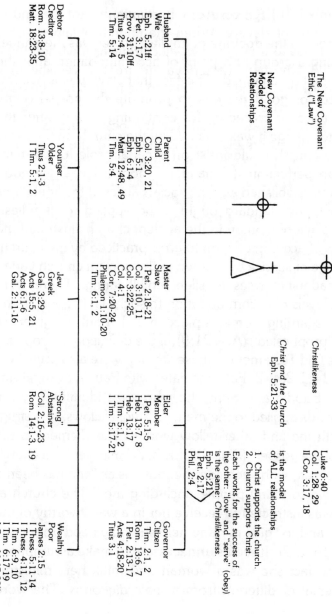

The New Covenant Ethic ("Law")

New Covenant Model of Relationships

Christlikeness
Luke 6:40
Col. 1:28, 29
II Cor. 3:17, 18

Christ and the Church
Eph. 5:21-33

is the model of ALL relationships
1. Christ supports the church.
2. Church supports Christ.
Each works for the success of the other: "love" and "serve" (obey) is the same: *Christlikeness*.
Eph. 5:21
I Pet. 2:17
Phil. 2:4

Husband
Wife
Eph. 5:21ff.
I Pet. 3:1-7
Prov. 31:10ff.
Titus 2:4, 5
I Tim. 5:14

Parent
Child
Col. 3:20, 21
Eph. 5:1
Eph. 6:1-4
Matt. 12:48, 49
I Tim. 5:4

Master
Slave
I Pet. 2:18-21
Col. 3:10, 11
Col. 3:22-25
Col. 4:1
I Cor. 7:20-24
Philemon 1:10-20
I Tim. 6:1, 2

Elder
Member
I Pet. 5:1-5
Heb. 13:7, 8
Heb. 13:17
I Tim. 5:1, 2
I Tim. 5:17-21

Governor
Citizen
I Tim. 2:1, 2
Rom. 13:6, 7
I Pet. 2:13-17
Acts 4:18-20
Titus 3:1

Debtor
Creditor
Rom. 13:8-10
Matt. 18:23-35

Younger
Older
Titus 2:1-3
I Tim. 5:1, 2

Jew
Greek
Gal. 3:29
Acts 15:5, 21
Acts 6:1-6
Gal. 2:11-16

"Strong"
Abstainer
Col. 2:16-23
Rom. 14:1-3, 19

Wealthy
Poor
James 2:15
I Thess. 5:11-14
I Thess. 4:11, 12
I Tim. 6:9, 10
I Tim. 6:17-19
I Cor. 11:17-22ff.

Frozen Accommodation

Inherent in the doctrine of implied power was the danger of holding a group at a point of accommodation after the social situation changed. The fact that slavery was accommodated for good reasons to promote the gospel ought not be used as precedent for continuing slavery after the power to change it was obtained by the church. In the same way the church could insist on a certain role for women, less than perfection, to maintain good order. Once good order was established and the social causes of the limitations removed, the standard ought to be applied to its fullest.

The place of women in the ancient church illustrated the varieties of accommodation to error practiced by the church. The range of service by women in the ancient church varied from leadership roles to silent childbearing. There were several levels of accommodation to social limitations on the church regarding women's place in it. 1. Four daughters of Phillip "prophesied" (Acts 21:9). If the definition of prophesy was the Old Testament's, these women were also preachers (I Cor. 14:1-25). 2. Full associates with Paul in evangelism, such as Euodia and Syntyche who were identified by the same words applied to the men, ". . .yokefellows, . . . struggled with me and other fellow workers like Clement in the cause of the gospel" (Phil. 4:2ff.). 3. A "minister" in a church at Cenchrea, with such commendations as "she has been a great help to many people, including me." The church at Rome was instructed to receive her in a way "worthy of the saints," and to "give her any help she may need from you" (Rom. 16:1, 2). It seems unnecessary to make assumptions from the fact she was a woman and think her "ministry" was menial or different from a male *diakonos*. The word "ministry" used was the same as Paul's in Second Corinthians in his discussion of ministry of reconciliation. 4. Women were allowed to pray or prophesy if they did so with their heads covered. The social accommodation was obvious. 5. Women were to keep silent in the churches. The context perhaps required silence because part of a pagan-type divination practice was being introduced by recent converts at Corinth. Whatever the reason for the command, it is obvious it had very limited application. Paul was not so inconsistent as to require women to both be silent and also pray and preach with their heads covered (I Cor. 14:33). 6. In the letters to Timothy, Paul laid down his most limiting restrictions on a woman. She was to keep silent, asking her husband at home if she did not understand, and she was not permitted to teach a man; in short, to make no public contribution to the growth of the church and to depend upon her faith in Christ and her childbearing to save her soul (I Tim. 2:15).

Such broad variance could exist in the same world church only when understood as accommodation to local circumstances. Unfortunately the local circumstances are not available to us in any detail. One thing was certain: the degrees of accommodation were mutually exclusive if applied to the same local church. What the Apostles would have insisted upon was a return to the standard of full Christlike service for all and to all, as soon as possible. The position of slave, or government, or of women, or Jew and Greek, must not be frozen at any one level of social accommodation. Steady progress toward Christlikeness for all was the basic law of the Apostles.

Full Christlikeness was the standard and the right of attainment for all. To fail to apply that rule would be a return to the frozen Torah of Moses. Jesus made it clear no statute

371

was to be understood apart from or applied contrary to the total thrust of the Law, and the reason for the statute. That included such definitive laws as the Sabbath (Mark 2:27). When the same principle was applied to the New Covenant, no passage of scripture, command or precedent may be applied contrary to the right of any person to become as fully Christlike as any other person in the church, subject to good order and temporary, local social realities.

Hesed to the Nations

The Christian was obligated to the nations simply because God had promised to bless them in Abraham, if for no other reason. When God agreed to bless someone and a servant was asked to deliver the gift, the servant partook of the obligation. All believers both individually and as part of the body of Christ were obligated to mankind.

> I am obligated both to Greeks and non-Greeks, both the wise and the foolish. That is why I am so eager to preach the gospel also to you who are at Rome.
>
> I am not ashamed of the gospel, because it is the power of God for salvation to everyone who believes: first for the Jew, then for the Gentile. For in the gospel a righteousness of God is revealed . . . (Rom. 1:14-17).

The church unconcerned with the salvation of the ethnics of the world was an unrighteous, covenant-breaking church. The individual who, having the opportunity to preach the gospel in any land, declined the opportunity, broke faith with God. What mankind needed more than anything else was reconciliation. The Lord Jesus had the power to feed and clothe all mankind. He knew the soul was of more value than the body. The church was to continue Christ's mission. The Apostles understood His mission. They established churches. The best help an Aramaic church can have for, let us say, a Galatian people was aid in establishing their own churches to care for their own people in their own way. What every land under heaven needed of highest priority was the gospel and the church. Imposed civilization, even with the best of intentions, was not the program of the Lord. Each society must restructure after the command of God. That restructure must be by its own Christian citizens. No church was supposed to stop the world mission to obtain the material blessing available because of Christ. Each generation must convert the next. The *hesed* to the next generation was a true faith in Christ. *Hesed* to the nations was taking them the message of eternal redemption in Christ.

Breach of Covenant

According to Jesus, love of God and love of one's neighbor was the foundation of all law. Breach of that law was the root definition of sin. Under the Treaty at Sinai, sin remained based on the same foundation, but grew to include breach of the 613, or applying any of the 613 in such a way as to breach the foundation law. Under the Christian Treaty, failure to be like Christ was breach of the covenant and therefore sin.

"Sin not unto death"

Since the Lord viewed all converts to Christ as "little children," (I John 3:7), immaturity was expected. Such immaturity was sin (I John 1:8). It was sin "not unto death"

373

(I John 5:16). Such sin was expected, although not approved. The Lord's Table provided a cleansing from sin and of the conscience. The fact the Table was there indicated the need for it. One making steady progress toward Christlikeness was growing in grace and in the Spirit. That growth was a type of perfection in itself. One was not put out of the covenant by simple breach of it, any more than the Israelite was put out of the covenant for simple trespass. He came to the sacrifices. Of course, God sought honest covenant-keeping rather than sin and restitution.

I desired *hesed,* not sacrifice (Hos. 6:6).

One was not in covenant in the morning, out of it at noon and back in it in the evening. It was because of the high goal set by God He tolerated the Corinthian church, full of sin and error as it was. Paul addressed them as the church of God, and as saints, people who had dedicated themselves to Christ (I Cor. 1:2). His efforts at correction implied both an acceptance of them with sins "not unto death," and of the norm, Jesus Christ's example.

"Sin unto Death"

"Sin unto death" was repudiation of the Lord, and His covenant. There was no hope for such a one, for there was no hope outside Christ's way. It was impossible for such a one to be brought again to repentance. After all, it was the gospel message that brought faith/repentance (Rom. 10:17). If he held the message to be false, and was not moved by the cross, how indeed was God to move him? (Heb. 6:5ff.).

There were two ways one could repudiate the covenant. 1). A complete break with Christ and the church was the

374

most obvious. It was called "fallen away" (Heb. 6:6), "severed from Christ" (Gal. 5:4), "fallen away from grace" (Gal. 5:4), "deliberately keep on sinning," (Heb. 10:26), "carried away" and "fall from your secure position," (II Pet. 3:17), "remove your lampstand" (Rev. 2:5), "denied my name" (Rev. 3:8), and "sin unto death."

John said, "Anyóne who welcomes him shares in his wicked work" (II John 2:11). The long course of human and Divine experience had shown some men kept commitments and others did not. Those who kept commitments with Christ were predestined for glory (Rom. 8:29, 30). Those who swore allegiance and did not keep it were destined for eternal exclusion from the presence of God (II Thess. 1:8, 9). In Hebrew predestination, only the results of choice were predestined. The word did not have reference to the decision-making process itself. God did not predestine which individuals might choose Christ, but He did predestine that all who did choose Christ would be saved.

2). The second way one could "fall away" was by utter neglect of covenant pledge. When one was baptized he placed upon himself a kind of self-curse. "May I die in water as those sinners of Noah's time if I prove faithless to the Lord of this oath." The Apostles spent a good many hours penning messages to their flocks urging them to be faithful. They stated clearly the consequence of neglect.

Paul: "By this gospel you are saved if you hold firmly to the word I preached to you. Otherwise you have believed in vain" (I Cor. 15:2).

Peter: "Be all the more eager to make your calling and election sure, for if you do these things you will never fall . . ." (II Pet. 1:10).

375

"If they have escaped the corruption of the world by knowing Jesus Christ, and are again entangled in it, and overcome, they are worse off at the end than they were at the beginning . . . turned their backs on . . . as . . . a dog returns to its vomit" (II Pet. 2:20).

Jude: "They are godless men who change the grace of our God into license for immorality, and deny Jesus Christ, our only Sovereign and Lord. . . . I want to remind you the Lord delivered his people out of Egypt and later destroyed those who did not keep their positions of authority . . . he has kept in darkness . . ." (Jude 4ff.).

John: "Be faithful even to the point of death and I will give to you the crown of life" (Rev. 2:10).

"and I saw the souls of those who had been beheaded because of the testimony of Jesus and because of the word of God" (Rev. 20:4).

Hebrews: "We must pay careful attention, therefore, to what we have heard, so that we do not drift away. For if the message spoken by angels was binding, and every violation received its just punishment, how shall we escape if we ignore such a great salvation?" (2:1ff.).

"Remember those earlier days after you received the light, . . . suffering . . . insult . . . persecution . . . because you knew yourselves you had better and lasting possessions. Do not throw away your confidence; it will be richly rewarded. You need to persevere so that when you have done the will of God, you will receive what is promised" (10:32ff.).

376

"See to it that none of you has a sinful, unbeliev-
ing heart, that turns away from the living God,
but encourage one another today, . . . so that
none of you may be hardened by sin's deceitful-
ness. We have come to share in Christ if we hold
firmly to the end the confidence we had at first"
(3:12ff.).

James: "What good is it my brothers, if a man claims to
have faith and has no deeds? Can such faith save
him? . . . you see, that a person is justified by
what he does and not by faith alone" (James
2:14ff.).

Jesus: "Depart from me, ye now are cursed. . . ." They
will answer, "Lord, when . . ." He will reply, "Whatever you did for one of the least of these brothers
of mine, you did for me" (Matt. 25:31ff.).

In the case told by Jesus, apparently some who thought
themselves saved and safely in Christ were utterly astounded
at the verdict. They "believed" in Christ. They called him
"Lord." Yet, they were lost. A person acquainted with
covenant would never be surprised at such a verdict. Indeed, the covenanter understood status as conditional.
One could not simply claim, as the Jews had, their status
protected them. Keeping covenant was as vital as entering
covenant.

Calvin R. Scoonhoven writing in analysis of the Book of
Hebrews correctly understood the issue of the book: perseverance as a condition to one's salvation.

In order for this emphasis not to become a meaningless
mockery, we must know that the writer is speaking of ultimate issues. It is not some reward that may be lost, rather it
is one's very soul. John Calvin wrote of the perseverance of

377

the saints, and it is precisely of this that the writer of this treatise speaks. Whether the word be perseverance or endurance, it is one's eternal destiny that is here involved. We must not here apply some external theological concept to this writer's formulations. Whether other Biblical writers are teaching what this writer teaches or not, we should never utilize the "analogy of faith" principle to make him say something other than what he really intends to say, and thereby force conformity to what we think he should say. This is precisely where hermeneutics and the application of certain false principles forthrightly frustrate the thinking an author's thoughts after him.[7]

Keeping covenant was essential to salvation. Works of faith were not the source of salvation (Heb. 5:8). The source of salvation was God in Christ. Christ was the essential condition to salvation. Faith and obedience were essential to get into and remain in Christ. Consequently the scripture said, "if we hold fast the confidence and hope" (Heb. 3:6). Holding fast to faith in Christ as the only source of life and hope was the believers' part in the covenant. For the Apostles it was never by faith alone. It was always faith and obedience (Rom. 16:28).

There were two standards of judgment by which God would evaluate for salvation at the judgment. The first was "in Christ."

If anyone's name was not found written in the book of life, he was thrown in the lake of fire (Rev. 20:15).

The other standard was covenant keeping by the believer.

So then, each one of us will give an account of himself to God (Rom. 14:12).

7. Calvin R. Schoonhoven, "The 'Analogy of Faith,' and the Intent of Hebrews," *Scripture, Tradition, and Interpretation*, Ed., W. Ward Gasque, Grand Rapids: Eerdmans, 1978, p. 97.

The dead were judged according to what they had done as recorded in the books . . . each person was judged according to what he had done (Rev. 20:12ff.).

Don't you know the wicked will not inherit the kingdom of God? Do not be deceived: neither the sexually immoral nor idolators, nor adulterers, . . . nor the greedy, nor swindlers will inherit the kingdom of God . . . (I Cor. 5:9ff.).

The Apostles tried to strike a reasonable balance between utter trust of Christ for salvation and acceptable faithfulness. According to the need of the audience they tended to emphasize first the one and then the other. Two things were certain: there was no salvation apart from Christ; and there was no salvation without individual faith in Him and obedience to him. Mutually for salvation was covenant.

He became the author of eternal salvation to all who obey him (Heb. 5:8).

The certainty of one's salvation rested in the faithfulness of God. That faithfulness must be complemented by a similar faithfulness in man. Paul used a hymn to express it clearly to Timothy.

> If we died with him,
> > we will also live with him.
> If we endure,
> > we shall also reign with him.
> If we disown him,
> > he will also disown us.
> If we are faithless,
> > he will remain faithful,
> > for he cannot disown himself (II Tim. 2:11-13).

When the harmonization of the concepts represented is presented, it would say,

If we have converted to Christ,
we shall have the life of Christ.
If we endure faithfully to the end,
we will reign with him.
If we renounce our faith
he will also renounce us as his own.
If we do not follow through on our commitments,
He will nonetheless judge by the agreed covenant.
God will never initiate a breach himself.

Ethnicity and God's People

The reason for choosing Abraham and his posterity was God's need for loyal servants for Messiah. God needed a band, a people upon whom He could depend. He separated the Israelites from their neighbors to indicate the need for His people to be attentive to their duty, not conformed to their neighbors. The people were chosen to service, not status. The people of God were to maintain their identity in every cultural circumstance. God led the Israelites through several social changes—always with the intent they should maintain their identity. They were once a shepherding tribe of wanderers, then an elite honored set of ethnic guests in Egypt. From there they became a deprived group of quasi-slaves locked into a pagan social system. They changed cultural status and became a wandering warlike band of rag-tags snapping at the borders of a wealthy land. From there they became a loosely held together confederation of conquering immigrants settling in uneasy truce with city-states unable to be conquered at the time. They became a powerful, if small, buffer kingdom reaping rich rewards because of their unique geographic location. They became a divided monarchy, and then a captive and dispersed set of expatriates living in many lands. At last they were a religious-cultural island in the sea of Hellenistic universal brotherhood. Their duty was to learn to maintain their identity as God's people in every changing circumstance. God needed a loyal people to serve Messiah when He came.

When Messiah came, He found His first disciples from this band of well trained (in terms of loyalty) men and women. They understood what it meant to be God's people. The early church was founded upon the dispora communities of Jews who maintained loyalty to Jehovah if not the Torah of Moses. Israel was the model for the church. The church was to go into every cultural circumstance found on earth. The church was to maintain its true identity amid the nations. Christ was the true identity for the church. God spent two thousand years preparing a people who could live as His People in every circumstance. The great commission sent into an Egyptian captivity again the people of God. This time, they would not be slaves but true "rulers," and uncompromisingly loyal to One God of the New Covenant.

Conclusion

Hesed was covenant keeping to the best interests of the other person. What *hesed* was to the Old Testament, Christlikeness was to the New. Jesus filled several words with the essentially same meaning as *hesed*. Love, serve, rule and submit were all redefined to mean contribution to the best interests of the other. The best interests of any person was reconciliation with God and one's neighbor. What was best for the community was peace with God and each other. What was best for a family was to aid each other to be successful.

The model of true service was Christ and the church. Christ aided mankind in the most helpful way. He died for them. In the same way all who found themselves in socially superior positions were to so aid the other as to imitate Christ's *hesed*. A husband, for instance, was to treat the wife as Christ treated the church. He loved the church. The church was to advance Christ's aims on earth. In the same way, the wife was to advance the husband's aims and welfare. All other socially inferior/superior relationships were to be modeled after Christ and the church.

Social accommodation to error may permit the church to limit the freedom of the individual in local and limited ways. Whatever was in the best interests of the church as it grew to Christlikeness was good stewardship. Such limitation was concession to error in society, and was not to become the rule in the church or the world. The social position of anyone, and especially women, was not to be frozen at an accommodation. When local and temporary situations allow it, each person was to be able to contribute to the growth of the church in as productive a way as any other member.

Since the basic need of mankind was reconciliation with God in Christ, world evangelism was the highest priority of the church. The church, as individuals and as a body were debtors to all the pagans on earth. An obligation was laid on the church to carry to the ignorant, the ill, those held in bondage, the message of salvation in Christ, and freedom under His New Reign.

Questions for Chapter Eight

1. *Hesed* meant a) faith   c) love
                b) faithfulness   d) pity

2. Explain the two elements making up *hesed*.
   a) _____ b) _____.
3. Why were there so many different English words translating *hesed*?
4. Comment: "We must give all the glory to God. We do nothing. It is sinful to use human ideas to serve God. One should never take the initiative, but pray for the Spirit to move."
5. T F God expects all believers to keep the Old Testament commands.
6. T F The basic idea in *hesed* was doing exactly what God said.
7. T F The servant who did only what a master told him was a good slave.
8. T F Rule, in the church, meant the authority to command obedience.
9. T F Obedience, in the church, meant doing exactly what one was told.
10. Define "stewardship."
_____
11. Define "service." _____
12. Define "*hesed*." _____
13. Define "love." _____
14. Define "submission." _____
15. Define "ruling." _____
16. What was the "law of the Spirit"? _____
17. When is a person most Spiritual? _____
18. What is "normal behavior" for a believer? _____
19. What was the standard functional definition of Christlikeness? _____
20. What was "social accommodation"? Give a Biblical example. _____

21. Differentiate between: "Sin unto death" and "sin not unto death."
22. Complete this, "Be thou _____ unto death and I will give to thee the crown of life."

PLEASE TURN THE BOOK OVER FOR ANSWERS.

1. b)
2. a) Keeping the covenant or expected behaviors.
   b) Keeping obligations in such a way the other person is benefited.
3. No single Greek, Latin or English word carried both concepts.
4. We give glory to God when we use our human initiative to do what He wants done. It is glorious for God to have His servants doing what He has asked them to do.
5. F The entire Old Testament passed from Law into history at the cross.
6. F It had the other idea also: doing it in such a way others are benefited.
7. F He was an "unprofitable slave."
8. F Rule meant exactly what serve and submit meant.
9. F Obedience meant doing what was best for the other person.
10. "Stewardship" was advancing the best interests of the owner.
11. "Service" was advancing the best interests of the master.
12. "Hesed" was advancing the best interests of one's partner.
13. "Love" meant acting in the best interests of another with affection.

14. "Submission" was subjecting what I wanted to what was best for others.
15. "Ruling" meant doing what would best edify or advance others.
16. Being like Christ.
17. When most like Christ.
18. Behaving in a given culture as Jesus would had He been born there.
19. Helping the other person be a success, with God and others (Reconciliation).
20. "Social accommodation" was limiting activities for a time in order to accomplish what God wanted.
    Stopping the common church meal at Corinth.
    Women keep silent.
    Circumcising Timothy.
21. "Sin not unto death" was making a mistake while trying to be a Christian.
    "Sin unto death" was repudiation of Christ by statement or utter neglect.
22. "faithful"

Chapter Nine

TYPES OF COVENANT THEOLOGY

As the age of the Apostles drew to a close, the documents of the New Testament Canon were completed. One of the last was the Book of Revelation. It was structured along lines of covenant formulary. In that way it was similar to several books circulating about the same time. Each of them were composed with similar presuppositions. Two were Jewish. Others were Christian. All had the parties, terms, and promises sections as provided by covenant formulary.

Extra-Biblical Covenant Formulary

The *Manual of Discipline,* a Jewish document, had three basic sections. The "dogmatic" or party section extended from chapter 3:1-5 through 4:1. The stipulations or "ethical" section was 4:2-6 and 5:9-11. The promises part was 4:6b through to the end of the book. Baltzer called the promises sections both the "blessings and curses" and the "eschatological" section.

The Damascus Document was similar to the Manual, and was an Essene-type constitution. Dogmatic section: 1:1—6:11. The Ethical Section: 6:12—7:4. The Eschatological Section: 7:5 to the end.

The *Epistle of Barnabas* was also divided into the three sections along covenant lines. The Dogmatic: Chapter 2 through chapter 17. The Ethical Section or Stipulations: 18:1 to 20:ff. The Blessings and Curses section: 21:1 to the end.

The Didache or the *Teaching of the Twelve Apostles,* was a small and very enlightening document circulating in Palestine in the early second century. The "Dogmatic" section is missing from the copy that survived.

386

The Second Epistle of Clement had the same three sections. Parties: Chapters one and two. Stipulations: 3:1 through 4:2. The Eschatological: 6:7—7:6.

There were several other documents using the "testament" motif for their formulary, including *The Jubilees* and the *The Testament of the Twelve Patriarchs.*[1]

The climate of the ancient church was alive with covenant idea. The wide distribution of documents reflecting the mindset precluded any assignment of the idea to purely Jewish perspectives.

Covenant and the Revelation

The Book of Revelation divided naturally into three parts. Each part dealt with materials usually found under the headings of parties, stipulations and promises. The parties were identified in the first five chapters. The author began with a vision of the throne of God. The Father, Christ and the Spirit were there. Lampstands were identified as seven churches. The seven churches were the parties in covenant with God. Each church received a message from Christ. At the end of each message the author was identified as the Holy Spirit. Chapter five pictured Jesus worthy to unroll the scroll. Christ was firmly in control of history. The covenanter need not fear God's ability to perform. The *parties* were identified as the Lord and the churches. Churches as well as individuals were parties to the covenant. Usually a commendation was given, but not always. Corrections needed by each church were identified. Recommendations, warnings, or demands were made. Each implied

---

1. Klaus Baltzer, *The Covenant Formulary,* London: Fortress Press, 1971, pp. 97-164.

a standard existed which was being met or not met. No commendation was possible unless a standard was understood and being met. No warning was understood without a standard which was not being satisfactorily met. Such talk addressed *stipulations*. *Promises* were put by the author into two categories: blessings and curses. Each positive promise implied the negative. One's eternal destiny was bound up in faithfulness to the covenant expectations of the God of history. The discussion of the churches ended the first part of the Apocalypse.

The second section of the book included chapter six and extended to chapter eighteen. The material in that section included seven seals, seven trumpets, the last three called woes, a dragon, a beast from the sea followed by a beast from the land, an additional seven bowls of God's wrath, ending with a scarlet woman/city. The stipulations of the covenant included both continuing to preach the message and remaining confident in God through every trauma pictured. It is doubtful whether the author intended each part of each seven to be specifically identified in history with an earthly power. With or without identity the impact was the same. The church would, along with mankind, undergo the difficulties created by wicked men and institutions. The church would be the target of serious attack. She was, in spite of all such terror, to keep her faith and conduct her mission. God was in firm control.

The last third of the book, from chapter eighteen through twenty-two, described the promises of the covenant. The very graphic assurances were intended to encourage the church to faithfulness when experiencing the difficulties pictured in the middle third of the book. A preview of how all would end was given. When all history was finished, and all the drama of the ages over, how would matters be? The Lord promised things would be as He now pictured. When it was all over, *human culture* without God, the best of all man's ideas and abilities together, would be like a burning city! (Rev. 18:1 to 19:10). What would *Christ* be? The Lord was pictured as a mighty conqueror, riding a white horse of victory, followed across the heavens by thousands and thousands of white clad warriors riding on white horses. He who once was a lowly babe, and once suffered mockery and death at the hands of wicked men will one day be the most splendid of all kings in victory (19:11-21). What of the *devil*? The devil was to be chained in darkness for a time, and then loosed. He was to do great damage, but in the end was captured and thrown into a lake of fire with his associates. "Do you," an ancient preacher would plead with his audience, "want to share his fate? Then do not share his life! If you wish to ride in victory with the Lord Jesus, come and surrender to Him now" (20:1-10). What of the *unbeliever*? How would it turn out for him? He was to be thrown into the lake of fire with his master (20:11-15).

What of the *church*? She had been terrorized by the dragon, beaten and left for dead in the streets, put through much trial, suffered her finest to be beheaded. What was her ultimate fate? She was to be a royal bride, fit for her wedding. She was Jerusalem the glorious. She was a combination of the beautiful bride and the holy city! What was more beautiful than that? (21:1-27). What of the *believer* himself? The believer was returned to Eden. The tree of life and the water of life were there. The second Eden was twelve times more wonderful than the first. Life with God was fully restored for the believer (22:1-16).

The closing of the last book of the New Testament repeated the great commission:

> The Spirit and the Bride say, "Come." And let him who hears say, "Come!" Whoever is thirsty, and whoever wishes, let him take the free gift of the water of life (22:17).

The Bible ended with a serious Treaty clause, one found in all ancient pacts. The parties of the treaty were forbidden to alter one word of the Treaty Text.

> Hear now, O Israel, the decrees and laws I am about to teach you. Follow them so that you may live and go in and take possession of the land that the Lord the God of our fathers, is giving you. Do not add to what I command you, and do not subtract from it, but keep the commands of the Lord your God that I gave you (Deut. 4:1, 2).

It seems very likely the writer had the above concept in mind for the people of the New Torah. Their promised land was far better. The way to it was essentially the same: faithfulness to the word of God.

> I warn everyone who hears the words of the prophecy of this book: If anyone adds anything to them God will add to him the plagues described in this book. And if anyone takes words away from this book of prophecy, God will take away from him his share in the tree of life, and in the holy city, which are described in this book (Rev. 22:18f.).

The assumptions of covenanted religion were reflected in the Revelation. While the Treaty idea was not explicit, the entire philosophic base of the book was covenantal. The heavy emphasis on steadfastness in suffering in confidence of God's ultimate victory was reflective of both the gospel of John and the book of Hebrews. The Revelation did not properly fall into typical apocalyptic literature. It was the capture of the apocalyptic vision-describing strength and applying it to the categories and emphasis of covenant. Great disservice was done to the Revelation when theologians assumed it was in typical apocalyptic tradition. It was not. Apocalyptic literature gave up on the Torah, the ability of men, the idea of a kingdom on earth apart from explosive intervention different from the first coming of Christ.[2] Typical apocalyptics did not believe in gradualism. Yet, that was precisely the way God worked. John's revelation was prophetic in the tradition of the Torah prophets. Christ was seated at God's right hand to reign until all His enemies were destroyed (I Cor. 15:25). He was to reign in and through the church on this earth. He would win with the church, His body, then He would return. For, you see, the sword held by the Master was in His mouth.

The Greek Disaster

The church spread throughout the known world. By the year four hundred, the Mediterranean Sea was all but a Christian lake. The Celtic peoples had strong churches in their areas. North Africa was being won. The warlike tribes of the north, in what is today Romania, Hungary, Yugoslavia, and Czechoslovakia, had contact with the gospel. Many sections of the tribes were already Christian.[3] The gospel was being preached as far as India in a regular way. The highland areas of Africa were converting. The powerful northern peoples of Ethiopia had accepted Christ in large numbers.

---

2. Walter Schmithals, *The Apocalyptic Movement*. Nashville: Abingdon Press, 1973, p. 87.

3. Kenneth Scott Latourette, *A History of Christianity*, New York: Harper-Row, Revised Edition, 1975, Vol. I, p. 98-102.

All was not well for the covenant in Greece. Three things wove the web of unhappiness. 1). The philosophy of Greece, represented in good measure by Plato, and popularized as gnosticism used categories of thought foreign to the Old Testament. The Greeks attempted a harmony of Moses/Christ with the categories of the Hellenists. That shift of frame of reference from covenant philosophy to naturalism/mysticism created almost five hundred years of bitter controversy. The discussion moved from the ethical being of God to the nature of God discussed in the rather rigid Greek format. Of course, no satisfactory solution was to be found. The church dissipated its energy in heresy battles that solved little. In the meantime, the evangelistic interests of the Greeks grew cold. Their great day was almost over as a vital force in world mission. 2). The capture of the government by a Roman general named Constantine revived the discarded and destructive concept of the Theocracy of God. He made Christianity the quasi-official state religion. His sons went further; they outlawed pagan religions in the Empire.[4] That further accelerated the decline of the true covenantal faith of the Apostles. In the end it meant a return to the Old Testament theology of citizenship and covenanted relationship to God being transmitted by the citizen/parent to the child. Eventually every child was Christian by law. There was, consequently, no real evangelism. The church became a nurture-oriented body. Babies were baptized at birth. The baptism was both a religious and national act. The duty of the church leadership was nurture. Personal conversion was a strange idea to those in the Christian covenant by reason of their parents' faith. 3). The serious attempt to

---

4. Latourette, *ibid.*, pp. 92-94.

enforce a Theocratic religion on all the ethnic sub-cultures created havoc for the ancient world. Everyone must become Christian, just as every Israelite was forced to be a good Torah abiding citizen in the Old Testament. The Theocracy of the Old Testament became the ideal in Christendom. Ethnicity was not allowed. The command of Christ to convert the ethnics of the world was changed to absorb all the ethnics of the world. Resistance to such cultural tyranny was fierce, and often futile.

One tragic result of the Byzantine imperialism was the breakoff of the Aramaic/Arabic peoples into Islam. Mohammed's emphasis was more anti-Greek than anti-Christian. The three marks of Islam reflected it. One language for the faithful: Arabic, not Greek. Against the trinity was advanced a high monotheism. Against the destruction of all literature of the ethnics was a new literature, the Koran. For over a thousand years the church would hold the old Theocracy as the ideal. Theologies developed to promote and defend that movement. The Old Testament was used to override the New. The Apostles were reinterpreted to harmonize with the concept of salvation by birth into a Christian commonwealth.

The Roman Glory and Failure

The Roman church did not accept the philosophy of Plato. Romans were more Hebraic in style. The Hebrews and the Romans were administrative rather than philosophy oriented. They were a straight-forward people. They did not care for abstract speculations.[5] That similarity helped

---

5. Michael Williams, *The Catholic Church in Action*, New York: Macmillian Co., 1934, p. 266.

stop the flow of Platonic philosophy into the western Mediterranean world. That much was good. The failure of the once great Roman church began when the city of Rome fell in 476 A.D. The loss of administrative control at Rome threw the entire western world into chaos. The churches were the chief stabilizing influence. The church became Rome, the City of God. Leaders in the empire, with limited access to each other, started congregations as best they could. They held together by administrative lines similar to the old Roman provincial administrative system. The now familiar Priest, Bishop, Archbishop, Pope system grew into being.

The theology of nurture again prevailed. The Theocracy of the Old Testament was taken over by the church itself. The people of the local churches were analogous to the citizenry in Israel. The Levites became the Priesthood. The Pope was a blend of the Davidic and Aaronic Kingly High Priest pictured by the prophets. When the Roman church obtained political control of a nation the Theocracy was complete. The State became new Israel. The church became the Priesthood of the nation. As in old Israel, religious freedom was eliminated. The religious and civil authorities worked together as in the Old Testament. The civil government enforced the religious program. The Old Testament dominated the New. The Apostles were interpreted as harmonious with the First Covenant. The New Covenant was seen as the moral extension of the ideal state, Israel. The trappings of office, the sacred clothing, the high status of clergy, the union of church and state, the use of the state to enforce religion was thoroughly Old Testament in spirit and form. In Roman theology, the church, meaning the Roman Catholic Church alone, was as authorized as Israel to change traditions, originate new expediencies, and on its own authority reinterpret the ancient and Apostolic practices. Israel produced the Old Testament as God's people, and the documents declared to be of God, it was said. In the same way, both the church and the New Testament shared power. The idea was carried in practice by the twin authorities of the Bible and tradition. "Tradition" referred to traditions approved by the Roman churches. At the bottom of all the theology lay the practice of interpreting the New Testament by the Old Testament. It was a revival, theologically, of Old Testament religion.

Lutheran Theology

There was little overt interest in covenant by the Lutheran theologians. The early orientation of Luther was Augustinian, i.e., Platonic. His belief in total depravity was to cause his break with the other Germanic theologian, Erasmus of Holland.[6] Under the influence of Melancthon Luther grew more Hebraic. To still the storm caused by the reorientation of their leader, the concept of Grace was used to integrate all theology. Although *b'rth* was used over 285 times in the Old Testament, Lutherans did not pay much attention to it.

> It (covenant) played a more prominent role in Reformed Theology than among Lutherans, perhaps because of the Reformed emphasis upon decree(s) of salvation.[7]

Another reason existed for the cool attitude toward covenant by Lutherans. There was a determined group of

---

6. Ewald M. Plass, *What Luther Says: An Anthology*, St. Louis: Concordia Press, 1959.

7. Julius Bodensiech, Ed., "Covenant," *The Encyclopedia of The Lutheran Church*, Minneapolis: Augsburg Publishing House, 1965, Vol. I, p. 627.

"re-baptizers" in Germany. One leader was a gentle teacher Pilgram Marpack. His approach was Christocentric with a strong theology of discontinuity between the two covenants.[8] The New Covenant did not support any concept of political Theocracy, he reasoned. Luther was determined to create a true Protestant political state. As a result, the Anabaptists, an early effort at Restoration theology, were held to be traitors to the state. They were hunted down in a most persistent way and put to death—men, women, and children. Marpack himself was tied to a wagon wheel and driven through the marketplace while great chunks of flesh were gouged out by pieces of metal welded to the wagon frame for that purpose. He was there burned at the stake.[9]

More recently Lutheran scholars have renewed interest in covenant as potential theological core. The radical dichotomy between the Old and New Testaments on the basis of Law and Grace was being questioned. Such writers as J. M. Myers in his *Grace and Torah*, W. R. Roehrs *Covenant and Justification in the Old Testament*, and Kline are examples.

There is indeed a sense in which the Old Testament, especially in the call of Abraham, and the exodus/Sinai episodes, portrays a conception of grace less "quid pro quo" than the New Testament.[10]

Reformed Federal Theology

The political/religious system of Rome broke up on the rocks of ethnicity, the very reason the Israelite Theocracy

---

8. William Klassen, *Covenant and Community*, Grand Rapids: Eerdmans, 1977, p. 124.

9. W. R. Estep, *The Anabaptist Story*, Nashville: Broadman Press, 1963, pp. 75-87, 142-145.

10. J. M. Myers, *Grace and Torah*, London: Fortress Press, 1975, p. 1.

failed. Northern Europeans had their own way of thinking and doing things. One universal language was not for them, even in the church of God. When Rome's old enemy, Greece, fell to the invading Moslems, whose army, incidentally included some determined Christian detachments from regions hostile to Greece's political ambitions, many scholars fled to Germany. The reformation was Greek in spirit. There seemed no way Rome could win in Northern Europe. Indeed she did not. Yet, in a sense, she did.

The main Protestant groups rejected her own political rule, claiming she was the anti-Christ. They rejected her heavy emphasis on works righteousness, so much so many almost became gnostics in reaction. They rejected the idea Rome was the true church. What Rome won was the theological assumption the Old Testament interpreted the New. Almost all groups adopted the Theocratic ideal. When Luther, Calvin, Henry the Eighth, and John Knox came into political power, they each used the state as Rome had. They put to death as political enemies their religious foes on the same theological authority claimed by Rome!

The main tradition interpreting the New Testament by the Old Testament was the Calvinists from Geneva. Their heavy emphasis on the unity of the two covenants overrode the Apostolic re-interpretations. The children of the Christian church were children of Abraham. Calvin was the source of two similar but competing theologies: Federal theology and the "analogy of faith" theology. The main one was Presbyterian and Reformed Federal Covenant Theology. There was but one covenant in the Bible they claimed, the Covenant of Grace. The name Federal was from a Latin word for covenant, *foederus*. Calvin had no real covenant orientation. It was his greatest theological blunder.[11]

---

11. Estep, *Op. cit.*, p. 87.

The covenant of all the fathers is so far from differing substantially from ours, that it is the very same. Only the administration varies.[12]

Calvin's chair at Geneva passed eventually to Turrentin.
He produced his own Institutes as Calvin had. They made
covenant explicit. His Institutes gave us Federal Covenant.
Turrentin's Institutes were used at Princeton by Archibald
Hodge. B. B. Warfield was a student and admirerer of
Hodge. Both men were leaders in their respective generations at Princeton. Princeton was America's most consistent
advocate of Federal Covenant. A defender of the Ecclesi-
astic Covenant of Grace was W. L. McCalla of Augusta,
Kentucky. He argued the Christian Church was but a branch
of the Abrahamic Church, part of the same covenant but in
different dispensations. Christian baptism was circumcision
under the second administration, and since circumcision
was practiced on children born of Abrahamic parents, so
baptism was to be administered to infants of Christian parents.
The issue of baptism was a covenant issue. All other issues
in religious controversy in that age were covenant issues,
he said.

The Jewish society before Christ and the Christian society
after Christ are one and the same church though in different dispensations, inasmuch that the latter is but a branch
of the former.
1. They had the same religion.
2. They had the same inspired name.
3. They had the same covenant.
The same injunctions have been laid upon the visible church
in all ages, and uniformly she has been subjected to the

---

12. John Calvin, *Institutes*, II:x:2.

same requirements. . . . They had substantially the same ordinances of religious worship. Circumcision, the Passover, and the Sabbath were primary ordinances amongst the Jews, and these were substantially the same as baptism, the Supper, and the Christian Sabbath.[13]

The same basic procedure was well established as a defense for the basic theological position inherited from Rome and Greece. Other authors have written similar defenses of infant baptism, the clergy, the Sabbath as Sunday, tithing, clerical clothing of distinction, the rather sharp distinction between the initiated scholarship and the laity, and the assumption the Old Testament rites carried over into the New Testament in direct substitutional fashion. That is, the forms changed between the covenants, but the meanings of the forms did not; that the Old Testament meanings override Apostolic reinterpretations. Writers advocating Federal Covenant included such notables as Nathan Rice,[14] John Murrey,[15] Calvin Knox Cummings,[16] and the translator of the Kittel *Theological Dictionary*, Geoffrey W. Bromiley.[17] All had the same presupposition. Covenant passed by physical descent, first through Isaac's and then through Christ's people. Faithfulness was taking up the

---

13. W. L. McCalla, *A Public Debate on Christian Baptism*, with Alexander Campbell, London: Simkin and Marshall, 1842, p. 111, 112. Reprinted Old Paths Book Club, Rosemead, California.

14. Nathan Rice and Alexander Campbell, *The Campbell-Rice Debate*, A. T. Skillman and Sons, 1843.

15. John Murrey, *The Covenant of Grace*, Sterling, Virginia: Grace Abounding Ministries, 1953.

16. Calvin Knox Cummings, *The Covenant of Grace*, Philadelphia: Great Commission Publications, 1974.

17. Geoffrey Bromiley, *Children of Promise. The Case for Baptizing Infants*. Grand Rapids: Eerdmans, 1979.

covenant of Christ as the Israelite descendants took up the Old Covenant. As a result, nurture dominated their theology, and the Old Testament tended to dominate the New.

Federal Covenant suffered greatly in England and elsewhere because it made children members of the covenant before they were saved. They were saved, because they were in the covenant, and yet saved "provisionally"— provided they took up the covenant faith in an act of "confirmation" upon reaching an age of accountability. The difficulty was highlighted in the rather long series of exchanges between Toombs and Baxter in 1646.[18] Baptist theology made heavy inroads in pedobaptist churches. The collapse of Federal Covenant was traced in North America by Dr. Peter DeJung in *The Idea of Covenant on New England Theology*.[19] The practice of declaring infants members of the covenant community by virtue of the faith of their parents, and yet reserving the right to pass upon the validity of their personal "experience" with the Lord before admitting them to the Lord's Table put an almost unbearable strain on the position. Practicing non-believer baptism on the basis of covenant and believer Communion on the same basis contributed to the adoption of Baptist theology by later generations. The issue was brought into sharp focus when John Cotton of New England baptized an infant whose parents had been baptized as infants but who never took up the faith and

---

18. John Toombs, *Anti-paedobaptism, or The Second Part of a Full Review of the Dispute Concerning Infant Baptism*, London, 1654. *An Exercitation About Infant-Baptism*, 1646.

Richard Baxter, *An Answer to Mr. Toombs His Valedictory Oration to the People of Bewdeley*, London, 1652.

19. Peter Y. DeJung, *The Covenant Idea in New England Theology*, Grand Rapids: Eerdmans, 1945.

who were not practicing church members.[20] What was the status of the child? Could it be baptized on the faith of the grandparents? Such theological entanglements brought any concept of covenant into disrepute in many parts of the country. Later generations used the word Testament when discussing the matter in order to disassociate themselves from the former difficulties. Detractors called the practices of New England Puritan Covenant the Halfway Covenant.[21]

Dispensational Covenant

In the middle of the last century a series of movements in theology toward a repudiation of all established church dogmas gained momentum. In one group, later known as the Plymouth Brethren, was a leader named John Darby. He believed the report of a woman who claimed Jesus appeared to her in a dream revealing a startling new understanding of prophecy. Margaret McDonald was the original source of dispensational theology according to Dave MacPherson.[22] To support the conclusions brought from the vision, a theology of dispensationalism arose. In it the Old Covenant was understood to be everlasting and co-existent with the New. One covenant with its set of promises was for the Jews. The other covenant with its own promises was for Gentiles. The real story of prophecy, which concerned the Jews, was interrupted by the failure of Christ to introduce the expected Davidic Kingdom during his lifetime. The Old Testament

---

20. John Cotton, *The Way of the Churches of Christ in America*, London, 1645.

21. E. Brooks Holifield, *The Covenant Sealed: The Development of Puritan Sacramental Theology in Old and New England*, New Haven: Yale University Press, 1974, pp. 169, 170.

22. Dave MacPherson, *The Incredible Cover-up*, Plainfield, New Jersey: Logos International, 1975, p. 47ff.

prophecies were suspended, as it were, during the church dispensation. At the end of a specified time, the Old Covenant was to be reinstated; Jesus was to rule in person in Jerusalem as both King and Aaronic High Priest. Blood sacrifices were to be continued in the rebuilt temple, etc.[23]

The prophecies of the Old Testament, they claimed, were meant to have been fulfilled in Christ, but were postponed until Christ's return. They will be literally and precisely fulfilled at that time. They had, as a result, two covenants, two true Israels, two real Jerusalems, two systems of prophecy, and three kingdoms of God. They distinguished sharply between the kingdom of heaven, the kingdom of God and the Church. The New Testament documents were not meant to be a total scripture for the church, but only certain chapters. Some chapters referred to the present kingdom and some to the millennial kingdom and some to the eternal kingdom. They had four gospels, such as Paul's gospel, the gospel of the kingdom, etc., each distinguished from the other. Their system included seven covenanted eras, called dispensations. They abandoned entirely the two covenant system of the Apostles.[24]

Writers in this tradition have been L. S. Chafer, *Systematic Theology* and *Dispensationalism*; John F. Walvoord, *The Rapture Question*; Arno G. Gaebelein, *Daniel*; and Hal Lindsey, commissioned to popularize the ideology by the leadership at Dallas Theological Seminary, *The Late Great Planet Earth*. Bibles using footnoted commentaries, such as the *Scofield Reference Bible* were published. A similar

---

23. L. S. Chafer, *Dispensationalism*, Dallas: Dallas Seminary Press, 1951. *Systematic Theology*. 1948.

24. William E. Cox, *An Examination of Dispensationalism*, Plainfield, New Jersey: Presbyterian and Reformed Publishing Company, 1980, pp. 17-50.

edition, the *C. C. Ryrie Reference Bible* aided their cause at the popular level.[25]

New Covenant Meant No Covenant

The second strain of theology tracing to John Calvin was represented by what Schoonhoven called the "analogy of faith" theology. Schoonhoven himself attributed the basic position to Luther[26] and not Calvin. There was some justification for that view, for Luther so repudiated any concept of conditionality beyond simple faith he disavowed both the Book of Hebrews and James. Certain strains of Baptist theology have struggled with the difficulty, Ironside in *Studies in Hebrews*, Chafer in *Systematic Theology*, Hewett in *Hebrews*, C. I. Scofield in his 1917 *Reference Bible*, and Ryrie's *Reference Bible* in the Acts 2:38 footnote.[27]

According to the "analogy of faith" theology, Christ's substitutionary death was the New Covenant. There was no real condition to salvation except Christ. The condition to salvation represented in Him was cared for at the cross. It was thus said, no condition existed for salvation in man other than hearing the message. When one heard the message and believed in it, he was saved quite apart from any other overt response whatever.

---

25. John F. Walvoord, *The Rapture Question.* Findlay, Ohio: Dunham Publishing Co., 1957.

Arno G. Gaebelein, *Daniel.* Grand Rapids: Kregel, 1955.

Hal Lindsey, *The Late Great Planet Earth.* Grand Rapids: Zondervan, 1970.

26. Calvin Schoonhoven, "The 'Analogy of Faith' and the Intent of Hebrews." *Scripture, Tradition, and Interpretation.* Edited by Gasque and LaSor. Grand Rapids: Eerdmans, 1978, p. 92.

27. H. A. Ironside, *Studies in Hebrews and Titus.* 1932, pp. 79-82.

Thomas Hewett, *Hebrews,* Grand Rapids: Eerdmans, 1960, pp. 106-111.

C. I. Scofield, *Reference Bible.* 1917, p. 1295.

L. S. Chafer, *Dispensationalism.* Dallas: Dallas Seminary Press, 1951.

The rule of "faith" was applied to all passages of scripture. As a result, no real condition to reward ever existed except faith. That was true, they said, in the garden of Eden, with Abraham, within the Sinai Covenant, among the prophets and most certainly in Christ. Faith and only faith was the condition to good grace with God in any age. Covenant was therefore pointless as theology. The entire concept was abandoned by Paul and the other Apostles, they claimed. Any deeds done in any covenant were vain "works" and had no real bearing on the relationship. What God looked for was the state of mind of the person when he responded to a command. The state of mind was faith. Any scripture that did not support the "analogy of faith" was reinterpreted, regardless of the damage done to the plain sense of it. Luther went so far as to cast from the Christian Canon both James and Hebrews!

Forms, whether covenanted or not, were held to be "works" and unrelated to salvation. The "faith," i.e., the mental state, saved; not the deed. One "received Christ" by prayer. An entirely new approach to conversion was developed. An emphasis on the sinfulness of the individual was designed to produce in him a "felt need" for relief. Heaven was declared to be a free and unconditional gift from God. A condition was made, but because it was simple faith, it was not a real "condition" of salvation. One came to feel saved when he asked Jesus to "come into his heart." After that brief prayer, the convert was assured he was saved. He was at the same time told to thank God for the salvation just extended. The life in the church was one long and serious effort to maintain that inner assurance of salvation. Without that introspective assurance, understood as the private witness of the Holy Spirit, there was no salvation. Works were denied to effect salvation at all, although the

404

churches holding the "analogy of faith" position work rather hard at defending the position and extending their church memberships.

The loss of confidence in governments, logic, international treaties, and the possibility of solution to problems from a rational approach pervaded western civilization beginning with the latter part of the twentieth century. The decline in constitutional law, the stability of marriage, and the shock of two world wars being fought by allegedly Christian powers added to the rise of individualism, existentialism and emotional solutions to problems. In that seedbed, the "analogy of faith" grew until it had achieved all but official status as authentic Christianity.

The Restoration Movement

John Locke was a Christian English philosopher who lived at the end of the Middle Ages. Europe was in transition from fixed to contract status; from the political philosophy of divine right of kings to constitutional monarchy. Locke was part of the movement that developed into Humanism on the one hand and the Scottish Common Sense philosophy on the other. He was an articulate spokesman for the idea of the Social Contract in western civilization. The political ideals of Locke received much more attention than his metaphysics. He was in the Newtonian, Aristotelian side of the ageless philosophic debate between the introspective approach of Plato and the "scientific" objectivism of Aristotle.[28] Locke was a political philosopher who saw the intolerance of the Christian states and sought a solution. His time in history

_____

28. Mont W. Smith, *The Philosophy of Education of Alexander Campbell*, Unpublished Master of Science Thesis for Butler University, Indianapolis, 1956, pp. 1-20.

was right, and he became famous for his works on Toleration and Civil Government. In the essay on Toleration he separated the church from the state in a rather crisp way. He was first and foremost a Christian philosopher. He saw a sharp distinction between the religion of the Old Testament and that of the New. His model constitution was based upon the ideal of covenanted or agreed relationships. In a political constitution, the state and the population agreed certain powers belonged to the state for good order and certain rights belonged to the citizen. His theory of the Social Contract was secular covenant. The American constitution traced back to John Locke. Alexander Campbell admired Locke.

Thomas Campbell and his son Alexander migrated from Scotland to America at the beginning of the nineteenth century. They had been Presbyterians but had dreams of a non-sectarian united Church of Christ, composed of all true disciples everywhere. Thomas Campbell presented a Declaration and Address in which he affirmed an Apostolic definition of the church. He mixed in a common sense way a concept of the church as a gathered community, a view of scripture, and a toleration that was almost one hundred and fifty years in advance of popular unity movements. He set his program down in a series of thirteen propositions.[29]

> Prop. 1. That the church of Christ upon earth is essentially, intentionally, and constitutionally one; consisting of all those in every place that profess their faith in Christ and obedience to him in all things according to the scriptures, and that manifest the same by their tempers and conduct, and none else; as none else can truly and properly called Christians.

---

29. Thomas Campbell, *The Declaration and Address*, St. Louis: Bethany Press, 1955, pp. 44-48.

Prop. 2. That although the Church of Christ upon earth must necessarily exist in particular and distinct societies, locally separate from each other, yet there ought to be no schisms, no uncharitable divisions among them. They ought to receive each other as Jesus Christ hath received them, to the glory of God. And for this purpose they ought to walk by the same rule. . . .

The next propositions were aimed at eliminating credal statements as tests of fellowship. Creeds were not rejected as teaching devices. The scripture and its own formulations were binding on believers. The authority of the Apostles was affirmed, and a hint of coming things was given when the Old Testament was identified as the constitution of Israel, and the New Testament the standard for Christians. That was a radical departure from typical covenant view. It was similar to Marpack's. It was revolutionary.

Prop. 3. In order to do this, nothing ought to be inculcated upon Christians as articles of faith; nor required of them as terms of communion, but what is expressly taught and enjoined upon them by the word of God. Nor ought anything be admitted, as of divine obligation, in their church constitution and management but what is expressly enjoined by our Lord Jesus Christ and his Apostles upon the New Testament Church, either in express terms, or by approved precedent.

Prop. 4. That although the scriptures of the Old and New Testaments are inseparably connected, making together but one perfect and entire revelation of the Divine will, for the edification and salvation of the Church, and therefore in that respect can not be separated; yet as to what directly and properly belongs to their immediate object, the New Testament is as perfect a rule for the particular duties of its members as the Old Testament was for the worship, discipline and government of the Old Testament Church, and the particular duties of its members.

Campbell's view of man was high. He was optimistic about mankind generally. In that regard he was more Hebraic than Greek. He had confidence in the common man to read and understand documents. His high view of man was reflected in propositions five and six.

> Prop. 5. With respect to the commands and ordinances of our Lord Jesus Christ, where the scriptures are silent as to the express time or manner of performance, if any such there be, no human authority has power to interfere, in order to supply the supposed deficiency by making laws for the church; nor can anything more be required of Christians in such cases, but only that they so observe these commands and ordinances as will evidently answer the declared and obvious end of their institution.

> Prop. 6. That although inferences and deductions from scripture premises, when fairly inferred, may be truly called the doctrine of God's holy word, yet are they not formally binding upon the consciences of Christians farther than they perceive the connection; and evidently see that they are so; for their faith must not stand in the wisdom of men, but in the power and veracity of God. Therefore no deductions can be made terms of communion, but do properly belong to the after and progressive edification of the Church. Hence it is evident that no such deductions or inferential truths ought to have any place in the Church's confession.

In harmony with the sentiment expressed in the Declaration, several synods or "associations" on the American frontier dissolved. The congregations which had supported the presbyteries "melted into the church at large."[30] The

---

30. Barton W. Stone, *Last Will and Testament of the Springfield Presbytery,* St. Louis: Bethany Press, 1955, p. 17.

Declaration and Address was delivered in 1809. The son of Thomas carried on the same sentiment. He delivered an address in 1816 to the Redstone Baptist Association called the Sermon on the Law. It made explicit the sentiment expressed in the Declaration and Address of his father. That address "threw down the gauntlet" before Federal Covenanters, and "analogy of faith" Lutherans and Baptists.

The Sermon on the Law

The Sermon on the Law represented an early example of what became known as Biblical Theology. It was a word study on Torah from the Hebrew and then from the Greek. Campbell concluded the basic Apostolic theology was one of discontinuity between the covenants, of abandonment and replacement. Nothing of the Old Covenant was binding on the Church of Christ but what the Apostles bound upon her. He denied the Law was needed to build into a sinner the consciousness of sin or guilt sufficient to bring repentance. The message of Christ, he maintained, was sufficient in and of itself to convert any person on earth. The Code of Moses was as likely to turn inquirers of Christianity away from religion as bring a sense of guilt. He implied the Apostles' doctrine and that alone was sufficient to edify to complete perfection in Christ.

He affirmed the unity and integrity of the Torah. There was no justification in dividing the Torah into Moral, Ceremonial, or Judicial parts. He defined with clarity what law meant and what "moral" meant. A "ceremony" could not be void of morality if the covenant of Moses enjoined it, Campbell argued. He objected to the baptism of infants on the basis of circumcision. He did not think tithing could be defended on New Testament grounds. He claimed the Old Testament was used to justify huge clergy-built institutions that divided the Church into quarreling sects. He did not use the word covenant frequently, but all the meaning of it was contained in his chosen word, testament. He was to become the champion of New Testament Church, and New Testament Christianity.[31]

When covenant was treated as quasi-constitution, the plain sense of the words must prevail, said Campbell. His hermeneutic was remarkably current. He insisted on words being defined, not dogmatically, but in context. The distinction between the covenants allowed him to avoid the allegorical pitfalls into which so many theologians fell. He insisted that figures of speech mean what they meant when spoken. He used parallelism extensively. He was one of the few published authors who distinguished between continuity of rite and rites in parallel. He knew and used the word synecdoche. By its understanding he was able to grasp the essential category system of both the Old and the New Testaments. He had the courage to reject the "analogy of faith" theology which was gaining in power in that age. He debated Baptist proponents, Federal Covenanters, a naturalist philosopher, Robert Owen of the New Harmony Utopia, and Bishop Purcell, the Roman Catholic leader from Cincinnati. He was the only minister to have been invited to address both houses of the American Federal Congress. He was a member of the Virginia State Legislature. Both Campbells were remarkable men. Robert E. Lee paid Alexander Campbell a very high compliment.

---

31. Alexander Campbell, *The Christian System*, 1835, reprinted by Standard Publishing, Cincinnati.

Christianity Restored, 1845, reprinted by Old Paths Book Club, Rosemead, California.

He was a man in whom were illustriously combined all the qualities that would adorn or elevate the nature to which he belonged. . . . A man who if sent to one of the many superior worlds would have suggested a grand idea of the human race.[32]

He did not wish to found a denomination but rather a denomination-wide movement back to the New Testament Church as model. He was not sectarian in attitude. He did not claim the churches which seemed to agree with his approach were the only true church. He did not aim to father a sect. He wanted all churches to dissolve the connections that maintained division in the world church fellowship. He held views on most theological matters. He never regarded one who disagreed with him, but who claimed Christ was Lord, to be his real enemy. He did not believe they were not Christian. They were simply brothers in error; in error if doing contrary to the covenant, but brothers in Christ and members of the one Church of Christ. In short, he appealed to the New Testament as authority and norm. He did not regard error in any specific point of theology as sufficient to override the basic loyalty one had to Christ. He did not believe in or practice the baptism of infants. Nor would he allow any unimmersed into membership in a restored congregation. But he held them to be Christian in spite of their error. The faith in Christ as Lord was too powerful to call such non-Christian. But that faith in Christ as Lord did not eliminate the New Testament norm for faith and practice. In that sense, he was a true prophet in the tradition of the Israelites. A prophet called the people to the norm, the covenant.

---

32. Benjamin L. Smith, *Alexander Campbell*, St. Louis: Bethany Press, 1930, p. 286.

Ashley Johnson was a generation younger than Campbell. He began a small correspondence school in Tennessee. Later it grew into a small institute called the School of Evangelists. Still later it became Johnson Bible College. Johnson delivered each fall a series of addresses on the two covenants. His students, if they graduated, heard the series four times. These lectures were published as *Sermons on the Two Covenants*. In the book, Johnson identified Campbell as having contributed a great deal to his thinking.[33] The sermons were stenographically recorded. They exhibit a wonderful rough-and-ready American style. Historians of Christian thought in years to come ought surely use those addresses as example of the presence of the Holy Spirit in the Church. For here was a man born and raised in rural America in its formative stage, and who, by independent study of the English text, came to conclusions startlingly close to those of Paul and John, as well as capturing the spirit and attitude of Jesus. He added a vital element to the American Reformation of 1830. The aim of that reform was to recapture the vitality and message of the first century. Those brave men wanted to have true covenant renewal in all the churches. They began what they called the Restoration Movement.[34] They wanted in the era of the New Covenant what Nehemiah wanted at his great oath renewal service (Neh. 10:1ff.).

One other recent author in covenant came to essentially the same conclusions of Campbell and Johnson. He was not in the tradition of the Restoration movement. Paul Jewett was and remained a Presbyterian. He believed in and supported Federal Covenant Theology, with modification.

---

33. Ashley Johnson, *Sermons on the Two Covenants*, 1899, reprinted by Gospel Light, Delight, Arkansas, p. 40.

34. James DeForest Murch, *Christians Only,* Cincinnati: Standard Publishing, 1962.

Three books by him suggested a journey of faith not unlike Campbell's. In *The Lord's Day,* he reasoned the name came from the Lord's Supper. And, as Campbell, the Lord's supper was practiced each first day of each week. Hence the name Lord's Day. In his *Male and Female,* he revealed a hermeneutic similar to Campbell's. He came to a far less rigid conclusion about women than was typical of his time, especially among "analogy of faith" and "restoration patternist" theologians.

His latest volume, *Infant Baptism and the Covenant of Grace* reasoned that "covenant theology, to be consistent with its essential emphasis on personal commitment and faith, must not only practice believer communion, (which it does) but also believer baptism (which it does not.)"[35] The three men, Campbell, Johnson, and Jewett were in a widening flow of scholarship who perceived the concept of covenant affected all theological questions. When the Bible was read as covenant documents, without the massive weight of human tradition obscuring the truth written there, the common man would be able to come to rather competent conclusions.

The Shape of Covenant Tomorrow

The word covenant has been used in very dissimilar ways. As a result, most scholars have assumed a cautious stance when the word was spoken. It was unlikely the word would be used as one understood it. The continued rise in popularity of "analogy of faith" Platonism, which all but repudiated

---

35. Paul K. Jewett, *The Lord's Day,* Grand Rapids: Eerdmans, 1971. *Man as Male and Female,* Grand Rapids: Eerdmans, 1975. *Infant Baptism and the Covenant of Grace,* Grand Rapids: Eerdmans, 1978. Front Cover statement by John D. W. Watts.

any norm from scripture, posed the single greatest threat to commonality of understanding or acceptance of the idea. Nonetheless, consensus has been slowly developing among world scholastic opinion.

The Bible itself is called Testament or Covenant. That fact alone guaranteed a fair hearing for the concept. International scholarship has agreed: some objective standard must exist for unity in the faith. Faith in faith is idolatry. Faith in an undefined name, even that of Jesus, is likewise idolatry. Redefining Biblical words to correspond to agreed presupposition is tacit rejection of the original. Consequently, if the Bible is understood as the standard or norm for faith and order, the concept of covenant has won. For if behaviors are judged by the scripture, covenant is functioning whether the term is used or not. All believers in Christ ought to accept all others upon honest allegiance to Him. The disciples of Christ ought then harmonize their faith and order along Apostolic lines. It is unnecessary to hold people who deviate from the covenant as outside the faith that saves. It is necessary that all owning allegiance to Christ standardize their faith and order by New Testament standards.

There are four main issues in covenant theology. The shape of covenant theology tomorrow will depend upon how matters go in these four areas. 1) The very concept of conditionality is a real issue. If mental state alone is the condition to salvation in Christ, then the attention given to covenant will drop seriously. The doctrine will be relegated to allegorical status and forgotten. 2) The question of superiority in covenant must be settled. The Old Testament either controlled the New, or the New reinterpreted and changed the Old. The entire question of separation of church and state is bound up in this issue. Another way of putting it is,

414

Can a child be born into the Christian church? Is his status, as far as covenanted relationship is concerned, dependent upon a personal affirmation of allegiance to Christ prior to any formal church relationship? In matters of church theology of ordinances, do the Apostolic meanings prevail? In what way is baptism related to circumcision? Is baptism an oath itself or the mere sign of a previous relationship—whether by "analogy of faith" or Federal Covenant birth? And finally, were the prophecies of the Old Testament fulfilled in the church, or are they separate from the history of the church and to be fulfilled in some form of National Theocracy of old Israel? To put it another way, do prophecies of the future root in the writings of the Apostles, or in the prophets? Do the Apostles have the authority to redefine Old Testament prophecies by their own present (A.D. 50) experience, or is the church a parenthesis in Jewish history? 3) The third major problem rests in the question of the relationship of the Canon to the Covenant. Does one seek to restore the culture of the first century or the gospel? That is, is the entire New Testament Canon the statutory covenant? Are there exhibited in the New Testament both cultural practices and covenanted ones? What may be more important, how does one determine what commands or practices of the Canon Text were cultural expressions of a principle in covenant, and what commands and practices are part and substance of the New Covenant itself? 4) What is the proper attitude toward covenant violators? Are they Christian if they do not hold to a covenanted relationship to Christ? Is there a basic difference between an error in establishing a covenanted relationship and an error in covenant keeping? In other words, are the unimmersed full members of the church and therefore proper subjects for unity, or are they

415

near-converts who are subjects for conversion? In addition, if one is held to be a brother, although in error, shall he be allowed full or only partial membership in a restored and covenant-keeping congregation? If one is admitted to be Christian without meeting the specified covenanted terms in the exact covenanted way, will not his admission to full status tend to reduce the covenant to mere theory? A new effort at a sane theology of error must be attempted by those claiming allegiance to Christ in a covenanted manner. What is done with these four issues will help determine the shape of Covenant Theology in the future.

One major difficulty is the almost utter lack of communication between the various groups. The theologians of the Churches of Christ are most competent, but fear that discussion of the issues with the "denominationals" as brothers will ratify the status quo. On the other hand the leadership of the "analogy of faith" groups reject any idea of sacramental theology, not distinguishing between covenanted sacrament and sacerdotal transmission of grace. Evangelical bookstores refuse to carry literature published by proponents of what they perceive as "works righteousness." Some forum of dialogue must be achieved where restoration covenanters of all types can communicate with the rest of the church without surrendering their basic assumptions as a condition to the discussion itself. The same must be allowed by covenanters. The idea of covenanted faith will not go away simply by tacit agreement not to define it. It is doubtful if unity is possible where two radically differing views on the basis of salvation exist in the world church. A hermeneutic allowing the scriptures to speak must be achieved as a matter of supreme urgency.

416

Conclusion

In this last chapter, the idea of covenant was traced from the Apostolic times to the present times in the broadest of categories. It was designed to give the student ability to recognize the classes of covenant theology.

A brief survey of writings produced or circulating in ancient times were examined in relation to covenant. The method used was an examination of covenant formulary. They were written in covenant style.

The Book of Revelation was examined and found to have been written in covenant formulary. That is, it was divided into three major data sections, each dealing chiefly with materials typically found under heading of parties, terms and promises. In the parties section, carried by seven letters to seven churches, it was found each letter had parties, terms, and promises in addition to the general structure of the book. Revelation ended with two aspects of typical Treaty summation. The great commission was repeated. A prohibition typical of ancient Treaties forbidding alteration of the Treaty Text was included.

The Greek and Roman experience with covenant was briefly described. In each case, there was dramatic return to the theology and style of the Old Testament. Each group attempted to create a Christian Theocracy after the model of the Davidic kingdom. It was a reversal of the Two Testaments. The Old Testament was held to be the ideal situation for a Christian Empire. It was not a return to all the stipulations of the Old Torah, but was a return to a Theocracy as ideal.

The Lutheran view of covenant was expressed in a brief way. Their heavy emphasis on Grace in contrast to Law

417

prevented their taking seriously a notion of covenant. They were the first source of the "analogy of faith" theology. One other reason for their failure to use covenant as the Apostles used it was their hostility in the early days to "restoration" type preaching of the Anabaptists. In reaction to Rome, to Geneva, and the "rebaptizers," Luther ran so fast he ran past Jerusalem!

Reformed Covenant Theology was called Federal Theology. The Geneva group produced a brand of covenant theology which emphasized the "descendant" aspect of covenant. They held a view which allowed the Old Testament to determine the theology of the New in certain given places. Along with Rome and the ancient Greeks, the Old Testament dominated the New. In that way, clergy, infant baptism, tithing, the use of Sunday as a day of Sabbath, clerical garb and such were authorized.

Dispensational theology was overt repudiation of the discontinuity of the covenants understood by the Apostles. This covenant view believed Jesus failed in his first mission, incorporated the church as a parenthesis in Hebrew history and found the Jews to be God's chief interest in historic revelation. The Old Testament was to be the ideal state in the millennial reign of Christ. They had four gospels, unlike the four found in the New Testament, seven "dispensational" ages, two co-existent covenants, two Israels of God, two tracts in revelation, and a hermeneutic wherein the Old Testament dominated the New.

Another view of covenant was called "No covenant." The only covenant in the new era, it was claimed, was between God and Christ, and was fulfilled on the cross. There was for these, no real covenant between Christ and the church. These churches believed in the "analogy of faith" view of

418

scripture and used it in all hermeneutics to eliminate any need of structured relationships to God. Theirs was a highly individualized, mystical, and "neo-gnostic" religion.

The last view examined was the Restoration understanding of covenant. In that theology, the Apostles were the authority over the Old and New Covenants. A system of continuity in salvation history was maintained throughout both Testaments. There was continuity in the church as God's Israel, and Jesus as Jehovah. A radical discontinuity between the Treaty inside each Canon was understood. A system of typology supported their basic Two Covenant view. In all matters, the New Testament ruled the Old. Both were inspired of God. One passed into inspired example and the other remained inspired Treaty.

Lastly, a judgment was given which linked the future of covenant thinking to four variables or live issues regarding covenant.

Questions on Chapter Nine

1. Material laid out in parties, terms and promises data
   was called
   a) Federal Covenant   c) Treaty
   b) Covenant Formulary   d) "Analogy of Faith"
2. The visions in Revelation of the seven churches meant
   a) Congregations are Party to covenant.
   b) God dealt with all people individually.
   c) There were new stipulations for each church.
   d) Once in grace always in grace.

3. Constantine did what for the church?
   a) Nothing   c) Made it the national religion
   b) Tolerated it   d) Persecuted it
4. T F The greatest common factor in Greek, Roman, and Protestant theology was a simlar view that the Old Testament was the Ideal.
5. T F The Apostles reinterpreted many Old Testament passages.
6. T F The Anabaptists did not believe in baptism.
7. T F When children were born into the church, "nurture"dominated all.
8. T F Federal Covenant used the Old Testament meanings for the New Testament.
9. The Apostles presented baptism as
   a) covenant birth   c) grace
   b) covenant sign   d) works
10. The most serious aspect of "dispensationalism" was
    a) They had two covenants both operative side by side.
    b) They believed in sprinkling babies.
    c) They believed the Old Covenant was done away.
    d) They did not believe in the New Covenant.
11. Campbell had a view of the two covenants emphasizing
    a) Water for baptism of infants
    b) Baptism took the place of circumcision
    c) Continuity between covenants
    d) Discontinuity between the two covenants
12. Campbell emphasized the need for a _____ in Unity.
13. T F Campbell believed unity was based on the Old Testament.
14. T F Campbell believed one who violated covenant was no longer a Christian.

15. T F Ashley Johnson was a Federal Covenanter.
16. Discuss the problem of holding a "norm" and allowing for breach of it without ratifying the error by implication.
17. Discuss why Federal Covenant was called "The Halfway Covenant."

PLEASE TURN THE BOOK OVER FOR ANSWERS.

14. F They were brothers in error.
13. F
12. Standard or norm
11. d) He held "continuity" in purpose, but discontinuity in Treaty Text.
10. a)
9. a) Birth into the covenant. The Spirit was the "sign" of the New Testament.
8. T
7. T If everyone was a church member by birth, nuture of the faithful was all there was to church leadership.
6. F The Anabaptists were those who believed in a separation of the two covenants with the New Testament the rule. Anabaptist meant they "rebaptized" people who had been sprinkled as infants.
5. T
4. T The idea of a national theocracy was understood as the natural result of conversion of all the people of a land.
3. c) Made it a national religion and changed its entire character.
2. a)
1. b)

15. F   He had a radical replacement of the Old by the New.
16. One must both be gentle to the erring, but must not teach the error as satisfactory church life. If the truth were taught, the need for eliminating errors would be eased a good deal. To call someone a brother in Christ is not to authorize his error. Or is it?
17. Because it allowed for infants to be part of the church, the Kingdom of God, and the people of the covenant when they did not have faith.

    Although full members of the church by birth, they were not allowed at the Lord's Table without an "experience" with the Lord.

Chapter Ten

CONCLUSION

This study was undertaken because of the confusion over the concept of covenant in the average church. The Bible was called the Old and the New Testaments or Covenants. It would be unfortunate if the words did not convey to the readers what they meant to the writer.

The basic procedure used throughout the study was historical. The idea of covenant was traced from the first book of the Bible through to the last. The assumption of the study was that one must take seriously the notion of covenant or risk creating a religion of one's own, calling it Christianity. The words carrying the basic ideas of covenant were examined in detail: b'rth- "covenant," alah- "oath," and hesed- "covenant keeping to the best interest of the other partner." A survey of the use of each of these and other covenant-related terms was undertaken. The idea of a formal Treaty with God was adopted as fundamental presupposition in the book. The Canon Texts of the Old Testament were all written with reference to the understood Treaty of Israel with God.

The philosophic concepts necessary to support the idea as God having formal, agreed, and duly sworn relationships based upon overt revelation of Himself to man were developed from the early Hebrew writings. The God of the Old Testament revealed in history in an objective, emperical, and verbal way. The religion of the Hebrews and of the Christians was based upon objective and certifiable events in history. The great events began with the appearance of God to Abraham. Based upon that intervention into human history, the covenant with Abraham arose. The Exodus of Israel from the Egyptian captivity was the event certifying the validity of the Old Covenant at Sinai. The life, death and resurrection of Christ certified the New Testament religion to be valid. Each major intervention in history brought a covenant after it. The validity of the covenant did not rest on the emperical usefulness of the treaty, but upon the facts that led to its creation.

Treaties were shown to have three basic elements: Parties, Stipulations, and Promises. The Old Covenant, and all others, for that matter, were viewed from the three perspectives. Conditionality as a concept was examined. The nature and consequence of breach of covenant was explored. It was found that God reacted immediately to some types of covenant breach and with considerable violence. On the other hand, a sacrificial system was provided to hold the people's faith intact and to support their need for cleansing of the conscience. The sacrificial system assumed breach of covenant would occur without rupture of the relationship.

The prophets were presented as God's lawyers of the covenant. They warned of loss, of doom, of the curses of the covenant if disobedience were steady or uncorrected. The prophets were historians and philosophers. They wrote histories wherein the value judgments were made on the basis of support for God and the Treaty as opposed to disloyalty or neglect of the Torah. Baalism was examined to indicate the thoroughly integrated society grown up around two competing philosophies: Revealed Religion as opposed to Naturalism. The latter prophets announced the end of God's patience. They invoked the witnesses to the treaty and put Israel before them. The doom of the nation was foretold. Israel was to go into captivity. She was to be brought out as further evidence of God's grace and covenant keeping.

When the New Testament came, it was emphasized Christ himself was the covenant. He was the parties to it. Anyone

424

who joined Christ by swearing allegiance to him according to specifications was said to be "in Christ." His life was the great summation of all God had wanted of mankind. To be like Christ in all essential matters fufilled the Stipulations of the New Covenant. To share with Christ all He was, and was to be, summed the Promises of the New Covenant.

God signed the new Treaty at Calvary in the blood of His Son. Man joined Christ when the mind, emotion, will and body were delivered to God in baptism in water. The benefits of the Kingdom were immediately his. One was saved by grace. He was saved by faith. He was saved by obedience to Christ. The receiving of Christ was a composited total response to the message of the gospel in the faith-repentance-baptism act. Salvation was presented as the co-operative covenanted faith wherein God had a part and man had a part.

The covenant-keeping required of the Christian was summarized. Details of the church, of the personal life, of holiness, of duty were only summarized, not detailed in this book. The summation took two forms, corresponding to the two classes of mankind: those in Christ, and those outside Christ. The duty of the church to those outside Christ was summed as participating in the "ministry of reconciliation." The duty of the believer toward the church, his own soul, and all human social order was Christlikeness. All men and women were to be treated as Christ would have treated them. All others were to be treated with the same kind of respect that would have been accorded Christ in the same circumstances.

The administration of the church was the administration of the "mystery of God," the gospel, the mission. Whatever advanced the purpose of God was good. The New Covenant was described in a major synonym for covenant, the "will of God." The will of God was that all men be saved and that all nations come to the law of the Spirit in Christ: Christlikeness toward others.

All relationships were to be modeled on the relationship of Christ and the church. Christ advanced the best interests of the church and the church advanced the glory and best interests of Christ. Male and female, bond and free, Jew and Greek, rich and poor, government and citizen, and all other social relationships were to look out for the interests of the others as matter of covenanted religion. The sacrificial system of the New Covenant was a life led of the Spirit and contribution to world reconciliation.

The Apostles had an understanding of two covenants, one following the other and replacing it. The two were related in a parallel way. One was the shadow. The other the substance which cast the shadow. In parallelism was found the secret of understanding the Apostles' use of the Old Testament history and Canon.

In the last chapter, a survey of several types of covenant theologies was given. These included the ancient Greek and Roman use of each Testament. The Lutheran, Calvinistic, Baptist, "dispensational" and Restoration views were summarized briefly. Finally, four problems about covenant were indicated. The future of covenant thinking was bound up in how each of those four problems was approached and solved.

It was the assumption of this book that Covenant was not allegorical to true religion or faith, but was the faith itself. This book takes the Treaty as real, dependable, and the basis of judgment.

426

Annotated Bibliography

Albright, William Foxwell. "The Hebrew Expression for 'Making a Covenant,'" *Bulletin of the American Schools of Oriental Research,* 121:21ff., 1951.

_____. *Yahweh and the Gods of Canaan.* Winona Lake, Indiana: Eisenbrauns, 1965.

A rather technical study for the advanced student. Requires some background in Old Testament vocabulary.

Allen, Donald B. "Deuteronomy: An Expression of Covenant and Responsibility." Unpublished Master's thesis, Lincoln Christian Seminary, 1980.

A typical and well done thesis on the concept of conditionality in the Old Testament. Has material summarizing ancient treaties. Good for beginning students.

Baltzer, Klaus. *The Covenant Formulary.* Philadelphia: Fortress Press, 1971.

A rather technical work, from the radical "form-critical" perspective of European scholarship. Carries many passages in Hebrew and Greek. Not for the beginning student. The interests discussed in the book are very narrow.

Bartchy, S. Scott. *Slavery in the First Century.* Missoula: University of Montana Press, SBL Dissertation Series, 1973.

A dissertation in typical European style: calling up of authorities to review opinions on a given idea or passage. An excellent work, but in a narrow field.

Baxter, Richard. *An Answer to Mr. Toombs: His Valedictory Oration to the People of Bewdeley.* London, 1652.

Berkhof, Hendrickus. *Christ, the Meaning of History.* Richmond: John Knox Press, 1966.

A philosophy of history wherein Christ is the central meaning. Not a technical work, not typically theological, no "point of view" that would seem odd to the average Christian. It is an alternative continental work which is not in the Bultmannian camp. A "conservative" theological work.

Bodenseich, Julius, ed. "Covenant," *The Enclyclopedia of the Lutheran Church*. Minneapolis: Augsburg Publishing House, 1965.

Bowen, Boone A. "A Study of Hesed." Unpublished Doctor's dissertation, Yale Divinity School, 1935.

Bright, John. *Covenant and Promise*. Philadelphia: Westminster Press, 1976.

Essentially a study of the covenant issue in Jeremiah. Not for the beginning student. It assumes the reader has an extensive background in both Biblical history and language. It attempts to place specific passages into their historic slot based upon certain presuppositions. An interesting work, for advanced students.

Brinsmead, Richard D. "Covenant," *Present Truth Magazine*, November, 1976.

An Australian from the typical Protestant "faith only" tradition, who is moving toward a "restorationist" position. An attempt to integrate covenant into total depravity theology.

Bromiley, Geoffrey. *The Children of Promise: The Case for Baptizing Infants*. Grand Rapids: Eerdmans, 1979.

A small book, for beginners, showing the typical arguments for infant baptizing. Nothing new is injected. A major weakness is that Bromiley did not refer to the Nehemiah event when discussing the "household" pedobaptist position. A strength of the book is that he frankly rests the position on the tradition of the church.

Campbell, Alexander. *The Christian System.* Cincinnati: Standard Publishing Company, 1835, reprint.

A topically organized series of summaries of Christian doctrine wherein the New Testament is regarded as the final authority. The individual sections had, for the most part, been previously published in the Millennial Harbinger. The language represents its age. A strength is that summaries are clear and competent. A weakness is that the documentation in many sections is lacking. It assumes the reader has a thorough knowledge of the Bible.

_____. *Christianity Restored.* Rosemead, California: Old Paths Book Club, 1845, reprint.

A description of Apostolic theology from the New Testament text only. An excellent review of essential hermeneutic tools is given in the first part. Good for either the beginning or the well-read Biblical scholar.

_____. "The Sermon on the Law."

An unusually competent study of the term "law" and "The Law" in the New Testament. A theology of the relationship of the two covenants wherein the New Testament is given priority.

Campbell, Thomas. *Declaration and Address.* St. Louis: Bethany Press, 1809, reprint 1955.

Ceram, C. W. *The Secret of the Hittites.* New York: A. A. Knopf, 1956.

A narrative review of the search for the ancient Hittite empire, together with an account of the language difficulties. A work for the beginner, in a narrow field, but whose conclusions have been supplemented by extensive later research.

Chafer, L. S. *Dispensationalism.* Dallas: Dallas Seminary Press, 1951..

_____. *Systematic Theology.* Dallas: Dallas Seminary Press, 1948.

Cotton, John. *The Way of the Churches of Christ in America.* London, 1645.

Cox, William E. *An Examination of Dispensationalism.* Plainfield, New Jersey: Presbyterian and Reformed Publishing, 1980.

Creham, Joseph. *Early Christian Baptism, and Creed.* London, 1950.

Cross, Frank M. *Canaanite Myth and Hebrew Epic.* Cambridge: Harvard University Press, 1973.

A very technical work requiring a knowledge of Hebrew to fully appreciate and understand it. Comparisons of certain Psalms and related passages with Canaanite poetry and mythology.

Cummings, Calvin Knox. *The Covenant of Grace.* Philadelphia: The Great Commission Publishing Co., 1974.

A typical pedobaptist, i.e., Federal Covenant explanation of the continuity of the covenants. Very little new data given. The basic same position restated. See N. Rice for an exhaustive case which this book merely summarizes. Emphasizes the unity of the Bible in the Federal format.

DeJung, Peter Y. *The Covenant Idea in New England Theology.* Grand Rapids: Eerdmans, 1945.

A review of the essential problems of Federal Covenant as they were worked out in New England. A splendid bibliography of the theological works of many early American churchmen. Centers in issue of sacramentalism, infant baptism, and the basis of salvation when the issues are placed within the Federal Covenant perspective.

Deracter, F. *Preparing the Way for Paul.* New York: Macmillan, 1930.

A study of the ancient world in pre-apostolic and apostolic times. An older account.

DeRidder, Richard R. *Discipling the Nations.* Grand Rapids: Baker, 1971.

Written in classic European style, without reference to form criticism, a very competent theology and history of covenant is given. A work all Bible students ought to read. DeRidder uses covenant as the integrating concept of world mission and the eternal purpose of God. Well documented, precise, with little "fat," the book is on target all the way.

Dissertations of Epictetus. Thomas W. Higgenson, tr. Roslyn, New York: Walter J. Black, Publisher, 1944.

Durant, Will. *A History of Greece.* New York: Simon and Schuster, 1939.

Dryness, William. *Themes in Old Testament Theology.* Downers Grove, Illinois: InterVarsity Press, 1979.

A general discussion of a variety of related themes from the Old Covenant. The author understands conditionality in the Old Testament and is not overly influenced by European thought and theological assumptions.

Estep, W. R. *The Anabaptist Story.* Nashville: Broadman Press, 1963.

A good book for beginners in an arena of history often neglected by historians. Good for beginners and scholar alike, with attention to the alternative theology repudiated by all major protestant groups until recently.

Gaebelein, Arno G. *Daniel.* Grand Rapids: Kregel, 1955.

A highly biased commentary which harmonizes sections of Daniel with the visions of Margaret McDonald. He ignores the local setting of Daniel, projecting most of it into the future in an odd way. An example of Dispensational hermeneutics at work. Not recommended for beginners, or anyone else.

Gleuck, Nelson. *Hesed.* New York: Hebrew Union Press, 1927.

This important work is the standard in its field. The foundational and definitive work in the word study. Most Bible scholars are accepting Glueck's conclusions as valid. He is a modern Hebrew scholar, previously associated with Albright in archeological work. He accepts the conclusions of radical form criticism, and writes from within that perspective.

Gunkel, Hermann. *The Legends of Genesis: The Biblical Saga and History.* Tr., W. H. Carruth. New York: Schocken, 1966.

A typical European Biblical scholar, accepting the basic conclusions of form criticism, but who attempts to show the rich meaning of the "legends" of the Hebrews Not recommended for beginners.

Hasel, Gerhart. *Old Testament Theology: Basic Issues in the Current Debate.* Grand Rapids: Eerdmans, 1972.

An excellent survey of current opinions about the Old Testament. It surveys the entire debate over whether the Old Testament is evidence of an evolution of religious thought, or an accurate record of God and the people of God. Good for the advanced student. An introduction to the issues for beginners. Good survey for college students interested in the presuppositions of opposing theological camps.

432

Hewett, Thomas. *Hebrews.* Grand Rapids: Eerdmans, 1960.
A commentary on Hebrews that does not take seriously the concept of conditionality. Accepts the analogy-of-faith presupposition. Not recommended.

Hillar, D. R. *Covenant: The History of a Biblical Idea.* Baltimore: Johns Hopkins, 1969.
A foundation study that should be in every scholar's library. An even-handed and steady work. Strong in that he understands the concept of covenant. Weak in that he failed to see the New Testament follow through on the idea. Recommended, but with due caution to facts to the contrary.

Holifield, E. Brooks. *The Covenant Sealed: The Development of Puritan Sacramental Theology in Old and New England.* New Haven: Yale University Press, 1974.
A history of the idea of "signs" and "seals" as understood by Federal Covenanters. A good introduction to sacramental theology and its courses among a brand of covenant theology. Well documented. Pulls together representative views on baptism and the Lord's Table from 1300 to 1900.

Hoven, Victor E. *Shadow and Substance.* St. Louis: Bethany, 1934.
An excellent study of typology by one who understands completely the concept of covenant and the place of parallelism in it. Most highly recommended for all, beginner and scholar. Well outlined, well documented, well written.

Huffman, Herbert B. "The Treaty Background of Hebrew YADA," *Bulletin of the American Schools of Oriental Research,* 181 (February, 1966).
An article in *BASOR (Bulletin of the School of Oriental Research),* and typical of that style. A survey of opinion,

many passages in the original language, with comment and comparisons. Not for the beginning student unless he can pass by the language barrier and read the conclusions from the English text.

Hulme, Edward M. *Renaussiance and Reformation.* New York: Century Publishing Company, 1917.

A fundamental history of the era. Not theologically oriented. The author was not a Christian as far as the text will indicate. A good, sound introduction to the time of the reformation and the social-philosophical winds blowing at the time.

Ironside, H. A. *Studies in Hebrews and Titus.* Loizeaux, 1932.

Written by a man that rejects on the basis of the analogy-of-faith what the author of Hebrews was really saying. An example of massive theological override of the text.

Iwald, H. J., quoted by J. I. Packer and O. R. Johnson, "Historical and Theological Introduction," Martin Luther's *Bondage of the Will.* Westwood, New Jersey: Revell, n.d.

Eichrodt, Walter. *Theology of the Old Testament,* Vol. I & II. Philadelphia: Westminster, 1961.

A sound and fundamental approach to the Old Testament. He is a Federal Covenant Theologian with a serious commitment to a continuity between the Old and New Testaments typical of that view. Nonetheless, his approach to the Old Testament gives unity and thrust to the whole. Recommended for all.

Jeremias, Joachin. *Jerusalem in the Time of Jesus.* London: SCM Press, 1969.

A good survey by a competent European scholar. German scholars as a group tend to have serious presuppositions about the origin and transmission of data in ancient times. Care must always be used when reading such. In this book, the data is well written and documented.

Jewett, Paul. *Infant Baptism and the Covenant of Grace.* Grand Rapids: Eerdmans, 1978.

A good study of the Federal Covenant view of baptism and the connectedness of the two covenants. Well researched, well organized, well written. Appeals for believer baptism. Tends to accept the analogy of faith, however. That may be due to conciliation toward his audience, rather than an acceptance itself. Recommended for all. He was on the same faculty as Bromiley. Each wrote about baptism from the Federal view, with the opposite conclusion. Jewett's is the better work.

_____. *The Lord's Day.* Grand Rapids: Eerdmans, 1971.

Highly recommended. A study of the Adventist view on Sabbath. A survey of ancient views. Well documented, well written. Good for beginner and scholar alike.

_____. *Man as Male and Female.* Grand Rapids: Eerdmans, 1975.

The weakest of the three books. A competent study of man and woman, attempting to maintain respect for Paul and the Bible amid calls for equality between the sexes. A good study. Good for beginner and advanced scholar. Well written, well organized, deals with the issues. Must be read with judgment.

Johnson, Ashley. *The Two Covenants.* Delight, Arkansas: Gospel Light, 1899, reprint.

The finest treatment of the subject in print, whether European, English, or American. In rural American style.

Good for beginners. Good for laymen. Good for scholars who can tolerate a style of scholarship different from their own. Used no source but the Bible. Did not call up authorities. They are sermons to the popular mind.

Johnson, Aubrey. *Hesed and Hasid.* Oslo: Fabritus and Sonnor, 1955.

A study much like Glueck's. Not for beginners. It is a word study from the form critical perspective. Is competent.

Josephus, Flavius. *Wars.* Chicago: Thompson and Thomas, 1901.

Kahen, Hasanein. *The Samaritans: Their History, Religion, and Customs.* Israel: Nablus, 1974.

A good survey of the history and literature of the Samaritans written by one who has lived there. Published in Samaria, the book covers the known history of the area from pre-Ezra times until today. A good general source.

Kittel, Gerhard, ed. *Theological Dictionary of the New Testament.* Tr. Geoffrey Bromiley. Grand Rapids: Eerdmans, 1964.

Klassen, Winham. *Covenant and Community.* Grand Rapids: Eerdmans, 1977.

A general history of the Anabaptist movement. Well written, good for the beginner in the area as well as the more advanced.

Kline, Meredith G. *By Oath Consigned.* Grand Rapids: Eerdmans, 1968.

This is a study of the treaty oath/curse concept applied to the Old and New Testaments. Kline supports the basic presuppositions of Federal Covenant.

_____. *The Structure of Biblical Authority.* Grand Rapids: Eerdmans, 1972.

This is not for beginners. It supports the concept the Bible was first a covenant. That is, covenant and Canon authority are implied when any discussion of Treaty is involved. A good well documented and well thought out text. One needs a very considerable experience in issues about Biblical Canon and authority to grasp all he says. An excellent book.

_____. *The Treaty of the Great King.* Grand Rapids: Eerdmans, 1963.

A general introduction to the ancient Treaties and their impact on the study of the Old Testament. A good beginning text. Well written, well documented, from a foremost authority. Kline was a student of the famous Von Rad, although he was more perceptive in Old Testament theology than Von Rad, as far as covenant was concerned.

Korosec, V. *Thethische Staatsuertrage Ein Beitrug zu iher Juristischen Wertung.* Leipsig: Rectswissen schaftliche Studen 60, 1931.

Ladd, George Eldon. *The Last Things.* Grand Rapids: Eerdmans, 1978.

Ladd is a pre-millennialist, but an opponent of dispensationalism. He has a hermeneutic that will not allow the use of two concurrent covenants in understanding scripture. He believes in the authority of the New Testament over the Old. He is not a Federal Covenanter.

_____. *The New Testament and Criticism.* Grand Rapids: Eerdmans, 1967.

A very readable and reasonable book for beginners in the entire problem of Biblical criticism. A fair, "conservative" and Biblical approach. An excellent book on

Criticism. Well written, including evaluations of most of the major writers in the recent history of theological issues.

_____. *The Pattern of New Testament Truth*. Grand Rapids: Eerdmans, 1968.

A good book describing the impact of one's presuppositions on how one understands the text of scripture. Ladd identifies the Greek perspective as a definite bias. He urges the Bible be read from the Hebrew perspective. His chief orientation in this book is support of the text against the assaults brought by religious evolutionists. Well written, an easy style that is common to all Ladd's works. For beginners and the well educated.

Latourette, Kenneth Scott. *A History of Christianity*. New York: Harper-Row, 1975.

The single greatest work on the history of Christian mission and impact. The author examines the impact of the church on the culture into which it penetrates and the impact of the culture on the church. This is the summa bonum of all mission history. Every student of the church ought to have this series. It is the very best.

Levi, Isaac. *The Synagogue: Its History and Functions*. London: Vallentine, 1964.

A general history written by a Jew in modern times. A good survey. Contains much background valuable for understanding the ancient church and the diaspora.

Limburg, J. "The Root 'RYB' and the Prophetic Lawsuit Speeches," *Journal of Biblical Literature*, 88, 1969.

Published by the Society of Biblical Literature, it is a very technical work, requiring a knowledge of the original languages as well as an appreciation of their methodology. A student could get the ideas of it in the English sections, however.

Lindsey, Hal. *The Late Great Planet Earth.* Grand Rapids: Zondervan, 1970.

The presentation of the theology of Dispensationalism as it applied to eschatology, in popular style. Well written, poor theology, terrible hermeneutics used in drawing conclusions.

Maimonides. "Isure Biah," *Babylonian Talmud,* Vol. XVIII, p. 202. Ed. I. Epstein. London: Soncino Press, 1948.

Maimonides is a writer found in the Talmuds. The Babylonian Talmud is a collection of Jewish writings which serve as the effective Bible of the modern Jew. Each section of the Talmud deals with a different matter. One who is not familiar with the Talmudic system is better advised to accept the conclusions of those who have researched the matters.

Mendenhall, George E. "Covenant Forms," *The Biblical Archeologist,* 15, 1954.

_____. *Law and Covenant in the Ancient Near East.* Pittsburg, 1955.

A fine monograph in which parallels between the Old Testament and the ancient treaties were given. This was the primary work that popularized the entire subject. It has a few pictures and some references. It is however, a secondary source.

Moran, W. L. "Love of God," *The Catholic Biblical Quarterly,* 25, 1963.

This article is one in a series found about that time relating what was thought to be "religious language" to typical diplomatic language of the ancient world. A good study, but filled, as these technical works are, with many original language passages.

Moulton, R. G. *Hebrew Literary Forms.* Boston: D. C. Heath Company, 1899.

A good, clear, exhaustive book on the varieties of Hebrew literature and their typical forms. Good for gaining a perspective as to what was "literal" and what was "figurative" type language. Excellent on parallelisms, indicating many different types. Not good for beginners, but almost essential for anyone who takes Bible study seriously.

Murch, James DeForest. *Christians Only.* Cincinnati: Standard Publishing Company, 1962.

A brief history of the "Restoration Movement" written by one who was influential in it. He is from the middle ground of the various groups. Well written, sympathetic and worthy.

Murrey, John. *The Covenant of Grace.* Sterling, Virginia: Grace Abounding Ministries, 1953.

A small, well written statement of the pedo-baptist theology of the one covenant. Is Calvinistic, and supports the Federal Covenant position. Nothing new is injected into the study.

Myers, J. M. *Grace and Torah.* Philadelphia: Fortress Press, 1975.

A fine book showing the covenant background of both Testaments. He demonstrates the abounding grace of God in the Old Testament as well as the New. He has a parallel of Romans with Deuteronomy that suggests a new approach to the study of covenant.

McCarthy, D. J. *Treaty and Covenant.* Rome, 1963.

The Roman Catholic scholar has done a fine job of describing the state of affairs among scholars on the topic

440

of Treaty as it relates to the Old Testament theology. The only real survey of opinion that is current.

McNeil, William H. *History of Western Civilization.* Chicago: University of Chicago Press, 1969.

A good, well written, modern, typical history of Europe and the West.

McPherson, Dave. *The Incredible Cover-up.* Plainfield, New Jersey: Logos International, 1975.

An historic survey of the origin and transmission of the "prophetic view" of the Bible. Traces the vision of Margaret McDonald thru Darby, Scofield, to Dallas Seminary and Hal Lindsey, A must for any who have been attracted to their work. Written in clear and well documented style, although his rage at the fraud cannot be hidden in the exposure of it.

Noth, Martin. *A History of Pentateuchal Traditions.* Englewood Cliffs, New Jersey: Prentice-Hall, 1972.

A review of the modern literature about the first five books of the Bible. Not for beginners. One needs a background in Biblical Criticism and the documentary hypothesis to appreciate the scholarship represented.

Oepke, A. "Jewish Proselyte Baptism," *Theologisches Wortenbuch zum Neuen Testament,* Vol. I, p. 535. For English translation see the *Theological Dictionary of the New Testament,* Vol. I, p. 535. Grand Rapids: Eerdmans, 1964.

A definitive article wherein the author challenges the former position that held proselyte baptism to have sprung from Christian practice. A foundational work. Some background in diaspora history is valuable, although not essential.

Pape, Dorothy R. *In Search of God's Ideal Woman.* Downers Grove, Illinois: InterVarsity Press, 1976.

> A good survey of what the Bible says about women. Has a good treatment of Jesus and women. It is one of several commendable sources discussing the subject. Well written. Scholarly.

Patten, Priscilla and Rebecca. *Before the Times.* San Francisco: Strawberry Hill Press, 1980.

> An excellent, if brief summary of the greater movements in Palestine before the time of Christ. An excellent series of maps, dynasties, lists of rulers, etc. Well done. In good standard English. For beginners and others.

Pearlman, Moshe. *The Maccabees.* London: Westenfelt and Nicolson, 1973.

> An excellent history of the family, together with the necessary background. Written in popular style, but very well documented. A foundational study in good flowing English.

Plass, Ewald M. *What Luther Says: An Anthology.* St. Louis: Concordia Press, 1959.

> A collection of sayings of the reformer. Not a complete review, but sufficient to indicate the basic currents of his theology.

Plato.

> The works of the ancients are available in any number of collections. Rarely can a complete works be found in one volume. Most works have selected what they believe are his representative works. The student will simply have to hunt up the various books on his own.

Plastaras, James. *Creation and Covenant.* Milwaukee: Bruce Publishing Company, 1968.

A Roman Catholic work from the radical form-critical perspective. He organizes his philosophy around the idea of covenant. One who is unfamiliar with typical modern Roman scholarship will find it difficult reading. Not for beginners.

Plutarch. *Consolations.* Tr. Louise R. Loomis. Roslyn, New York: Black, 1951.

Rice, Nathan. *The Campbell-Rice Debate.* Cincinnati: A. T. Skillman, 1843.

Rice was the most competent of all the debaters to face Campbell. He presented an excellent case for pedobaptism. His supporting data was excellent. His presentation was clear and competent. No author since Rice has added much to the discussion.

Richardson, Alan R. *A Theological Wordbook of the Bible.* New York: Macmillan, 1953.

A good text on key words of the Bible. Richardson required his committee to use the Hebrew antecedent word in defining Greek terms. That procedure insured a better study than typical of Protestants.

Ringgen, Helmer. *Israelite Religion.* Philadelphia: Fortress Press, 1966.

A survey of the Old Testament from a typical German modern methodology. Well documented, but without much cohesion. His acceptance of "developmental" religion weakens the work, however. Not for beginners. Not well presented to American readers. An excellent sourcebook for theologians. Good word studies. Typical European scholarship: excellent detail, poor philosophy and poor theological orientation.

Robinson, John A. T. *The Body: A Study in Pauline Theology.* London: SCM Press, 1977.

A very short, precise British work supporting sacramental theology in an age of individualism. A must for men who wish to think as did the ancient church. An excellent study of the terms *sarx* and *soma* as used by Paul.

Rowley, H. H. "Jewish Proselyte Baptism and John's Baptism," *Hebrew Union College Annual,* 1940.

A technical article that reviews previous literature on Jewish baptism. He assumes the Federal Covenant presuppositions to be true. A good typical Protestant work.

Russell, David S. *The Jews from Alexander to Herod.* London: Oxford University Press.

An excellent history of the Jews.

Schoonhoven, Calvin R. "The 'Analogy of Faith' and the Intent of Hebrews," *Scripture, Tradition, and Interpretation,* ed. W. W. Gasque and W. S. LaSor, Grand Rapids: Eerdmans, 1978.

An excellent article, well written, without rancor, with care for detail without being overcome by it. A must for serious students of the "faith only" position. Needs to be read and reread to cover all the implications of this very careful presentation.

Schmithals, Walter. *The Apocalyptic Movement.* Nashville: Abingdon, 1973.

A sound German work. He understands the clash between the prophetic and the apocalyptic movements in Hebrew history. He is not "fundamentalistic," in the theological sense. A sound, well written and well translated work. For beginners and others.

Scofield, C. I. *The Scofield Reference Bible.*

Violates good hermeneutics. Violates the rule of Bible translation without theological comment. Not worthy.

Smith, Benjamin L. *Alexander Campbell*. St. Louis: Bethany Press, 1930.

A good, readable biography of the remarkable nineteenth century theologian and church builder.

Smith, Mont W. "The Philosophy of Education of Alexander Campbell." Unpublished Master's thesis, Butler University, 1956.

A typical Master's thesis on a limited topic.

Tarn, Sir William W. *Hellenistic Civilization*. Chicago: Meridian Books, 1961.

A good, readable study of the topic for general audiences.

Taylor, T. M. "The Beginnings of Proselyte Baptism," *New Testament Studies*, II 3 (1956).

An article which attempts to trace the evidence for a practice from typical sources. Not foundational. One of several such works. Well done.

Thayer, J. H. *Greek-English Lexicon*. New York: American Book Company, 1886.

Toombs, John. *Anti-Paedobaptism or The Second Part of a Full Review of the Dispute Concerning Infant Baptism*. London, 1654.

Available through interlibrary loan only. This is a primary source. An early example of the handling of the problem.

Torrence, T. F. "Proselyte Baptism," *New Testament Studies*, 1945.

Another typical review of the evidence.

Von Rad, Gerhart. *Old Testament Theology*. New York: Stalker and Company.

A typical European theological work, assuming the validity of the documentary hypothesis. He did not support the implications of the Treaty discoveries. His heavy continental background disarmed him. He was however recognized as one of the all time greats in Old Testament studies. Not for beginners.

Walvoord, John F. *The Rapture Question*. Findlay, Ohio: Dunham Publishers, 1957.

An example of how an alien agenda can warp plain statements of scripture. The defense of the immediate coming of Christ has produced a theology unknown to the Apostles and the church until Margaret McDonald's time.

Warfield, Benjamin B., quoted by J. I. Packer and O. R. Johnson, "Historical and Theological Introduction," Martin Luther's *Bondage of the Will*. Westwood, New Jersey: Revell, n.d.

Warfield was a Federal Covenanter who fought the early fight for the "fundamentalist" position on the errancy and inerrancy question.

Wead, David W. "The Centripetal Philosophy of Mission," *Scripture, Tradition, and Interpretation*, ed. W. W. Gasque and W. S. LaSor. Grand Rapids: Eerdmans, 1978.

An innovative and perceptive examination of missions as it relates to Old Testament prophecy. An excellent work.

Weinfeld, Moshe. "Covenant," *Encyclopaedia Judaica*, Vol. V. Jerusalem: Keter Publishing House, 1972.

Wellhausen, Julius. *Die Composition des Hexateuchs*. Jahrbucker duer Deutch Theology 21, 1876.

Any work by Julius Wellhausen will reflect the very radical form-critical assumption. He was a believer in the evolution of Hebrew religion, and assumed the Bible writers merely reflected the then current religious ideas of then ancient near east.

Westerman, C. *Isaiah Forty-Sixty Six*. Philadelphia: Westminster, 1969.
   A treatment of Isaiah from the assumption of dispensationalism.

White, W. C. *The Chinese Jews*. Toronto: Toronto University Press, 1966.
   A fine presentation of the fact the Jews extended their synagogal system into China hundreds of years before Christ. Well written. For general audiences.

Williams, Michael. *The Catholic Church in Action*. New York: Macmillan, 1934.
   A good readable review of the history of the Roman Catholic Church from one sympathetic to it.

Wilson, William. *Old Testament Word Studies*. Grand Rapids: Kregel Publishing, 1978.

Wiseman, D. J. *The Vassal-Treaties of Esarhadden*. London, 1978.
   A foundational work. Necessary for any who wish to go into a near-primary source. It will be instructive for all Bible students. Somewhat technical, but very readable.

Wood, Leon J. *A Survey of Israel's History*. Grand Rapids: Zondervan, 1970.
   A typical evangelical textbook on the Old Testament. Good for general audiences. Full of historical backgrounds to the text. Identifies critical texts. Supports the validity and truthfulness of the text as is. Is the opposite of Wellhausen in basic approach. An excellent college text for beginners.

writers who reflected the then current religious ideas of ancient Israel and ...

Westermann, C. *Isaiah 40-66*. Sixth. Sr. Philadelphia: Westminster, 1969.

A treatment of Isaiah from the assumption of diverse authorship.

White, W. C. *The Chinese Jews*. Toronto: Toronto University Press, 1966.

A fine presentation of the fact the Jews extended their synagogal system into China hundreds of years before Christ. Well written. For general audiences.

Williams, Michael. *The Catholic Church in Action*. New York: Macmillan, 1934.

A good readable review of the history of the Roman Catholic Church from one sympathetic to it.

Wilson, William. *Old Testament Word Studies*. Grand Rapids: Kregel Publishing, 1978.

Wiseman, D. J. *The Vassal Treaties of Esarhaddon*. London, 1958.

A foundational work. Necessary for any who wish to go into a near primary source. It will be instructive for all Bible students. Somewhat technical, but very readable.

Wood, Leon J. *A Survey of Israel's History*. Grand Rapids: Zondervan, 1970.

A typical evangelical textbook on the Old Testament. Good for general audiences. Full of historical background to the text. Identifies critical texts, supports the validity and truthfulness of the text as both the opposite sites of Wilhausen in basic approach. An excellent college text for beginners.

Index of Scriptures

Index of Subjects